Web Design for Libraries

Web Design for Libraries

Charles P. Rubenstein

AN IMPRINT OF ABC-CLIO, LLC
Santa Barbara, California • Denver, Colorado • Oxford, England

Library of Congress Cataloging-in-Publication Data

Rubenstein, Charles P.
Web design for libraries / Charles P. Rubenstein.
pages cm
Includes bibliographical references and index.
ISBN 978-1-61069-343-1 (paperback) — ISBN 978-1-61069-344-8 (ebook)
1. Library Web sites—Design--Handbooks, manuals, etc. I. Title.
Z674.75.W67R835 2014
025.0422—dc23 2014014594

ISBN: 978-1-61069-343-1
EISBN: 978-1-61069-344-8

18 17 16 15 14 1 2 3 4 5

This book is also available on the World Wide Web as an eBook.
Visit www.abc-clio.com for details.

Libraries Unlimited
An Imprint of ABC-CLIO, LLC

ABC-CLIO, LLC
130 Cremona Drive, P.O. Box 1911
Santa Barbara, California 93116-1911

This book is printed on acid-free paper ∞

Manufactured in the United States of America

This textbook is dedicated to
my parents who gave me the opportunity to continue my education,
my wife Rose who has encouraged me and made it possible for me to write this text,
our sons—Jaron, Adam, and Scott

Stephanie, Jaron's wife, who has
given Rose and I two grandchildren
Alyssa Michelle and Noah Meyer, and
Elizabeth, Scott's wife, all of whom
have made our lives worthwhile.

I am also indebted to my students at Pratt-SILS who have helped
shape these contents,
and to my editor Blanche Woolls and all the folks at ABC-CLIO
who have guided me through the process of bringing this text to life.

Contents

List of Figures xix
Preface..... xxix
Welcome to *Web Design for Libraries* xxix
About the Red Rose Library (http://www.redroselibrary.com) xxix
Why This Book?..... xxx
Where Can I Find Library Web Page Examples? xxxi
CSS, XML, HTML5, and CMS xxxii
About Using Templates xxxii
Typographical Conventions xxxiii
1 Quick Start in Web Design..... 1
Welcome to *Web Design for Libraries!* 1
Operating Systems and Browsers..... 1
Setting Up a Website Shell Directory 2
Creating a Website 3
Using Microsoft's Word to Create Easy Web Pages 4
About File Sizes 4
HTML Page Structure..... 6
The Web Document Type 6
Elements and Containers..... 7
Using HTML, Title, and Body Tags 8
Creating a Red Rose Newsletter Web Page..... 11
Adding the Preformat Tag..... 11
Adding the Paragraph Tag 11

Adding the Center, Bold (Strong), and Underline Tags 13

Adding the Image Tag 14

Creating Structure with Table Tags 15

Recap of HTML Elements Used in Chapter 1 18

What's Next? 18

URLs Cited 20

Chapter 1 Review Exercises 22

Chapter 1 Fill-In Questions 22

Chapter 1 Multiple-Choice Questions 22

Chapter 1 Design and Discussion Questions 22

2 Hypertext Markup Language (HTML) 23

File-Naming Conventions 24

Uniform Resource Locators (URLs) 24

The Anchor Element (a) 25

Web Browsers 25

Saving a Web Page from the Internet 28

Website Design 29

About Browsers and HTML Standards 31

Document Type Definitions (DTD) 31

Top-Ten Library Home Page Links 32

Web Page Graphics 35

What's Next? 36

URLs Cited 36

Chapter 2 Review Exercises 38

Chapter 2 Fill-In Questions 38

Chapter 2 Multiple-Choice Questions 38

Chapter 2 Design and Discussion Questions 38

3 The HTML Document 39

The HTML Document and Header Information 39

HTML Tags, Elements, and Attributes 39

Well-Formed Markup Tags 40

Basic HTML File Structure 41

HTML Elements and Their Attributes 41
HTML Head Section 44
Document Header Information. 44
Document Title Element. 44
Your Website's Base URL 45
Default Fonts for Your Page. 46
Defining Color Values 46
Describing Your Page with Metadata. 47
In-Page Cataloging 48
Telling Search Engines: Don't Index This Page 49
Setting a Freshness Date for Your Page 49
Don't Cache—Get Me the Latest Page 49
Redirecting Your Patrons to a New Website 50
Adding an ISBN Number 50
Your Page's Relationship to Other Documents 50
What's Next? 50
URLs Cited 51
Chapter 3 Review Exercises. 52
    Chapter 3 Fill-In Questions. 52
    Chapter 3 Multiple-Choice Questions. 52
    Chapter 3 Design and Discussion Questions 52
4 Displaying Text in Your HTML Document 53
Using Comments. 53
The Body of Your HTML Document 54
Document Heading and Block Formatting Elements 60
Forcing Line Breaks 61
Making Text into Paragraphs 61
Division and Span Elements 61
Horizontal Rules 62
Centering Text 63
Using the Preformat Element for Easy Text Display 64
Representing Quoted Text as a Block. 65

Character Formatting 66
Displaying Text in Boldface 66
Displaying Text in Italics 66
Changing Font Typefaces 67
It's All about the Fonts 67
Using Multiple Attributes in a Font Tag 70
Special Characters (Entities) 70
Text Format Tricks Enhance Your Web Page 71
What's Next? 71
URL Cited 72
Chapter 4 Review Exercises 73
    Chapter 4 Fill-In Questions 73
    Chapter 4 Multiple-Choice Questions 73
    Chapter 4 Design and Discussion Questions 73
5 Images and Linking to Other Web Pages 75
Graphics and Copyright 75
Clipart Collections 75
Subscription and Fee-Based Royalty-Free Clipart 77
Graphic File Types 79
Lossy and Lossless Image Compression 79
Spicing Up Your Web Page with Clipart 80
Relative and Absolute File Addresses 80
Missing Images and the alt Attribute 81
Sizing Your Images and Multiplying Them 82
Boxing in Your Images 84
Adding Space around Your Images 85
Aligning Your Images and Text 85
Hyperlinking: Locally, Globally, and Internally 86
Hypertext and Hypergraphics: Linking to Images and Other Web Pages 87
Relative Links within a Web Page: The name Attribute 90
Opening a New Browser Window 90
Adding Your Email Address to Your Web Page 90

What's Next? .91
URLs Cited .91
Chapter 5 Review Exercises .93
Chapter 5 Fill-In Questions .93
Chapter 5 Multiple-Choice Questions .93
Chapter 5 Design and Discussion Questions .93
6 Cascading Style Sheets and Floating Images .95
Cascading Style Sheets .95
Adding Inline style Attributes to HTML Elements .95
Using Border Attributes with Horizontal Rules .96
Internal Cascading Style Sheets .97
Adding style—One Page at a Time .98
Changing Multiple Defaults with style on a Single Page .100
Defining style within Elements Using Classes .100
Fully Defined Element Class Method .101
Generic Class Method .101
Other Class Acts .103
Using External Style Sheet Files .103
Updating Our Red Rose Library Home Page .104
Styling Paragraph Indents and Margins .106
Background Images .107
Image Borders .108
Text Boxes and Borders .110
Dropped Caps .111
Floating Images for Newsletter Designs .112
Additional CSS Resources .113
What's Next? .113
URLs Cited .114
Chapter 6 Review Exercises .115
Chapter 6 Fill-In Questions .115
Chapter 6 Multiple-Choice Questions .115
Chapter 6 Design and Discussion Questions .115

7 Lists, Lists, and More Lists 117
Three Basic Lists 117
Unordered Lists 117
The List Item 118
Ordered Lists 118
Nesting Lists 119
Definition Lists 121
Creating Lists with Style 124
What's Next? 125
Chapter 7 Review Exercises 126
Chapter 7 Multiple-Choice Questions 126
Chapter 7 Design and Discussion Questions 126
8 Tables and Their Creative Uses 127
Building a Table 127
Designing a Calendar 130
Adding Table Captions and Headings 131
Spanning Table Rows and Columns 133
Applying Tables to Red Rose Library Web Pages 134
Using Cascading Style Sheets to Create Tables 136
Style Sheet Table Element Equivalents 137
What's Next? 141
URL Cited 141
Chapter 8 Review Exercises 142
Chapter 8 Multiple-Choice Questions 142
Chapter 8 Design and Discussion Questions 142
9 Forms for Patron Interactivity 143
What Uses Might Your Library Have for Forms? 143
Creating Web Forms 144
The form Element 144
The input Element 145
The select Element 146

The textarea Element 147
Adding Color to a textarea Box Form 147
Action Button Types 147
Server-Side Processing: Making Forms Work with CGI 149
How the CGI Can Work for You 149
Online Surveys 151
Forms Processing Using Simple Email Techniques 151
Making It Work with JavaScript: Client-Side Processing 154
Using Forms Graphics in Calendar Pages 154
SuDoKu Anyone? 156
What's Next? 156
URLs Cited 156
Chapter 9 Review Exercises 158
Chapter 9 Multiple-Choice Questions 158
Chapter 9 Design and Discussion Questions 158
10 Web Page Navigation, Image Mapping, and Marquees 159
Web Page Navigation Techniques 159
Image Maps 161
Image Map area Attributes 162
Adding Navigation to the Red Rose Library Page 165
Marquees 166
Section 508 168
What's Next? 168
URLs Cited 169
Chapter 10 Review Exercises 170
Chapter 10 Multiple-Choice Questions 170
Chapter 10 Design and Discussion Questions 170
11 More Fun with CSS 171
HTML Doctypes 171
About the CSS Specification 172
CSS Rules 172
Block-Level and Inline-Level HTML Element Types 173

Default Element Styles 174
External Style Sheets and the link Element 174
Media Attributes 176
Media Blocks 179
Avoid Using title Attributes in the link Tag 179
Internal Style Sheets and Inline Styling 181
ID Selectors 183
Checking for IE Browser Type: Conditional Comments 184
Boxes and Borders 184
Box Margin Shorthand 184
What's Next? 186
URLs Cited 187
Chapter 11 Review Exercises 188
Chapter 11 Multiple-Choice Questions 188
Chapter 11 Design and Discussion Questions 188
12 XML 189
What Is XML? 189
XML Applications or Vocabularies 190
Basic Web Document Requirements 190
The XML Document 191
The XML Prolog 191
Encoding: The Unicode Transformation Format 192
XML Comments and Style Sheets 193
Doctypes and DTDs 193
EAD, TEI, and Other Library-Oriented Vocabularies 194
Internal DTD Subsets 197
The XML Body 197
The XML Epilog 197
Creating XML Documents without Using DTDs 198
A CSS-Structured XML Cookbook 198
XML Document Construction 199
Creating an *XML-Like* Document 201

The XML Document Tree 203
XML Namespaces 205
XML Dublin Core Metadata Set (DCMES) Tree Diagrams 206
XML-Like Presentations: Using CSS to Create an XML Document 206
Creating HTML Element Styles in CSS 209
External CSS Style Processing in *XML-Like* Documents 212
Which to Use: .htm or .xml Extensions? 214
Browser XML Tree Displays 214
Creating XML Document Type Definition Vocabularies 215
XML Element Declarations 216
ALL and EMPTY Content Specifications 216
Children and Mixed Element Specifications 217
Content Specification Element Occurrence Rules 217
The Cookbook DTD Element Set 218
Parsed and Non-Parsed Character Data 218
Creating an Internal XML DTD 219
Creating an Unordered List Document Type Definition 220
External XML DTDs 222
The Dublin Core DTD 223
XML Element Attributes 224
XML Attribute Declaration Syntax 225
Required, Fixed, and Implied Attribute Defaults 225
String, Enumerated, and Tokenized Attribute Types 226
XML Character and Entity References 226
XML Entity Declarations 227
DTD Parameter Entity Syntax 228
External Entity File Syntax 229
Internal cookbook DTD 229
Using Multiple DTDs 230
Why Use Namespaces? 232
HTML 5—The Future Is Near! 235
What's Next? 236

URLs Cited .236
Some XML Vocabulary Namespaces for Science and Math .237
Review Exercises .239
Chapter 12 Review Exercises .239
Chapter 12 Multiple-Choice Questions .239
Chapter 12 Design and Discussion Questions .239
13 Content Management Systems, Mobile Applications, and Things That Go Bump in the Night .241
Content Management Systems .241
What Is Content? .245
Basic Content Management Process .245
CMS Web Design Methodology .247
CONTENTdm Digital Collection Management Software .247
How CONTENTdm Works .248
The CONTENTdm Content Management System .249
DreamHost and Common CMS Systems .252
WordPress: The Popular Blog and Bibliography Collection CMS .254
Should You Use WordPress.com or WordPress.org? .254
Planning Your WordPress Theme .256
Other DreamHost CMS Options .258
Social Media and "Web 2.0" .260
Web Page Usability .262
Mobile Applications .263
The Ubiquitous QR Code .263
Up and Coming Buzz Words to Consider .265
We Covered a Lot of Things, but Not Everything .266
URLs Cited .266
Textbooks .269
Chapter 13 Review Exercises .270
Chapter 13 Multiple-Choice Questions .270
Chapter 13 Design and Discussion Questions .270

Appendix A HTML Element Syntax 271
Appendix B HTML Entity Relationship Characters 283
Appendix C Cascading Style Sheets: CSS Properties and Syntax 291
Index 299

List of Figures

Chapter 1

Figure 01-01	Creating Subfolders in a Folder (Directory)	2
Figure 01-02	Website with Common Subfolders	3
Figure 01-03	Red Rose Library Newsletter (**code0103.doc** = **redrose1.doc**)	4
Figure 01-04	Word Document Saved as a Web Page (**code0104.htm**)	5
Figure 01-05	Viewing a Text File Directly as a Web Page (**code0105.htm**)	6
Figure 01-06	Basic Skeleton of an HTML Page (WordPad view: **code0107.htm**)	9
Figure 01-07	Browser View of Basic Web Page (**code0107.htm**)	10
Figure 01-08	WordPad View of Newsletter HTML File (**code0109.htm**)	10
Figure 01-09	Browser View of Newsletter HTML File (**code0109.htm**)	11
Figure 01-10	Using the **pre** Element (WordPad view: **code0110.htm**)	12
Figure 01-11	Web Page Using **pre** Element (**code0111.htm**)	13
Figure 01-12	Adding Paragraph Tags to Preformatted Pages (**code0113.htm**)	14
Figure 01-13	Effect of Paragraph Tags on Preformatted Pages (**code0113.htm**)	15
Figure 01-14	Styling with **center**, **b**, and **u** Elements (**code0115.htm**; adds formatting)	16
Figure 01-15	Web Page with **center**, **b**, and **u** Elements (**code0115.htm**)	17
Figure 01-16	Adding the **img** Tag (**code0117.htm**)	17
Figure 01-17	Web Page with Graphic (**code0117.htm**)	18
Figure 01-18	Adding a Basic Table (**code0119.htm**; adds table elements)	19
Figure 01-19	Web Page Table with Borders [**border="1"**] (**code0119.htm**)	19

Figure 01-20 The Red Rose Web Page [**border="0"**] (**code0120.htm**) 20

Figure 01-21 Web Page with All Content Inside of a Table (**code0121.htm=redrose.htm**) 21

Chapter 2

Figure 02-01 Naming Your Files 24

Figure 02-02 Lynx View of Figure 01-21—Red Rose Library Newsletter 27

Figure 02-03 Adding the **alt** Attribute to **img** Tags (**code0204.htm**) 28

Figure 02-04 Lynx View of Image with **alt** Attribute (**code0204.htm**) 28

Figure 02-05 Suggested Website Directory Tree Structure 30

Figure 02-06 Suggested Website Windows™ Folder Structure 30

Figure 02-07 Library Home Page with Top-Ten Page Links (**code0207.htm**) 33

Chapter 3

Figure 03-01 Nesting HTML Element Tags 41

Figure 03-02 Structure of an HTML Document 42

Figure 03-03 Structure of an HTML Page (**code0304.htm**) 43

Figure 03-04 Default **html** Tag and Its Attributes (**code0304.htm**) 43

Figure 03-05 Inserting the **title** Tag (**code0306.htm**) 45

Figure 03-06 Browser Showing Page Title (**code0306.htm**) 45

Figure 03-07 Sixteen Common Web Page Color Names and Their Values (**code0307.htm**) 47

Figure 03-08 Example of In-Page Cataloging: Dublin Core Metadata Parameters 48

Chapter 4

Figure 04-01 Adding Comments to Your Code 54

Figure 04-02 Using Comment Delimiters to "Ignore Code" (**code0403.htm**) 55

Figure 04-03 Using Comment Delimiters—Browser View (**code0403.htm**) 55

Figure 04-04 Pagetutor.com ColorPicker II by Joe Barta 57

Figure 04-05 Changing the Web Page's Background Color (**code0406.htm**) 57

Figure 04-06 Creating a Solid Colored Background (**code0406.htm**) 58

Figure 04-07 Replacing Background Color with Graphics (**code0408.htm**) 58

Figure 04-08 Creating a Tiled Graphic Background (**code0408.htm**) 58

Figure 04-09 Default Hyperlink Colors (**code0409.htm**) 59
Figure 04-10 Customized Hyperlink Colors (**code0410.htm**) 59
Figure 04-11 Heading Examples (**code0411.htm**) 60
Figure 04-12 Using the Paragraph Element (**code0412.htm**) 60
Figure 04-13 Comparing the **div** and **span** Elements (**code0413.htm**) 62
Figure 04-14 Acquiring **div** and **span** Styles Inline (**code0414.htm**) 62
Figure 04-15 Examples of Horizontal Rule Coding (**code0415.htm**) 63
Figure 04-16 Viewing the **pre** Tag in a Browser (**code0416.htm**) 64
Figure 04-17 Viewing a Blockquote (**code0417.htm**) 65
Figure 04-18 Using Blockquotes (**code0418.htm**) 65
Figure 04-19 How Boldface Characters Are Displayed (**code0419.htm**) 66
Figure 04-20 How Characters Look in Italics (**code0420.htm**) 67
Figure 04-21 Monotype Text Display (**code0421.htm**) 67
Figure 04-22 Inline **font size** Changes on Your Browser (**code0422.htm**) 68
Figure 04-23 Inline **font face** Changes on Your Browser (**code0423.htm**) 69
Figure 04-24 Inline **font color** Changes on Your Browser (**code0424.htm**) 70
Figure 04-25 Nested **font** Changes on Your Browser (**code0425.htm**) 71
Figure 04-26 Special Entity Characters 71
Figure 04-27 Enhancing Your Web Page with Format Tricks (**code0427.htm**) 72

Chapter 5

Figure 05-01 Web Page Clipart URLs 76
Figure 05-02 Flaming Text Sample Logos (**code0502.htm**) (from: **http://www.flamingtext.com/start.html**) 77
Figure 05-03 FlamingText.com "Old Stone" Logo Creator Screen (**code0503.htm**) (from **http://www.flamingtext.com/net-fu/forms/old-stone-logo.html**) 78
Figure 05-04 Flaming Text Red Rose Library Logo (Romeo Font, **img002.jpg**) 78
Figure 05-05 Relative and Absolute Addressing in **img** Tags (**code0505.htm**) 81
Figure 05-06 Adding Information with the **alt** Attribute (**code0506.htm**) 82
Figure 05-07 Adjusting Image Height to Fit Your Space (**img001.jpg**, **code0507.htm**) 83

Figure 05-08	Boxing in Your Images (**code0508.htm**)	84
Figure 05-09	Adding Horizontal Space between Your Images (**code0509.htm**)	85
Figure 05-10	Aligning Text and Images (**code0510.htm**)	85
Figure 05-11	Flowing Text around Images (**code0511.htm**)	86
Figure 05-12	Hypertext, Hyper graphics and the name Attribute (**code0512.htm**)	88
Figure 05-13	Using the **mailto:** Hyperlink (**code0513.htm**)	91

Chapter 6

Figure 06-01	Inline Horizontal Line **style** Examples (**code0601.htm**)	96
Figure 06-02	Inline Style Syntax	99
Figure 06-03	Changing **h1** Style Definitions (**code0603.htm**)	100
Figure 06-04	Using an Internal Style Sheet (**code0604.htm**)	100
Figure 06-05	Fully Defined Element and Generic Class Definitions (**code0605.htm**)	102
Figure 06-06	Sample Home Page (**code0606.htm**)	105
Figure 06-07	Web Page Results from Either Internal or External CSS Techniques (**code0607int.htm** = internal style sheet technique; **code0607ext.htm** and **0607style.css** = external style sheet)	106
Figure 06-08	Defining Paragraph Classes (**code0608.htm**)	108
Figure 06-09	Softened Logo for Watermarking Your Page (**img005.jpg**)	108
Figure 06-10	Style Sheet Watermarking (**code0610.htm**)	109
Figure 06-11	Images with Fancy Borders (**code0611.htm** = **bio.htm**)	110
Figure 06-12	Styling Text and Image Borders (**code0612.htm** = **history.htm**)	111
Figure 06-13	Dropped Caps (**code0613.htm**)	112
Figure 06-14	Floating Images (**code0614.htm**)	113

Chapter 7

Figure 07-01	The Unordered List Elements (**code0701.htm**)	118
Figure 07-02	Ordered Lists (**code0702.htm**)	119
Figure 07-03	Nesting Ordered Lists (**code0703.htm**)	119

Figure 07-04 Nesting Ordered and Unordered Lists (**code0704.htm**) 120

Figure 07-05 A Children's Room Hypergraphic List Quiz (**code0705.htm, quiz.htm**) 121

Figure 07-06 The Definition List (**code0706.htm**) 122

Figure 07-07 A Program Page Template (**code0707.htm, programs.htm**) 122

Figure 07-08 Template for an Event (**code0708.htm, 1401prog.htm**) 123

Figure 07-09 Lists with Style and Class (**code0709.htm**) 124

Chapter 8

Figure 08-01 One-Cell Tables (**code0801.htm**) 129

Figure 08-02 Red-Bordered Tables (**code0802.htm**) 130

Figure 08-03 Basic Table Construction Syntax 130

Figure 08-04 Two-Cell and Four-Cell Tables (**code0804.htm**) 131

Figure 08-05 Simple One-Row, Seven-Cell Table (**code0805.htm**) 132

Figure 08-06 Simple One-Week Calendar Table (**code0806.htm**) 133

Figure 08-07 One-Week Children's Room Activity Calendar (**code0807.htm**) 133

Figure 08-08 Simple Calendar for September 2014 (**code0808.htm**) 134

Figure 08-09 Using **colspan** for Odd and Even Column Rows (**code0809.htm**) 134

Figure 08-10 Web Page Periodical Table (*Source:* WebElements.com) 135

Figure 08-11 Basic Directions Page (**code0811.htm**) 136

Figure 08-12 Table Directions Page (**code0812.htm**) 136

Figure 08-13 Table Directions Page without Border="0" (**code0813.htm=where.htm**) 137

Figure 08-14 One-Day Calendar Page (**code0814.htm=workshop.htm**) 138

Figure 08-15 Weekly School Program Planner (**code0815.htm=program.htm**) 139

Figure 08-16 Style Sheet Table Based on W3 Example (**code0816.htm**) 139

Figure 08-17 Seven-Column CSS Table (**code0817.htm**) 140

Figure 08-18 CSS One-Week Table Template (**code0818.htm**) 140

Figure 08-19 CSS One-Month Table Template (**code0819.htm**) 141

Chapter 9

Figure 09-01	Check Box, Radio, and Text Buttons (**code0901.htm**)	145
Figure 09-02	Adding Style to Form Buttons (**code0902.htm**)	145
Figure 09-03	Adding Drop-Down (**select**) Lists to Your Form (**code0903.htm**)	146
Figure 09-04	Drop-Down Form for Hotel Reservations (**code0904.htm**)	146
Figure 09-05	Adding Text to Your Form (**code0905.htm**)	147
Figure 09-06	Adding Color to the Textarea (**code0906.htm**)	148
Figure 09-07	Adding Color to a Scrollbar in the Textarea (**code0907.htm**)	148
Figure 09-08	Adding Action Buttons to Your Form (**code0908.htm**)	149
Figure 09-09	Email Form Elements (**code0909.htm**)	152
Figure 09-10	Outlook Express Email Generated by Form in FireFox Browser	153
Figure 09-11	Simple JavaScript URL Selection Form (**code0911.htm**)	155
Figure 09-12	First Quarter 2006 Form Calendar (**code0912.htm**)	155
Figure 09-13	2007 Annual Calendar—Form in Portrait Mode (**code0913.htm**)	156
Figure 09-14	SoDuKu Module Using Nested Tables (left, **code0914.htm**) and Using Input Buttons and Color (right, **code0915.htm**)	157

Chapter 10

Figure 10-01	Hypertext Navigation Bar (**code1001.htm**)	160
Figure 10-02	Stylized Hypertext Navigation Bar (**code1002.htm**)	160
Figure 10-03	Home Page with Logo and Hypertext Navigation Bar (**code1003.htm**)	161
Figure 10-04	The Navigation Bar Image (**navbar.jpg**)	162
Figure 10-05	Correlation between Hyperlinks and Files (**code1005.doc**)	163
Figure 10-06	Image Mapping a Navigation Bar (**code1006.htm**)	164
Figure 10-07	Adding Navigation to the Red Rose Library Page (**code1007.htm**)	165
Figure 10-08	Adding Hyperlinks and Real File Names (**code1008.htm**)	166
Figure 10-09	Restyled Hyperlinks for a "Finished" Look (**code1009.htm**)	167
Figure 10-10	Adding Marquees to Your Page (**code1010.htm**)	168

Chapter 11

Figure 11-01	Example of CSS Rule Syntax	173
Figure 11-02	Example of a Default DTD Table	174
Figure 11-03	Using Multiple Style Sheets in the Head of an HTML Document	175
Figure 11-04	Effect of External CSS Changes on the Body Background Color	176
Figure 11-05	Embedded Style Codes Including Media Block	180
Figure 11-06	Screenshot of Alternate Style Sheets (Eric Meyer's Complex Spiral Demo) **http://meyerweb.com/eric/css/edge/complexspiral/demo.html**	181
Figure 11-07	Inline or **class** Attributes and the DTD Stack	182
Figure 11-08	Stripping Inline or **class** Attributes from the DTD Stack	183
Figure 11-09	Example Using **class** and **ID** Selectors	183
Figure 11-10	Using Conditional Comments to Adjust for Different IE Versions	184
Figure 11-11	Browser Window Box Definitions (from "CSS, DHTML & Ajax," fourth edition by Jason Teague, Peachpit Press; Figure 6.1 page 160)	185

Chapter 12

Figure 12-01	Basic HTML Document Requirements	191
Figure 12-02	The HTML DOCTYPE Declaration	194
Figure 12-03	Basic XML Document Structure	198
Figure 12-04	Basic Hierarchical Structure for a Cookbook	199
Figure 12-05	Basic HTML Recipe for a Cookbook (**code1205.htm**)	200
Figure 12-06	HTML Recipe Browser Display (**code1205.htm**)	201
Figure 12-07	Element Nesting for Well-Formedness	202
Figure 12-08	Semantic Recipe Elements (**code1208.htm**)	202
Figure 12-09	Browser View of Semantic Recipe Elements (**code1208.htm**)	203
Figure 12-10	Establishing Tree Structure Rules	203
Figure 12-11	Tree Diagram Modules with Structure Rules	204
Figure 12-12	Basic **books** Tree Diagram	204
Figure 12-13	Basic **cookbook** Tree Diagram	205
Figure 12-14	Basic **recipe** Tree Diagram	205

Figure 12-15 Basic **play** Tree Diagram 206
Figure 12-16 Basic **records** Tree Diagram 206
Figure 12-17 Basic **Dublin Core Metadata Set** (DCMES) Tree Diagram 207
Figure 12-18 Adding Inline Style Code to the **cookbook** Document (**code1218.htm**) 208
Figure 12-19 The **cookbook** Document with Inline CSS Styling (**code1218.htm**) 208
Figure 12-20 The **cookbook** Document with CSS Block Style (**code1220.htm**) 209
Figure 12-21 Equating HTML and **recipe** Document Elements 209
Figure 12-22 Internal CSS Style Declarations (**code1222.htm**, also **xmlstyle.css**) 211
Figure 12-23 Results of Internal CSS Style Declarations (**code1222.htm**) 212
Figure 12-24 Linking to External CSS Style Files (**code1224.htm**, **code1224.xml**) 213
Figure 12-25 The **.xml** Extension and Browser Tree Structure (**code1225.xml**) 214
Figure 12-26 Collapsing the Browser's Tree Display (**code1225.xml**) 215
Figure 12-27 Content Specification Occurrence Rules 217
Figure 12-28 Basic **cookbook** Internal DTD (**code1228.htm**) 220
Figure 12-29 Internal DTD Subset Syntax 221
Figure 12-30 XML Document with Internal DTD (**code1230.xml**) 222
Figure 12-31 General **Dublin Core Metadata Set** (**DCMES**) Tree Diagram 223
Figure 12-32 External DTD Coding Basic Dublin Core **record** (**dc.dtd**) 224
Figure 12-33 Some Predefined Entity and Character References 227
Figure 12-34 Basic Internal Subset DTD Structure for a Cookbook 229
Figure 12-35 Possible XML Cookbook Document (**cb.dtd**, **code1235.xml**) 230
Figure 12-36 XML Cookbook Document IE Display (**code1235.xml**, **cb.dtd**, **xmlstyle.css**) 231
Figure 12-37 Combined Firefox and IE Namespace Styles (**model.css**) 234
Figure 12-38 Firefox and IE Namespace Style Coding 235

Chapter 13

Figure 13-01 "Book" Database Tables for a Microsoft Access Relational Database 243

Figure 13-02	Title/Author/Publisher Links for a Microsoft Access Relational Database	244
Figure 13-03	Intranet Roadmap with Highlighted Section (from **http://www.steptwo.com.au/products/roadmap**)	246
Figure 13-04	The CONTENTdm Windows-Based Project Client Interface (Spreadsheet View)	248
Figure 13-05	CONTENTdm Web Browser Administration Interface, Server Tab	250
Figure 13-06	CONTENTdm Web Browser Administration Interface, Collections Tab	251
Figure 13-07	CONTENTdm Digital Collection Process	252
Figure 13-08	CONTENTdm Web Browser Administration Interface, Items Tab	253
Figure 13-09	Two Phases of DreamHost CMS Setup	253
Figure 13-10	WordPress Quick Setup at **https://signup.wordpress.com/signup**	255
Figure 13-11	Differences between Websites on WordPress Sites	256
Figure 13-12	WordPress "Twenty Ten" Default Template	257
Figure 13-13	WordPress Widgets Administration Page	257
Figure 13-14	Anatomy of a WordPress Theme	258
Figure 13-15	The Seven Key Features of Web 2.0 (from: **http://webapprater.com/general/7-key-features-of-web-2-0.html**)	260
Figure 13-16	Popular Social Network Logos and URLs	261
Figure 13-17	Anatomy of a QR Code (from **U.S. Patent # 5726435**)	264
Figure 13-18	150 × 150 pixel QR Code for the Red Rose Library Website (**http://www.redroselibrary.com**)	265

Preface

Welcome to *Web Design for Libraries*

Librarians communicate with their patrons and staff in many ways. These include signs and posters in the library, newsletters to the local community, and now, with web pages via the World Wide Web. Each mode of communication has its own strengths and weaknesses. Each provides opportunities for you to put your best foot forward. Each is also a publication that requires some common branding elements such as logos and consistent names.

Posters, newsletters, and other printed materials are fixed publications that cannot easily be modified once created. The web is a dynamically changing "instant" publication with web pages that can be (and are!) changed nearly instantaneously and updated as errors are discovered, events end, or changes are needed. Most of us know how to use word processors to create print materials. Your goal then, with the help of this text, is gaining the knowledge of the language of web pages, the HyperText Markup Language (HTML) needed to present your information on web pages for the entire world to see.

Being creative online involves planning, HTML coding, and publishing web pages. In cyberspace, your page can link to other pages, other websites, and even your library's online public access catalog, or OPAC, and content management system. More than merely a text, *Web Design for Libraries* is a gentle introduction into web design and publishing that takes you on an adventure into the creation of a website for the Red Rose Library.

About the Red Rose Library (http://www.redroselibrary.com)

Rather than obtaining permissions to publish dozens of other library's web pages, we will develop a (mythical) Red Rose Library website that has many of the services that you probably have in your brick-and-mortar library and want to feature on your web pages. After looking over dozens of online library pages (see "Where I can find Library Web Pages" later) and thinking about what kinds of "stuff" might be on, or linked to by, a library website a list of "standard" items was created. In no real order these consisted of links from the library's home page to inside or internal page content links covering Ready Reference Q&A, a children's section, a young adult's section, a general patron section, an OPAC and/or online databases link, a link to the library's online collection(s), the hours of operation, special events, calendar, library board and staff contacts (including special budget vote information), newsletters and archive, links to the local library system, and links to your community and governmental agencies. Once you have completed the task of evaluating what you want to display, based on the techniques in this text you will easily create your own library web pages.

Key to your success in this adventure is your creativity, and CONTENT! Great prose makes great pages. Sad, but true, not everyone is a writer or poet, and not everyone is an artist. However fancy your page format is, be aware that like a blank sheet of paper without good content, your website could be a wasteland of information-empty files. Although professional-looking graphics and marketing techniques are not everyone's cup of tea, clipart is easy to find and use, if you make sure you have copyright permissions! And talking to your library's newsletter editor or public relations person (or a friend at another library performing these functions) will give you lots of ideas on content, and how to market your library programs.

In this text, through the development of a variety of pages for the "Red Rose Library," you will be guided to creating your own web pages. Linking these pages together will create a website that will function internally on your library's intranet, or when posted on a web server, be accessible externally on the Internet for patrons anywhere in the world. From paper designs to working websites you'll find tips and techniques on every page where you will discover how to present your library through the broadcast medium of the World Wide Web.

Why This Book?

So you saw this really neat web page while surfing the Internet and said how great it would be if your library had a page that looked just like that one . Well, it is certainly possible and in buying this book you have indicated you are up for the challenge.

While there may be several very complicated pages, sections and chapters that you will not be able to replicate because they contain high-level computer science techniques, or others that may use special graphics such as flash movies, after following the procedures and tips in this text you will be able to create very functional web pages that can do nearly everything "professional" pages can do.

This text is intended to be used as a stand-alone user-friendly workbook for individuals who have no programming background with an interest in the rapid development of professional-looking websites. What you need to begin is lots of paper for designing your page layout. You'll also need lots of words, articles, and other content and ideas. Finally, you'll need a computer and familiarity with creating and using files and folders in a Microsoft Windows™ environment. You'll need a text processor and Internet browser installed on your computer. Although you can use any plain text editor like Microsoft's Notepad, and any browser (see examples in Chapter 2), examples in this text were created using Microsoft WordPad™ and viewed with Mozilla's Firefox™ (Version 23) in the Microsoft Windows™ 7 environment. "Cut and paste" techniques and templates are used throughout the text as examples of how to create pages without the need to really learn the HTML markup language and all are downloadable from the text's demonstration website.

Finishing this web design text doesn't mean you are an instant webmaster any more than having oil paints and canvas, an easel, and brushes means you can paint like a Picasso. What you will get is the feeling that you know how web pages fit together, how to create them, and about the way various web page tools work with markup languages to make your web pages come alive.

In fact, our goal is that in the time it takes you to go through each chapter you will see the creation of web pages for the "Red Rose Library" and using those techniques you could easily configure pages for use in your library. Each page will be simple enough for a novice to create and yet have enough choices to make HTML-aware folks happy with their results.

You will be able to create your own personal web page and one for your library or even a basic library system website. You supply the time to practice these techniques, add the content, design, and structure you want; we'll supply the tools, techniques, and markup code snippets that will permit you to design web pages and sites that combine text, graphics, animation, and multimedia using markup language techniques to control the layout and flow of your information.

The text's focus is on the creation of HTML pages useful in libraries and information centers as demonstrated using the mythical Red Rose Library as a demonstration site. Screenshots and code sets/files will be created and Uniform Resource Locator (URL) links to them will be included in each section of the text. We will show you how to add style to a single page or your whole website using program language-like style cascading style sheet (CSS) coding.

After completing the text, or participating in an instructor-led workshop, the reader will understand the web design cycle from content development to publishing on the web, will learn the most essential topics in web page development, will be able to develop complex websites in a short period of time, and will realize some of the benefits and limitations of using HTML to create web pages.

The good news is that after working through the exercises in this text you will be able to create web pages which can be published on any web server to show the world all the great things you have in your library.

At your public library, do you have a web server as part of your local government or school board's electronic resources? If you do, you should see if they can set it up for you to use to publish your pages.

Where Can I Find Library Web Page Examples?

Not all libraries are on the web, but most public libraries in the United States that have websites can be located using the searchable, and regularly updated, "Libweb" at **www.lib-web.org.**

On the Libweb directory, last updated in December 2012, are links to over 8,000 library server web pages from not only the United States but from over 146 countries as well. You'll find library websites that vary from single web page to elaborate presentations offering everything from digital collections to OPAC, some with email and interlibrary loan options. The more sophisticated sites have at least two levels of access: general public and password-protected areas for authorized registered users. Those websites with some level of online accessible digital collection are typically interconnected with a special e-commerce or transaction server that also enables the librarian to process forms and permits document purchases. Not content with only offering the public libraries, Libweb also has lists (and hyperlinks) to academic libraries, national libraries and library organizations, state libraries, regional consortia, and special and school libraries. You'll also find links to library websites in Europe, Africa and the Middle East, Asia, Australia, New Zealand, and the Pacific, Canada, Mexico, the Caribbean, Central America, and South America.

CSS, XML, HTML5, and CMS

Although not for those who are not willing to dive into the computer science and coding ends of the pool, chapters on more advanced CSS techniques, the eXtensible Markup Language, XML, that adds a new dimension to your coding—homemade markup elements, and HTML5 which melds HTML, XML, and CSS into an even more powerful future-looking tool are covered so that you can understand the basics of their usage. We close the text with an overview of what content management systems, CMS, are, and some examples of their use in libraries and information systems. As you are still here, GOOD! I didn't want to scare you off, but rather to indicate that from the meager beginnings of understanding HTML and how to create your own web pages, websites, and web presence, to HTML5 and CMS, this text can be your guide to improving your library's visibility and usability in the brave new world of Web 2.0.

About Using Templates

Some are of the opinion that the easiest way to create their own web pages would be to use an already coded template page. To satisfy their needs, all the examples used in the text and a variety of template styles may be found in the **template** folder on the Red Rose Library demonstration website at:

http://www.redroselibrary.com/template

To use these sample web pages and templates, save the **template.zip** file on your desktop and extract the **code** folder onto your hard disk. Then whenever you need a template or code example, decide which file to use, open the file up in a text-processing program, change the titles, put your text (etc.) in it, and add in images or the HTML destinations (links) for your text or graphics as appropriate. Saving the **code** folder and then copying the individual files or giving them a different file name will allow you to reuse the template files without resaving them from the website. (If you accidentally overwrite the original files, relax. Exact copies are still on the website for you to download.)

Typographical Conventions

To make your use of this text easier we have adopted some typographic conventions. When HTML element or attribute names are used, the name of the **element** or **attribute** is shown in bold. We also type all filenames and website addresses (e.g., **filename.htm** or **http://www.redroselibrary.com**) in bold. Graphics used in this text, unless otherwise noted, were created by the author, used with permission, or obtained through the Clipart.com link on the Red Rose Library page. This low-cost service is discussed in Chapter 2. The company permits royalty free personal and/or commercial use of their graphics, and others, as long as not more than five images appear on any given web page.

1

Quick Start in Web Design

Welcome to *Web Design for Libraries!*

Our task in this first chapter is to give you the tools to jump right into creating a web page so you don't have to wait too long to have a page up and running. The remainder of the text is designed to ease you into good design of web pages using common HyperText Markup Language (HTML) techniques without expensive software. We will actually be working with a version of HTML called the Extensible HyperText Markup Language—XHTML, but will call it HTML throughout the text. Once you have mastered the HTML/XHTML and basic cascading style sheet (CSS) techniques, you will be ready for the more advanced chapters on CSS and the eXtended Markup Language (XML), which bridges the gap between from the mostly static HMTL or XHTML to database-driven dynamic web pages of XML and HTML5. In that chapter you find out how to create your own elements and use them to design new tags and even new vocabularies of markup language elements. A ton of information on these topics and their standards can be found at **http://www.w3.org**—the place for all things World Wide Web. Once you have a bit of XML under your belt, you will be better able to understand a bit of how content management systems work.

But we are getting way ahead of ourselves.

What if all you needed for a rapid web page design was to create a word-processed document and then quickly turn it into a simple web page?

In this age of instant gratification we all want to see results quickly and effortlessly. By the time it takes you to finish this Quick Start chapter, you will have learned a quick and easy way to create web pages that you can use on your individual computer, on a CD-ROM, on your library intranet, or on an Internet web server for viewing by the entire world.

Operating Systems and Browsers

To avoid having to learn a new (and possibly expensive) program, and recognizing that according to statistics on operating systems—your computer system's basic controlling software—compiled by the W3schools for May 2014 (see the full analysis at **http://www.w3schools.com/browsers/browsers_os.asp)** only about 10% of users have Mac and 5% have Linux computers with the remainder running a version of

Microsoft™ Windows, we will use the popular Microsoft™ Word software program, which has a built-in word to web page converter. We can also create HTML pages manually, from "scratch," using Microsoft™ WordPad and simple HTML elements to "tag" your information. Mac and Linux users can use similar plain text software available for their systems.

When the author's "Crash Course" version of a web design text came out in 2007, Microsoft™ Internet Explorer was used as our standard web page viewer or "browser" as it was the most popular browser at that time. Even though it still comes installed with their Microsoft™ Windows operating system, the May 2014 survey shows only about 9% of all users use the Microsoft™ Internet Explorer web browser. Instead, almost 60% of all users use Google™ Chrome (**http://www.google.com/chrome)** and 25% use Mozilla™ Firefox (**http://www.mozilla.org/products/firefox/)** web browsers. Both are free! And both work on most computers. Safari (http://www.apple.com/safari/), an Apple™ "I" product browser, has been used by about 4% of users since 2011.

Although we will only show results using Microsoft™ Windows Chrome or Firefox software, rest assured that the results will be quite similar—although not guaranteed—using Mac and Linux browser versions.

Good to Know: In addition to the computer operating system statistics noted earlier, you can see the W3Schools analysis of the use of all popular browsers over the years at:

http://www.w3schools.com/browsers/browsers_stats.asp

Setting Up a Website Shell Directory

As you will be saving your work on a computer or server somewhere either locally or through your Internet service provider, it is best to create a website "shell" folder on your computer's desktop that you can use to collect all the bits and pieces you'll be using such as graphics and pictures, audio and other multimedia files, primary and secondary web pages, and other information. This will keep them in one space. Creating this shell requires a few simple steps.

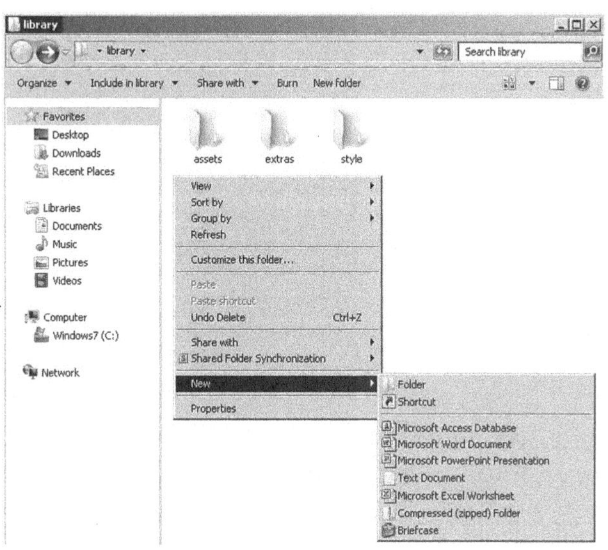

Figure 01-01. Creating Subfolders in a Folder (Directory)

To create a directory or folder that will be our website location and container for all our files on your computer desktop, right-click your mouse anywhere on your desktop. Then select "New" and then "Folder" from the drop-down menu that appears. A new folder will appear on your desktop. Use the name **library** for your overall shell directory. Then press "Enter."

Next create a subfolder (subdirectory) inside of **library** named **assets.** This is where all of your page's graphic, picture, audio, and other multimedia files will be stored. This strategy makes it easy to reference your links to digital multimedia items so you will always know where they are. Figure 01-01 shows the "New" drop-down menu after adding two more subfolders to our structure named **style,** which will be used for style definition files, and **extras,** for documents and other files that we might want to have accessed by our web pages.

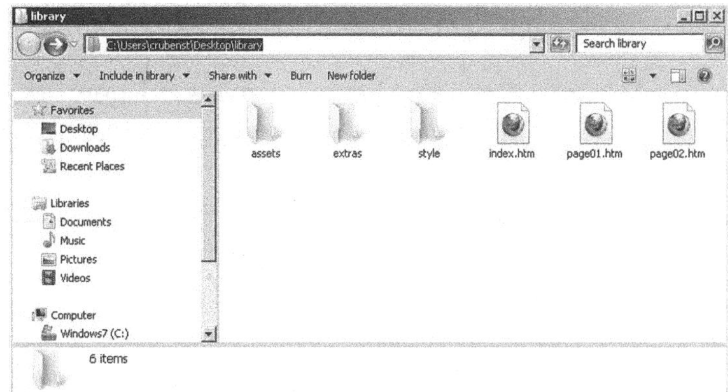

Figure 01-02. Website with Common Subfolders

The folder model we will use for our library website has a single directory with all web page HTML files and one set of assets, style, and extra subfolders supporting these HTML files inside of it as noted in Figure 01-02.

Creating a Website

The website you will be creating is merely a series of web pages, including the first or home page, often called the index page, as your library's presence on the Internet. You will want to have some or all of the following library topics and information available on your website:

Address information (phone number, fax, maps, and directions)
Hours of operation
Special events
Library board and staff
Library newsletter and archives
Links to local library systems, state library systems
Volunteer page
Ready reference section
Children section
Fiction and non-fiction sections
Audio and video resources (CD-ROMs, DVDs, cassettes, and VHS tapes)
Young adult section
OPAC (online public access catalog)
Online databases and digital collections

For this quick start exercise we will start with only five items on your website's home page: address information, hours of operation, children's room, young adult services, and special events. We will be calling our library the Red Rose Library and will want to include a logo graphic on at least our first web page, typically our home page.

The Red Rose Library
18 Rose Street
New York, New York 10010
Telephone +1 212 555-7673

First Quarter 2014 Newsletter

Open Weekdays 9:00am – 9:00pm Weekends 11:00am – 6:00pm
Come visit us– we're right across from Town Hall

For Young Adults:
Young Adult Services for those in the Red Rose High School - assistance in researching end-of-semester reports, science fair projects, and how to use online databases.

The Children's Room - *our even younger adults:*
*Mommy and Me reading programs: Monday-Wednesday-Friday 10:00am – 12:00noon.
*"Tuesdays We Read" program for kindergarten through second grade 3:30pm – 4:30pm.
*Computer and Internet Instruction: Thursdays from 3:30pm – 5:30pm.
NEW for 2014! Children's Videos Section (*next to the audio tapes section*)
Come in Fridays after 3:30pm and borrow any children's video for the whole weekend!

Special Events
(Sorry - our January trip to Radio City Music Hall has sold out.)
Annual Trip to the American Museum of Natural History and the Hayden Planetarium.
Sign up now! The bus to New York City will be leaving on Sunday February 23, 2014 at 6:00am. Trip cost is $50, which includes bus tickets, snacks on the bus, lunch at the Museum, and a souvenir. Be sure to make your reservation early - this trip sells out fast!

The Cultural Committee of the Friends of the Rose Library is co-sponsoring this bus trip.

The Red Rose Newsletter - C. Rubenstein, Editor

Figure 01-03. Red Rose Library Newsletter (**code0103.doc = redrose1.doc**)

If you have a newsletter for your library patrons, your library's home page could look much like a simple word-processed newsletter. For the fictitious Red Rose Library we have created a simple newsletter that you can see as Figure 01-03. The content for this newsletter corresponds to a word document file called **fig0103.doc.**

Using Microsoft's Word to Create Easy Web Pages

Creating a word document page layout is often easy as you know how to do it! What you may not be aware is that the later versions of Microsoft's Word have the ability to save your word-processed document as a web page with an **.htm** file extension that can be instantly viewed using your browser! The downside of this technique is that speed often results in not exactly a what-you-see-is-what-you-get (WYSIWYG) result, and minor changes require returning to the original file rather than editing the HTML web page. Another challenge is that there are lots of "droppings" due to Word's desire to keep its entire proprietary markup commands when converting to simple HTML. This will be shown after a discussion of file sizes because file sizes directly affect the overall speed of patron retrieval of your web pages.

About File Sizes (Bytes)

If we look at the size of the files, for the previous page (**code0103.doc = redrose1.doc**) we see the doc file is 26,624 bytes. When saved directly as a web page, its **.htm** file (**code0104.htm = redrose1.htm**) is 11,627 bytes plus another 4,520 bytes for the graphics and other files saved in a **redrose1_files** folder. Note: when you save your files on your computer, the exact number of bytes may vary, but the relative sizes will not. A plain text version of the doc file (**code0103.txt**) is even smaller—only 1,555 bytes! Even when we add our HTML tags and links, the manually configured html file you will have designed at the end of this chapter (**code0105.htm = redrose.htm**) will be less than 5 kilobytes, including the red rose image. OK, I won't use these number games too often, but they are important.

File sizes are often critical because some of your patrons may still be accessing the Internet, and thus your web pages, via a dial-up connection to their Internet Service Provider (ISP). Where cable modems, digital subscriber line (DSL), and Wi-Fi connections are typically too fast to worry about this magnitude of file size, dialup modems are very slow and you will want to give your patrons the information they need as quickly as possible, or they may go to another site!

The quick "Word to Web page" method uses more space and must be edited in the original, Word document file, but it still gets the job started. Or does it? After Word converted the newsletter from **.doc** into **.htm** format, when we look at the result (**code0104.htm = redrose1.htm**) as seen in Figure 01-04 we find that the rose images have shifted and now cover up some of our text.

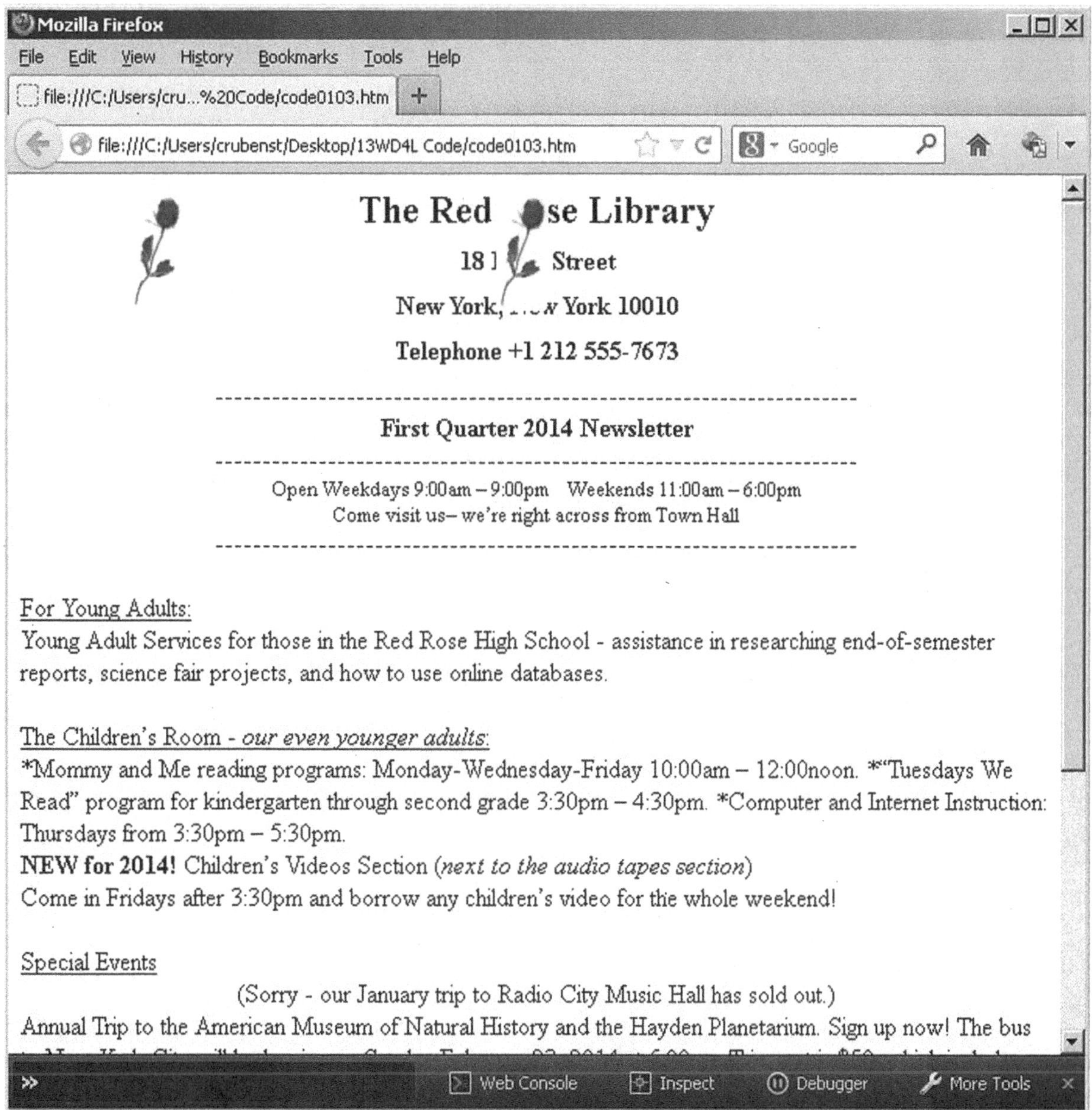

Figure 01-04. Word Document Saved as a Web Page (**code0104.htm**)

The other, not so quick, way to get your page online uses WordPad (or a similar plain text software program) to take the plain text information from your Word document newsletter and create a pure text file (**code0103.txt** = **redrose1.txt**). We can then try to force this text into an HTML file by changing its extension from **.txt** to the **.htm** file extension. Your operating system will probably suggest not doing this, but accept the change of extensions anyway. This will result in a browser display of a non-graphic, continuous stream of words that looks something like Figure 01-05.

OK, it doesn't look pretty. But it does have all the text content of the original word-processed page without wasting a lot of file download time. Clearly, this is not a page

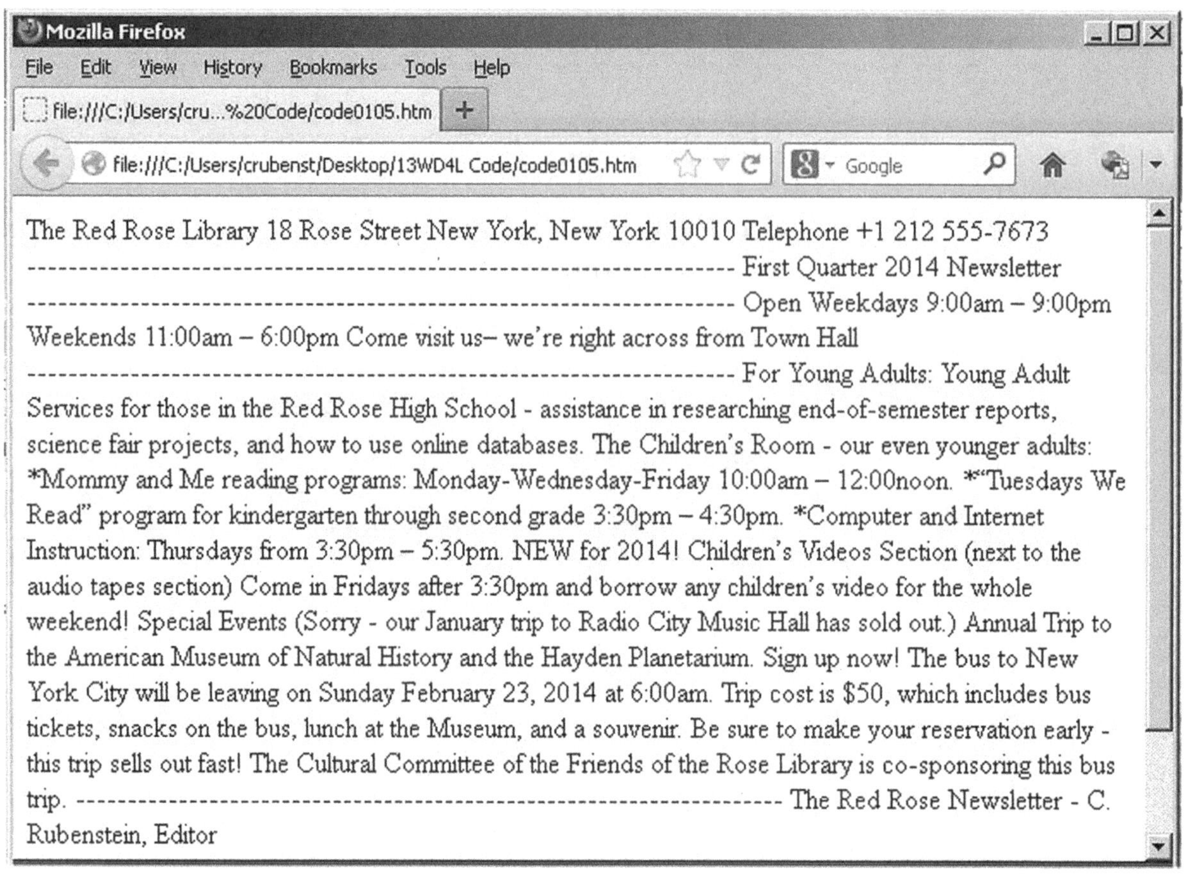

Figure 01-05. Viewing a Text File Directly as a Web Page (**code0105.htm**)

that would have your patrons coming back for more. It's time to turn to some very basic markup elements to create your page using HTML Page Structure.

HTML Page Structure

The Web Document Type

Although not needed for most browsers, W3 recommends the use of a document type declaration as the very first thing in all HTML documents to identify the precise "language" being used. To be fully compatible with future versions of HTML, we will begin every web page with a DOCTYPE declaration statement.

<u>**Good to Know:**</u> In the absence of a DOCTYPE declaration, your browser may presume that you are using the HTML 4.01 glossary of elements. Although we will be calling our work here HTML, it is actually XHTML as we are advocating using the HTML element set with XML/HTML5 rules wherever practical. *PLEASE don't let your browser make any decisions for you.* Including the DOCTYPE declaration as the very first line of *all* your web pages will assure the browser translates your code properly.

We will use the simpler, more "user-friendly" HTML5 version that looks like:

<!DOCTYPE html>

The HTML5 specification is not yet final, but most of today's browsers are ready for it and the fully defined XHTML DOCTYPE is quite a bit more complicated and would look like:

<!DOCTYPE html PUBLIC "-//W3C//DTD XHTML 1.0 Strict//EN" "http://www.w3.org/TR/xhtml1/DTD/xhtml1-strict.dtd">

We will analyze what the parts of this more complete DOCTYPE mean in Chapter 2. Please note that we will *not* show the DOCTYPE in most code display figures. Be aware that it does need to go first in your file and that the code files that we create will all include the DOCTYPE code line. You won't notice anything "wrong" if you leave the DOCTYPE out, unless you try to validate, or certify that your web page complies with web standards. Then you will see a warning message indicating that your browser presumes that you are using (typically) HTML 4.01 and will use that language's vocabulary to check your elements. Sadly, the HTML 4.01 syntax does not require closing empty element tags. These XML-compliant tags will then show up as "errors" even though the browser will display them properly.

Your validator will also scold you about the lack of character encoding. We will not include character encoding in our web page files and thus your validator program will argue, naturally, that you have not included any character encoding. The code needed to add this information requires the HTML **meta** element:

> Good to Know: Speaking of errors. I used the Web Developer 1.2.5 to validate the Word-converted newsletter **code0104.htm = redrose1.htm** as seen in Figure 01-04 and found, using the Validate HTML Local Tool, that the Word-to-Web Page method produces an HTML document with 101 errors (!), most important of which is the lack of a DOCTYPE declaration. But as noted previously, this is merely an *easy* way to create a web page from a document file. No one said it was a *valid* way to create HTML.

<meta http-equiv = Content-Type content = "text/html; charset = windows -1252" />

We will discuss **meta** elements in Chapter 3 when we discuss optional elements inside the HTML document's **head** area. Not to worry. Your browser will normally default to the **windows-1252** character coding anyway, and you will most likely not see any difference between files with, or without, this code line in your document.

Elements and Containers

After the DOCTYPE declaration, all HTML pages must begin and end with the basic element named **html** that informs the browser that the contents in the file are tagged with HTML elements. These element names are incorporated into HTML tag commands, which can be thought of as switches that turn on and off a particular way your text or images are displayed. Tags usually consist of an opening and a closing tag. I like to think of elements as "containers" so I remember to close inner containers before closing outer ones.

Opening tags contain the name of the element and one or more optional "attributes" that can further stylize your display. Closing tags contain only a slash preceding the element's name. These tags surround your text to produce the desired display features.

The basic structure of HTML documents includes elements that exist in tags. The opening tag contains any additional optional, or required, attributes or sub-elements of the element and their values.

<elementname attribute1="value"> = *AN OPENING TAG EXAMPLE*

The attribute values become style defaults during the time that the element is surrounding text, and cease their styling when the closing tag is reached in the document. Note that the closing tag only contains the element's name as closing the element's "container" closes all of its attributes.

</elementname> = *A CLOSING TAG EXAMPLE*

The correct way of using HTML element tag sets is to surround the content you wish to define by the opening element tag with its attributes and then close these changes using the closing tag (which has no attributes):

<elementname attribute1="value"> Your Text **</elementname>**

Using the HTML, Title, and Body Tags

The first element listed in a markup language document is called the *root element*. In the case of an HTML document, this would be the **html** element. The simple **html** root element **%lt;html>** is all that is needed for most web pages; however, the "official" **html** opening tag for an XHTML document is actually:

<html xmlns="http://www.w3.org/1999/xhtml" lang="en" xml:lang="en">

We will analyze what the attribute parts of this XHTML html opening tag mean in Chapter 2.

As noted earlier, using the HTML5 DOCTYPE means we do not have to use this fully defined **html** opening tag in our pages.

The basic HTML document begins with an **html** opening tag and has a **head** area that usually contains a **title** tag and then a **body** tag that opens your content area. Thus for the "First Quarter 2014 Newsletter" you should have an initial HTML document structure that looks like Figure 01-06. Please note that we are NOT showing the DOCTYPE declaration and using the simple html element without XHTML attributes to simplify the initial code examples. Also note that your text editor display will not have HTML element tags in bold. That was done here to highlight changes more clearly in the figures. Please recall that the code actually begins with the line: **<!DOCTYPE html>**

Notice the symmetry of the opening and closing element tags in the preceding figure. Proper nesting order is essential so that your browser knows when to start and stop its job of styling your text. Note that although the file name appears in the

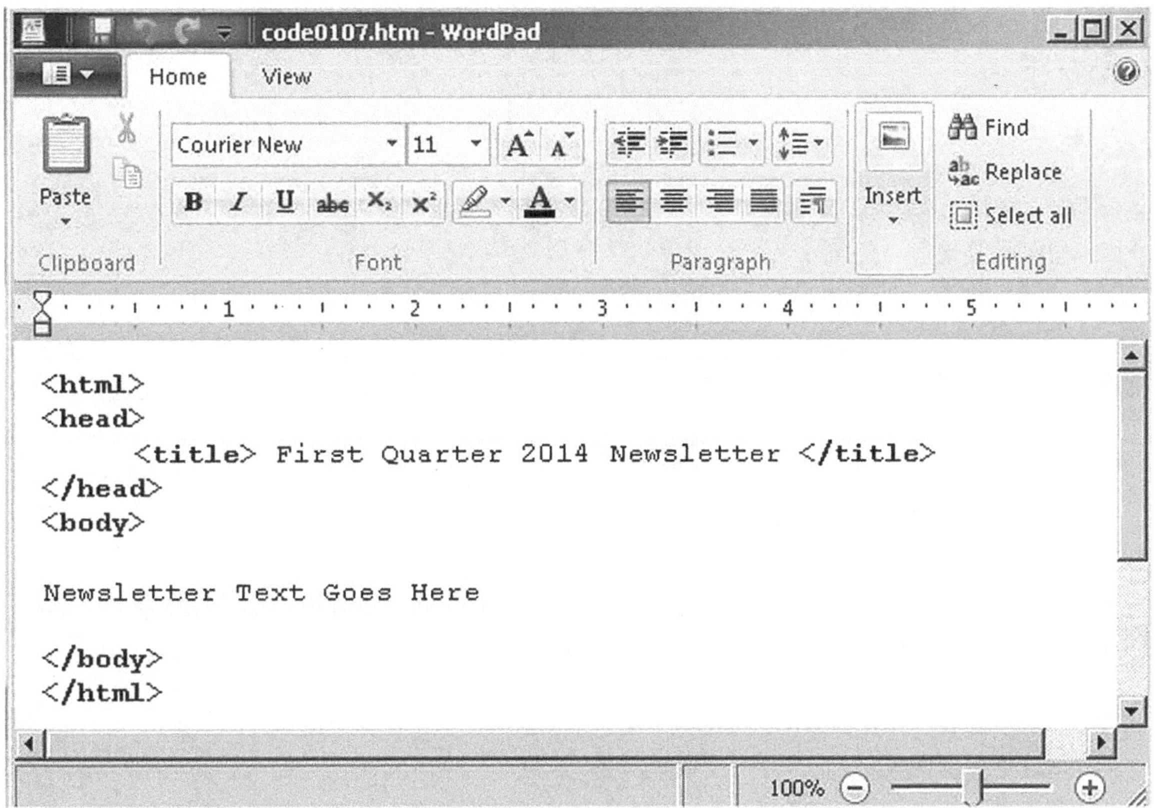

Figure 01-06. Basic Skeleton of an HTML Page (WordPad view: **code0107.htm**)

text editor window, the page's title appears in the browser window at the top to the left of the pointer to announce the name of your page. This simple file structure would be displayed as in Figure 01-07.

> **Good to Know:** We will be using only lowercase letters for our elements and other HTML names in the XHTML style. Attributes and their values are also written in lower case as will be seen later. This convention is for upward compatibility to future browsers that follow stricter XML and HTML5 guidelines.

> **Good to Know:** Browsers do not interpret line spaces or even multiple spaces between words the way a word processor does. Extra spaces and lines (carriage returns) are ignored, and this results in displaying text as a continuous line of plain text. We will need to enlist the help of some additional markup elements to create a more realistic, and more attractive, web page.

Add the contents of newsletter's text file (**fig0103.txt = redrose1.txt**) to this basic HTML file structure overlaying the "Newsletter Text Goes Here" line after the opening **body** tag to create the WordPad file of Figure 01-08 (the added text is shown in bold).

The result is an otherwise still pretty ugly web page that we already saw as Figure 01-05 but, in Figure 01-09, one that has a title appearing in the browser window.

Clearly this simple solution does not yield an attractive, or easily readable, web page. We have all the content and none of the formatting that we are seeking.

First Quarter 2014 Newsletter - Mozilla Firefox

File Edit View History Bookmarks Tools Help

First Quarter 2014 Newsletter

file:///C:/Users/crubenst/Desktop/13WD4L Code/co

Google

Newsletter Text Goes Here

1 Web Console Inspect Debugger More Tools

Figure 01-07. Browser View of Basic Web Page (**code0107.htm**)

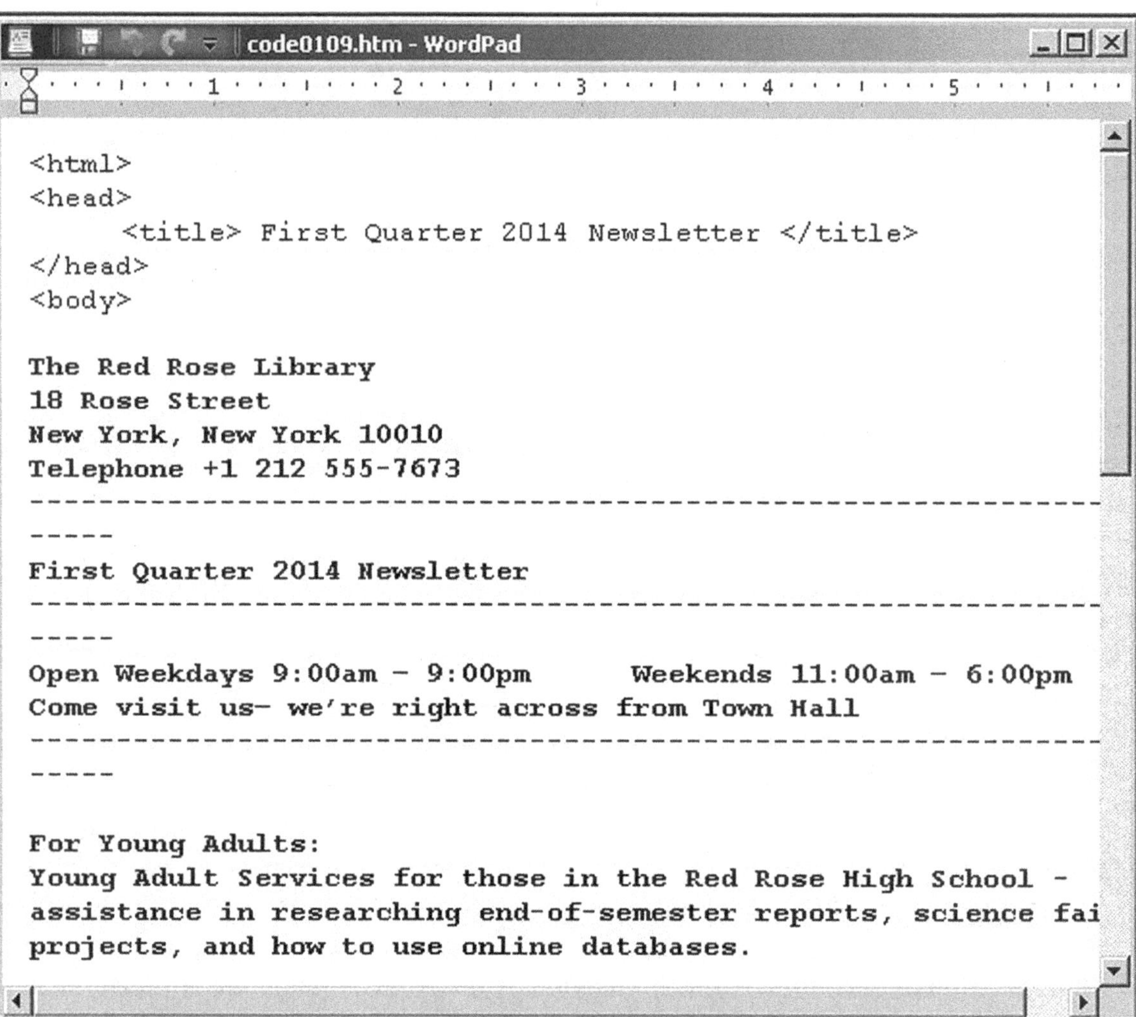

```
code0109.htm - WordPad

<html>
<head>
     <title> First Quarter 2014 Newsletter </title>
</head>
<body>

The Red Rose Library
18 Rose Street
New York, New York 10010
Telephone +1 212 555-7673
----------------------------------------------------------------
-----
First Quarter 2014 Newsletter
----------------------------------------------------------------
-----
Open Weekdays 9:00am - 9:00pm      Weekends 11:00am - 6:00pm
Come visit us- we're right across from Town Hall
----------------------------------------------------------------
-----

For Young Adults:
Young Adult Services for those in the Red Rose High School -
assistance in researching end-of-semester reports, science fai
projects, and how to use online databases.
```

Figure 01-08. WordPad View of Newsletter HTML File (**code0109.htm**)

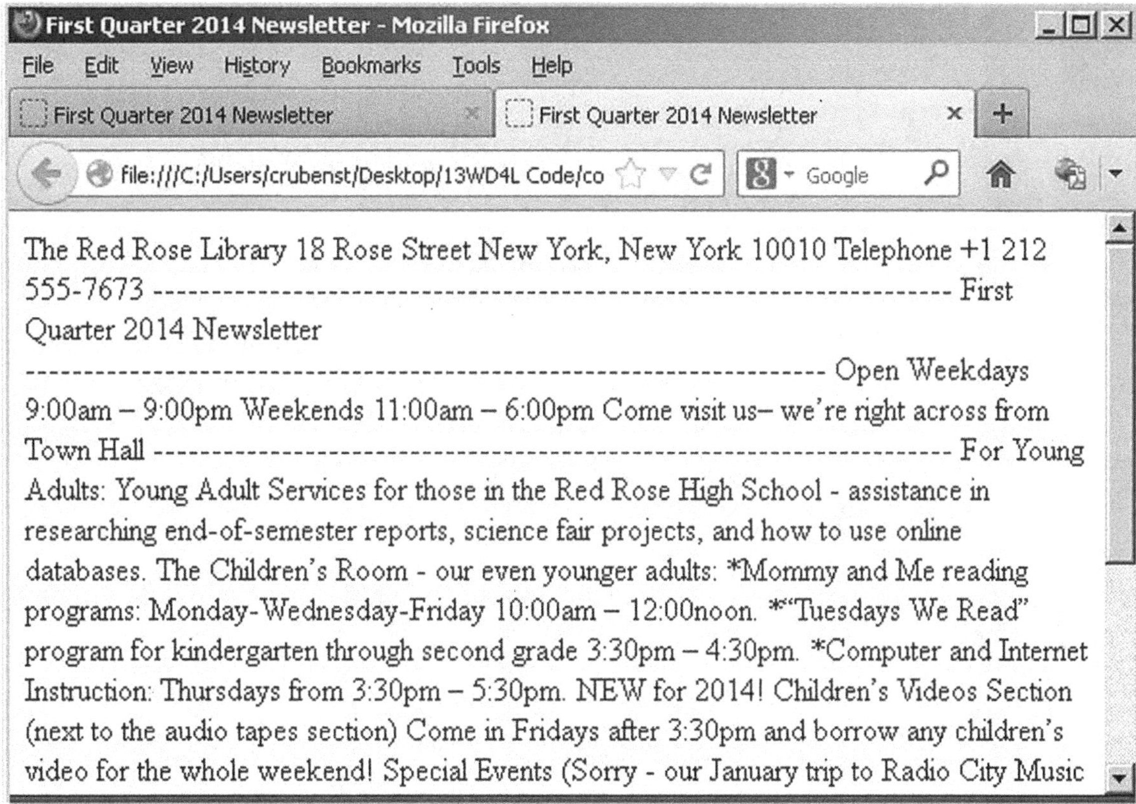

Figure 01-09. Browser View of Newsletter HTML File (**code0109.htm**)

Creating a Red Rose Newsletter Web Page

Adding the Preformat Tag

To keep the word-processed structure we have in our newsletter, we look to the HTML **pre** element to create separate headlines and sentences. By merely adding an opening **<pre>** tag before our text and a closing **</pre>** tag after text in a plain text file that has line spaces, tabs, end of line and space (used to be called "carriage returns" and "line feeds") dramatically changes the way the browser displays our content as shown in Figure 01-10.

The addition of just the **pre** tag set to our plain text results in a file whose browser display closely resembles that of the original except it does not have bold or underlining. We're getting closer to the desired effect, but the text for each paragraph still runs across the page and does not wrap, and there still are no rose logos on the page in Figure 01-11.

Adding the Paragraph Tag

Although the **pre** tag added some structure, as seen earlier, paragraphs tend to run wild with the text running off the page to the left. Adding the paragraph tag **p** will take

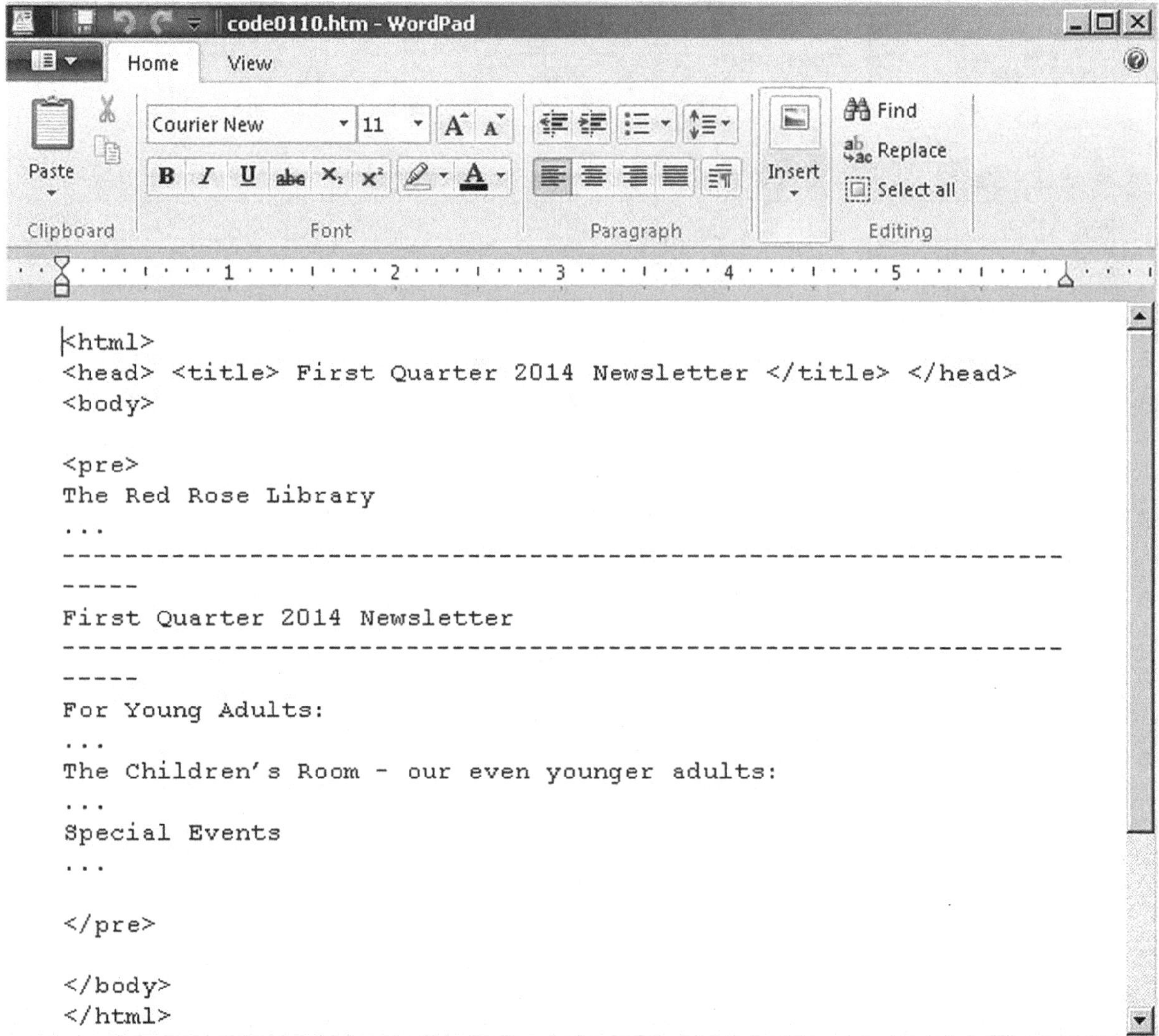

Figure 01-10. Using the **pre** Element (WordPad view: **code0110.htm**)

care of that problem. To make this change easier to visualize, remove the **</pre>** from the end of the file and place it just before the "For Our Young Adults" line. Then add paragraph opening **<p>** and closing **</p>** tags at the start and end of each paragraph, and also around each "heading" to achieve a page that has text wrap to the size of the browser window. Note that many browsers do not *require* a closing paragraph tag, but as it is required to use proper nesting of elements and tags when using more advanced techniques, we will use that style here to prepare our files for eventual upgrading to XML and HTML5.

To make surrounding text by the paragraph tags easier to see in our HTML file, we often use the TAB key as shown in the plain text document of Figure 01-12. Recall that your browser ignores tabs and extra spaces, so we can use these freely to show us what we are trying to do and to separate various parts of our document for future processing.

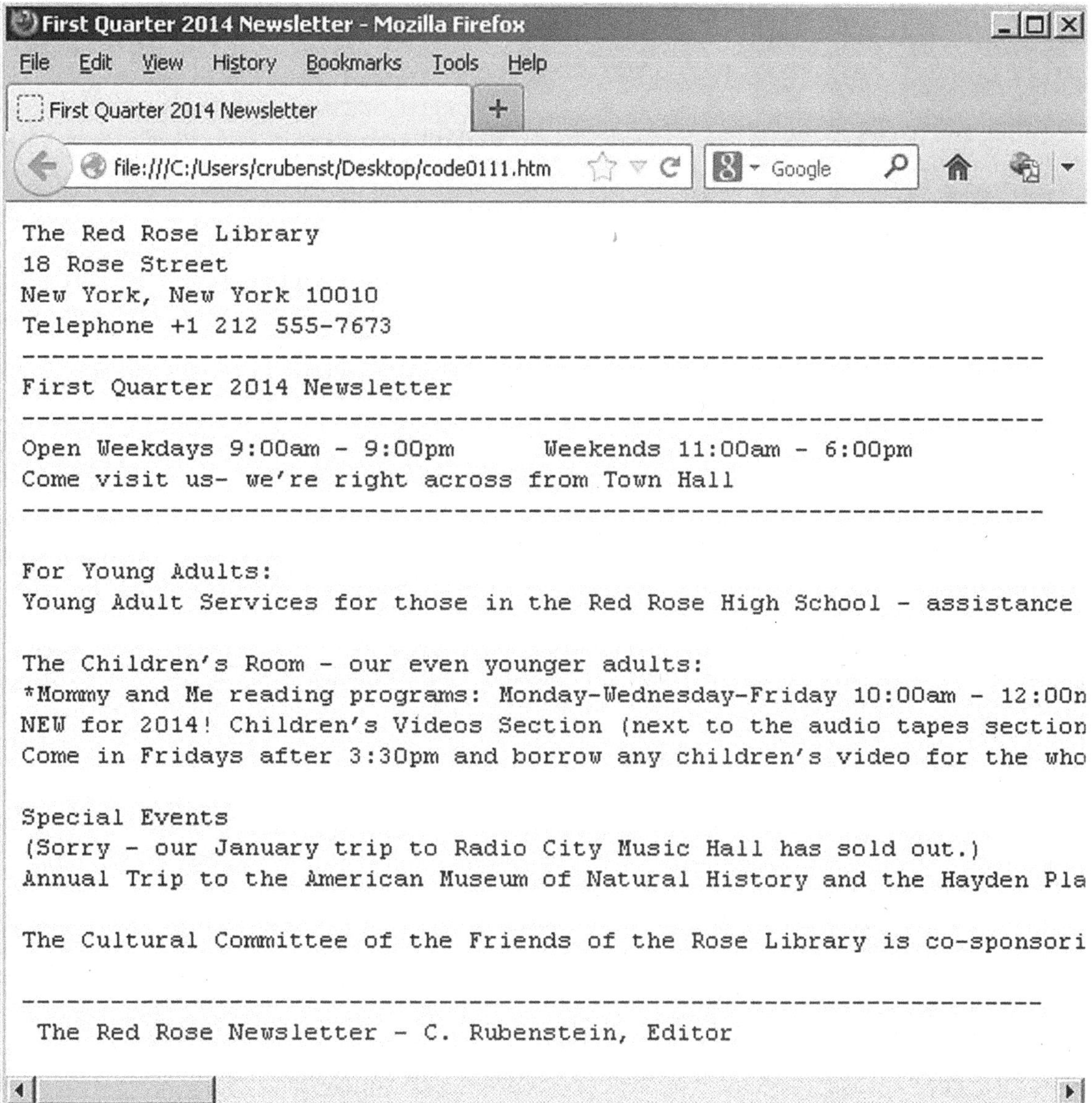

Figure 01-11. Web Page Using **pre** Element (**code0111.htm**)

Adding paragraph tags to our plain text file is a simple way to get our text file to look better when viewed in a browser as a web page as is shown in Figure 01-13.

Adding the Center, Bold (Strong), and Underline Tags

Three elements that can be used to further enhance our web page are named **center, b** for bold, and **u** for underline.

Using these simple tags will give text the basic look found in your original document. Figure 01-14 shows the (highlighted) location of these elements properly using both opening and closing tags as necessary to create our HTML file.

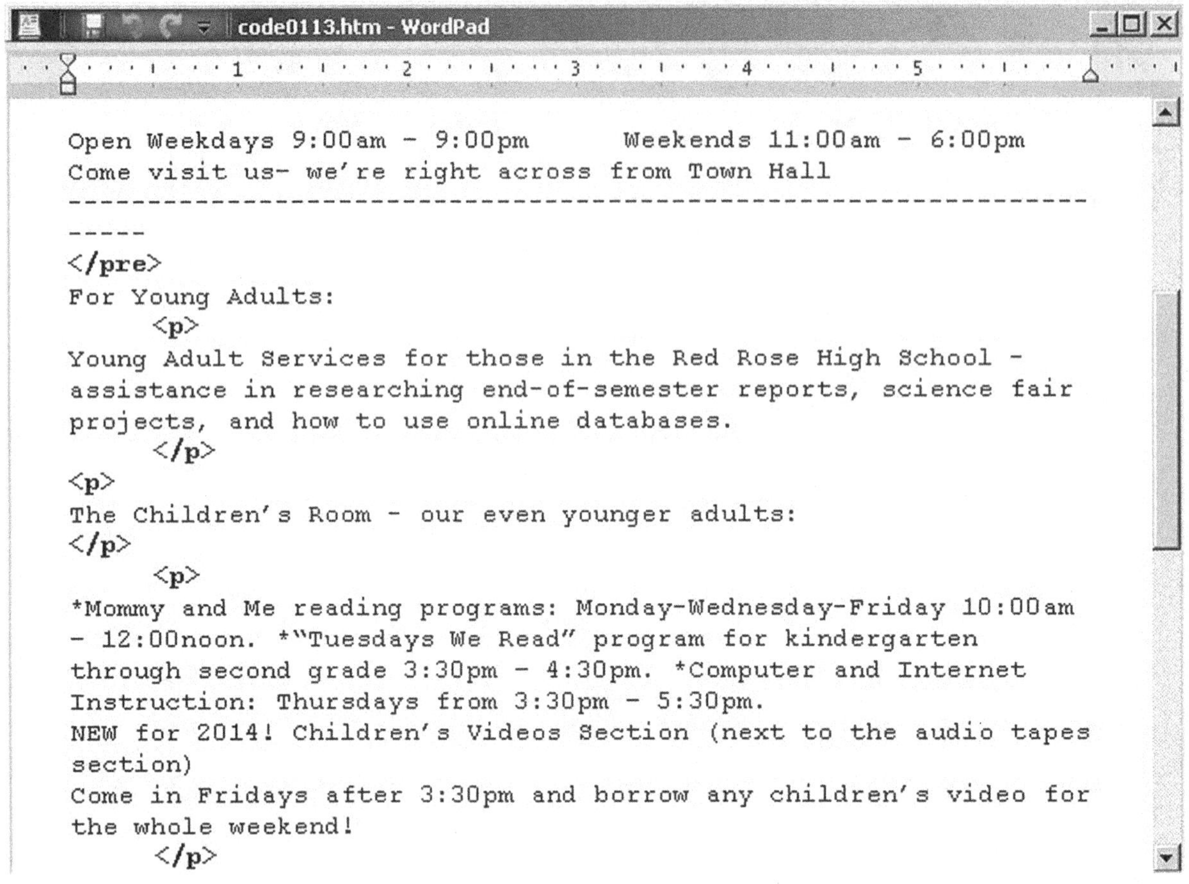

```
Open Weekdays 9:00am - 9:00pm      Weekends 11:00am - 6:00pm
Come visit us- we're right across from Town Hall
-----------------------------------------------------------------
-----
</pre>
For Young Adults:
      <p>
Young Adult Services for those in the Red Rose High School -
assistance in researching end-of-semester reports, science fair
projects, and how to use online databases.
      </p>
<p>
The Children's Room - our even younger adults:
</p>
      <p>
*Mommy and Me reading programs: Monday-Wednesday-Friday 10:00am
- 12:00noon. *"Tuesdays We Read" program for kindergarten
through second grade 3:30pm - 4:30pm. *Computer and Internet
Instruction: Thursdays from 3:30pm - 5:30pm.
NEW for 2014! Children's Videos Section (next to the audio tapes
section)
Come in Fridays after 3:30pm and borrow any children's video for
the whole weekend!
      </p>
```

Figure 01-12. Adding Paragraph Tags to Preformatted Pages (**code0113.htm**)

Figure 01-15 shows the improvement in the browser's display by using these elements to create our web page.

Good to Know: Although the bold element **b** can be used in your web pages, it has been deprecated (a fancy word meaning that it is no longer recommended for new web pages) and you will more than likely see the **strong** element tag used in its place. Here again, many browsers will not worry about it if you use **b** rather than **strong,** but I need you to realize that as the markup languages "mature," they often drop older element names for new ones or even for new ways to create them. Indeed, pages incorporating CSS techniques use style commands within the paragraph tag to center text instead of the **center** tag. It is likely that validation tools will consider the use of some deprecated elements as errors. Once again, for our purposes, and especially at this early stage in web design, we will make use of these elements as they *are* accepted by most browsers.

Adding the Image Tag

Figure 01-16 shows how to place an image on the web page (**code 0117.htm**) where the rose graphic **img001.jpg** is stored in the **assets** folder by using the **img** element. Unlike most of our tags, an **img** element does not enclose or contain any information—it merely puts a graphic on your page. The **img**

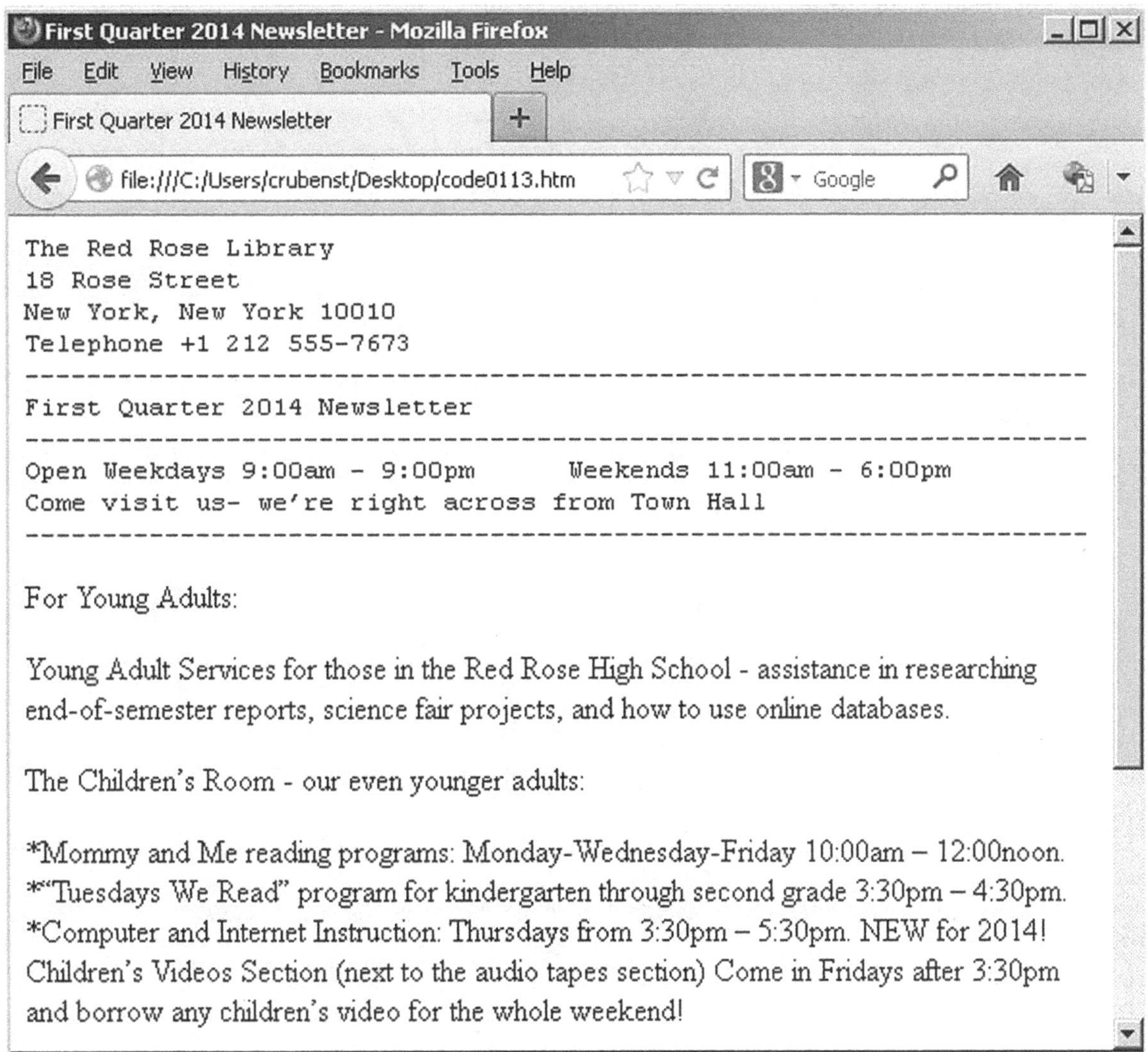

Figure 01-13. Effect of Paragraph Tags on Preformatted Pages (**code0113.htm**)

tag is called an empty, or a single-ended, tag. We'll see more of how to use the image element in Chapter 5, including the use of the **alt** attribute, which adds a title to the image.

Figure 01-17 shows the resulting single rose graphic centered on our almost complete web page.

Creating Structure with Table Tags

Figure 01-18 (a text editor window with highlighted text) shows the use of **table** elements (**table, tr, td**) to add a second rose graphic to our web page (**code0119.htm**) where the rose graphic images are positioned on either side of text by placing the graphics and text into a table. This simple table technique uses a **tr** tag set to create a single row and three sets of **td** tags to create three "columns." Note that the opening **table** element has a **width** attribute as well as a **border** attribute.

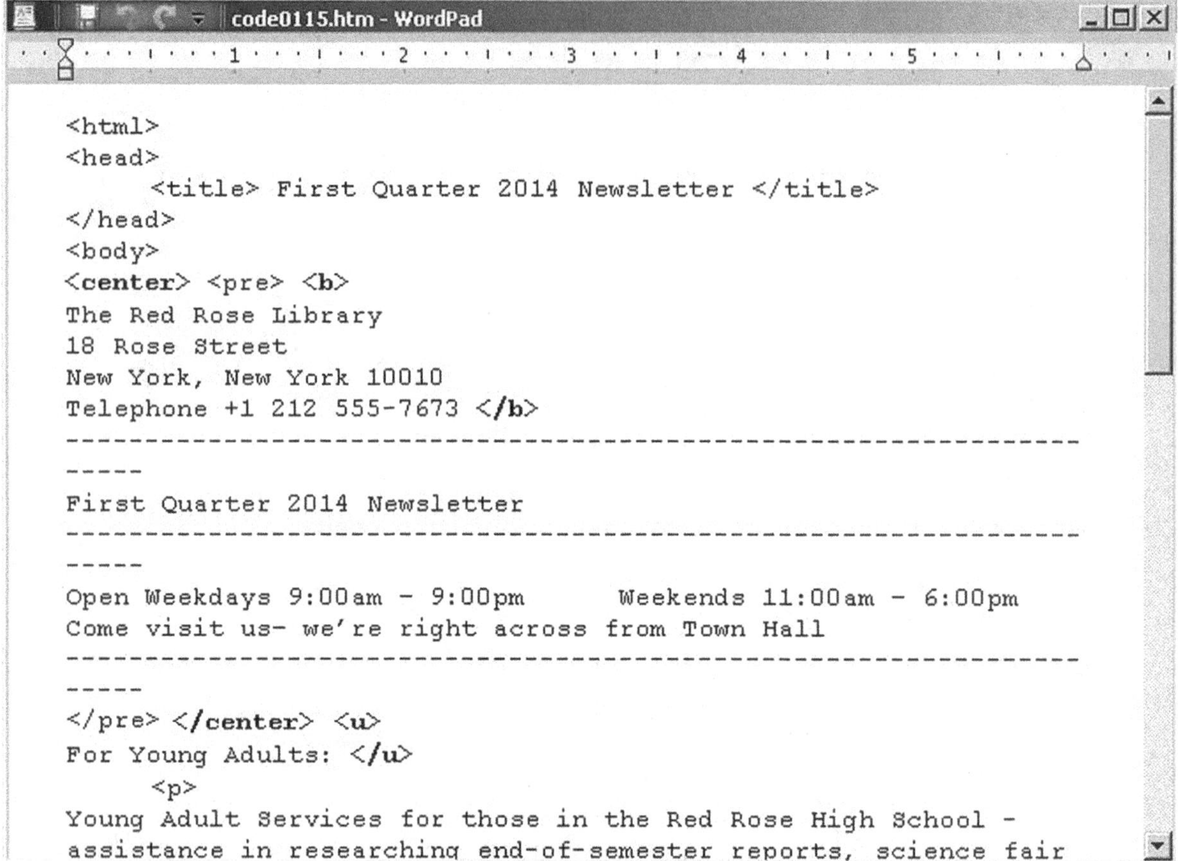

code0115.htm - WordPad

```
<html>
<head>
      <title> First Quarter 2014 Newsletter </title>
</head>
<body>
<center> <pre> <b>
The Red Rose Library
18 Rose Street
New York, New York 10010
Telephone +1 212 555-7673 </b>
-----------------------------------------------------------------
-----
First Quarter 2014 Newsletter
-----------------------------------------------------------------
-----
Open Weekdays 9:00am - 9:00pm      Weekends 11:00am - 6:00pm
Come visit us- we're right across from Town Hall
-----------------------------------------------------------------
-----
</pre> </center> <u>
For Young Adults: </u>
      <p>
Young Adult Services for those in the Red Rose High School -
assistance in researching end-of-semester reports, science fair
```

Figure 01-14. Styling with **center, b,** and **u** Elements (**code0115.htm;** adds formatting)

Please don't concern yourself with the fact that you may have no idea what is happening here.

Chapter 8 will take all the magic out of creating table structures that give form to our pages.

Figure 01-19 shows the result of using these table elements. Using the **border** attribute set to the value "1" allows us to see how the table is designed (**border="1"**) to show the two rose graphics. Your initial web page is almost finished; the borders just need to be "hidden" from the viewer.

In Figure 01-20 the border attribute is changed to "0" (**border="0"**) to position the two rose graphics on either side of the text, but without showing the actual table structure border.

Of course, an even better result might occur if all of our text was included in the table as shown in Figure 01-21. If you would like to investigate how this happens, please feel free to look at the code in the file **code0121.htm.**

Note that we removed the dashed lines and replaced them with the **hr** or horizontal rule elements to get a nicer header look in the final design. If you aren't ready to make that change in your page yet, don't fret; these techniques will be discussed in later chapters.

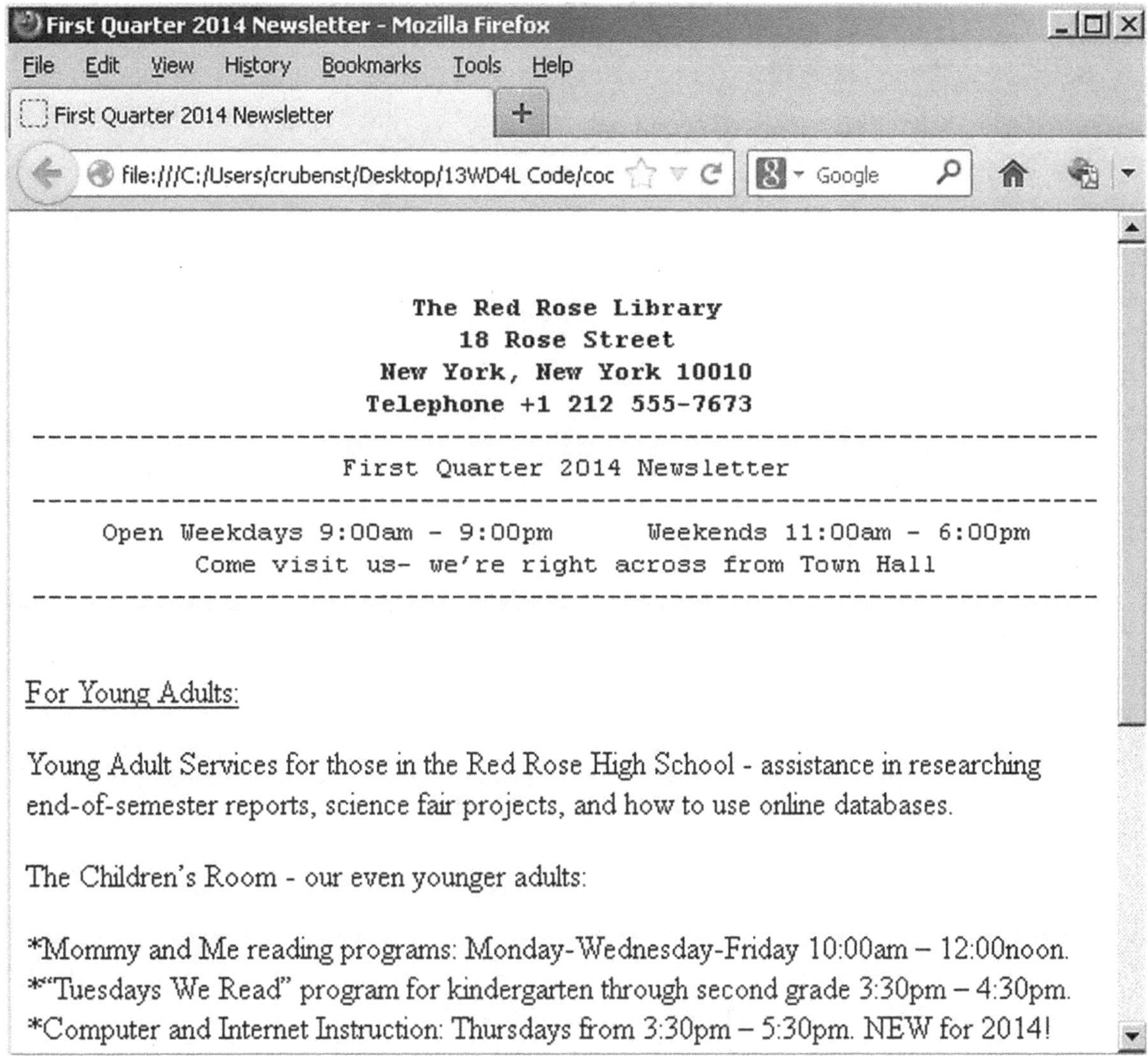

Figure 01-15. Web Page with **center, b,** and **u** Elements (code0115.htm)

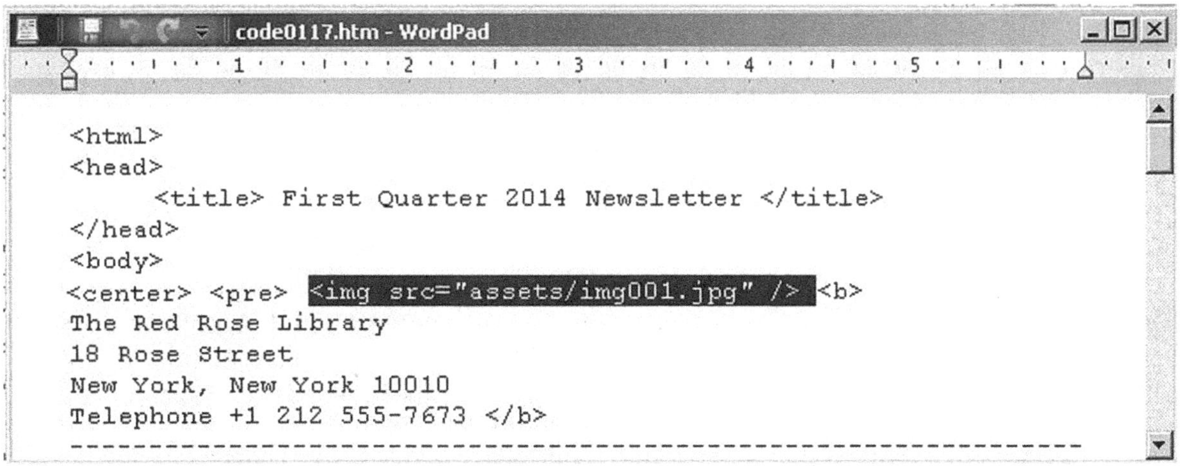

code0117.htm - WordPad

```
<html>
<head>
     <title> First Quarter 2014 Newsletter </title>
</head>
<body>
<center> <pre> <img src="assets/img001.jpg" /> <b>
The Red Rose Library
18 Rose Street
New York, New York 10010
Telephone +1 212 555-7673 </b>
-------------------------------------------------------------------
```

Figure 01-16. Adding the **img** Tag (**code0117.htm**)

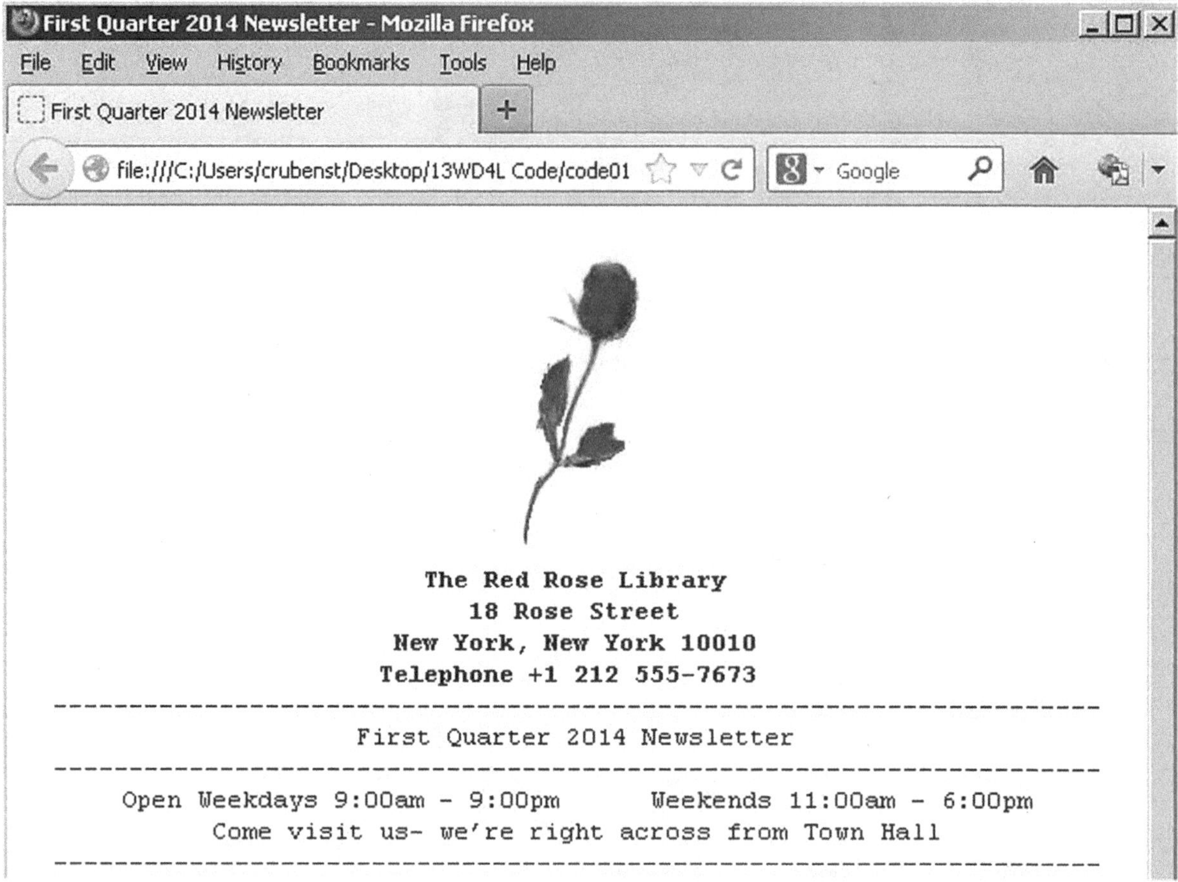

Figure 01-17. Web Page with Graphic (**code0117.htm**)

Recap of HTML Elements Used in Chapter 1

Well you made it. Hopefully most of your hair is on your head and your headache is subsiding, but you were able to create a simple newsletter for your library using **html, title, body, pre, p, center, b, u, img** and **table, tr,** and **td** tags! You also learned a little about deprecated tags, HTML page validation (and that for our pages it's not so important right now) and that most browsers ignore tabs, additional letters, and line spaces so they need to be fooled into letting our pages look more word-processed. And this is only your first chapter.

What's Next?

In the next few chapters these basic HTML elements will be reviewed in a bit more detail. Examples of a variety of content specific web pages that you might want to have in your library will be created as examples of their potential use. These examples will use additional sets of HTML elements, whose specific use (syntax) is covered in Appendix A, HTML Element Syntax, while showing you how to create web pages you might want to use in your library's website. Note that although to reduce the cost to you, the reader, color is not used in the print version of the text; the online

```
<html>
<head>
     <title> First Quarter 2014 Newsletter </title>
</head>
<body>
<center><pre>
<table width="640" border="1">
<tr>
<td> <center> <img src="assets/img001.jpg" /> </center>
</td>
     <td>
<pre> <center> <b>
The Red Rose Library
18 Rose Street
New York, New York 10010
Telephone +1 212 555-7673 </b>
     </td>
<td> <center> <img src="assets/img001.jpg" /> </center>
</td>
</tr>
</table>
```

Figure 01-18. Adding a Basic Table (**code0119.htm;** adds table elements)

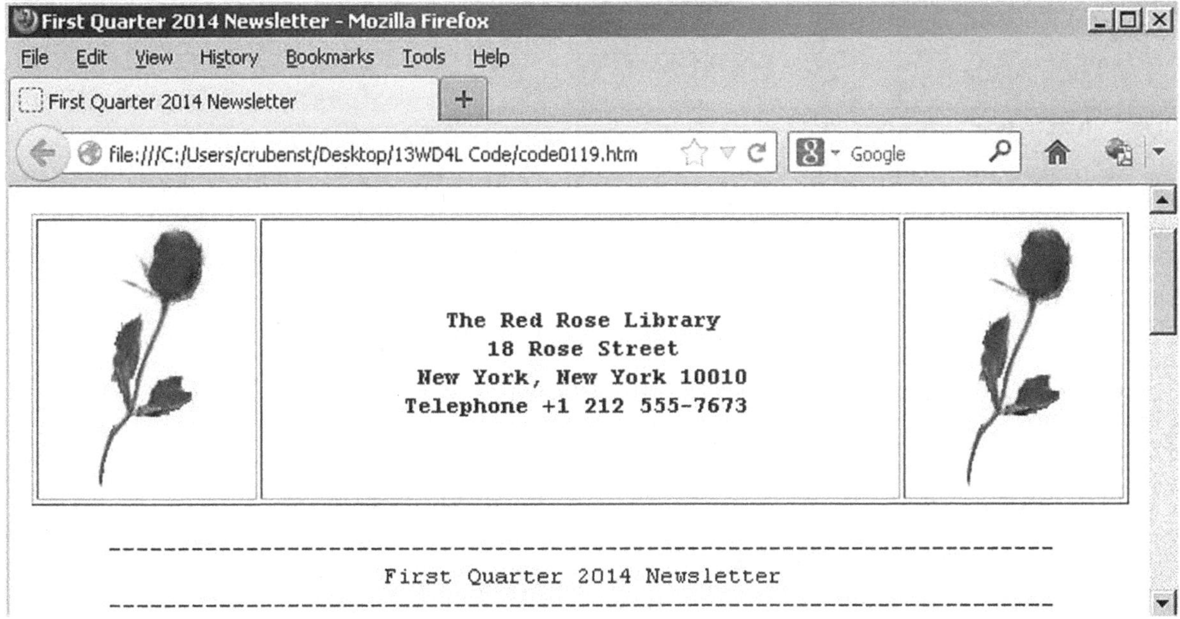

Figure 01-19. Web Page Table with Borders [**border="1"**] (**code0119.htm**)

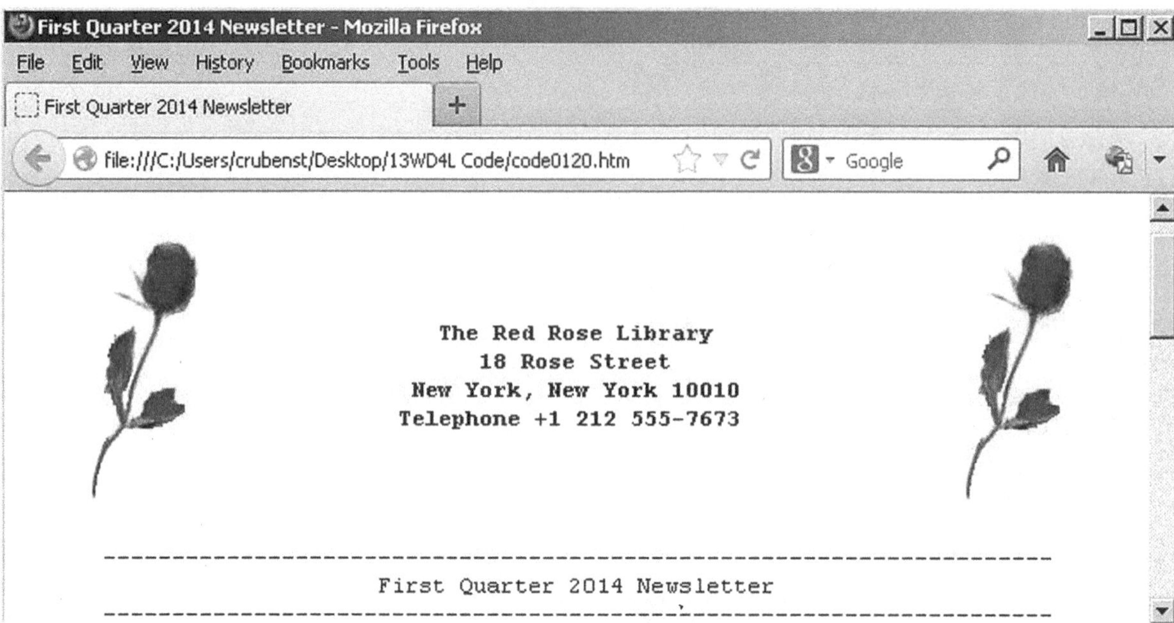

Figure 01-20. The Red Rose Web Page [**border="0"**] (**code0120.htm**)

website (www.redroselibrary.com) and the eBook all have color versions of the figures in all the chapters.

For now, we want to recap the websites that were discussed in this chapter, and provide some review exercises for you to master.

URLs Cited

"The" place for all things World Wide Web

http://www.w3.org

Statistics on operating systems used for accessing the web

http://www.w3schools.com/browsers/browsers_os.asp

Statistics on browsers used for accessing the web

http://www.w3schools.com/browsers/browsers_stats.asp

Google™ Chrome free web browser software download page

http://www.google.com/chrome

Mozilla™ Firefox free web browser software download page

http://www.mozilla.org/products/firefox/

The Red Rose Library Website and "archives"

http://www.redroselibrary.com

The Red Rose Library
18 Rose Street
New York, New York 10010
Telephone +1 212 555-7673

First Quarter 2014 Newsletter

Open Weekdays 9:00am - 9:00pm   Weekends 11:00am - 6:00pm
Come visit us- we're right across from Town Hall

For Young Adults:

Young Adult Services for those in the Red Rose High School - assistance in researching end-of-semester reports, science fair projects, and how to use online databases.

The Children's Room - our even younger adults:

```
*Mommy and Me reading programs: Monday-Wednesday-Friday 10:00am - 12:00noon.
*"Tuesdays We Read" program for kindergarten through second grade 3:30pm - 4:30pm.
*Computer and Internet Instruction: Thursdays from 3:30pm - 5:30pm.
NEW for 2014! Children's Videos Section (next to the audio tapes section)
Come in Fridays after 3:30pm and borrow any children's video for the whole weekend!
```

```
Special Events
(Sorry - our January trip to Radio City Music Hall has sold out.)
Annual Trip to the American Museum of Natural History and the Hayden Planetarium.
Sign up now! The bus to New York City will be leaving on Sunday February 23, 2014 at 6:
Trip cost is $50, which includes bus tickets, snacks on the bus, lunch at the Museum,
and a souvenir. Be sure to make your reservation early
- this trip sells out fast!

The Cultural Committee of the Friends of the Rose Library is co-sponsoring this bus tri
```

The Red Rose Newsletter - C. Rubenstein, Editor

Figure 01-21. Web Page with All Content Inside of a Table (**code0121.htm = redrose.htm**)

Chapter 1 Review Exercises

(Answers to all Review Exercises are posted in the online website to this text.)

Chapter 1 Fill-In Questions

1. When setting up your folders for a website, the graphics, music, and video files can be most easily found if they are saved in the ______ subfolder.
2. It is easy to create a website for your library or information center if you start with a ______.
3. We avoid using word processor to web page conversions to _____ file size.
4. Using standard plain text files as web pages is a/an _____ idea.
5. HTML pages should start with the _______ element.

Chapter 1 Multiple-Choice Questions

1. To easily create the appearance of a word processed page use the following element:

   a) style b) strong c) pre d) u
2. To make text appear bold use the following element:

   a) style b) strong c) pre d) u
3. To make text appear underlined use the following element:

   a) style b) strong c) pre d) u
4. To create a "column" in a table element use the following element:

   a) style b) tr c) td d) u
5. To easily view the structure of a table use the following attribute:

   a) style = "0" b) style = "1" c) border = "0" d) border = "1"

Chapter 1 Design and Discussion Questions

1. Identify some specific challenges to creating web pages from word-processed documents.
2. Describe how HTML elements work.
3. Can you use deprecated elements and techniques? Should you?
4. What is the importance of using lowercase letters in writing your element names, attributes, and variable values?
5. We have noted that there are several browsers being used today and that their popularity changes over time. As each browser uses a different set of software to display your web pages, what does this imply you should do before you publish a website to your patrons that might use different types of browsers and computers?

2

Hypertext Markup Language (HTML)

As we saw in Chapter 1, nearly all HTML elements have three parts, a starting tag with the elements name and often a variety of special "attribute" commands that modify the default use of the element, inside a pair of angle brackets: **<element . . .>,** your encapsulated content to be styled, and an ending tag with a slash preceding the elements name only, even if attributes were described in the opening tag, also inside a pair of angle brackets **</element>.** We call this standard configuration the element's syntax:

Standard HTML Element Tag Set Syntax:
<element attribute1="value" attribute2="value">
your content to be styled goes here
</element>

Attributes and styles are optional. They can be added to the starting tag as shown earlier to modify the way elements re-create your document. We'll see these in use later, but the horizontal rule and image elements are special element types that define a style or action but they don't surround content. The **hr** and **img** are empty elements that generate what are called "empty tags." Standard HTML browsers do not require empty elements to have ending tags. For upward compatibility to XML, or HTML5, empty element tags should have either a standard closing tag or a slash before the ending bracket of its opening tag: **<element />**:

HTML Empty Element Tag Set Syntax:
<element attribute1="value" attribute2="value"> </tag>
Or the more preferred
<element attribute1="value" attribute2="value" />

Each element's specific structural, presentational, and semantic behavior are predefined within your browser by built-in default values called document type definitions (DTDs). We'll investigate DTDs further later in this chapter, but generally speaking, the DTD defines the particular attribute value that the browser will use when no other commands are given to change the default value. The opening tag's new attribute values do not erase the default DTD values, but rather stack new ones on top of the existing defaults. Ending the attribute change with the closing tag restores the default the new attribute value was stacked upon.

File-Naming Conventions

During the earliest years of the web, web servers used an 8.3 file name specification where all filenames were to have no more than eight lowercase alphanumeric characters plus a three-alphabetic character extension to indicate the file's type or application. The filename **"document.doc"** indicates the resource named "document" is a **doc** or Microsoft Word™ file. These original web servers were programmed to return either a file named "default.htm" or the more common "index.htm" as the first, or default, opening page of a website. Today's web servers and their operating systems permit files to have "long filenames" as well as "long extensions." This results in the most common opening page filename becoming **"index.html."** Note the four-character extension. It is now also common, but not required, to have long filenames for HTML pages and the documents and graphic files they require.

As our websites will be relatively small to start with, and we don't know which server platform you will be using to mount your site, it is recommended that you keep to the original 8.3 file-naming standard as shown in Figure 02-01.

8.3 File name: **file0124.htm** **←Yes!**

Long File Names: **File Version_24.htm** **← We won't use long names here!**

Figure 02-01. Naming Your Files

Uniform Resource Locators (URLs)

The uniform resource locator or URL is a subset of the more general uniform resource identifier scheme that permits linking a web page on one web server to a file on another web server. A web server's full URL has several distinct parts; the first part describes the method of transferring information via a particular set of standard instructions (called protocols such as http and ftp), the next gives the web server's full name, and finally we see the name of the file or resource to retrieve. The fully defined or absolute URL for the Red Rose Library website is:

http://www.redroselibrary.com

The absolute URL for the rose image file (**img001.jpg**) stored in the **assets** folder in our example library website is:

http://www.redroselibrary.com/assets/img001.jpg

Links to a file on your own web server located "relative" to the current or index page would not need the **http://www.redroselibrary.com/** preface. So if you are on your index.htm page and want to use the rose image in the **assets** folder on the same web server, the URL would look like:

assets/img001.jpg

The location on the web where the file **filename.htm** would be located on the web server **www.servername.com** is fully described using the following URL:

http://www.servername.com/filename.htm

The Anchor Element (a)

The anchor or **a** element has several uses depending on the attributes included in its opening tag. It is used to create a hyperlink to a relative or absolute URL web file or location when the encapsulated text (hypertext) or graphic (hypergraphic) is clicked. Either the **href** or **name** attribute is required in the opening tag:

HTML Anchor Element Tag Set Syntax:
<a href="URL" attribute2="value"> text or graphic**</a>**
or
<a name="name" attribute2="value"> text or graphic**</a>**

As with most elements, there are other attributes that can be used within the anchor element's opening tag. Most common of these is the **target "value"** used to open the URL cited in the current or a new browser window depending on the value used.

Hyperlinking locations within a web page (e.g., **paragraph3**) are defined on that page with the anchor element using the **name** attribute. You would insert **<a name="paragraph3">** tag just before the location on a relatively "long" web page. When accessed, that portion of the page would be placed at the top of the browser's viewing window.

If you are on the *same web page* as the location you wish to go to, you hyperlink there using the "relative" addressing mode inside the anchor tag:

<a href="# paragraph3"> go there**</a>**

The "absolute" URL location on the web where the **<a name "paragraph3">** tag would be located, in the file **filename.htm,** on the web server **www.servername.com** is fully described using the following anchor tag:

<a href="http://www.servername.com/filename.htm#paragraph3"> go there
</a>

Now is a good time to remind you that web server URLs and file names are often case sensitive. Be sure to carefully copy the upper and lowercase letters of any Internet address.

Web Browsers

Before continuing the construction of more pages for your library, it is important to learn the names of and understand the most common web browsers, some of which were mentioned in Chapter 1. Nearly all browsers in use today are graphic user interface (GUI) browsers that give the common "what-you-see-is-what-you-get" (WYSIWYG) display and printout. There is also another, less commonly used plain text browser called Lynx, which is used by the sight-impaired. We will look at how this browser "displays" your web page a bit later in this chapter.

When the "Crash Course" version of this text came out in 2007, Microsoft™ Internet Explorer was used as our standard web page viewer or "browser" as it was the most popular browser at that time. Even though it still comes preinstalled with the Microsoft™ Windows operating system, nowadays only about 13% of all users use the Microsoft™ Internet Explorer web browser.

As stated in Chapter 1, almost 60% of all users use Google™ Chrome web browsers and another 25% use Mozilla™ Firefox web browsers. Both are free, and both work on most computers. The full analysis of browser usage is on the **http://www.w3schools.com/browsers/browsers_stats.asp** website. Although we will primarily show results using Microsoft™ Wordpad or Mozilla™ Firefox software in this text, rest assured that results will be quite similar—although not guaranteed—using similar Mac and Linux text editor and browser versions.

As noted earlier, the most popular browser is currently Google™ Chrome. Chrome is available for download at:

http://www.google.com/chrome

No longer available, Netscape's Navigator was the dominant web browser in terms of usage share in the 1990s but had its last release, version 9, in 2007 and was discontinued in 2008. With computer systems rarely lasting more than five years, it is safe to presume that your patrons won't be using this browser. In 2003 the Mozilla Foundation separated from Netscape and its product the second most popular browser, Mozilla™ Firefox, claims to yield faster downloads, higher security, and includes more spyware and pop-up blockers than Microsoft's Internet Explorer. It is available for download at:

http://www.mozilla.org/en-US/firefox/fx/#desktop

Interestingly enough, the default starting page for both the Chrome and Firefox browsers is the Google Search page.

Coming in at a surprisingly low 13%, the next most popular GUI browser, Microsoft's Internet Explorer, now in version 10, is available for downloading at:

http://www.microsoft.com/en-us/download

With usage at 4% for Safari (often used on mobile devices) and 2% for Opera, it is safe to presume that your patron will not be using these.

All GUI browsers are nearly identical in their treatment of web pages as well as in their application design and structure. Most are available in Microsoft Windows, Macintosh, and Linux operating system flavors and in different languages as can be discovered on the web pages noted earlier. That said, it is a good idea to set up a computer in your library technical area that has all five of these most popular browsers on it for testing your web page look and feel.

Still available and useful for your sight-impaired patrons, Lynx is a text-based web browser that creates an 80-column text output. Note that as Lynx is a non-GUI browser, it ignores the preformat tag (**pre**) in our file. When calling graphics files, the **img** element tag must include the **alt** attribute to provide information on what the graphic represents; otherwise, your patron will just get the filename of the graphic appearing which probably won't give your patron any idea as to what the image represents. Lynx browsers are often used in conjunction with voice synthesizers to enable your blind and sight-impaired patrons to "see" web pages. Lynx text browser software, currently in version 2.8.7, can be downloaded from the distribution site hosted by the Internet Software Consortium (**http://lynx.isc.org**).

Several online services will let you see how your web page would appear in the Lynx browser. The nongraphic, 80 characters across, web page output that would be "seen" by a Lynx browser for the Red Rose Library web page (Figure 01–21) looks like Figure 02-02 as processed by the service at:

http://www.delorie.com/web/lynxview.html

Figure 02-03 shows the code snippet where the **alt** attribute needs to be added to your **img** element tag with the value **Red Rose Logo**

The Lynx browser displays the **alt** value **Red Rose Logo** wherever the image element is found on the page as shown in Figure 02-04. With GUI browsers the **alt** attribute value normally appears in a drop-down box when your cursor is positioned over graphics that use **alt** attributes.

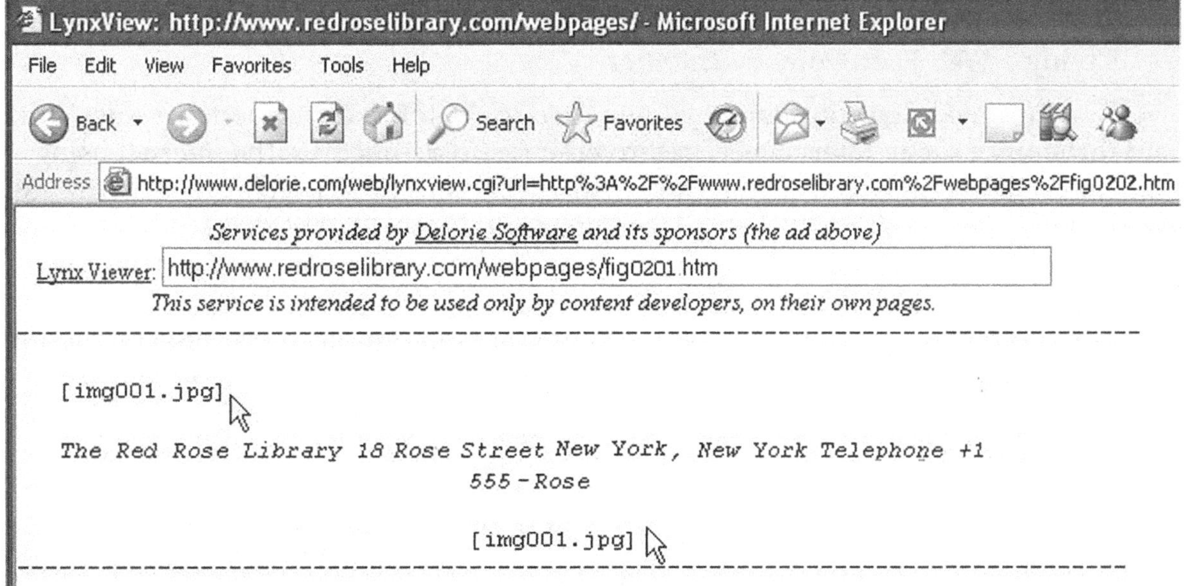

Figure 02-02. Lynx View of Figure 01-21—Red Rose Library Newsletter

code0204.htm - WordPad

```
<html>
<head>
      <title> First Quarter 2014 Newsletter </title>
</head>
<body>
<center>
<table width="640" border="0">
<tr>
<td>
      <img align="right" height="100" alt="Red Rose Logo"
src="assets/img001.jpg" /> </td>
```

Figure 02-03. Adding the **alt** Attribute to **img** Tags (**code0204.htm**)

Services provided by Delorie Software and its sponsors (the ad above)

Lynx Viewer: http://www.redroselibrary.com/webpages

This service is intended to be used only by content developers, on their webpages

Red Rose Logo

The Red Rose Library 18 Rose Street New York, New York Telephone +1 555-Rose

Red Rose Logo

Figure 02-04. Lynx View of Image with **alt** Attribute (**code0204.htm**)

Saving a Web Page from the Internet

It is presumed that your library is connected to the Internet via modem or network card through either an Internet Service Provider (ISP) or directly to the Internet using a high-speed leased line connection. Of course, that connection could also be a wireless Wi-Fi (IEEE 802.11) or a 3G, 4G, or LTE cellular one. However, the "access point" that establishes the wireless signal creates a connection between your computer and the Internet, so the result is the same.

What happens next, happens in the computer, and you need not understand all the steps. You will have an opportunity to refer back should you need to review the information. With the options for libraries increasing, it is suggested that you check with your IT staff, or the computer vendor that created your Internet connections to see how your specific facility is constructed.

Open your browser and type a URL (e.g., **redroselibrary.com**) into your browser's address line. Your browser will automatically add the default **http://** access preface, and if not already there, the default **www** URL preface that indicates the request is not to your computer's local drives (as we'll be doing when we create our own pages), but to a web server accessed using the hypertext transfer protocol (**http**) on the World Wide Web at the web server's URL: **http://www.redroselibrary.com,** the full address of the sample website! In a matter of seconds, your browser displays the web page you requested in its window. But what really happened?

A website's opening page is normally **index.htm** or **index.html** unless otherwise specified (e.g., **http://www.redroselibrary.com/1stpage.html**). Your browser initially sends a request to the web server named by the URL or address name of a website (e.g., **www.redroselibrary.com**) requesting the default or specified file. The server sends that file to your browser using the hypertext transfer protocol (HTTP). Then the browser assembles, formats, and displays the file on your computer monitor according to established HTML rules (DTDs) that are already stored inside its browser software program.

As you probably already know, you can save someone else's online web page and all its related files by clicking on Files on your browser's taskbar and then selecting Save As. Saving a web page this way normally creates a "long name" file with an **htm** or **html** extension (e.g., **index .htm**), as well as a folder with all the associated files (e.g., **index_files**) needed to re-create that web page for offline use (i.e., without going onto the Internet to reconstruct the display). This file set is all that is needed to view that web page anytime, anywhere. (Be sure to get permission if you want to reuse the graphics or content of someone else's web pages.)

> <u>Good to Know:</u> If you click View on your browser's taskbar and then select Source, you can see the contents of the displayed page's HTML coding. Even if your displayed web page uses several pictures, sound, or other multimedia files, all you will see in this file is plain text. Portions of that text are surrounded by special markup codes, the HTML element tags. Looking more closely, in the areas where you have graphics on the page, you'll see several **<img . . . />** markup tags. On "reading" these markup codes, your browser will actually request additional files one at a time until all images in the HTML file are stored in a temporary Internet file folder on your computer. Then your browser will assemble all requested files and display them as a formatted web page.

Website Design

As there is no standard for good website design, we will define the one we used in Chapter 1 to make it easier for you to put your site together and to reduce the number of graphics files. First we'll open a new folder, give it an eight-character long name, say **webpages** and place it on the desktop so you can access it quickly.

Good web page design suggests reducing the space you use for files on your server by having only one instance of a file on your website. The easiest way to do this would be to have a separate folder, with all of your images, which can be shared by your web pages. We will use the **assets** folder for all graphic, audio, or other media files. As we plan on using style sheets to give a uniform look and feel to our web pages, we will also want to have a **styles** folder. In this design all HTML pages would be in the website's **library** folder, which would also contain **assets** and **styles** folders. If you wish, you can include other semantically named folders for other specific files such as a **pdf** folder or a **text** folder. Figure 02-05 shows the "tree" diagram of this type of folder or directory structure.

Figure 02-06 shows the Windows Explorer view of the suggested standard **library** folder or directory structure.

webpages *(overall container directory)*
\ **index.htm** *(home page with hyperlinks to ALL your pages)*
\ **page01.htm** *(first topic web page)*
assets *(subfolder for all graphics and other media)*
\ **img001.jpg**
\ **logo.gif**
\ **...** (etc. - *all data, assignment, and graphic files)*
style *(subfolder for all cascading style sheets)*
\ **style.css**
\ **...** (etc. - *all stylesheet files are placed in this folder)*
extras *(subfolder for miscellaneous files)*
\ **article.pdf**
\ **...** (etc. - *all other miscellaneous files)*

Figure 02-05. Suggested Website Directory Tree Structure

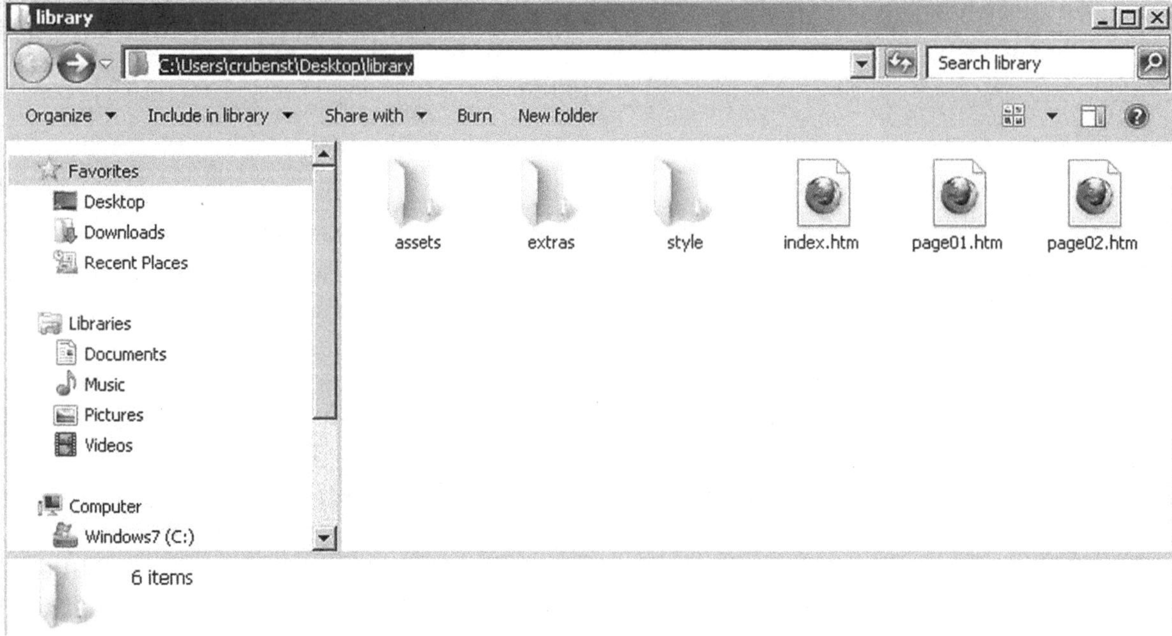

Figure 02-06. Suggested Website Windows™ Folder Structure

About Browsers and HTML Standards

Today's browsers bring your web pages to life. Browsers are a combination of graphical user interfaces, protocol interpreters, and markup language interpreters. Graphical user interfaces are designed to display images (e.g., **jpg, gif,** and **png** which will be discussed later in our coverage of the **img** element). The browser is an interpreter for a variety of **ftp, http,** and other Internet protocols. It functions as a markup language interpreter based on a built-in set of rules for formatting text and other digital objects (e.g., graphics, animation, sound, and movies) according to standardized rules.

Document Type Definitions (DTD)

Each browser's built-in document type definition (DTD) rule set includes decoding rules for HTML elements, their common attributes, and display styles. Modification of these rules is accomplished by using inline style commands, attributes, or style sheet techniques.

Some browsers do not recognize or display all standard HTML elements and others don't recognize some of the attributes of some elements. Still other browsers have their own set of special HTML extensions not supported by the HTML standards. We'll review some techniques for modifying the look and feel of your page using inline style declarations, in-file style definitions, and external style files. These are cascading style sheet (CSS) techniques that overlay the DTD default element attribute values in your browser.

HTML DTDs are composed of element tag sets that compose a variety of levels (e.g., HTML Level 4.01 and XHTML 1.1) and types (e.g., Strict, Transitional, and Frameset) as defined by the W3C—the World Wide Web Consortium, an international industry consortium dedicated to building consensus around web technologies. The latest W3C HTML 4.01 recommendations (dated December 24, 1999) may be viewed at:

> Good to Know: HTML, which provides the *structure or content layer* of the web document, and CSS, which adds the visual and aural *layout or presentation layer,* are two of the core technologies for building web pages. HTML, CSS, and JavaScript (which we will not discuss here which provides an additional "scripting" layer is called the *behavior layer* as it allows interaction between the patron and the page) are the basis of building web pages and web applications.

http://www.w3.org/TR/html401/

You may have heard of HTML5. Not yet an approved web standard, this fifth edition of HTML intends to marry HTML, XHTML, CSS, and XML in a seamless way. HTML5 received Candidate Recommendation status (one of the last steps before becoming a web standard) on December 17, 2012, and promises to be a great leap forward in simplifying web page design in the future.

Extensible HyperText Markup Language (XHTML) is, as its name suggests, an extension of the basic HTML rules. Designed specifically for use with information appliances such as cell phones and PDAs, to create web pages that look good on a small screen, it is a variant of HTML that uses the syntax of XML, the Extensible Markup Language. We are actually using the XHTML syntax in this text, making sure to only use lowercase element and attribute names, nest element tags, and so on. The latest W3C XHTML 1 specification is the Second Edition of XHTML 1.0, a reformulation of HTML 4 as an XML 1.0 application (dated January 26, 2000, and revised August 1, 2002) may be viewed at:

http://www.w3.org/TR/xhtml1/

The Extensible Markup Language (XML), on the other hand, goes one step further allowing you to define new and unique DTDs (yes new HTML tags that *you* create!) that supplement the HTML standards built into your browser. Finding aids and specialty markup language DTDs for music and science are designed using customized XML element DTDs that define the way your browser will treat specially tagged content. Once these specialized XML DTD vocabularies are accepted in a particular field, they become de facto standards for specific web page uses.

Good to Know: EAD, the Encoded Archival Description vocabulary, is one library standard based on XML techniques. It was adopted by the Society of American Archivists (SAA) and the Library of Congress in 1996 as an efficient way to represent archival collection database information.

Additional information on the EAD Standard DTD including the latest 2002 version of the EAD DTD Vocabulary and lots of other EAD information may be viewed through the Library of congress portal at:

http://www.loc.gov/ead/

The SAA has created an EAD Roundtable website to promote the implementation and use of encoding standards for dissemination of archival information at:

http://www2.archivists.org/groups/encoded-archival-description-ead-roundtable

Your web page will use a DOCTYPE declaration to specify which DTD the browser should use for your pages. We'll see how that is done in Chapter 3. For those curious enough to want to immerse themselves into all things HTML and web, they can visit the WC3 website at:

http://www.w3.org/standards/techs/html#w3c_all

Top-Ten Library Home Page Links

Although the goal of this chapter was to provide mostly background and setup suggestions, we didn't want to leave it without at least showing you a hypothetical library home page that contains the top-ten links that every library should consider having on its home page. Each of these would link to at least one more HMTL page on your library's website.

Figure 02-07 shows a possible home page design with the top-ten links called out in it. In later chapters you will see how these "linked" pages are constructed.

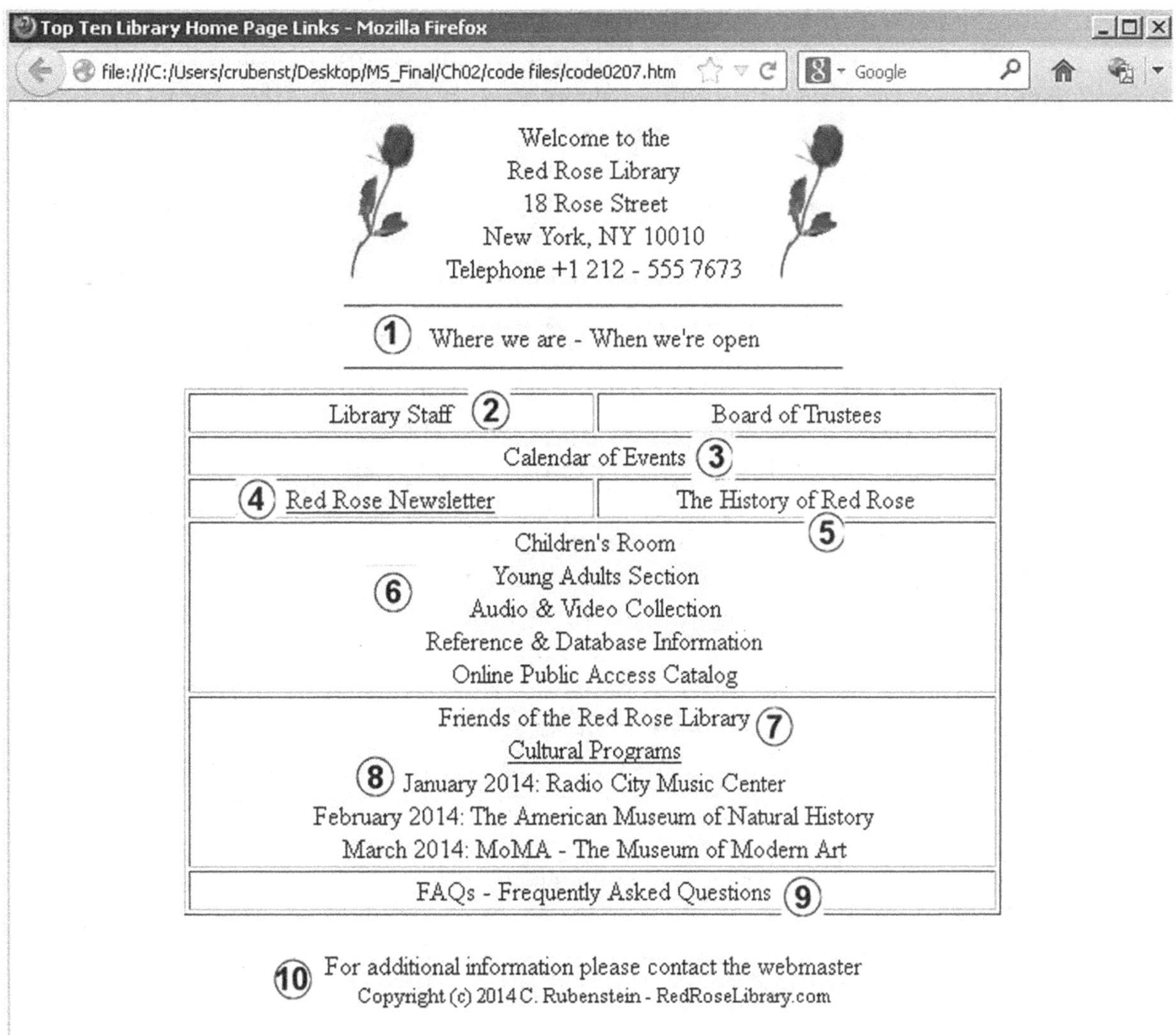

Figure 02-07. Library Home Page with Top-Ten Page Links (**code0207.htm**)

This home page file will be a work in progress for a final home page, and a bit advanced for now. Although the page is pretty bland with only a pair of rose images to brighten it up now, we will see it come alive as we go through the next chapters using HTML elements that bring life into your pages. As we create the underlying web pages, we will come back to this page to link the new files into this page.

Note that the newsletter link in the figure is highlighted in blue and underlined. This is the HTML DTD default hyperlink standard. Yes, we can change this by using techniques developed in a later chapter! In Chapter 1 you already put together a basic HTML Newsletter page (Figure 01–21) and thus have already created, and can link to, an HTML version of the fourth item in this set of Top-Ten Page Links.

Note that there is no hierarchy intended by the topic location on this list.

1. **Location and Hours of Operation**
   If you build it they may come, but they need to know where to go and when you are open!

2. **Library Staff and Board of Trustees Contact Information**
   As library professionals we already know that communication is the key to keeping information flowing between staff and patrons. Be sure to include your staff's "**@yourlibrary.com**" email addresses, but not any personal information. Some pages, to avoid the problem of web tools used by email address sellers, spell out the email addresses. Using "**webmaster_at_your library.com**" is one example of how this might be done. Don't forget your Board of Trustees. Post public information about the Board, its members, and its meetings. Note that your Board is usually made up of volunteers (even if they may be elected) that devote much of their efforts to making it possible for the e-library to grow and succeed. Reward them with their own web page and photo galleries. Don't release any of their personal information, but a library-based email will let them be in touch with patrons, too.
3. **Calendar of Events (Keep It Current!)**
   Here's where you keep all the current programs on one page so that your patrons can plan their life around your library.
4. **Your Library Newsletter**
   Posting your library's current newsletter as well as an archive of past issues will let your patrons as well as your Board and staff plan for the future based on your past programs. Newsletters are often posted in **doc, html,** and/or **pdf** formats. Most newsletters are created using a word processing program, like Word, but many librarians don't like the fact that a downloaded word processed file could be altered and thus no longer be a true archiving tool.

   In Chapter 1 you saw some of the basic techniques for creating an HTML version of your newsletter. Unfortunately, it takes a fair amount of effort to create an HTML rendering of even a simple newsletter. One solution would be to create a **pdf** file using a word processor plug-in "text to **pdf** file converter" to preserve the look and feel of your original newsletter. Some of these **pdf** file creation software applications are free. Others, like the most popular Adobe Acrobat Publisher, can cost a few hundred dollars. Either way, the freely available, multi-platform, Adobe Acrobat Reader software can be used to read any standard **pdf** file. The latest versions of Adobe Reader (currently Version 11.0.03) for any operating system platform, and in many languages, can be downloaded from:

   http://get.adobe.com/reader/otherversions/

5. **History of Your Library**
   A brief overview with major milestones reached and major capital programs under way will give your patrons an insight into your library's importance to the neighborhood and its rightful place as your community's information resource and provider. Don't forget to include a photo archive of its construction or original buildings and personnel.

6. **List of Departments**
   Once they know what programs you have that they want to be involved with, let your patrons contact the staff person in charge so that they can volunteer or register for your activities.
7. **Friends of the Library (FOL)**
   If you have one, your FOL group should also get their 15 minutes of fame. Offer them the same benefits of patron communication you give to your Board members.
8. **Trips and Special Programs**
   Many libraries have trips and/or special fee-based programs; some use them for fund-raising. Place these prominently on your home page so your patrons can easily sign up for them. You might even consider a photo gallery archive for past programs.
9. **Frequently Asked Questions (FAQs)**
   FAQs should be online in one place. Accumulate these and place them on one or more pages for online access. This way your patrons won't need to go into the building to find out answers to common problems, such as:

   How can I get (or renew) a library card?
   What are the policies for on-site computer use?
   How can I get a library web email address?
   What databases can I access from home?
   How can I get answers to reference questions?

10. **Webmaster Contact Information and Copyright**
    Again, with communication in mind, you should include a line at the bottom of your home page that will permit the person viewing it to email you or the person helping with your website and also to understand that the page(s) are copyrighted.

Web Page Graphics

As you probably recall from your own searching of websites, ease of finding what you want quickly is important. Also important are your web page's graphics. Since you won't be spending time doing original artwork, you may wish to purchase some software or subscribe to one of several online clipart collections.

Purchasing a clipart collection, such as PrintMaster®, provides tens of thousands of images on CDs or DVDs for a one-time purchase price and is often easier than doing online searches. The software allows you to browse the collection offline, and you can also browse the included print catalog of images. PrintMaster® is only one of Broderbund's graphics and publishing products, which include ClickArt® and the Print Shop®. Some CD/DVD vendors also have online access to even more art work. For more information, or to order one or more of these packages, check out its website at:

http://www.broderbund.com

An additional benefit to purchasing one or more of these CD/DVD packages is that you can, after using them for your library web pages, put them into circulation for your patrons to use! Just be careful to read and understand any copyright restrictions they might include on the use of the art work.

Several online clipart collections are available. The Animation Factory hosts an online subscription service for a wide variety of clipart and animated graphics, backgrounds, videos, and PowerPoint templates. Subscriptions to its services are available from $59.95 to $199.95 per year. Check out its website at:

http://www.animationfactory.com/en

Clipart.com makes available downloads of up to 250 clipart images per week at rates of $12.95 per week to $139.95 per year. For more information on its over 10 million images, or to order a subscription, check its website at:

http://www.clipart.com

Also online are a variety of vendors for what are known as stock photos; professionally photographed standard images of babies and workers, farms and cities, tricycles and airplanes, and everything in between. iStockphoto™ provides a service that permits you to upload and download royalty-free stock images. This is not an inexpensive service with each download 5–35+ credits for low resolution, 7–55+ credits for medium resolution, or 17–75+ credits for high resolution stock photos. With credits costing $1.50–$1.75 based on bulk purchases, a small (400 × 300) image would cost around $8. For more information, go to its website at:

http://www.istockphoto.com

What's Next?

In this chapter we focused on the **"8.3"** naming convention and explained the **DTD.** We also addressed the **html** element and saw how the **alt** attribute can be used to add a text description to your **img** elements.

In Chapter 3, the process of completely defining HTML concepts and elements and linking them to HTML web pages will give you the understanding of how to work with the various elements you used with a "leap of faith" in Chapter 1. Some readers will decide to skip over Chapter 3 now and return to it at a later date if they need to incorporate header information in their HTML pages.

URLs Cited

Statistics on browsers used for accessing the web

http://www.w3schools.com/browsers/browsers_stats.asp

Google™ Chrome free web browser software download page

http://www.google.com/chrome

Mozilla™ Firefox free web browser software download page

http://www.mozilla.org/en-US/firefox/fx/#desktop

Microsoft™ Internet Explorer free web browser software download page

http://www.microsoft.com/en-us/download

Lynx™ free text web browser software download page

http://lynx.isc.org

Safari™ free text web browser software download page

http://www.apple.com/safari

Delorie web page viewer service page

http://www.delorie.com/web/lynxview.html

W3C HTML 4.01 standard web page

http://www.w3.org/TR/html401/

W3C XHTML 1 standard web page

http://www.w3.org/TR/xhtml1/

Library of Congress EAD standard web page

http://www.loc.org/ead/

SAA EAD Roundtable web page

http://www2.archivists.org/groups/encoded-archival-description-ead-roundtable

W3C All HTML version standards web page

http://www.w3.org/standards/techs/html#w3c_all

Adobe™ Acrobat Reader free pdf reader software download page

http://get.adobe.com/reader/otherversions/

Broderbund™ clip art software download page

http://www.broderbund.com

AnimationFactory™ clip art subscription page

http://www.animationfactory.com/en

Clipart™ clip art subscription page

http://www.clipart.com

iStockPhoto™ clip art subscription page

http://www.istockphoto.com

Chapter 2 Review Exercises

Chapter 2 Fill-In Questions

1. The built-in rules that a browser uses to display an HTML page are called ______.
2. Most HTML elements require an opening tag and a closing tag. Those that do not are called ______ elements.
3. The default web page on a web server is named _____.
4. To make our lives easier, we put all our graphics and media files in the _____ folder.
5. Sight-limited patrons can surf the Internet using the _______ plain text browser.

Chapter 2 Multiple-Choice Questions

1. The most popular web browser in use today is:

   a) Firefox b) Opera c) Chrome d) IE

2. The current standard version of HTML is:

   a) XML b) XHTML c) HTML5 d) HTML 4.01

3 There are no copyright restrictions on graphics and the like downloaded from the web.

   a) True b) False

4. To create a "drop-down text" box when your patron's mouse goes over a graphic image on your web page, add the following attribute to your **img** element opening tag:

   a) style b) class c) alt d) text

5. One of the best ways to protect the email addresses of your staff and Trustees, and others that you post on your website is to:

   a) not do anything, this is not a problem. b) not include them at all.

   c) give incorrect addresses d) replace "@" symbols with "at" or "_."

Chapter 2 Design and Discussion Questions

1. Identify some specific challenges to creating web pages using the browser you are most familiar with.
2. What does a basic HTML document look like?
3. Describe the 8.3 file-naming standard and give an example.
4. Prepare a sketch of how you would like your library home page to look.

3

The HTML Document

From time to time, even in the best of worlds, we have to "pay our dues" in order to go on with what we would rather be doing. In Chapter 3 you will be paying your dues by looking into the structure of an HTML document. It isn't glitzy. It isn't exciting. In fact, this chapter which covers basic HTML elements and the structure of the web page is quite boring.

To those of you who just want to "just do it" please feel free to skip this chapter and jump ahead to Chapter 4. Return some night when you can't fall asleep and review the finer details of HTML's defining elements described herein.

The HTML Document and Header Information

The HTML document is your web page. Ideally, the page you create using text editors or high-end software programs should work on all browsers. That concept is called *interoperability* and it is the essence of HTML's design. Unfortunately, technology seldom functions ideally, and not all browsers interpret HTML elements the same way. Regardless of what browser they normally view web pages on, good web page designers will test the formatting of their pages on at least the top three browsers: Google's Chrome, Mozilla's Firefox, and Microsoft's Internet Explorer.

The basic HMTL page and its header have little to show you. They do their work behind the scene. If you can bear with us until Chapter 4, you'll have the information you need to create web page headers and be ready to add content and display text on your page. To create effective web pages it is important to understand the tags that elements and attributes create as well as the basic HTML file structure, fonts, and color values.

HTML Tags, Elements, and Attributes

Each HTML "command" is an element type. To provide for future upgradeability to XML, each element type must be written in ***lower case***. As we saw in Chapter 2 an HTML "tag" consists of the element name placed inside of a pair of angle brackets. For example, the opening tag for HTML **preformat** element is **<pre>**. The **preformat** element's closing tag is placed after the text or object the element operates on. The closing tag has a slash preceding the element name in angle brackets, in this case **</pre>**.

Opening tags may include one or more optional "attributes" that stylize the element for the specific set of text they enclose. In Chapter 1 we saw that the table element used the border attribute. Its opening tag was **<table border="1">** indicating that the table was to be displayed with a 1 pixel thick border. A pixel is the smallest graphic element that can be seen on a computer monitor. Note that the element attributes defined in the opening tag are NOT included in the closing tag. Thus, although the opening tag for a table with border attributes includes the border attribute, its closing tag does not and is simply **</table>**.

"Nesting" is the technique of using tags inside of other tags, such as bold inside of center, for better styling of our content. We need to be careful to NOT "overlap" tags or we may end up confusing the browser into prematurely closing tags we still want open. It is good practice when you open a series of tags (**<tag1><tag2><tag3>**) to close them in the reverse order that they were opened in (**</tag3></tag2></tag1>**) as you'll see later in this chapter.

Several HTML elements do not actually surround content (e.g., the line break **br**, horizontal rule **hr**, and image **img** elements). These "empty tags" do not require a closing tag, but to maintain upward compatibility, empty tags will be "self-closed" by adding a space after the element name and then a slash in their *opening* tag **
. The **img element is an empty tag that *must* have the **src** attribute inside its opening tag to describe the location or source of the graphic file. The rose graphic stored as **img001.jpg** in the **assets** sub folder was placed on our page using the tag:

<img src= "assets/img001.jpg" />

Note that in the **img** tag we are using the relative addressing scheme to find the rose graphic file on the same server where the current page is found in the assets folder. It is also important to note that values are enclosed in the "straight" quotes of a plain text file rather than the "curly quotes" provided by most word processors. The use of straight quotes (") is essential as browsers do not recognize the curly quote (") as a value delimiter.

The element's name, which major elements the element can contain and/or where the element might be located, and the element's common attributes will be noted in the text before each element usage example. Often, in the description of the element, information is included on typical uses and values of its common attributes.

Well-Formed Markup Tags

Good markup language practice encapsulates content between "non-overlapping" opening and closing element tags. Such proper nesting of tags is essential in well-formed pages that can easily migrate to XML as well as to avoid confusing the browser. Examples of good and improper nesting are shown in Figure 03-01.

In the second case, **tag1** and **tag2** are turned "on" and then **tag2** turned "off" before **tag1** has been turned "off" resulting in an unreliable interpretation of what you want the browser to do. NEVER let a browser make decisions on how to display your content. Improper nesting will result in browser confusion with unpredictable stylization and display of your content.

Well-Formed, Proper Nesting of Tags ← *USE THIS STRUCTURE!*

```
<tag1> stuff, stuff, stuff          ←Open Tag1
          <tag2> text, text, text   ←Open Tag2
          </tag2>                   ← Close Tag2    ← Good Form!
</tag1>                             ← Close Tag1
```

Overlapping, Improper Nesting of Tags ← **NEVER use this!**

```
<tag1> stuff, stuff, stuff          ←Open Tag1
          <tag2> text, text, text   ←Open Tag2
</tag1>                             ← Close Tag1    ← BAD, Tag2 still OPEN!
          </tag2>                   ← Close Tag2
```

Figure 03-01. Nesting HTML Element Tags

Basic HTML File Structure

Quite often, when you download an HTML file from someone else's website, your browser will review the file and add a line noting the "DOCTYPE" of the file. The DOCTYPE declaration is critical on your web pages to avoid having your browser try to figure out what HTML type and level you are using without this extra line.

Once you have provided your HTML document with the root **html** element opening and closing tags, it is time to consider the overall structure of your HTML document. HTML documents have three specific sections, the document type and root, the head, and the body.

As noted earlier, the HTML **root** element, prefaced by a DOCTYPE declaration, surrounds the entire document. As can be seen in Figure 03-02, the **root <html>** is followed by the **head** element and section and the **head** section is followed by the **body** element and section. The **root** element container is closed with the **</html>** tag to fully close your document.

The **head** contains page definition information and other metadata (the data about the data in your document). Most of the elements that can be found in the **head** are shown in Figure 03-02. The majority of your page's content, and all of the other HTML elements, are found in the **body** of your markup file. Each element must be written in lower case and have a closing tag to be upward compatible.

In Chapter 1 we saw the HTML model structure used in Figures 01-06, 08, 10, 14, 16, and 18. Figure 01-10, for example, is repeated here as Figure 03-03.

Although at the end of your web page file, when your browser runs out of content, it automatically closes all open elements; the closing **body </body>** and **html </html>** tags should be included to properly close your HTML documents.

HTML Elements and Their Attributes

Following the XML concept that the first (outermost) or "root" element contains everything else in the document, you should always begin and end your HTML

```
<!DOCTYPE html>                          ← DOCTYPE declaration line
<html>                                   ← Root element opening tag
  <head>                                 ← Head element opening tag
      <title> Web Page Title </title>    ← Title element tags and content
      <base ... />                       ← Base element empty tag
      <basefont ... />                   ← Basefont element empty tag
      <meta ... />                       ← Meta element empty tag(s)
      <link ... />                       ← Link element pointing to other files
  </head>                                ← Head element closing tag
  <body>                                 ← Body element opening tag
      Your content would continue written here, left to right, in English.
  </body>                                ← Body element closing tag
</html>                                  ← Root element closing tag
```

Figure 03-02. Structure of an HTML Document

document with an **html** element. The **<html>** tag comes right after the **DOCTYPE** declaration line. Note that **DOCTYPE** and other browser *commands* are always written in uppercase. The **html** root element contains the **head** and **body** elements and all of your web page content and stylization. The root element closing tag **</html>** should be placed at the end of the document.

In addition to the **version** attribute, the **html** element can be modified using **lang** (language) and/or **dir** (text direction) attributes to inform the browser what language you are using and which document type definition (DTD) should be written into the browser's HTML rules area.

The two-letter ISO639-1 and three-letter ISO639-2 Standard HTML native language attribute codes are maintained by the Library of Congress. The two-letter ISO639 code for English is **en** (this is the browser default value) with the three-letter value being **eng.** For other language values, additional information on the ISO639 standards can be found at:

http://www.loc.gov/standards/iso639–2/php/code_list.php

As noted earlier, to assure upward migration to XHTML and XML all attribute values are enclosed in straight quotes. Unless otherwise noted, the browser's default text direction is **ltr** (left to right). Thus, the opening **html** tag, with either the default tag **<html>**, or the fully defined element tag with its default attributes called out **<html lang="en" dir="ltr">**, would result in the standard English text display of Figure 03-04.

Some languages, like Hebrew, read from right to left. The HTML opening tag with two-letter language values would therefore read **<html lang="he" dir ="rtl">**

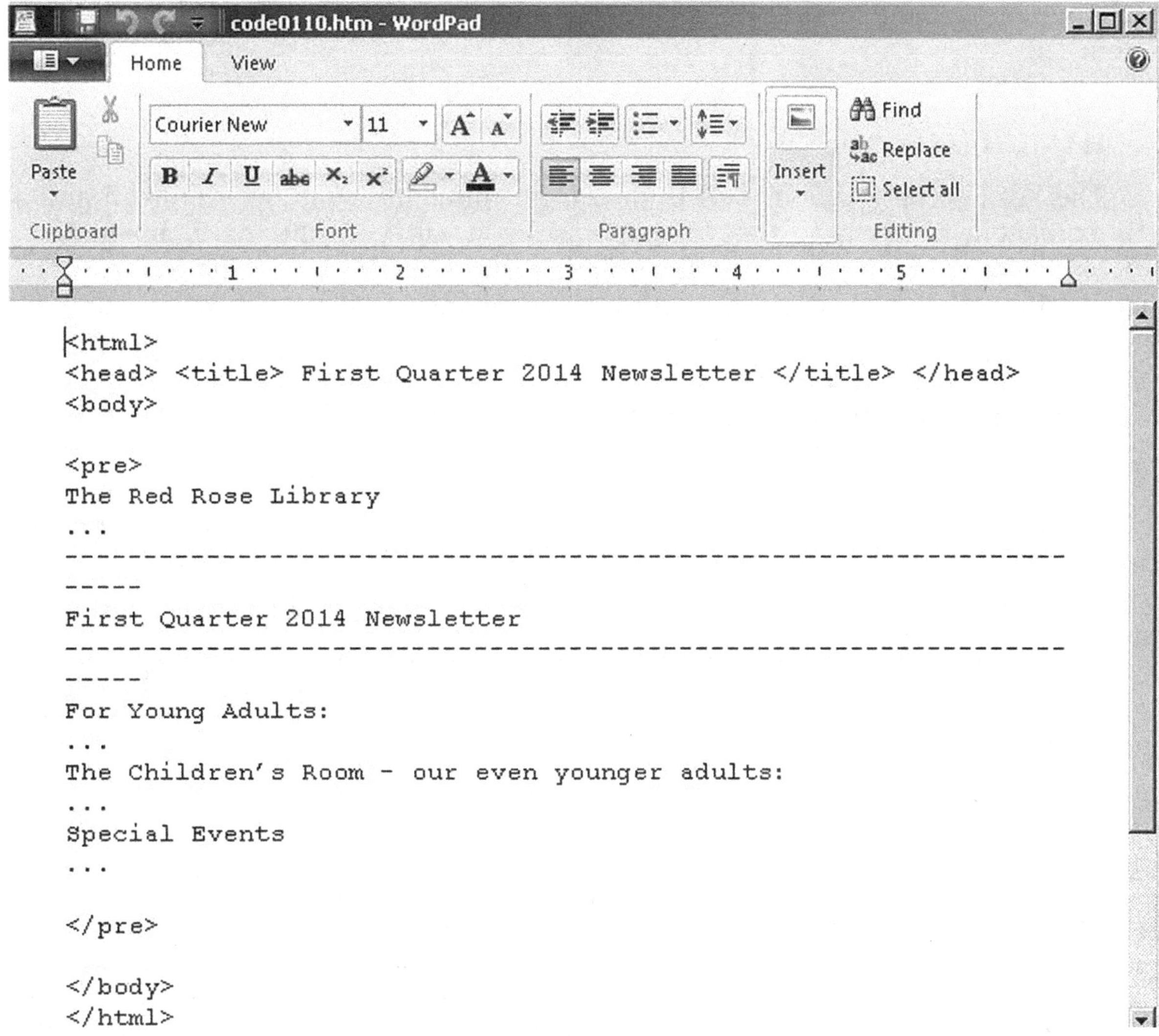

Figure 03-03. Structure of an HTML Page (**code0304.htm**)

CODE:

Either the Browser Default: **<html>** Content is written using English characters, margin at the left. **</html>**	or the fully defined **html** tag: **<html lang="en" dir="ltr">** Content is written using English characters, margin at the left. **</html>**

Yields the **RESULT**:

Content is written using English characters, margin at the left.

Figure 03-04. Default **html** Tag and Its Attributes (**code0304.htm**)

to change the default language to Hebrew and the text direction on the page to right to left.

HTML Head Section

The head section of your HTML document minimally includes the **head** and a **title** element inside the head area. In many cases you will see additional elements here, notably the character encoding declaration that is established by a **meta** element. The **meta** and most of the optional element types contained in the **head** portion of your HTML document are empty elements; that is, although they may have several attributes and can be a rich source of information for your document, they do not encapsulate anything. Only the **title** element of those elements on the listing in Figure 03-02 surrounds any content with opening and closing tags.

You won't see anything happen differently with, or without these tags! Your *browser,* however, will be given information it needs to go to another website or to set the font or URL for your page, or a *search engine* will be told what contents you have on your web page. In Chapter 6 we will add the **style** element to our **head** section to allow page-level and website-level changes to a variety of element defaults using cascading style sheet (CSS) techniques that alter the browser's DTD rules. Although beyond the scope of our text, **script** elements can also be found in the **head** that invoke **JavaScript** and other scripting language style changes.

Document Header Information

The **head** element encloses the header information in your HTML document. The **head** contains general information about the document and can contain the **title, base, basefont, meta, link, isindex, nextid** elements. It is located inside the root **html** element.

With the singular exception that the **title** element displays the title in your browser's title window, elements in the document's **head** are **not** displayed when the web page is displayed. Any number of element tags (above) can appear in the **head,** in any order, but only the **title** element is typically used, despite the need to have character encoding via the **meta** element that is required to fully validate HTML documents.

In addition to character encoding, it might be expected that the use of the **meta** element to create the Dublin Core description of your web page would become more widespread in the future as cataloging of web pages becomes necessary. We will look at this in-page cataloging concept later on in this chapter.

Document Title Element

The **title** element specifies the title of your document that is displayed in the browser's title window. It can contain only character data (CDATA); that is, no other tags or elements can be in your title. Although not required to be included in your web page, the **title** tag must be inside the **head** section if you are using it. When you do not use the title element, the browser will display the full URL and file name of your page, including path instead of just displaying the page's title. We already saw this in

```
<html>        ← Open the html document
  <head>   ← Open the head section
<title>Your Library's Home Page</title> ← Insert title Tag
<!-- Other head elements go here -->   ← Add Comments
  </head>   ← Close the head section
<!-- The rest of the document is here --> ← Add Comments
</html>       ← Close the html document
```

Figure 03-05. Inserting the **title** Tag (code0306.htm)

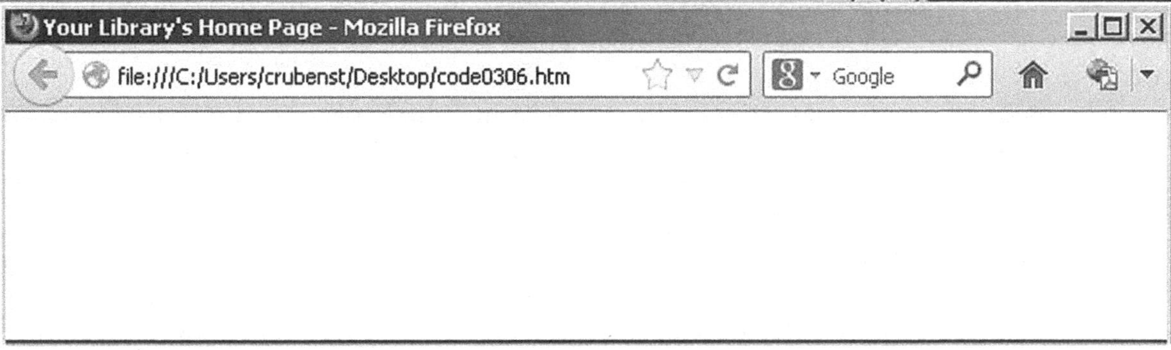

Figure 03-06. Browser Showing Page Title (**code0306.htm**)

Chapter 1, in Figure 01-06, without the **title** tag, and Figure 01-09 with the **title** tag. To add a **title** tag to your web page, insert the **title** tags and its content inside the **head** of your document as illustrated in Figure 03-05.

Note the "Tag Structure for Adding Comments" in the code mentioned earlier. Adding comments is a very important way to remind yourself, and others working on your page in the future, what you had in mind for a certain set of codes. We will review commenting more rigorously in Chapter 4. Figure 03-06shows the contents of a file **code0304.htm** that uses the above code. While this file yields only a blank web page, it demonstrates how using a **title** tag makes your page more attractive and defines its intended contents as that of **"Your Library's Home Page."**

Your Website's Base URL

The **base** element is an empty element that is placed inside the **head** and does not require a closing tag. It uses the required **href** attribute to specify the server and folder address of the current document. If the **base** element is absent, the browser assumes the **href** addresses in your HTML document point to documents on the same server. If your website is in the folder **lib** on the server **www.yourserver.org**, the base tag would look like:

<base href="http://www.yourserver.org/lib/" />

Default Fonts for Your Page

The **basefont** element is also an empty element that does not require a closing tag. You can use it inside the **head** section to set the default font characteristics for all the text in your HTML document. You can override the browser's standard default text attributes for **size, color,** and **face,** or even a **basefont** default attribute by using **font** element tags around specific text. This technique is more fully described in Chapter 4, with the more elegant style sheets methods described in Chapter 6. Although either technique will change the appearance of specific text inside of your document, please note that both the **basefont** and **font** tags that specify size, color, and face attributes will be phased out in lieu of **style** sheet definitions in future HTML versions.

The **basefont**'s **size** attribute can be used to reset the default font size value of **3** to any number between **1** and **7** (where 1 is the largest and 7 the smallest font size). You can also use "+" or "–" number values to change the font size *relative* to whatever the current font size is.

The **color** attribute can override the default **black** text color by changing the **color** attribute to **red** for example. Adding a font **size** value of **6** resulting in the tag:

<basefont color="red" size="6" />

The **font face** attribute permits changing the face (e.g., Arial, Times) using a comma-separated list of font names. If you provide several font face names, your browser will try to match the face in the order given. Should your computer NOT have a particular font installed on it, the browser will go one by one through your list to try to match the font. If it does not find any of your fonts, it will decide what font you wanted. Don't let this happen! The last font face of your listing should be a generic "serif" or "nonserif" face name to at least keep the general text look what you had intended.

Please recall that attributes can be listed in any order, but do not all need to be listed in an opening tag.

Defining Color Values

The 16 common **color** values are defined by either their color **name** or their RGB (red-green-blue) two-digit hexadecimal (Hex) values preceded by the pound sign (**#**). Two-digit hexadecimal numbers are used to describe the "amount" of each color using the 16 Hex numbers (0, 1, 2, 3, 4, 5, 6, 7, 8, 9, a, b, c, d, e, and f) for 256 shades of each basic color. In Figure 03-07 we see that the color **white** contains the full color spectrum as its two-digit Hex number equals all the **red,** all the **green,** and all the **blue** we can display or **#ffffff.** At the other extreme is **black** (the absence of color), or **#000000.** Pure **red** contains only red, no green and no blue and thus has the value **#ff0000.** The full

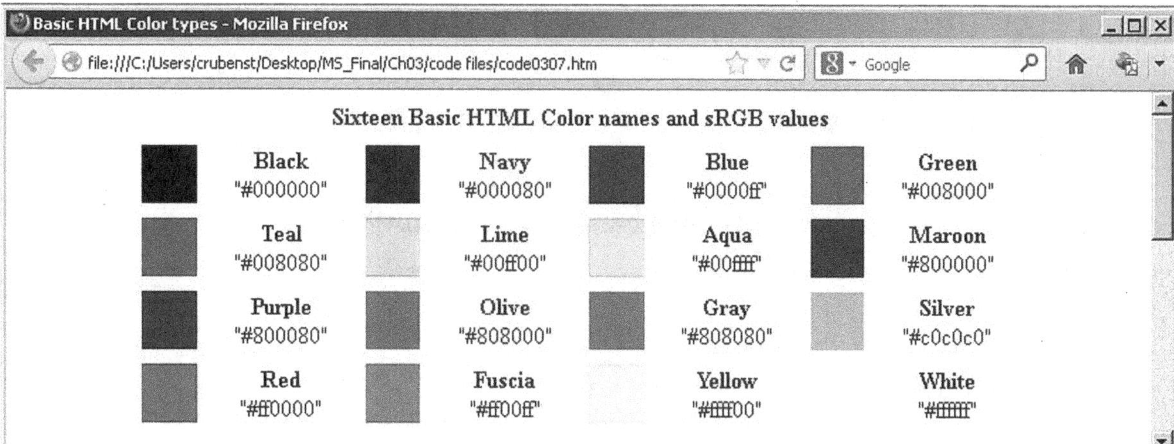

Figure 03-07. Sixteen Common Web Page Color Names and Their Values (**code0307.htm**)

set of hexadecimal values from **black** to **white** (**#000000** through **#ffffff**) can be used to generate a 24-bit color map with 16.7 million colors!

Examining the 16 common web page colors and their RGB values of Figure 03-05, we note that when the **green** hexadecimal value is **ff** and **red** and **blue** are both **00,** the resulting color **#00ff00** is NOT green but **lime** (**green** being rendered by **#008000**) as illustrated in Figure 03-07.

Unfortunately, color palettes are not consistent between browsers. To help you decide how best to colorize your web pages, use a color chart or **body** attribute creator service like that offered by

Some online color chooser and color chart services:

http://www.w3schools.com/tags/ref_colorpicker.asp
http://www.colorschemer.com/online.html
http://color.online-toolz.com/tools/color-chooser.php
http://www.colorpicker.com/
http://www.visibone.com/colorlab/big.html

Not only will these web pages let you see the full spectrum of web colors you can use, but they will also give the specific **#rrggbb** numeric code, and show how the colors show up on your test browser. You should be aware that how your browser looks does not guarantee how your page will look to patrons with other browsers, or if they have created alternate color palettes that change the appearance of these codes installed on them.

Describing Your Page with Metadata

The **meta** element is an empty element that hides inside the **head** and does not require a closing tag. This element allows you to include a variety of metadata (the data about your data) in your web page. The **meta** element that establishes character encoding, although not required, is the only other element common to minimal HTML documents that can achieve HTML validation. As we noted earlier, it is not needed for our documents, but should you wish to include it, add the line noted in bold just after the **title** in the head as illustrated here:

```
<!DOCTYPE html>
<html> <head>
<title> Page Title Here . . . </title>
<meta http-equiv=Content-Type content="text/html; charset = windows-1252" />
. . .
</head>
```

The **http-equiv** attribute has several values. In this instance it establishes the **Content-Type** with the content of the document defined as **text/html** and the character set the browser should use to be **windows-1252.** In the above coding it defines the **Content-Type** of the document as **text/html** and the character set the browser should use to be **windows-1252.**

In-Page Cataloging

The **meta** tag is particularly interesting as it can also be used to supply lots of data about your page in the form of descriptors and keywords that search engines find particularly easy to work with. In effect, by using **meta** tags one can look at a web page as if it were a book and describe the ownership and creator of the page, and other characteristics of your page.

Good practice suggests librarians in libraries and information centers *should* be using the Dublin Core ISO Standard 15836 metadata elements (**http://www.dublincore.org/**) to identify the content of their web pages using the **meta** element with its **name** attribute to describe specific Dublin Core (DC) parameters and the **content** attribute to provide keywords for each parameter. The suggested DC metadata set in an HTML document's head section might include one or more of the typical Dublin Core **meta** tags shown in Figure 03-08.

The full vocabulary of 15 Dublin Core Metadata Elements (Version 1.1) can be found at:

```
<head> ...
<meta name="dc.title" content="Red Rose Library Web Site" />
<meta name="dc.creator" content="Charles Rubenstein" />
<meta name="dc.subject" lang="en" content="Library Web Site" />
<meta name="dc.description" content="Red Rose Library Web Site" />
<meta name="dc.date" content="07/01/13" />
... </head>
```

Figure 03-08. Example of In-Page Cataloging: Dublin Core Metadata Parameters

http://dublincore.org/documents/dces/

If all the **meta** element tag accomplished was to provide a Dublin Core profile for a web page, that would be sufficient to make the **meta** element worthwhile to use.

You might wish to include several non-Dublin Core elements in your pages that are available as values for the **meta** element **name** attribute. These metadata include information about your email address (value="**email**"), the URL of your site (value="**url**"), or can even add keywords to your page (value="**keywords**"):

```
<meta name="email" content="webmaster@redroselibrary.com" />
<meta name="url" content="http://www. redroselibrary.com" />
<meta name="keywords" content="Library Website, web pages, City, State" />
```

When a software program creates a web page, it may insert an additional **meta** tag **name** attribute value to note the page's creation (**name="generator"**) by that specific software application:

```
<meta name="generator" content="Adobe GoLive" />
or
<meta name="generator" content="Microsoft Word 14" />
```

Telling Search Engines: Don't Index This Page

You should know that a search engine can index the contents of your pages so that its users can find your page content more quickly. This means that information found in *your* web pages, for example, names of your board of trustees, goes into the search engine's database and can be used for retrieval by others. If you have a small library, this is not a likely scenario for your library's web pages. However, if you **don't** want search engines to index the content of your pages, so that your board's names cannot be retrieved, the following **meta** element **name** value tells search engines to pass over the file:

```
<meta name="robots" content="noindex" />
```

Setting a Freshness Date for Your Page

A web page is worthwhile only if it is kept up-to-date. If you want to automatically delete dated information, set an expiration date for your page following the model below with the **meta name** attribute value as **expires** noting your **content** to expire on the **date, time GMT** value as shown here:

```
<meta name="expires" content="Wed, 26 Nov 2014 23:59:59 GMT" />
```

Don't Cache—Get Me the Latest Page

To instruct your patron's browser to ignore cached (saved) pages and request the latest files from your server, use the **http-equiv** attribute with the value **pragma** and a **content** attribute with a **no-cache** value:

```
<meta http-equiv="pragma" content="no-cache" />
```

Redirecting Your Patrons to a New Website

To redirect a viewer from one web page (perhaps an original page that has been relocated either elsewhere on your server or onto another server) to another, use the **http-equiv** attribute with the value **refresh** and set the **content** attribute to show the amount of time your patron will see the current web page (in seconds). After a semicolon, provide the protocol and full URL name of where the browser should go to get the next page as shown here:

```
<meta http-equiv="refresh"
content="10;url = http://www.somewhereelse.com/newpage.html" />
```

After a delay of about 10 seconds, the browser will automatically redirect itself to the new server at **http://www.somewhereelse.com** to open and display the **newpage.html** file it finds there. In Chapter 10 we'll examine other ways to use the **http-equiv** attribute to create a variety of other page transitions.

Adding an ISBN Number

Lastly, the **meta** element **scheme** attribute can be used to identify the ISBN number for a document, or the web page referring to it. A review web page about *Wynar's Introduction to Cataloging and Classification*, ninth edition, by Arlene Taylor, might use:

```
<meta scheme="ISBN" name="identifier" content="1-56308-857-5" />
```

Your Page's Relationships to Other Documents

The **link** element is used to establish a relationship to other web documents. It is found inside the **head,** it requires the **href** attribute, and it accepts **rel** and **type** attributes. This element is commonly used to link your web page to another page that has support information needed for the proper displaying of your content. Chapter 6 will review style sheets and you'll see the reason you might need to link a CSS file named **default.css** saved in the **styles** folder on your website. The style sheet information **type** in the file is noted by the value **text/css** with the file location indicated by the **styles/default.css** hyperlink address:

```
<link rel="stylesheet" type="text/css" href="styles/default.css" />
```

What's Next?

In this chapter you reviewed the structure of the HTML document and saw it included three sections, the **html** root element, the **head,** and the **body.** You looked deeper into the various default and configurable subelements of the **head,** specifically the **base, basefont,** and **meta** elements. You saw each element has a variety of default attributes which can, if desired, be revised to better stylize the look of your web pages.

In Chapter 4 we will illustrate the use of the elements that change the way text displays in your browser. You'll see how HTML can format your text using examples you would expect to find on your library website.

URLs Cited

Two-letter ISO639-1 and three-letter ISO639-2 Standard HTML native language attribute codes

http://www.loc.gov/standards/iso639-2/php/code_list.php

Some online color chooser and color chart services

http://www.visibone.com/colorlab/big.html
http://www.w3schools.com/tags/ref_colorpicker.asp
http://www.colorschemer.com/online.html
http://color.online-toolz.com/tools/color-chooser.php
http://www.colorpicker.com/
http://www.visibone.com/colorlab/big.html

Dublin Core Metadata Elements (Version 1.1)

http://dublincore.org/documents/dces/

Chapter 3 Review Exercises

Chapter 3 Fill-In Questions

1. You should test your HTML pages on these three browsers: ______. If you overlap HTML element tags, the result is ______.
2. The HTML page **title** element is always placed within the _____ of the file. The default language and text direction for an HTML document is _____.
3. There are _______ web safe, standard colors.

Chapter 3 Multiple-Choice Questions

1. All HTML element names should be written in:

   a) lowercase b) uppercase c) mixed fonts d) upper and lower case
2. All HTML attributes and their values should be written in:

   a) lowercase b) uppercase c) mixedfonts d) upper and lower case
3. When nesting tags, the order is:

   a) first opened, first closed b) first opened, last closed

   c) last opened, first closed d) arbitrary
4. If you use the DOCTYPE command in your HTML document, it is located in the:

   a) last line of document b) head section

   c) first line of document d) body section
5. The DC parameters in a **meta** element are always found in the:

   a) last line of document b) head section

   c) first line of document d) body section

Chapter 3 Design and Discussion Questions

1. Create a Dublin Core meta tag set using the code for Figure 03-08 for the five DC metadata parameters shown for your library web page.
2. Why should you consider using the DC parameters on all your library web pages?
3. Describe why you might need to redirect a patron from one page URL to another and give an example.

4

Displaying Text in Your HTML Document

Now that you understand the structure and header portion of your HTML document, it is time to see how we can display text. You will learn what you can do in your document, locally and globally, to change the way text is displayed by surrounding the text with a variety of stylizing elements. While you need to understand these elements, you will see how they tell the computer to center something, to make a paragraph, or other commands, which you do without thinking while working with a word processing program. However, you won't need to be as fast in creating your web page as you might think you needed to be in writing a proposal for funding. Your web page won't need as much work once you have it started as it will seem right now when you are trying to absorb a great deal in a short time. Please note as indicated earlier, we will include the **<!DOCTYPE html>** declaration in each of our web page code files, but will not show that line in our figures. Also note that should you decide to validate any of our sample code files, you will often see the character encoding and one or more warnings about attributes that are obsolete and should be rendered by cascading style sheet (CSS) techniques that we will review in Chapters 6 and 11. Please don't be concerned. These "errors" are not ones that will affect the way your browser displays the web page.

Before we begin, you need to know how to remind yourself what, or why, you used a particular method in a section of your page through adding comments to your HTML document.

Using Comments

Comments can be included anywhere in your HTML document to explain why a particular set of tags or items were included, or suggest future enhancements. You must surround the text with the comment delimiter set "**< ! - -**" and "**- - >**" to indicate that comments and notes—not HTML elements—are being presented in the document. These comments can be anywhere, inside or outside the **html** element tag set. All the text and/or element tags occurring between these two delimiters will not be decoded.

They will be completely ignored by your browser. Comments can appear anywhere text would normally be allowed. As an example:

< ! - - comments about blah-blah-blah . . . **- - >**

Bearing in mind that your browser does not normally display extra spaces, tabs, or lines, the text and even HTML element lines between comment delimiters can be broken, and the comment's angle brackets separated from the text and/or markup commands you intend to be ignored. This makes it much easier reading the encapsulated content as demonstrated in Figure 04-01.

As HTML tags can exist within a comment structure, you can temporarily delete text and all its formatting by inserting the comment opening delimiter set and ending delimiter set around all the information you want to "comment out" or want your browser to ignore. Let's see if we can create a page that uses some of the tags we used in Chapter 1 to show how it is done. The code for a simple web page (**code0403.htm**) with commented-out text and HTML elements, where characters in **bold** are not displayed, could be as shown in Figure 04-02.

Note that in the browser view of Figure 04-03 whatever text in **code0403.htm** was surrounded by the comment delimiters is not displayed, and any tags present are not parsed (decoded) by the browser.

The Body of Your HTML Document

From a **head** filled with a **title** and one or more "invisible" empty tags, whose effects are not always apparent, your HTML document opens into the **body** of your page. The **body** element encloses the text and tags comprising the main body of your document.

Inline Comments

```
        <!-- Filename: index.htm Created by CR, on 07/01/14 -->
```

Comment Delimiters with Tabs

```
        <!-- Filename: index.htm    ← Remember: Browsers ignore extra spaces & tabs!
                Created by CR, on 07/01/14 -->
```

Separating the Comment Delimiters using line breaks and tabs

```
        <!--                        ← Remember: Browsers ignore breaks & tabs!
                Filename: index.htm
                Created by CR, on 07/01/14
        -->
```

Figure 04-01. Adding Comments to Your Code

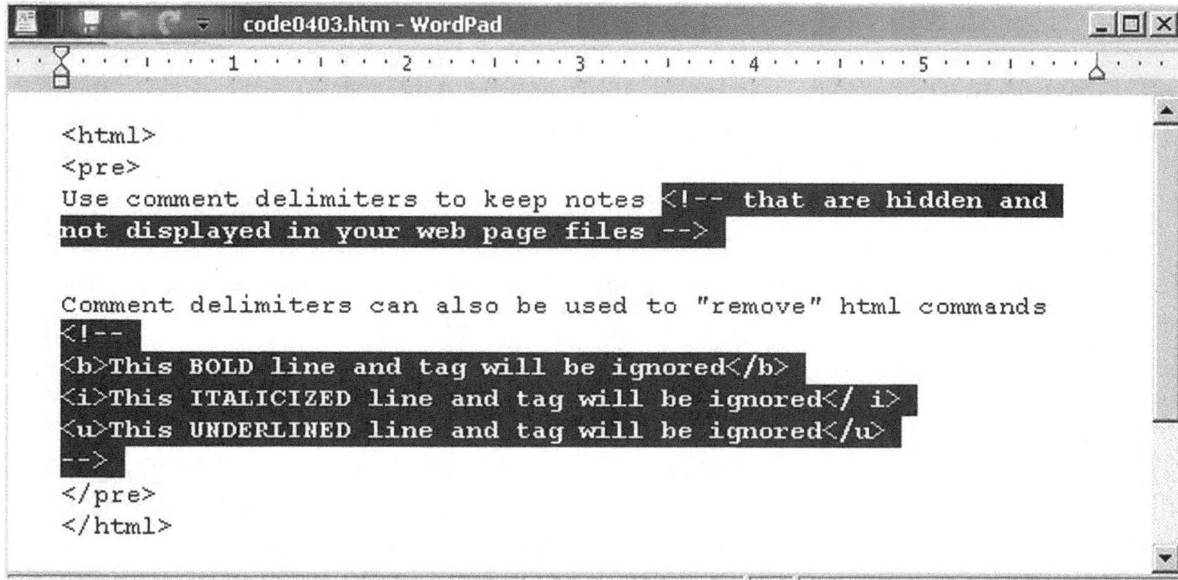

```
<html>
<pre>
Use comment delimiters to keep notes <!-- that are hidden and
not displayed in your web page files -->

Comment delimiters can also be used to "remove" html commands
<!--
<b>This BOLD line and tag will be ignored</b>
<i>This ITALICIZED line and tag will be ignored</ i>
<u>This UNDERLINED line and tag will be ignored</u>
-->
</pre>
</html>
```

Figure 04-02. Using Comment Delimiters to "Ignore Code" (**code0403.htm**)

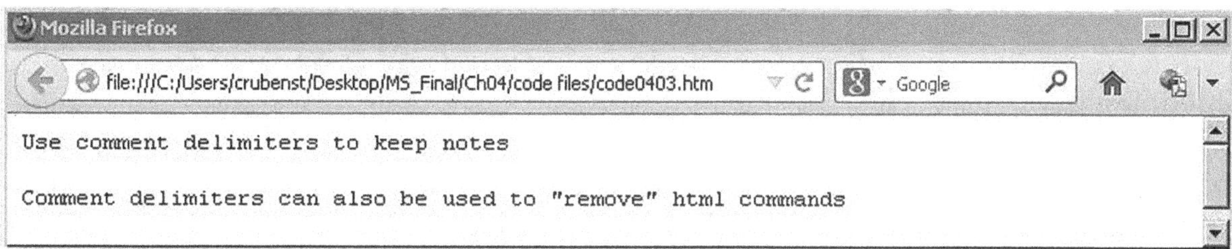

Figure 04-03. Using Comment Delimiters—Browser View (**code0403.htm**)

Your **head** supplied a **title** to your page and a variety of "hidden" metadata and information about your document. The major portion of your HTML document consists of information surrounded by element tags in the **body.** Elements within the **body** tell the browser how to control appearance and formatting (rendering) of your page's content. Content must be surrounded by one or more (properly nested) elements that determine what will be done to display the text and graphics of your document.

The displayed text in the **body** section can contain one or more header elements, paragraphs, horizontal lines, tables, hyperlinks, and images. It can keep its preformatted spacing, be displayed as a quote, in a list or interactive form.

The **body** element itself can be modified by adding a variety of attributes (**background, bgcolor, text, link, vlink,** and **alink**). We can specify a URL pointing to an image file to be used to create, or tile, the background of the document-viewing area with the attribute **background="URL"** or change the color of the page's background with attributes, for example, background color: **bgcolor="aqua"** text color: **text="black",** or the various visited and unvisited hyperlinks **link, vlink,** and **alink** by changing those attribute's values.

In HTML documents, as noted in Chapter 3, when a color is specified the attribute's value is the red-green-blue hexadecimal triplet **#rrggbb** derived from standard color tables using those numbers or standard names. These three 2-digit hexadecimal numbers are each capable of displaying 8 bits or one of 256 possible levels of color (red, green, and blue) creating a 24-bit color palette with 16.7 million colors! This is the same palette used by most common scanners and graphics creation programs. In Chapter 3 we noted that to speed your use of colors in your HTML document, several free online services permit creation of color combinations without worrying about which numeric coding to use. Another one of these is Joe Barta's Color Picker version 2.0:

http://www.pagetutor.com/colorpicker/picker2

This two-panel web page seen in Figure 04-04 provides an interactive Color Picker II widget on the left side panel whose results are shown on the right side Testing Site panel. The tool is available for downloading to work off line and can help you fine-tune the hex color codes for your own web page. Feel free to experiment with the effect of various text colors on different background colors as well as change the attribute colors of the various hyperlink types. You can also modify the font **size** and **face** and even choose a background image file. Simple enough for anyone to use, either insert hex number triplets (if you have them) or simply click on the color chart to immediately see the results in the right-hand pane. Once you are satisfied with your results, record the hex code values and insert them into your opening tag for inline redefining of the **body** element's default values.

> Good to Know: The Color Picker tool shows element names in uppercase at the bottom of the Testing Site panel. We *ONLY* use *lowercase* names in this text to maintain future compatibility with XML and HTML5 web page designs. Also note that Color Picker is now in version 3.1 on the website (at http://www.pagetutor.com/colorpicker/), which incorporates the lowercase names convention. Either version can be used, but I like the way version 2.0 works a bit more.

The default color of a browser web page background is **white** (color value **#ffffff**). If you wanted to change the **white** background color to **aqua,** you could use the **body** element's **bgcolor** attribute with the color value **#00ffff.** The section of HTML code that would generate a solid **aqua** background along with content noting this change is shown in Figure 04-05.

The file with this coding example (**code0406.htm**) generates a solid colored background that can be seen in Figure 04-06.

To create a graphic background is equally simple using the **body** element with the **background** attribute pointing toward an image file. Depending on the size of the graphic you could, as we will see here, see more than one copy of the image as the page background. The code for using a single red rose graphic **img001.jpg** that has been stored in an **assets** folder to create a multiple "tiled" image backdrop (the attribute's default) for your web page using the **background** attribute with an image value (**background="assets/img001.jpg"**) is seen in Figure 04-07.

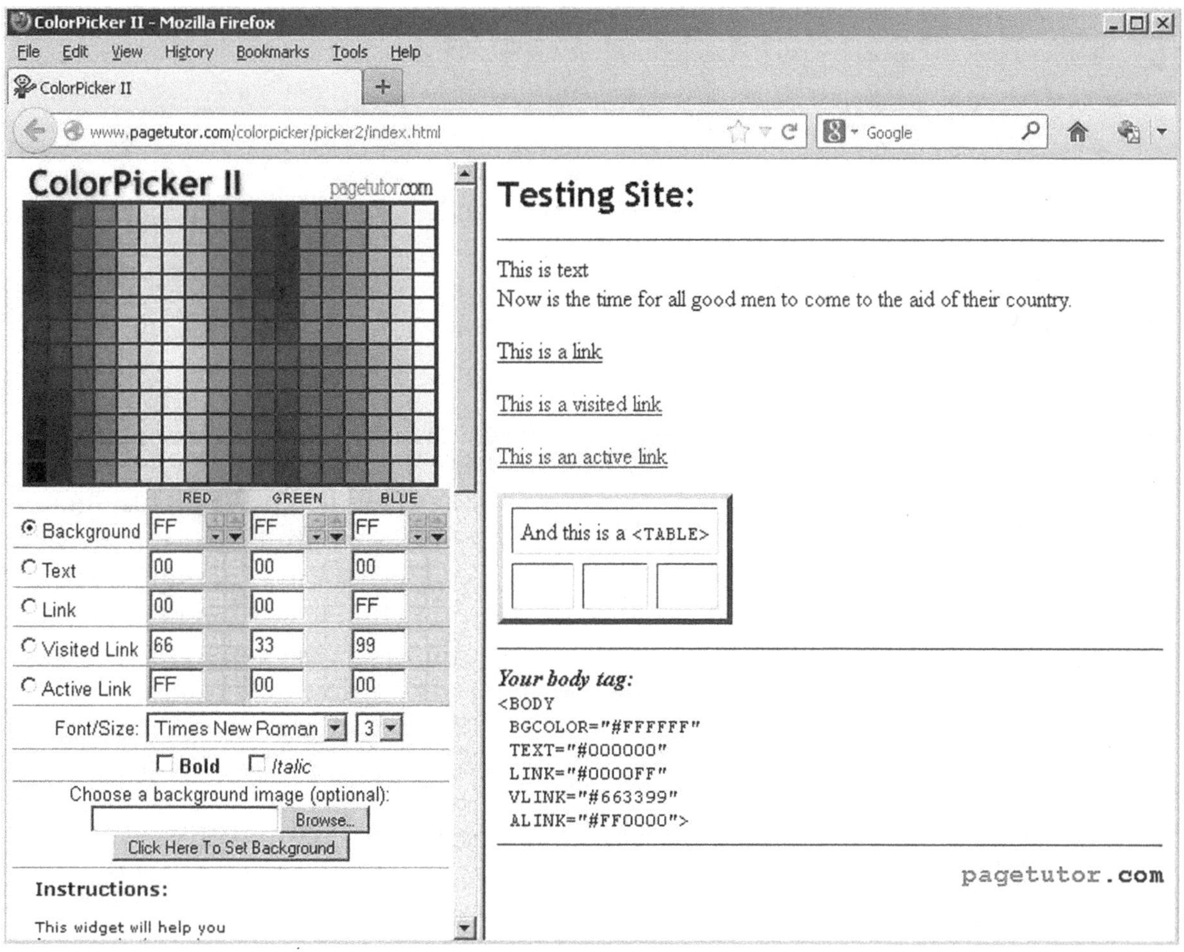

Figure 04-04. Pagetutor.com Color Picker II by Joe Barta

```
<body bgcolor="#00 ff ff">
        <! - - Web Page Background Color = aqua - ->
  Changing the body's bgcolor attribute (default="white") <p />
  Yields the <b>RESULT</b>: <p />
  The background is now colored "aqua"
        <! - - The rest of the document goes here - ->
</body>
```

Figure 04-05. Changing a Web Page's Background Color (**code0406.htm**)

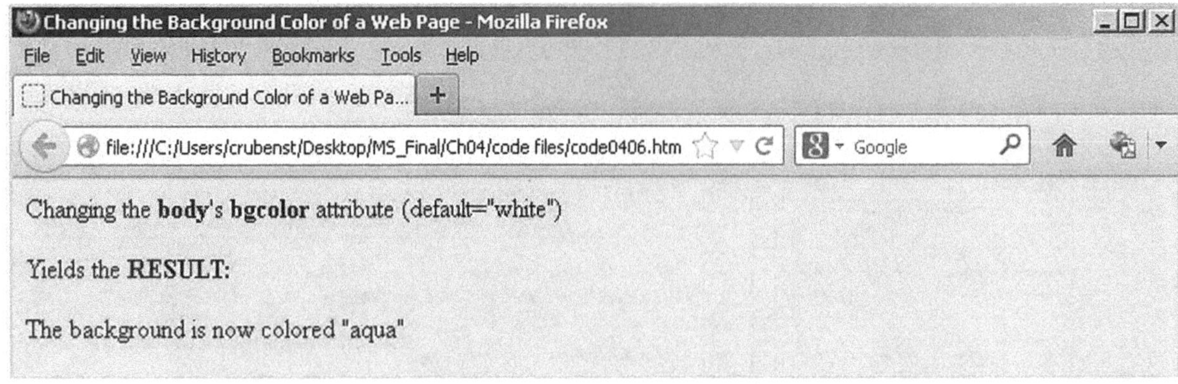

Figure 04-06. Creating a Solid Colored Background (**code0406.htm**)

```
<body background="assets/img001.jpg">
<!-- The background of this page is made up of a single graphic
repeated to fill the background -->

        <! - - The rest of the document body goes here - - >

</body>
```

Figure 04-07. Replacing Background Color with Graphics (**code 0408.htm**)

The file **code0408.htm** generates the multiple rose image background example of Figure 04-08.

This figure illustrates one reason for trying out your pages before putting them online! Clearly, this particular rose image is much too small to be a single image background as well as too powerful for any tiled background. Should you want to use this

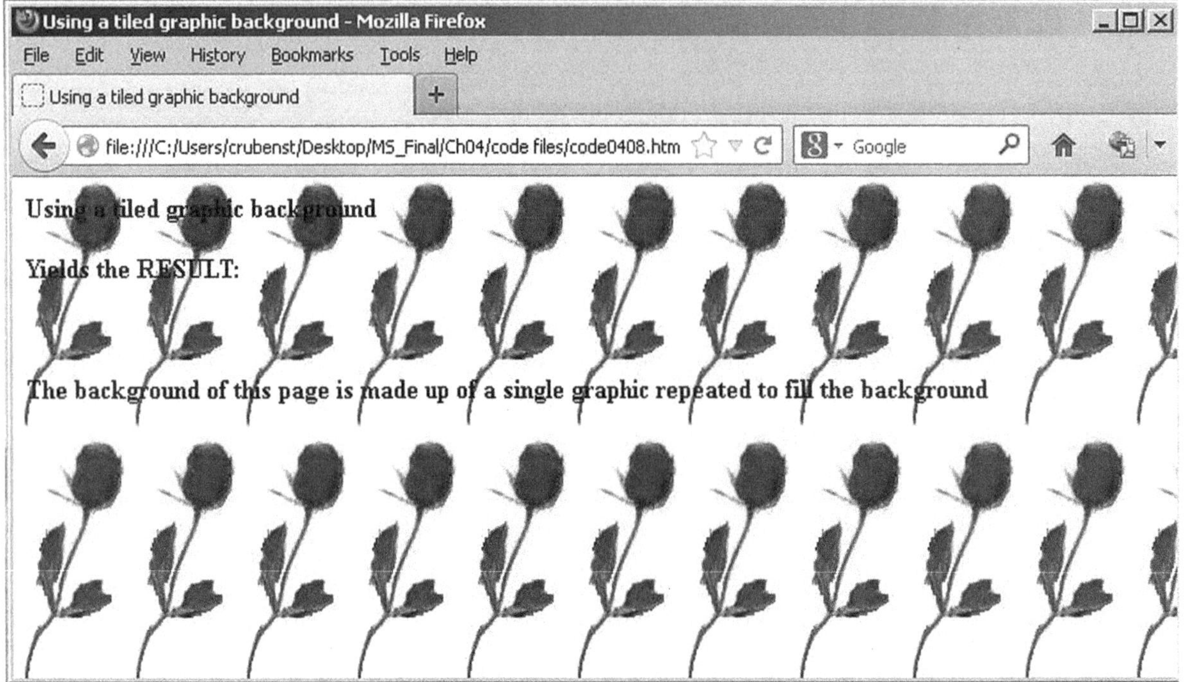

Figure 04-08. Creating a Tiled Graphic Background (**code0408.htm**)

technique on your web pages, how to correct this challenge will be discussed in Chapter 5 where we will look at working with images in more depth.

The **body** tag can also include **link, vlink,** and **alink** attributes. These are attributes used to control the way that hyperlinks are seen on your web page. Normally, unvisited **link** hyperlinks are by default colored blue and are underlined. The active **alink** hyperlinks are by default colored purple and are also underlined. These defaults are illustrated in Figure 04-09.

In Figure 04-10 we see that using the **body** tag we can change the display characteristics such that the unvisited **link** hyperlinks are colored red and the visited **vlink** hyperlinks are colored green. Note that once you try a link the colors may change.

We can also define the active or **alink** hyperlink characteristics. In Chapter 6 we'll find out how we can define these links using **style** or style sheet concepts. For now you can change the way that hyperlinks and text are displayed simply using the previously mentioned attributes within the **body** element tag. Of course now that you know how to do these as inline attribute changes, it is time to tell you that CSS will be handling most of these stylizations in the future and will make this inline technique obsolete.

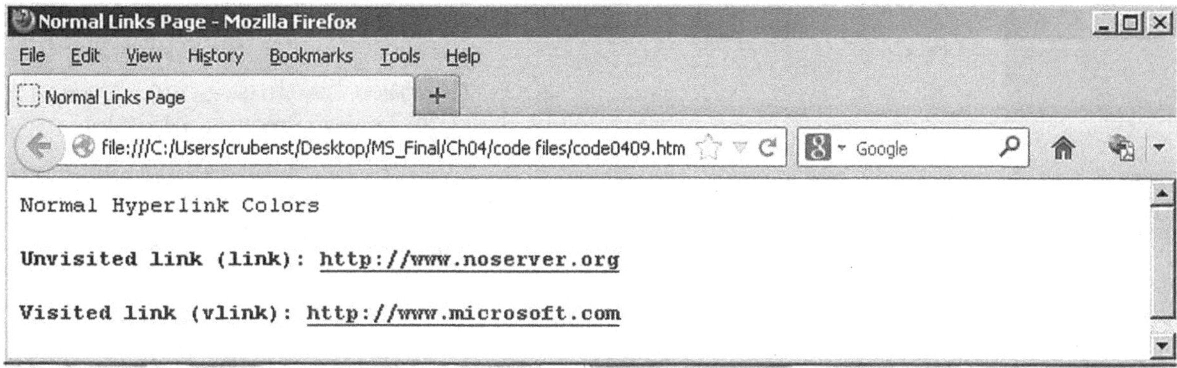

Figure 04-09. Default Hyperlink Colors (**code0409.htm**)

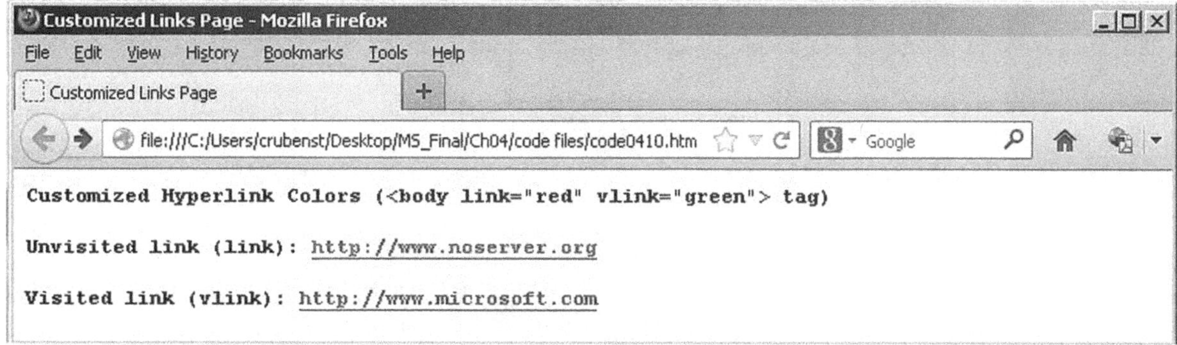

Figure 04-10. Customized Hyperlink Colors (**code0410.htm**)

Document Heading and Block Formatting Elements

Your web pages can be improved by applying heading elements to create titles, and block formatting elements to stylize whole blocks of text. Formatting elements can modify text formats, too, and they are quite useful in creating line breaks and new paragraphs and for creating horizontal lines on your web page.

Heading elements are used to create different font sizes and styles as is typically seen in headlines of a newsletter. Heading tags define six distinct levels of heading from **h1,** the most important, to **h6,** the least important. Each default heading style includes a paragraph break before and after the specific heading style change as seen in Figure 04-11.

The content inside of the heading tags can contain a wide variety of elements such as the hyperlink anchor **a,** images **img,** line breaks **br,** and other text style elements (**b, em, strong, code, samp, kbd, cite, tt, var, i,** and **u**). You can place your heading tags inside the **body,** in a **blockquote,** and even inside of a **form.** HTML can be used to create interactive web pages that generate a response from a patron filled-in form as we will see in Chapter 9. You may also use **align, style,** and **class** attributes in the heading tags as can be seen in Figure 04-12.

The **h1** heading is the top-level heading displayed as a large bold-faced font. At the other extreme, **h6** is the smallest pre-defined heading style, typically used for footnotes like the page copyright or emailing the web-master information. Although Figure 04-11 only shows heading elements encapsulating text, the heading elements can also include a variety of stylizations, hyper-links, and even images.

It is important to note that the heading tags insert a paragraph (carriage return and line feed) on closing the heading tag. That is why the phrase "Other text" does not appear in line with the header and is displayed in the default font size. Another way of handling headings, that permits inline changes of font sizes, is through the use of the **font** element's **size** attribute as shown later in this chapter in Figure 04-22.

CODE:	RESULTS:
<h1>Top-level heading</h1>Other text	**Top-level heading** Other text
<h2>Second level heading</h2>Other text	**Second level heading** Other text
<h3>Third level heading</h3>Other text	**Third level heading** Other text
<h4>Fourth level heading</h4>Other text	**Fourth level heading** Other text
<h5>Fifth level heading</h5>Other text	**Fifth level heading** Other text
<h6>Sixth level heading</h6>Other text	**Sixth, lowest level heading** Other text

Figure 04-11. Heading Examples (**code0411.htm**)

CODE:
This is the start of a new paragraph using an empty tag.<p />
RESULTS:
This is the start of a new paragraph using an empty tag.
CODE:
<p align="center">This is a new paragraph using open and close tags and centering the text.</p>
RESULTS:
This is a new paragraph using open and close tags and centering the text.

Figure 04-12. Using the Paragraph Element (**code0412.htm**)

Forcing Line Breaks

The **br** element is an empty tag that causes a line break to be inserted in the displayed text at the point of its insertion, but does not add a line space as we see the paragraph element **p** doing. The empty or single-sided line break element opening tag is written <**br** />. The line break **br** can be used just about anywhere in your HTML document—even inside the preformatted text **pre** element. The line break element can also be used with **clear, style,** or **class** attributes.

The line break's **clear** attribute controls how text, which is aligned with images, behaves when a line break tag is encountered. The default **clear** attribute causes a new line to start below the image, back to the original margin. A value of **left** tells the browser that you want to break to a clear left margin, **right** to a clear right margin, and **all** to a full clear line.

Making Text into Paragraphs

The paragraph element **p** is used to separate the text in the **body** of your HTML document, list, **table,** or **form** into paragraphs. The opening and closing paragraph tags show the end of the current paragraph and the start of a new paragraph and insert line spaces before and after the surrounded paragraph of text. Some browsers allow the use of an empty paragraph tag to end the previous paragraph and start a new paragraph. If your favorite does not, avoid problems by using a paragraph end/start tag set: **</p><p>.** Either way the paragraph attributes can be used to change text display at the paragraph level. Text, line breaks, character formatting (style tags like **b, u,** and **i**), hyperlinks, and images can all exist inside paragraphs. Like the line break, the paragraph tag can be used with **clear, style,** or **class** attributes. Paragraphs cannot exist within each other as the browser would close the paragraph when it saw the **</p>** code. The effect of creating the end of paragraph within a paragraph, or avoiding paragraph tags altogether, can be approximated by using a pair of line breaks:

.

Division and Span Elements

Up until this point all text was dealt with as a series of continuous characters formed into lines and paragraphs using **br** and/or **p** tags. We will learn later in this chapter how to use the **font** element to stylize text. But what if we want several paragraphs of text to have the same attribute look and feel? Paragraphs cannot nest inside of each other. To repeat the same paragraph style we would have to repeat the desired attribute value changes to make their content look alike. This is tedious and we might forget to include one or more changes. Is there a way to define the styles for several paragraphs at one time? Yes, there is! The block-level **div** element can define text in divisions with paragraph-like breaks (sort of super paragraph elements) and similarly, the **span** element is used to stylize sections of text inline without any line break effects.

The **div** element is used to format small sections, or divisions, of text on a web page treating them as a single block. The **div** is surrounded by implied line breaks just like heading and paragraph tags. It can contain any element that can exist within the HTML body element, so it is a great choice for stylizing several paragraphs with a single attribute change. For further fine-tuning of attributes, one can nest **div** elements inside of **div** elements.

The **span** element can be used to style sections of text inline just like the **div,** but it renders the text without any line breaks. Because neither the **div** nor **span** element has any default formatting, they are most likely going to contain a **style** or **class** attribute. To replace the deprecated **center** element, the **div** element is typically used with at least the **align="center"** attribute.

Figure 04-13 shows some sample text surrounded by default **div** and **span** elements to demonstrate the basic differences between the two elements. To stylize the text to be colored **red** before and after the **div** and **span** segments we use the **font** element with a **color** attribute. The **font** element will be more fully described later in this chapter.

CODE: **<font color="red">** This red text line is before the div starting tag.**</font>** **<div>** This text is surrounded by the div element. ... **</div><font color="red">** This red text line is after the div ending tag and before the span starting tag.**</font>** **<span>** This text is surrounded by the span element. ... **</span><font color="red">** This red text line is after the span ending tag.**</font>**

This red text line is before the div starting tag.
This text is surrounded by the div element. Note that although it has neither a line break before, or after it, as a block-level formatting element there is a paragraph break before and after this line.
This red text line is after the div ending tag and before the span starting tag. This text is surrounded by the span element. Note that as it does not have a line break before, or after it, the next line continues right here, at the end of this line. This line is after the span ending tag.

Figure 04-13. Comparing the **div** and **span** Elements (**code0413.htm**)

Although all the HTML elements within the **div** element *do* acquire its **style** definition, Figure 04-14 illustrates that when an **align** attribute is placed in a **span** tag, the surrounded HTML content does *not* acquire the **align** attribute. From this we can easily determine that the **align** attribute is not included in the DTD design of the **span** element, thus it has no default value, and—at least within HTML4.01—cannot have any effect on text alignment.

CODE: **<font="red" >** This red text line is before the div starting tag.**</font>** **<div align="center">** This text is surrounded by the div align="center" element tag (breaks after each line). ... **</div><font color="red">** This red text line is after the div ending tag and before the span starting tag.**</font>** **<span align="right">** This text is surrounded by the span align="right" element tag (breaks after each line). ... **</span><font color="red">** This red text line is after the span ending tag.**</font>**

This red text line is before the div starting tag.
This text is surrounded by the div align="center" element tag (breaks after each line).
Note that it has neither a line break before or after it.
It is a block-level formatting element with a line break before and after this section. Also note that alignment is throughout the section.
This red text line is after the div ending tag and before the span starting tag. This text is surrounded by the span align="right" element tag (breaks after each line).
Note that it does not have a line break before or after the tag.
The next line continues right here, at the end of this line. Also note the absence of any alignment to the right... This red text line is after the span ending tag.

Figure 04-14. Acquiring **div** and **span** Styles Inline (**code0414.htm**)

Horizontal Rules

In addition to generating a line break, the horizontal rule **<hr />** element is an empty tag that causes a horizontal line to be rendered on the screen, usually at the full width of the screen. The **hr** tag, normally inside of the body of your document, can also be used inside of the preformat

(pre), **blockquote,** or **form** portions of your document. It can be used with **align, width, size,** and **noshade** attributes.

The **align** attribute, which can have the value **left, right,** or **center,** defines how the rule will be aligned on the page. The tag **<hr align="center" />** creates a centered line.

The **width** attribute specifies the width of the horizontal rule, either in pixels or in percentage of screen width, and can have the values **###px** or **###%.** The tag **<hr width="450px" />** creates a line 450 pixels wide regardless of the screen window width. The default for the **width** attribute is that the horizontal rule is centered. A more elegant use of the **width** attribute makes the rule scalable to the browser's window using <**hr width="50%" />** to create a centered line that is always half the width of the screen window regardless of the actual width of the browser window.

The **hr** element's **size** attribute specifies the thickness of the rule line, in pixels. The **noshade** attribute displays horizontal rules as solid black lines rather than in the default line style, which creates a shadow-box or shade effect.

Figure 04-15 shows a variety of horizontal rule attribute values and how they are displayed in a browser.

Centering Text

The **center** element is an older (deprecated) shorthand notation for the more properly used **div** element opening tag **<div align="center">** that can be used to center a block of text as well as other elements such as paragraphs, tables, images, and headings on a web page. It can contain text, character formatting, hyperlink, headings, and images. It can be used inside the HTML **body, blockquote, form, table,** or list elements. The **center** tag includes a default paragraph tag as part of its opening and closing element set.

Although still in active use, the **center** element is a deprecated element in future HTML definitions, which means it is being replaced by the use of the **div** element with an **align** attribute. If you are worried about future browser versions not displaying your work properly, note that the two lines of HTML code given next are equivalent, and most browsers still permit either, but try to use the div version for upward compatibility of your web page whenever possible:

<center>
This displays as a centered line as if in between two paragraph tags**</center>**

CODE:	RESULT:
Default Rule: <hr />	
Rule Width = 50% : <hr width="50%" />	Rule Width = 50%
50% Rule - Left : <hr width="50%" align="left" />	50% Rule - Left
50% Rule - Right : <hr width="50%" align="right" />	50% Rule - Right
50% Rule - Center : <hr width="50%" align="center" />	50% Rule - Center
50% Rule - Size = 6 : <hr width="50%" size="6" />	50% Rule Size = 6
50% Rule - Size = 16 : <hr width="50%" size="16" />	50% Rule Size = 16
Width = 50%, noshade : <hr width="50%" noshade />	Rule Width = 50%, noshade
Size = 6, Width = 50%, noshade : <hr width="50%" size="6" noshade />	50% Rule Size = 6, noshade
Size = 16, Width = 50%, noshade : <hr width="50%" size="16" noshade />	50% Rule Size = 16, noshade

Figure 04-15. Examples of Horizontal Rule Coding (**code0415.htm**)

similarly:
<div align="center">
This displays as a centered line as if in between two paragraph tags **</div>**

Using the Preformat Element for Easy Text Display

Your HTML browser usually ignores extra spaces and tabs as well as additional character spaces, tabs, or line spacing of the content in your HTML document. As we saw in Chapter 1, not only can the **pre** element be used to quickly display your content with a minimum of effort, but it also allows you to *retain* all the line breaks and character spacing you have in your plain text HTML document. As with most of the tags in this chapter, you can use the **pre** tag inside the HTML **body, div, blockquote, form, table,** or list elements. The preformatted content can contain text, character formatting, images, and hyperlinks.

Using the **pre** element instructs your browser to display blocks of text in a fixed-width font retaining all spacing and allowing hyperlinks within the text. It displays this content with a default serif font face, which may be different for different browsers. As with most block formatting elements, the **pre** element automatically inserts a paragraph tag before and after the text it surrounds

As all text spacing is retained using the **pre** element, there is no need for the paragraph and line break tags as would be required if one of the mono-spaced fonts described later in this chapter was used. The use of preformatted text in a web page can help you quickly post your message, but it is not at all an elegant way to create web pages with a word-processed look and feel as is demonstrated in Figure 04-16.

You can use the **pre** tag only with the **width** attribute. The **width** attribute has a default of 80 characters and can be used to specify the maximum number of characters in a line of text. This forces a line break once the character width is reached that has an appearance of a wrapped text.

You need not worry about the width attribute as it, as with most of the alignment and spacing elements and attributes, is deprecated in exchange for the much greater flexibility in web page design possible when using the style sheet techniques of chapter 6.

CODE:

```
<pre>
Using the preformat tag, your text will display


on the screen in a fixed-width font
          keeping line
 and character spacing



    when displayed by your browser or printed.
</pre>
```

RESULTS:

```
Using the preformat tag, your text will display


on the screen in a fixed-width font
          keeping line
 and character spacing



    when displayed by your browser or printed.
```

Figure 04-16. Viewing the **pre** Tag in a Browser (**code0416.htm**)

Representing Quoted Text as a Block

Although the **blockquote** element is normally used to display one or more blocks of text as quotations or citations, it is often used to add a word processor style to your page without resorting to the somewhat more difficult use of tables (see Chapter 8). The **blockquote** can be nested, and it can also be used inside of tables and lists to give your text a more word-processed appearance. You can nest a variety of HTML elements inside of a **blockquote** (including other **blockquotes**) such as headers, horizontal rules, and lists, and can include a **blockquote** inside of forms, tables, and list elements.

The **blockquote** can be used to create a single-line quote as seen in Figure 04-17 but it is more typically used to create indented paragraphs as shown in the Red Rose Library example in Figure 04-18. It can also be used to indent lists (see Chapter 7) and other HTML elements. As shown in the browser views of both Figure 04-17 and Figure 04-18, the opening **blockquote** tag will insert a paragraph tag before the "quoted" text and again after the closing **blockquote** tag, to separate the quoted information from the rest of the text on the page.

Anytime we "force" a look onto an HTML page we need to keep the differences in browser rendering in mind. If you are using the **blockquote** element set to create a certain word-processed look and feel, you need to view it not only in your usual browser, but also in other popular browsers to make sure it looks the way you want it to for all your patrons.

CODE:

```
The following text is a quote: <blockquote> Yada, yada, yada
means yada, yada, yada. </blockquote> As was noted quite
often on the TV series Seinfeld...
```

RESULTS:

```
The following text is a quote:

        Yada, yada, yada means yada, yada, yada.

As was noted quite often on the TV series Seinfeld...
```

Figure 04-17. Viewing a Blockquote (**code0417.htm**)

CODE:

```
Annual trip to the American Museum of Natural History and the Hayden Planetarium <blockquote> Sign up now!
<br /> The bus to New York City will be leaving on Sunday Febuary 23rd at 6:00am. <br /> Trip cost is $50 which
includes bus tickets, snacks on the bus, lunch at the Museum, and a souvenir. <br /> Be sure to make your
reservation early as this is a fast sell out! </blockquote> The bus trip is sponsored by the Cultural Committee of the
Friends of the Rose Library.
```

RESULTS:

```
Annual trip to the American Museum of Natural History and the Hayden Planetarium

   Sign up now!
   The bus to New York City will be leaving on Sunday Febuary 23rd at 6:00am.
   Trip cost is $50 which includes bus tickets, snacks on the bus, lunch at the Museum, and a souvenir.
   Be sure to make your reservation early as this is a fast sell out!

The bus trip is sponsored by the Cultural Committee of the Friends of the Rose Library.
```

Figure 04-18. Using Blockquotes (**code0418.htm**)

Character Formatting

Although block formatting can be used to stylize your text, the paragraph breaks that go before and after **blockquote** tags provide unnecessary and unwanted line spaces that can be distracting. Like all elements, character formatting elements work like switches to turn style on and off for the specific text they surround. These allow you to display bold, italics, or underlined text within in paragraphs, sentences, or even individual characters on your page.

Displaying Text in Boldface

Two elements display surrounded text in boldface. These are the boldface **b** and the strong **strong** elements. The more common boldface or bold **b** tag (which is deprecated) denotes a physical element that adds emphasis to text where the **strong** tag adds emphasis to text with a semantic element name. Most common elements can modify content inside of the boldface tags, and most common elements can contain boldface elements.

Encapsulating individual letters, words, and sentences with a character element allows instant, and temporary, resetting of the character display anywhere on your web page. These elements can have either a physical name that notes their displayed look, or a semantic name that explains their typical function. The first set of these elements is used to display text in boldface.

Whereas the **b** element is clearly a physical element formatting tool used to create boldface text, the **strong** element is a semantic element that uses a name that more clearly denotes its effect on text. Figure 04-19 shows that both the **b** and **strong** elements cause the marked text to be rendered in boldface with no difference in way text is displayed.

CODE:	Results:
Bold in HTML is <b>really, really</b> easy.	Bold in HTML is **really, really** easy.
Strong in HTML is also <strong>really, really</strong> easy.	Strong in HTML is also **really, really** easy.

Figure 04-19. How Boldface Characters Are Displayed (**code0419.htm**)

Displaying Text in Italics

Just as there are several elements that can be used to display text in boldface, there are also several that display italicized text. The four elements are the element that denotes the physical italics change to your text **i** and three semantic names that are used to italicize text, emphasis **em, cite** which notes book or text citations, and **var** which represents variable names in a program. These elements behave very much like the boldface elements and can contain or are found inside of the elements listed earlier. The use of the four different elements **i, em, cite,** and **var** to display the text surrounded by them in italics is shown in Figure 04-20.

CODE:	Results:
The following text is <i> an italicized font</i> and this text is not.	The following text is *an italicized font* and this text is not.
The following text is <em> an emphasized font</em> and this text is not.	The following text is *an emphasized font* and this text is not.
The following text is <cite> a citation font</cite> and this text is not.	The following text is *a citation font* and this text is not.
The following text is <var> a variable name font</var> and this text is not.	The following text is *a variable name font* and this text is not.

Figure 04-20. How Characters Look in Italics (**code0420.htm**)

Changing Font Typefaces

On occasion you might want to vary, or substitute, a different typeface instead of using the default or base font's typeface. HTML tags can be easily used to display text in a fixed-width font, like we did when we used the **pre** element where we wanted to retain line and character spacing inside the tags, but this time in line, without the need to insert paragraph tags before and after the text.

The teletype **tt,** keyboard **kbd,** computer code fragments **code,** and sample elements **samp** mark text typically displayed in a fixed-width (non-proportional) monotype typewriter style font as shown in Figure 04-21 and can be used much like the boldface and italics elements covered earlier.

CODE:	Results:
This text is <tt>in the physical teletype font</tt> and this text is not.	This text is `in a physical teletype font` and this text is not.
The following text is <kbd>in a keyboard font</kbd> and this text is not.	The following text is `in a keyboard font` and this text is not.
The following text is <samp> in a sample font</samp> and this text is not.	The following text is `in a sample font` and this text is not.
The following text is <code>in a code font</code> and this text is not.	The following text is `in a code font` and this text is not.
The following line shows these styles are equivalent:	The following line shows these styles are equivalent:
<tt>font</tt> <kbd>font</kbd> <samp>font</samp> <code>font</code>	`font font font font`

Figure 04-21. Monotype Text Display (**code0421.htm**)

It's All about the Fonts

Speaking of fonts, perhaps the most popular and flexible of character-level elements is the **font** element. Even though the font element is deprecated and expected to be discontinued in future HTML versions, it is very easy to use and much simpler than the more customizable style declarations that we will look at in Chapter 6. Obsolete or not, it is commonly used to create inline type size, color, and face changes.

The popular and versatile **font** element allows inline changes of text style, without the paragraph separation created using header or **blockquote** tags. Encapsulating individual letters, words, and sentences with a **font** element allows instant, and temporary, resetting of the size, typeface, and color of text anywhere on your web page. The attribute changes toggle off at the appearance of the font closing tag **</font>.** We'll see that several attributes can be included in a single font tag, or, as shown in Figure 04-22, selected attributes can be individually, sequentially, turned on and off as needed by nesting **font** tag sets inside of each other.

CODE: a. Using absolute font sizes: font size = "n" (the 0 is in default size 3)

```
0<font size="1">1</font> <font size="2">2</font> <font size="3">3</font> <font size="4">4</font>
<font size="5">5</font> <font size="6">6</font> <font size="7">7</font> <font size="6">6</font>
<font size="5">5</font> <font size="4">4</font> <font size="3">3</font> <font size="2">2</font>
<font size="1">1</font> 0
```

Results: a. Using absolute font sizes: font size = "n" (the 0 is in default size 3)

0 1 2 3 4 5 6 7 6 5 4 3 2 1 0

CODE: b. Making text relatively smaller: font sizes = "-n" (the 0 is in default size 3)

```
0<font size="-1">-1</font> <font size="-2">-2</font> <font size="-3">-3</font> <font size="-4">-4</font>
<font size="-5">-5</font> <font size="-6">-6</font> <font size="-7">-7</font> <font size="-6">-6</font>
<font size="-5">-5</font> <font size="-4">-4</font> <font size="-3">-3</font> <font size="-2">-2</font>
<font size="-1">-1</font> 0
```

Results: b. Making text relatively smaller: font sizes = "-n" (the 0 is in default size 3)

0 -1 -2 -3 -4 -5 -6 -7 -6 -5 -4 -3 -2 -1 0

CODE: c. Making text relatively larger: font sizes = "+n" (the 0 is in default size 3)

```
0 <font size="+1">+1</font> <font size="+2">+2</font> <font size="+3">+3</font> <font size="+4">+4</font>
<font size="+5">+5</font> <font size="+6">+6</font> <font size="+7">+7</font> <font size="+6">+6</font>
<font size="+5">+5</font> <font size="+4">+4</font> <font size="+3">+3</font> <font size="+2">+2</font>
<font size="+1">+1</font> 0
```

Results: c. Making text relatively larger: font sizes = "+n" (the 0 is in default size 3)

0 +1 +2 +3 +4 +5 +6 +7 +6 +5 +4 +3 +2 +1 0

Figure 04-22. Inline **font size** Changes on Your Browser (**code0422.htm**)

In our discussion of headings, **size="#"**, specified the size of the font with values of #ranging from 1 to 6. However, unlike heading tags where the larger the number, the smaller the font (recall that **h#** creates different sized headings, with **h1** the most important, and **h6** the least important), the **size** attribute has larger numbers giving larger text. Including a + or – before the **size** value makes the size change relative to the **basefont size** which has a default value of **3**. As seen in Figure 04-19, sections b and c, **font size 1** is the smallest font size and **font size 7** is the largest font size. Any +/– changes are relative and limited to these maximum and minimum values. That is why the default size of the **basefont** is so important.

Now that we understand a bit about changing the size of our text, we can investigate how the **face** attribute can be used to select one or more typefaces or font names to stylize your text. The browser will check to see which of these type faces, in the order you have listed them,

<font face="name1, name2, name3">

is available on your computer and then the browser will display the text in this typeface—if it finds it!

The generic font families have a font type as well as typical names. Figure 04-23 shows a browser view of the major font face types.

The **serif** font face is most often seen in Times New Roman (**font style example**) and Palatino (**font style example**) styles and it is the default browser font face. Arial (**font style example**) is a common **sans-serif** font face and is typically more readable than a serif font. There are **cursive** font faces with a variety of script names as well as **monospace** (**Courier font style example**), the style used with the **pre** element. Note that **font face** is an inline tag that does not add paragraph breaks

> Caution! As with so many special element attributes, you must use the **font face** attribute carefully. If none of the typefaces you requested are installed on the user's computer, the browser default font will be used, and that could spoil your desired effect. This effect is noted in Figure 04-23, **Results line c** (arrow), where the default cursive font, isn't quite cursive! It's a bold sans-serif font. You can get really creative results using font with font faces until you get the hang of using the style and CSS techniques discussed in Chapter 6.

The **font** element's **color** attribute is, as before, a predefined name or a triplet of hexadecimal numbers. The added magic here is that as an inline tag, **font color** can be changed at will, even changing colors for single characters one at a time—a neat trick, when added to the **font size** attribute—to keep your Children's Room patrons happy. As seen in Figure 04-24, **Results line b** near the bottom of the figure (arrow), best viewed in your browser as the colorful stylization, does not show up well in a black-and-white figure.

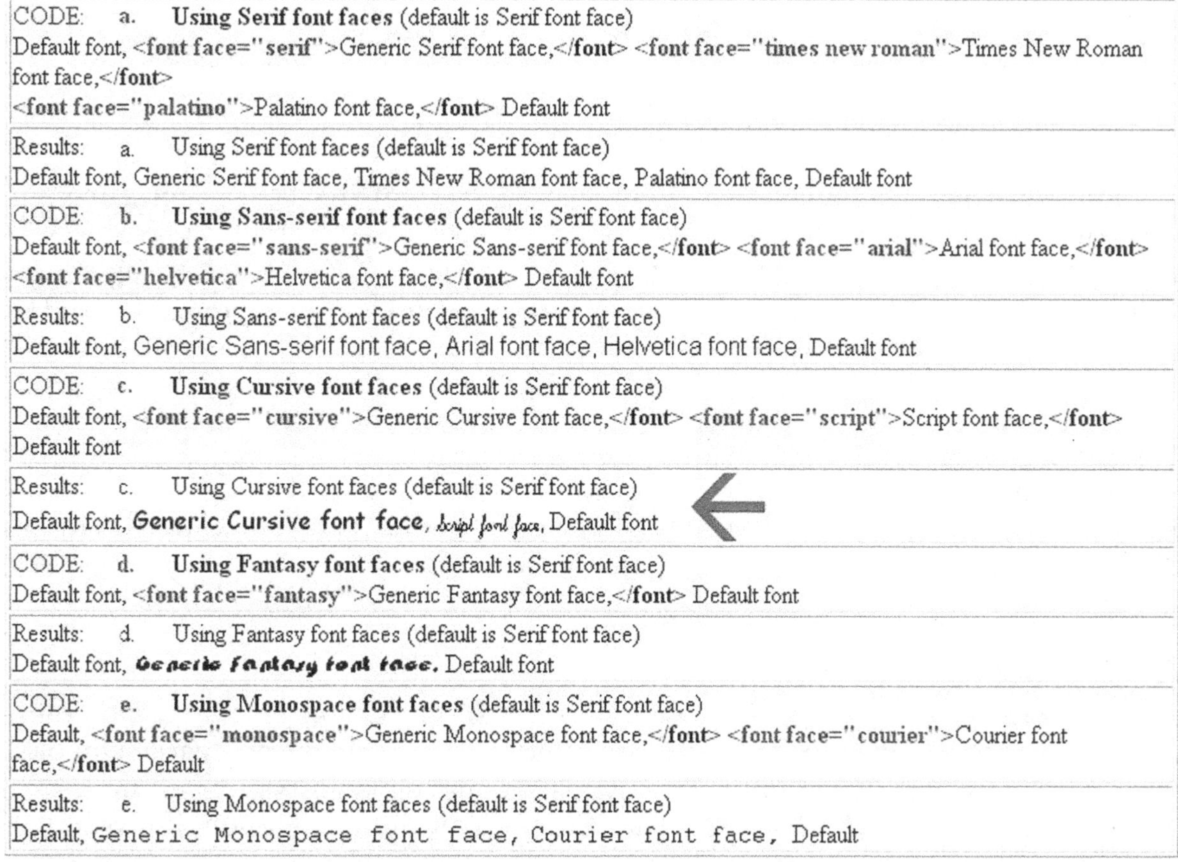

CODE: a. **Using Serif font faces** (default is Serif font face)
Default font, <**font face="serif"**>Generic Serif font face,</**font**> <**font face="times new roman"**>Times New Roman font face,</**font**>
<**font face="palatino"**>Palatino font face,</**font**> Default font

Results: a. Using Serif font faces (default is Serif font face)
Default font, Generic Serif font face, Times New Roman font face, Palatino font face, Default font

CODE: b. **Using Sans-serif font faces** (default is Serif font face)
Default font, <**font face="sans-serif"**>Generic Sans-serif font face,</**font**> <**font face="arial"**>Arial font face,</**font**>
<**font face="helvetica"**>Helvetica font face,</**font**> Default font

Results: b. Using Sans-serif font faces (default is Serif font face)
Default font, Generic Sans-serif font face, Arial font face, Helvetica font face, Default font

CODE: c. **Using Cursive font faces** (default is Serif font face)
Default font, <**font face="cursive"**>Generic Cursive font face,</**font**> <**font face="script"**>Script font face,</**font**>
Default font

Results: c. Using Cursive font faces (default is Serif font face)
Default font, **Generic Cursive font face**, *Script font face*, Default font

CODE: d. **Using Fantasy font faces** (default is Serif font face)
Default font, <**font face="fantasy"**>Generic Fantasy font face,</**font**> Default font

Results: d. Using Fantasy font faces (default is Serif font face)
Default font, ***Generic fantasy font face***, Default font

CODE: e. **Using Monospace font faces** (default is Serif font face)
Default, <**font face="monospace"**>Generic Monospace font face,</**font**> <**font face="courier"**>Courier font face,</**font**> Default

Results: e. Using Monospace font faces (default is Serif font face)
Default, `Generic Monospace font face, Courier font face,` Default

Figure 04-23. Inline **font face** Changes on Your Browser (**code0423.htm**)

```
CODE:    a.    Changing Font Colors in line (base color is black #000000)
Black (default) #000000: <font color="black">Black</font>, Navy #000080: <font color="navy">Navy</font>,
Blue #0000ff: <font color="blue">Blue</font>, Green #008000: <font color="green">Green</font>,
Gray #808080: <font color="gray">Gray</font>, Red #ff0000: <font color="red">Red</font>,
Fuchsia #ff00ff: <font color="fuchsia">Fuchsia</font>, Yellow #ffff00: <font color="yellow">Yellow</font>,
White (it really is!) #ffffff: <font color="white">White</font>
```

```
Results:    a.    Changing Font Colors in line (base color is black #000000)
Black (default) #000000: Black, Navy #000080: Navy, Blue #0000ff: Blue, Green #008000: Green,
Gray #808080: Gray, Red #ff0000: Red, Fuchsia #ff00ff: Fuchsia, Yellow #ffff00: Yellow, White (it really is!) #ffffff:
```

```
CODE:    b.    Children's Room Example Using Size and Color:
<font color="black" size="1">W</font><font color="navy" size="2">e</font><font color="blue"
size="3">l</font><font color="green" size="4">c</font><font color="gray" size="5">o</font><font
color="red" size="6">m</font><font color="fuchsia" size="7">e</font> <font color="yellow"
size="6">2</font> <font color="black" size="5">T</font><font color="navy" size="4">h</font><font
color="blue" size="3">e</font> <font color="green" size="2">C</font><font color="gray"
size="1">h</font><font color="red" size="2">i</font><font color="fuchsia" size="3">l</font><font
color="yellow" size="4">d</font><font color="black" size="5">r</font><font color="navy"
size="6">e</font><font color="blue" size="7">n</font><font color="green" size="6">s</font> <font
color="gray" size="5">R</font><font color="red" size="4">o</font><font color="fuchsia"
size="3">o</font><font color="yellow" size="2">m</font> <font color="black" size="1">!</font>
```

```
Results:    b.    Children's Room Example Using Size and Color

        welcome   The Chil rens Roo !
```

Figure 04-24. Inline **font color** Changes on Your Browser (**code0424.htm**)

Using Multiple Attributes in a Font Tag

Putting these three **font** attributes (**color, size,** and **face**) together can spice up your web page as **font** tags can be nested for interesting effects. The example in Figure 04-25 displays your content (we'll use the term "stuff" in this example) using a single multiple attribute tag and then shows the effect of nesting **font** tags using **red,** size **+2 (3+2 yields size 5),** and **arial font face** values. It turns on each and then closes all attribute changes one at a time returning to the default basefont.

Note that as shown here the attributes can change one at a time, or be nested. This set of commands result in "Stuff1" displayed as **red,** size **+2,** and **Arial.** "Stuff2" is **red** and size **+2,** but in the default **basefont** face style. "Stuff3" is **red** in the default **basefont** style size and face, "Stuff4" is completely displayed in the **basefont.** "Stuff5" shows all attributes turned on and off using a single tag.

Special Characters (Entities)

Your HTML browser can display a number of special characters that could otherwise not be part of your web page. These include the registered trademark symbol®, the copyright symbol ©, the ampersand symbol &, and a blank space character that is used for adjusting the space between text that is normally ignored by your browser. The angle bracket characters (used in creating the tag structure) must also be generated by entity relationships as they would otherwise be parsed (reviewed by your browser) for the element names and commands contained within them. Entity characters include the most often used ones in Figure 04-26.

A more complete listing of special characters entity relationships may be found in Appendix B.

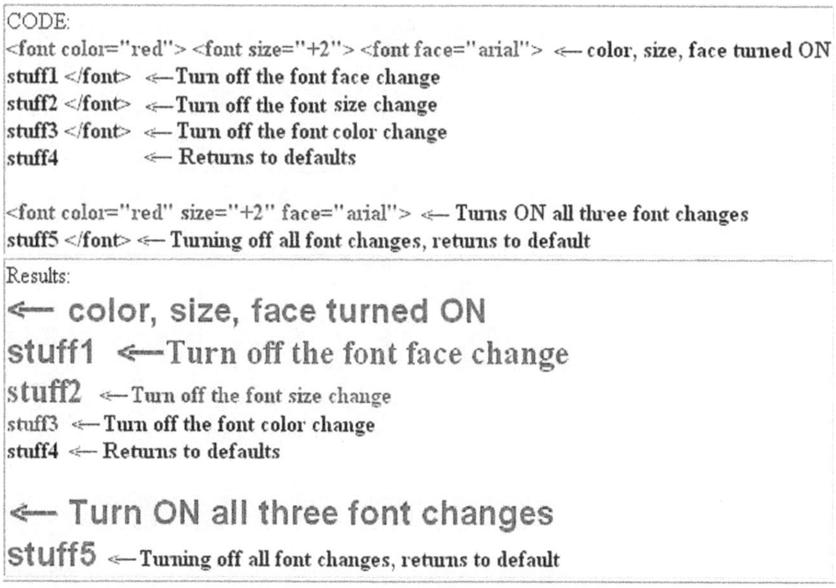

```
CODE:
<font color="red"> <font size="+2"> <font face="arial"> <— color, size, face turned ON
stuff1 </font>  <—Turn off the font face change
stuff2 </font>  <—Turn off the font size change
stuff3 </font>  <—Turn off the font color change
stuff4          <— Returns to defaults

<font color="red" size="+2" face="arial"> <— Turns ON all three font changes
stuff5 </font> <— Turning off all font changes, returns to default
```

Results:

<— color, size, face turned ON
stuff1 <—Turn off the font face change
stuff2 <—Turn off the font size change
stuff3 <—Turn off the font color change
stuff4 <— Returns to defaults

<— Turn ON all three font changes
stuff5 <—Turning off all font changes, returns to default

Figure 04-25. Nested **font** Changes on Your Browser (**code0425.htm**)

Text Format Tricks Enhance Your Web Page

Using the neat tricks we have added to our repertoire in this chapter we can enhance the Red Rose Library Newsletter page we saw back in Chapter 1 with color, size, and font face variations as well as with bold and italics as seen here in Figure 04-27.

What's Next?

Chapter 5 continues our quest for HTML elements and their use by giving you the tools for perhaps the most important of HTML elements—those dealing with hyperlinking and displaying images.

®	The registered trademark symbol ®
©	The copyright symbol ©
&	The ampersand symbol &
	The blank space character (non-breaking space)
<	The "less than" (angle bracket) symbol: <
>	The "greater than" (angle bracket) symbol: >

Figure 04-26. Special Entity Characters

Welcome to the

Red Rose Library

18 Rose Street
New York, NY 10010
Telephone +1 212 - 555 7673

Where we are - When we're open

Library Staff	Board of Trustees
Calendar of Events	
Red Rose Newsletter	The History of Red Rose

Our children's RoOm!

YOUNG ADULTS SECTION

Audio & Video Collection

Reference & Database Information

Online Public Access Catalog

Friends of the Red Rose Library
Cultural Programs
January 2014: **Radio City Music Hall**
February 2014: **The American Museum of Natural History**
March 2014: **MoMA - The Museum of Modern Art**

FAQs - *Frequently Asked Questions*

For additional information please contact the webmaster
Copyright (c) 2014 C. Rubenstein - RedRoseLibrary.com

Figure 04-27. Enhancing Your Web Page with Format Tricks (**code0427.htm**)

URL Cited

Online and downloadable web page color chooser

http://www.pagetutor.com/colorpicker/picker2

Chapter 4 Review Exercises

Chapter 4 Fill-In Questions

1. You can keep portions of your HTML page from being viewed by ______. The element that is used to create a solid background for your web page is ______.
2. The default style for a hyperlink is _____.
3. The hr element is used to create _____ on your web page.
4. The Times New Roman font family is an example of a _______ type font.

Chapter 4 Multiple-Choice Questions

1. HTML comments are placed between the <!-- and _____ delimiters.

   a) // b) > c) /> d) -->

2. If the HTML color code for black is "000000" the code for white is:

   a) ff00ff b) 00ff00 c) ffffff d) 00ffff

3. Largest headline text element is the:

   a) h7 b) h2 c) h1 d) h4

4. The HTML document line break element is the:

   a) b b) end c) br d) body

5. The **strong** element displays the same way as the:

   a) b b) end c) br d) body

Chapter 4 Design and Discussion Questions

1. Write the HTML code to set the font color and font size for several sentences, words, and individual characters.
2. When should you consider using nested font tag sets rather than a single font tag with multiple attributes on your library web pages?
3. Describe why you might decide to use deprecated HTML elements rather than newer ones, or waiting until Chapter 6 to try to understand the use of style sheets for many content placement challenges.
4. Describe how you can avoid using the paragraph element and achieve the same spacing result (without using Chapter 6 methods).
5. Describe how you can stylize more than one paragraph with a single opening tag.

5

Images and Linking to Other Web Pages

This chapter begins with using graphics you may download from someone else's website to use on your web pages. You will advance to helping your static HTML pages come alive with the use of inline images and hyperlinks. In this chapter you'll see how to use these techniques to insert images on your page and to create hypertext links, and you'll see how to activate images to achieve hyperlinking to other web pages with graphic images.

Graphics and Copyright

Having tools such as Adobe Photoshop, Corel's Paint Shop Pro, or Microsoft's Paint program won't make you an artist, but starting from the myriad of clipart available on the Internet (using Google or Yahoo! to find the treasure troves, see the next section), or digital photographs that you can take or find, you should be able to find several graphics that suit your library website needs. *The challenge here is to make sure you aren't violating copyright with the images you select.*

Good to Know: If you take a photo or create a graphic yourself, you can probably use it without restrictions. Of course, if the photo is a picture of a painting you may have some copyright issues, but in general, city scenes and photos of staff or others ***who have granted you permission to use their image*** are good to use on your web page. In fact, they give a more personal look to otherwise commercial looking photos. But, be very careful if you use graphics from someone's website without their permission as you may be guilty of copyright infringement. Also use clipart collections described in the next section carefully as they have certain license restrictions for commercial use.

Clipart Collections

Clipart graphics come in many shapes and sizes. They come as freely usable public domain or as subscription or royalty fee–based clipart. Some of the clipart collections available via the web do allow truly free use: free of cost, free of royalty, and free of copyright restrictions. Some have a small subscription charge, and still others have a license fee for each file you download. You must read the fine print! In most cases web graphics are downloaded by right-clicking on the clipart or photo, selecting "Save as" from the pop-up menu, and then selecting the place on your computer (preferably a new folder on your desktop or the assets folder in your website folder so you can find them later!) to save the file.

1. FREE Clipart without major advertising distractions:

Free Clipart Pictures.Net **http://www.free-clipart-pictures.net**

Pages and pages of free categorized clipart – many used in this text!

Microsoft® Clipart **http://office.microsoft.com/en-us/images**

Royalty-free *clip art*, photos, illustrations, animations, sounds, borders, icons, backgrounds, and more for Microsoft Office products

Flaming Text **http://www.flamingtext.com/start.html**

Create logos, download fonts. Under 'More': clipart, buttons, arrows, bullets, etc.

2. FREE Clipart with software downloading and sponsor offer selection required:

Freeze.Com **http://www.freeze.com**

No fees, clipart under Home/Office tab. Also offers software, music, video.
Uses InstallIQ™ downloading software which includes optional sponsor offers (be careful to select only the offers you want!)

3. FREE Clipart with major sponsor and advertising distractions:

All Free Clipart **http://www.free-clipart.net**

Animated gifs, backgrounds, clipart and icons

4. Subscription and Fee Based (Royalty Free) Clipart URLs

Animation Factory **http://www.animationfactory.com**

Animated royalty free images and templates, etc. ($60 to $200/year)

Broderbund **http://www.broderbund.com**

CD-ROM Clipart Collections and software (prices vary)

Clipart.Com **http://www.clipart.com**

Millions of clipart and photos, etc. ($13/week to $140/year)

iStockphoto **http://www.istockphoto.com**

Royalty free stock photos. (with $5 and higher PER PHOTO license fees)

Figure 05-01. Web Page Clipart URLs

Among the over 67 million (!) free clipart websites that you can find, if you do a Google search, several have thousands of high-quality, royalty-free clipart images in hundreds of categories that could be usable on your library web pages.

I am particularly grateful to Mehmet Emin Ericek, webmaster at **http://www.free-clipart-pictures.net** who was kind enough to give me permission to use the pages and pages of free categorized clipart on his website in this text.

To most of us free means without any charge, BUT you may have to register and give your name and email, or navigate around sponsor advertisements, or download special software to access them. Figure 05-01 shows just a few of these free treasure troves of clipart. Please beware! Free may be without cost, but you may find a great many pop-up pages after you finish on the main page because many free sites are sponsored and have pop-up pages of sponsored site ads. You'll probably want to avoid these free sites—unless their sponsor's ads have something you might to purchase.

Subscription and Fee-Based Royalty-Free Clipart

Other sites require subscriptions for access to royalty-free clipart that you can then use even after cancelling your subscription. The Animation Factory hosts an online subscription service for a wide variety of clipart and animated graphics, backgrounds,

Figure 05-02. Flaming Text Sample Logos (**code0502.htm**) (from: **http://www.flamingtext.com/start.html**)

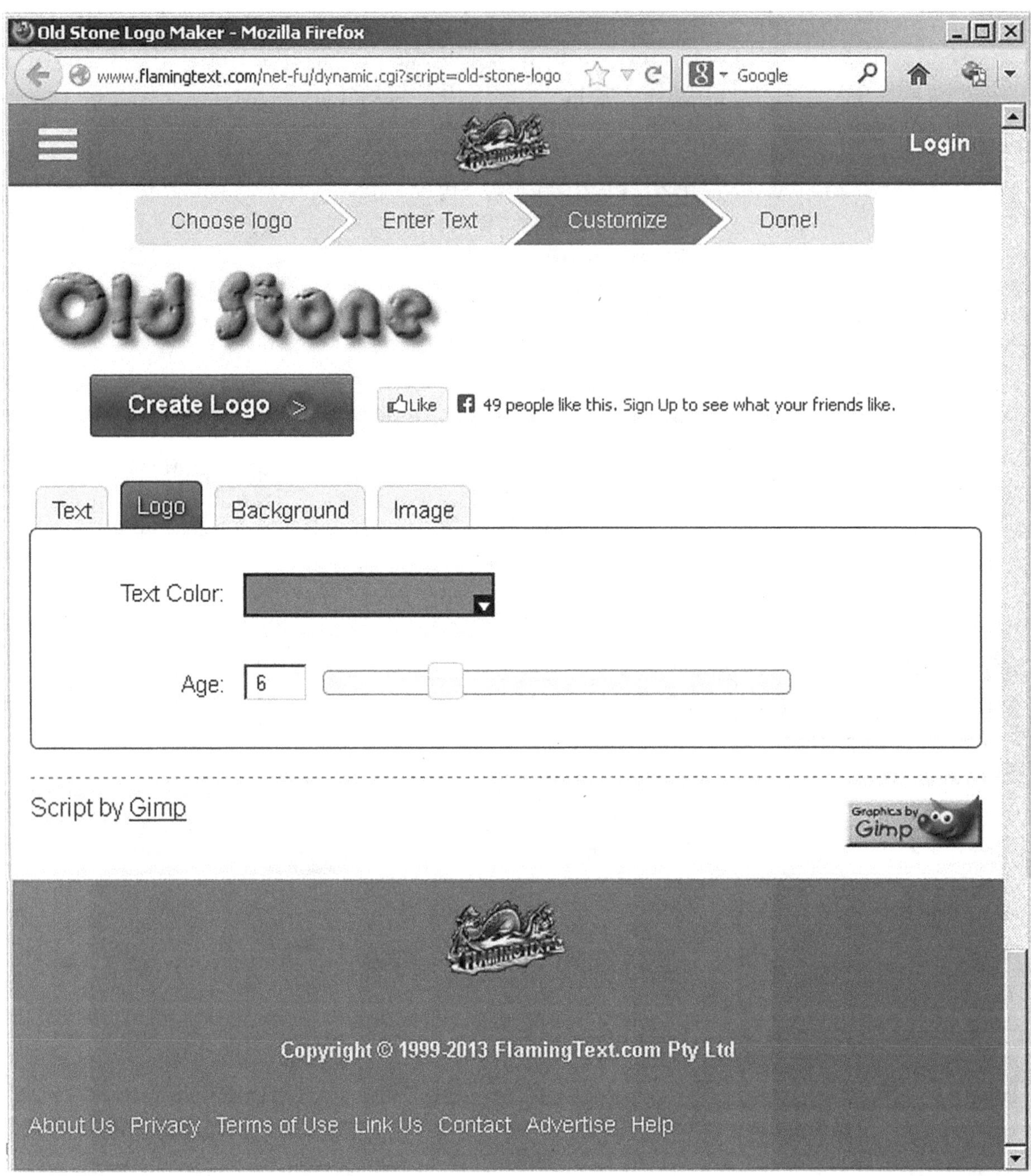

Figure 05-03. Flaming Text.com "Old Stone" Logo Creator Screen (**code0503.htm**) (from **http://www.flamingtext.com/net-fu/forms/old-stone-logo.html**)

Red Rose Library

Figure 05-04. Flaming Text Red Rose Library Logo (Romeo Font, **img002.jpg**)

and PowerPoint templates. iStockphoto, a rather expensive non-subscription service, permits you to download professionally taken royalty-free stock images whose cost is based on the photo's low, medium, or high resolution and physical image size. Other vendors, such as Broderbund, have CD-ROM Clipart Collections along with a variety of graphics and publishing software products that help you use them. Many include online access to additional art work. Several of these not-so-free resources are found in Figure 05-01, section 4. Even these fee-based services often have free samples of their contents that you should review before paying for any services.

Flaming Text (see Figure 05-01, section 1) is a really interesting site that offers clipart, buttons, arrows, bullets, and others, but I like it best as it allows you to create logos online—for free! Its online heading generation program permits adding style to text without the use of a "paint" program. The results are great, and did I mention, it's free!

Create a vast variety of heading types using the Flaming Text fonts and styles of Figure 05-02 (this black-and-white figure doesn't do justice to the vibrant colors and shades you'll see online).

To show how this type of online tool can be used in enhancing your library website we selected the Flaming Text Old Stone font for our example. The tool's online screen looks as seen in Figure 05-03.

Inserting the parameters: Text String=Red Rose Library, Font Size=55, Font=Romeo and Text Color=R: 255, G: 0, B: 0 as seen in the figure, press the **Create Logo** button to create the library logo (**img002.jpg**) seen in Figure 05-04. What an easy way to create logos or headers!

If you expect to be using this type of heading tool a lot, or require animation or other premium services, you can become a Flaming Text member ($20–50/year).

Graphic File Types

Today's browsers only support and display three graphic file types. These have the extension **gif** (Compuserve's Graphics Interchange File—pronounced jiff), **jpg** or **jpeg** (Joint Photographic Editors Group—pronounced jay-peg), or **png** (Portable Network Graphics—pronounced ping). The **png** file type was created in the late 1990s to offset potential legal issues surrounding the **gif**'s use of patented LZW (Lempel, Ziv, and Welch) lossless compression algorithm that threatened to create a per use charge for **gif** file images. This, hardly enforceable effort, has not yet occurred.

Lossy and Lossless Image Compression

The more common JPEG graphic file standard analyzes an image and uses non-patented mathematical "lossy" compression algorithms to compress a photo or complex graphic such that it faithfully represents the image but without keeping all the pixels needed to reconstruct an image. The *lossless* **gif** thus typically creates a larger file than a **jpg.** Most images look about the same in either **gif** or **jpg** versions, but the **gif** format can be animated to look like a short cartoon.

For small icons and simple line graphics (or animations) the 8-bit, 256 color palette **gif** is an excellent choice. For photos you get best results with the 24-bit, 16.7 million color palette **jpg** compression. Typically you will use whichever file type gives us a good graphic image in the smallest file size, or whatever the file type you obtained or downloaded was. Even though more and more patrons are going online via a high-speed connection, you should always pay attention to file size where you can. As the **png** has the best features of both **gif** and **jpg,** it is often seen on newer web pages.

Spicing Up Your Web Page with Clipart

OK, so now you have some artwork, photos, or clipart with a **gif, jpg,** or **png** file type that you want to use on your pages. Let's see how you can get these graphics to do what you want them to on your page.

Recall that the **img** element is an empty HTML element used to insert a graphic image from a file either on your computer, or more likely a web server somewhere into a web document. This insertion is inline and does not generate line or paragraph breaks before or after the image insertion.

Images are not embedded inside of HTML documents, as they are with word-processed documents or PowerPoint slide shows, but rather one or more separate files are retrieved by the browser using the **img** element's **src** (source) attribute which are stored as temporary files on your hard disk and then assembled by the browser on your local computer into a web page. When you close the web page, the images are no longer needed and may be deleted.

Let's look at the **img** element's attributes and see how they can be used to enhance the way your browser displays images.

Relative and Absolute File Addresses

The file location source attribute **src** is required to be present in all **img** tags. This attribute tells your browser where to look for the file of the image you want to insert on the page. If you are using a standard website structure for your website, it is most convenient to locate all of your images in an **assets** folder. When the image file you want is located on your website, the files can be addressed relative to where your HTML document is. If we presume your document is in a folder on your desktop named **library,** which contains a subfolder called **assets** where the red rose graphic **img004.jpg** is stored, the **img** tag's **src** attribute with a relative address

<img src="assets/img004.jpg" />

could be used. *Notice there is no mention of the outer folder* **library** *as we are looking for the file relative to where the current HTML document is located.* This "relative" addressing technique permits your website to be developed on your desktop or on a removable USB or hard drive. Your browser would look for the image files in an **assets** folder within the folder or directory *wherever* your HTML document is *currently* located. If you transfer this folder structure to another media, or folder, all the relative addresses will be valid as they are not fixed to any particular computer location or path.

If we presume your document is in the root folder on a web server, which contains a subfolder called **images** where **img003.jpg** is stored, the **img** tag's **src** attribute requires the full uniform resource locator (URL). The **img** element then uses the "absolute" addressing scheme to locate the file:

<img src="http://www.solutionsmall.com/images/img003.jpg" />

The result, your image being displayed on your web page, is shown on the right in Figure 05-05.

The absolute addressing method is best used when the image is NOT on your website as it fully describes the file's location and path. The **img** tag using the absolute address of the **img004.jpg** file in the **assets** folder in the **library** folder on your computer's desktop might be:

> <u>**Good to Know**</u>: You will find that many websites store their media files in an **images** folder rather than an **assets** folder as we are doing here. There is no problem using either, or even another folder name—as long as you are consistent in doing so or you won't know where your files are.

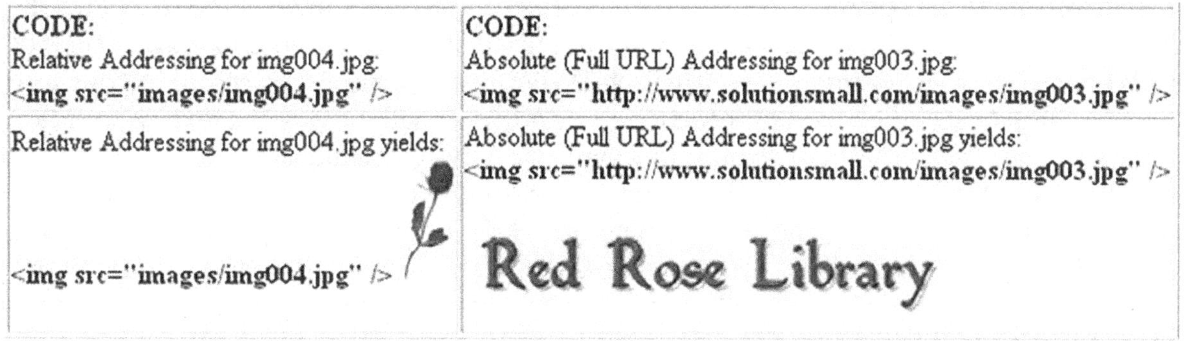
CODE:
Relative Addressing for img004.jpg:
<img src="images/img004.jpg" />
CODE:
Absolute (Full URL) Addressing for img003.jpg:
<img src="http://www.solutionsmall.com/images/img003.jpg" />
Relative Addressing for img004.jpg yields:
<img src="images/img004.jpg" />
Absolute (Full URL) Addressing for img003.jpg yields:
<img src="http://www.solutionsmall.com/images/img003.jpg" />
Red Rose Library

Figure 05-05. Relative and Absolute Addressing in **img** Tags (**code0505.htm**)

<img src="C:\Documents and Settings\LibraryName\Desktop\library\assets\ img004.jpg" />

However, if you decided to change the location of this folder, using absolute addressing you would need to use the new path or your browser would not find your files. Relative addressing doesn't much care where the folder set is located. Whenever possible you should use relative addressing to avoid future file location problems unless the file is in a folder on someone else's website on the Internet, where you would have to use absolute addressing with the fully described URL. If you use someone else's HTML files, remember that if they change their folder structure you may never find what you are looking for again <grin>, but your patron will see a "file not found" error. As noted in the next paragraph each browser has a way to deal with images not found.

Missing Images and the alt Attribute

As shown in Figure 05-06, when your browser goes to a website for resources and finds that the location or name of a file on that website, described with either a relative

CODE: Relative Addressing for image004.jpg: <img src="images/image004.jpg" alt="Red Rose" />	CODE: Absolute (Full URL) Addressing for image003.jpg: <img src="http://www.solutionsmall.com/images/image003.jpg" alt="Red Rose Library Logo" />
Relative Addressing for image004.jpg yields: [x] Red Rose	Absolute (Full URL) Addressing for image003.jpg yields: [x] Red Rose Library Logo

Figure 05-06. Adding Information with the **alt** Attribute (**code0506.htm**)

or an absolute address, has changed, your browser may show a rectangle space with a broken link icon where the graphic belongs (Chrome and IE), may show the value of the **alt** attribute as later described (FireFox), or it may show nothing at all—just an empty space. The Internet Explorer browser displays missing graphics in a rectangle with not only the broken link icon, but also the **alt** value message and is the browser display shown in Figure 05-06.

Broken links happen most often when an external server's images are used and the other website has modified where it stored the original files, or when you make a typo or folder name error in the **img** tag **src** attribute. When you use the **alt** attribute in your **img** tag, a strongly recommended best practice, your browser will display the text information "value" associated with this attribute in the missing image area as shown in this figure. Another pair of attributes you might want to consider when seeking files from other folks' web servers are the **height** and **width** attributes. Set these values in pixels matching the actual size of your image. When you use these, and the image is not where you told your browser to find it, the browser will make a space equal to the image's size on your web page. This will make the layout look more like it would look if the image was located.

The **alt** attribute can be used to add information about the image when your mouse pointer hovers over the image. When the image is also used to hyperlink to another website (see "Hypertext and Hypergraphics: Linking to Images and Other Web Pages" later in this chapter), it is common to add that URL in the **alt** attribute. The information appears for a few seconds in a textbox near the pointer.

The **alt** also adds to your web page's accessibility as voice output readers or Lynx (non-graphic) browsers can use the **alt** attribute to inform their user what the image represents.

Sizing Your Images and Multiplying Them

The **img** tag's **width** and **height** attributes mentioned earlier can not only create an actual size space on the page for your image, but it can also be used to shrink, or even enlarge, your graphic to fit a particular size space. The **img** element tag itself, as it is a true inline element, can be repeated as if it were merely a character on a line.

As shown in Figure 05-07, the **width** attribute defines the width of the displayed image in pixels, the smallest graphic element on a screen. Similarly, the **height** attribute defines the height of the displayed image in pixels. When only one dimension is used, the current aspect ratio of the image is maintained. The red rose **img001.jpg** graphic is 69 pixels in width and 154 pixels in height.

CODE:

```
Original: <img src="assets/img001.jpg" /> 77: <img src="assets/img001.jpg"
height="77" /> 39: <img src="assets/img001.jpg" height="39" /> 77, 154, 308, 39's:
<img src="assets/img001.jpg" height="77" /> <img src="assets/img001.jpg" /> <img
src="assets/img001.jpg" height="308" /> <img src="assets/img001.jpg" height="39" />
<img src="assets/img001.jpg" height="39" /> <img src="assets/img001.jpg"
height="39" />
```

RESULTS:

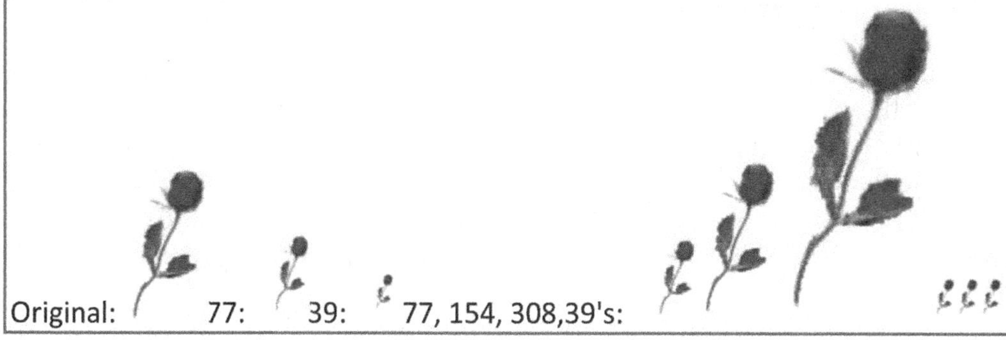

Original: 77: 39: 77, 154, 308,39's:

Figure 05-07. Adjusting Image Height to Fit Your Space (**img001.jpg, code0507.htm**)

Specifying **height="77"** will have the browser automatically adjust the width to produce a 35 × 77 displayed image size. Using **height="308"** the image is stretched to give a 138 × 308 image size. A similar result would occur if we fixed the **width** attribute in pixels allowing the height of the image to be automatically adjusted according to the image's aspect ratio. Both the **width** and **height** attributes can also use percent **###**%values such as **width="10%"** or **height="500%"** to permit your web page to be scalable, that is, for it to fill the browser window at a certain percentage of the full height or width regardless of how small or big the browser window is.

As you can also see in Figure 05-07, web images are not very scalable. Even when the height is doubled (308 pixels), the image starts to become "fuzzy" or pixilated. This is due to the image's pixels being merely repeated to accommodate stretching of the height and width resulting in a very poor image quality when the browser fits the image into a much larger defined space.

In the few instances where you want a fully defined image space, both the **width** and **height** attributes can be used in a single **img** tag. The benefit of using both is that the image size is maintained while the image file is being processed by your browser. As noted earlier, if both attributes are included, and there is a broken link to the image, the size that the graphic would have used is displayed on the browser.

Using the **width** and **height** attributes to change the size of a graphic only forces a temporary size change in your browser window. Using the resize function on an art program like Paint Shop Pro or Adobe PhotoShop is the most efficient way to shrink or enlarge an image. Use these program's special mathematical calculations for resizing affects the actual file size.

Our 69 pixel wide and 154 pixel high red rose graphic (**img001.jpg**), for example, contains well over 10,000 pixels, but it is compressed into a JPEG file size of only 3 kilobytes (kb). The file size for a 32 wide by 72 high graphic (**img004.jpg**) should be about 1.5 kilobytes, BUT resizing using attributes still requires that the full 3 kb file be retrieved regardless of the displayed image size.

Also demonstrated in this figure is the ability of the **img** tag to display images inline, without line breaks before and after images.

Boxing in Your Images

Notice in Figures 05-05 and 05-07 that there was no border around the images. The **img** element's **border** attribute default is **0** pixels. It can be set to **1** for a one pixel border or for larger values (in pixels) for as thick a border as you might want! Figure 05-08 shows some sample border thicknesses as well as the spacing (about 2 pixels) that is used to automatically separate inline images. A few caveats: first note that placing a thick, black, border around a photo can yield an "in memoriam" effect. Of course that might be what you are intending! Also, as we'll see later in this chapter, when we use hypergraphics, an image which is hyperlinked to another page or website, the color of the border takes on the color scheme defined for all hyperlinks. As you might already guess, the border attribute has been replaced by CSS techniques in newer web pages.

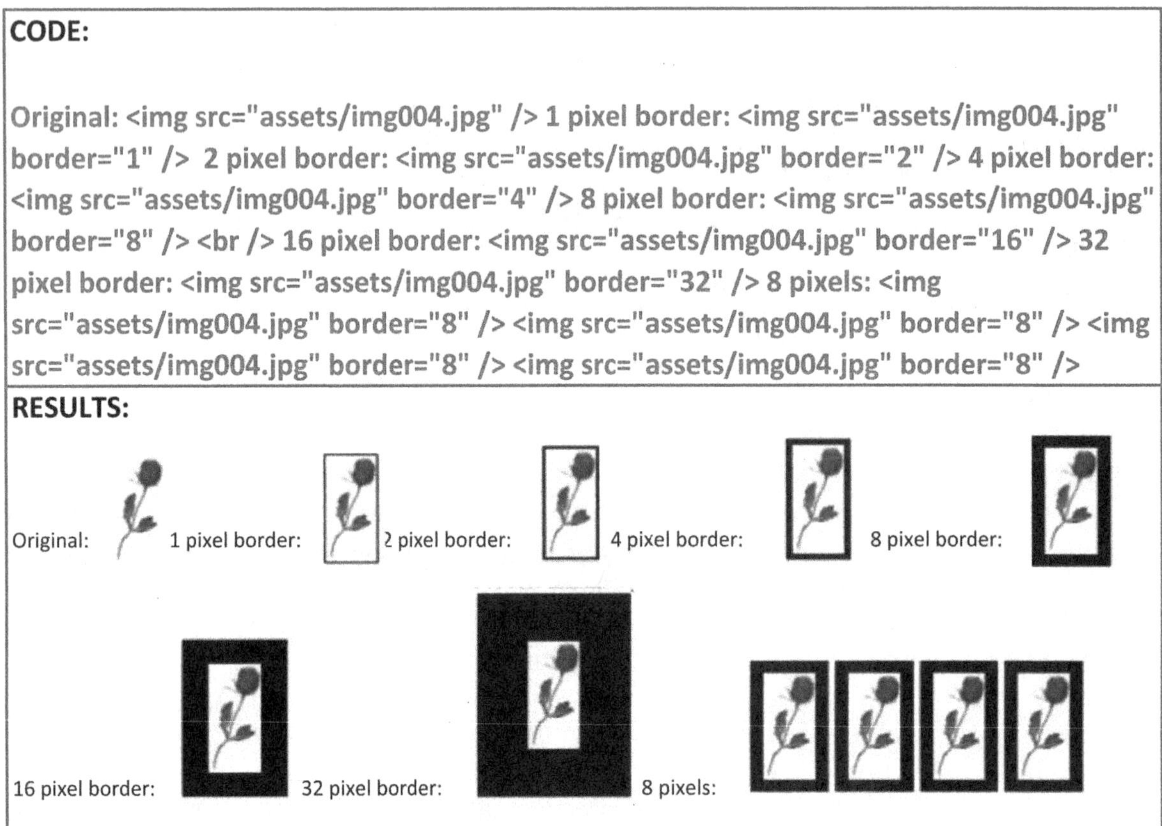

CODE:

```
Original: <img src="assets/img004.jpg" /> 1 pixel border: <img src="assets/img004.jpg"
border="1" />  2 pixel border: <img src="assets/img004.jpg" border="2" /> 4 pixel border:
<img src="assets/img004.jpg" border="4" /> 8 pixel border: <img src="assets/img004.jpg"
border="8" /> <br /> 16 pixel border: <img src="assets/img004.jpg" border="16" /> 32
pixel border: <img src="assets/img004.jpg" border="32" /> 8 pixels: <img
src="assets/img004.jpg" border="8" /> <img src="assets/img004.jpg" border="8" /> <img
src="assets/img004.jpg" border="8" /> <img src="assets/img004.jpg" border="8" />
```

RESULTS:

Figure 05-08. Boxing in Your Images (**code0508.htm**)

Adding Space around Your Images

Although your browser automatically includes a small 2 pixel whitespace around each of your images, it may not be enough of a separation to suit your page's needs. The **hspace** and/or **vspace** attributes can be used to position the image on the page using the value **#,** in pixels (#), as seen in Figure 05-09.

Aligning Your Images and Text

Now that we can position the image by defining the horizontal and/or vertical margins surrounding them, what if we didn't want our text to appear flush with the bottom of our images all the time? As shown in Figure 05-10, when the image is larger than the text line, the **align** attribute defines where the image will be located relative to adjacent text. This attribute can define the image location as the top (default), the middle, or bottom, right, or left of the text line.

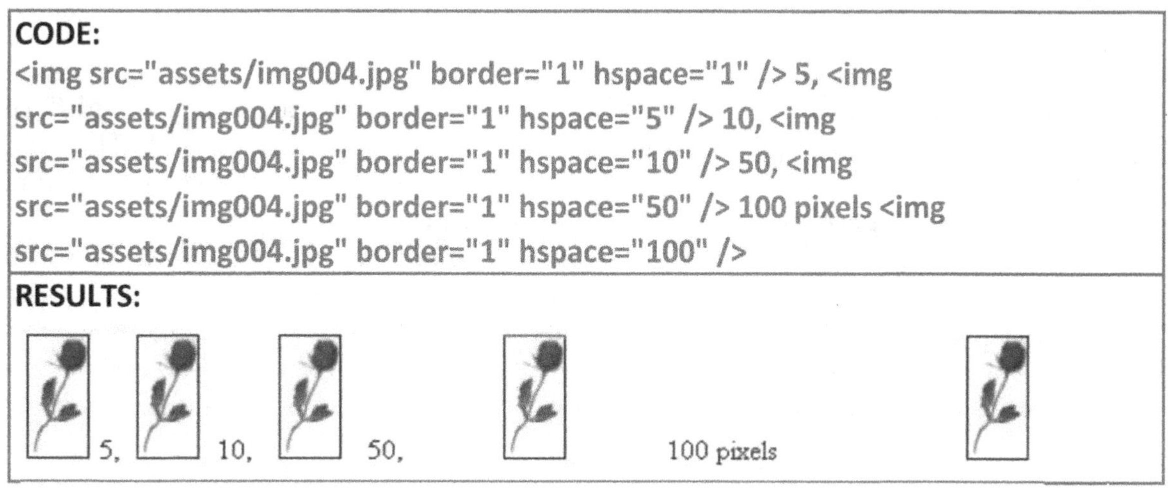

CODE:

```
<img src="assets/img004.jpg" border="1" hspace="1" /> 5, <img
src="assets/img004.jpg" border="1" hspace="5" /> 10, <img
src="assets/img004.jpg" border="1" hspace="10" /> 50, <img
src="assets/img004.jpg" border="1" hspace="50" /> 100 pixels <img
src="assets/img004.jpg" border="1" hspace="100" />
```

RESULTS:

Figure 05-09. Adding Horizontal Space between Your Images (**code0509.htm**)

RESULTS:

```
<img src="assets/img004.jpg" border="1" align="top" /> Text at TOP, Image at Left

<img src="assets/img004.jpg" border="1" align="middle" /> Text at MIDDLE, Image at Left

<img src="assets/img004.jpg" border="1" align="bottom" /> Text at BOTTOM, Image at Left
```

Figure 05-10. Aligning Text and Images (**code0510.htm**)

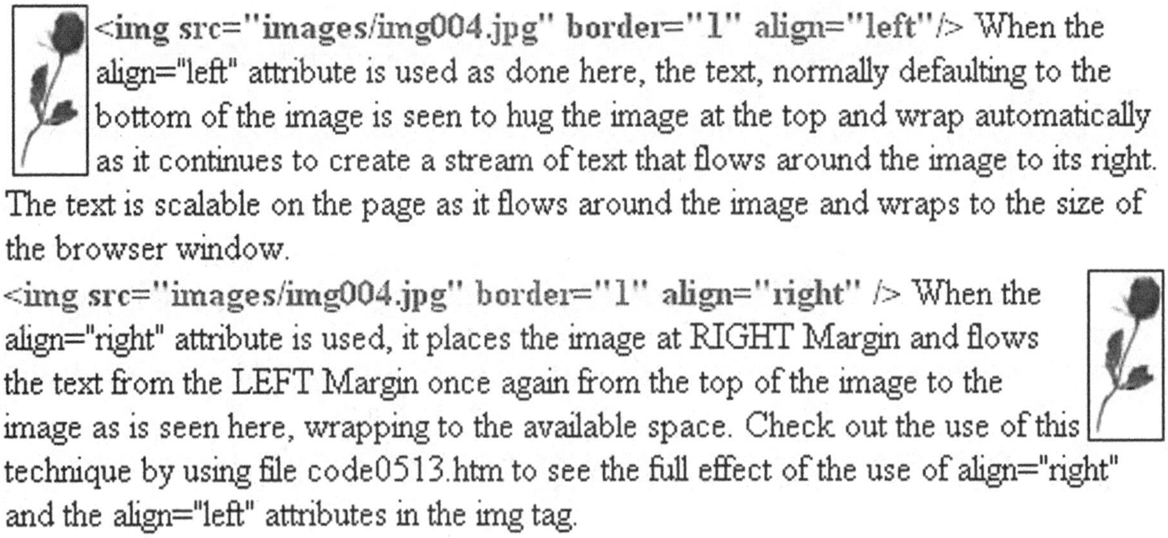

<img src="images/img004.jpg" border="1" align="left"/> When the align="left" attribute is used as done here, the text, normally defaulting to the bottom of the image is seen to hug the image at the top and wrap automatically as it continues to create a stream of text that flows around the image to its right. The text is scalable on the page as it flows around the image and wraps to the size of the browser window.

<img src="images/img004.jpg" border="1" align="right" /> When the align="right" attribute is used, it places the image at RIGHT Margin and flows the text from the LEFT Margin once again from the top of the image to the image as is seen here, wrapping to the available space. Check out the use of this technique by using file code0513.htm to see the full effect of the use of align="right" and the align="left" attributes in the img tag.

Figure 05-11. Flowing Text around Images (**code0511.htm**)

When the **align** attribute is used with its right or left values (**align="right"** or **align="left"),** it creates text that seems to flow around images as in Figure 05-11.

This technique is used quite often in the creation of newsletters. Of course the **img** attributes of **border, vspace,** and **hspace,** as well as **width** and **height** can all be used with the **align** attribute (in any convenient order) giving an appearance of a word-processed newsletter. Try it with your own images and text and see if you don't agree that it is a great way to simulate word processing in HTML documents without resorting to the table element that we'll review in Chapter 8. (As the table element is being phased out in later HTML versions, this "trick" will no doubt become a standard presentation alternative.)

Hyperlinking: Locally, Globally, and Internally

A book is typically read sequentially, page after page, from the beginning to the end. Sometimes textbooks are read by selecting chapters out of sequence to cover material in a class, but here, too, the pages are usually turned one by one in order.

The magic of the web is due to its ability to "randomly" select the path and page that one wishes to go to in any order. The web page's target or link may be internal, to a section or paragraph in the current web page, local, to a page on your local computer or server, or global or external—anywhere on the Internet.

The HTML anchor element **a** is used when you want to redirect your web page user to an internal, local, or global web page using

<u>Good to Know:</u> The **body** element can be used to modify the way hyperlinks are displayed before and after visiting their links. In Chapter 6 we'll see that the **style** element will be used more and more in future HTML versions and web pages to change the default link colors and decorations as well as what happens when the mouse pointer hovers over hyperlinks.

hypertext or hypergraphic links. The anchor opening tag must include either the **href** or the **name** attribute. When used to surround text, the text is highlighted to identify it as hypertext link, typically underscored and in blue.

Hypertext and Hypergraphics: Linking to Images and Other Web Pages

We reviewed the basics of relative and absolute addressing in the last section when we looked at how the **img src** attribute is used. The anchor **a** element's **href** is a hypertext transfer protocol (http) reference link that works in much the same way as the image's **src** attribute as it points the browser to either relative or absolute addresses for a web page or graphic image file. The text between the anchor element opening and closing tags becomes hypertext and when clicked on, your browser gets the file at the URL value of the **href** attribute. Clicking on a hyperlink signals the browser to load a new page or display an image from the same server (relative addressing), or retrieve a file from a web location defined by a full URL (absolute addressing).

As you can see, Figure 05-12 is a full-page screenshot. I strongly recommend that you view it on your browser using the file **code0512.htm** since it is a very complex figure. This figure contains nearly all the coding we can use for hyperlinking on an HMTL page in one place. We will use it to see how to retrieve graphic files to display by themselves on your browser, how to link to other files and websites using both text (hypertext) and graphics (hypergraphics), and how to navigate within the same web page using the anchor's **name** attribute.

Just as we saw when we were loading images onto our web page, it is always easier to hyperlink to local files using relative linking. But if we want our patron to go from the current web page to a file on another server, we need to use absolute addressing. Let's see how we direct the browser to view an image file named **img003.jpg** that is in the subfolder called **assets** in the web server root folder on the Solutions Mall website. The anchor tag's **href** attribute requires absolute addressing using the full URL that describes exactly where the file is. To suggest that your patron view that image you might use a snippet of code as shown in Figure 05-12, **line b:**

Click **<a href="http://www.solutionsmall.com/images/img003.jpg">**here **</a>** to display the Image File **img003.jpg**

If your patron was a volunteer who was viewing your Friends of the Red Rose Library page and you wanted them to visit the American Library Association (ALA) website for information on improving the library's program, you might use Figure 05-12, line f:

Visit **<a href="http://www.atyourlibrary.org">** http://www.atyourlibrary.org **</a>** the ALA @ Your Library™ website for program ideas

> **Good to Know:** Note that placing the anchor tag around the spelled-out URL allows the page to be printed out and still allows your patrons know where you wanted to have them hyperlink to.

Perhaps the most exciting aspect of linking is that you can also link graphics to web pages. Let's say that you want to show the

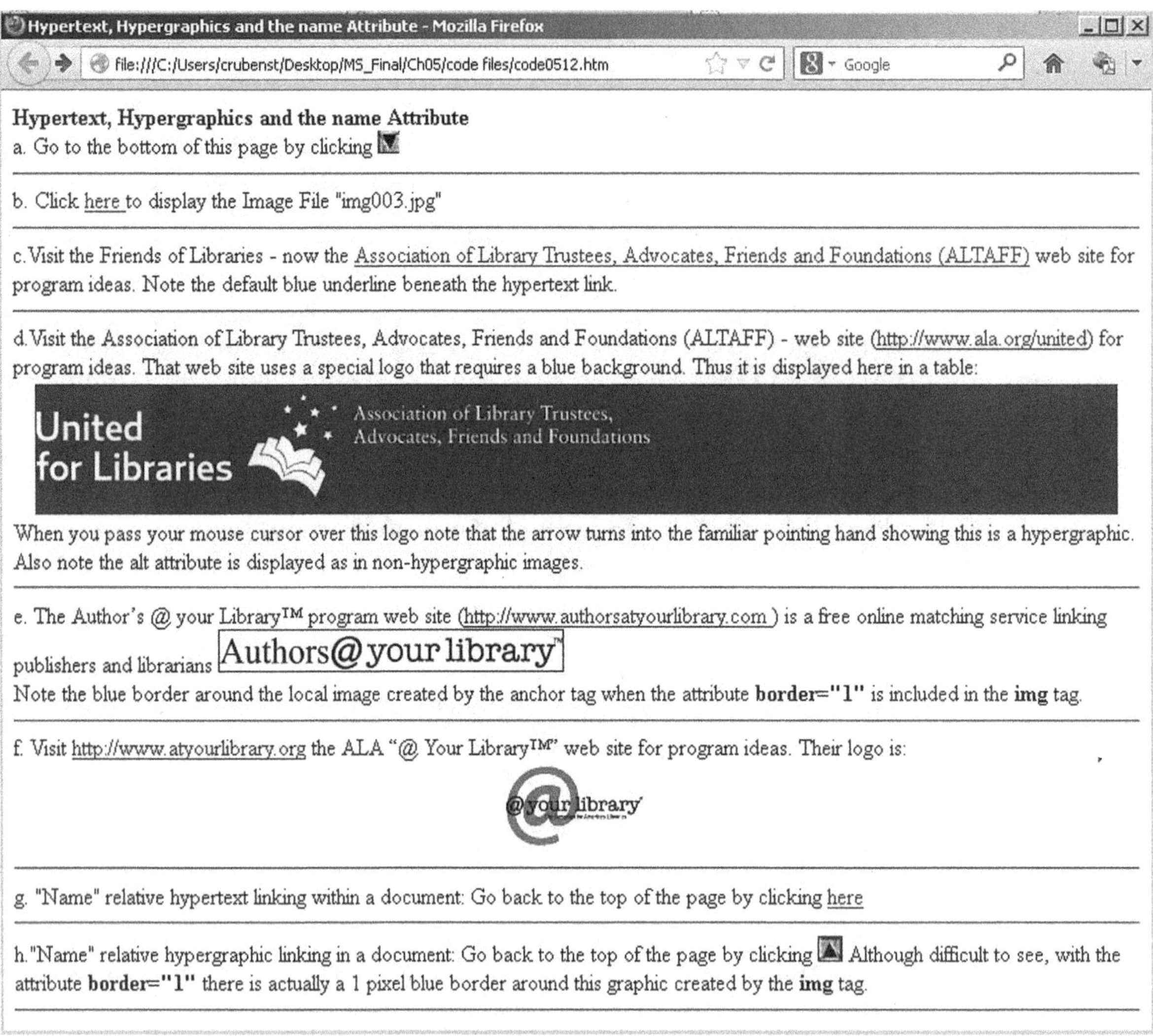

Figure 05-12. Hypertext, Hyper graphics and the name Attribute (**code0512.htm**)

@ Your Library™ logo on your web page and have the logo link to the ALA website. Figure 05-12, section f shows the result, but how did we know where to get the logo? Clearly you could email the owner of the website (we'll see how you can set that up for your web pages in the next section) or web master—the person responsible for the pages, for permission to save the logo on your website. But what if you don't want to save it on your website? First go to the web page that you found the logo on. Using the Firefox browser you would click on Tools, Web Developer, and then Page Source. The source code for the page will open in a **notepad**-like text editor and you can search for the page's **img** tag for the logo source code. This is probably a poor example to use as the logo does not save on right-clicking, and the page source is much more complex than we need it to be as an example that would not give you any challenges to complete. Once you find it, copy and paste the tag information.

You can change the **height, width,** and **alt** information in this tag as needed to size it for your page. We can modify the other attributes in the HTML file, add some text, and surround the new **img** tag by an anchor link to the full URL of the website as in Figure 05-12, code lined:

> <u>**Good to Know:**</u> This was a particularly difficult page to use as the best way to find the logo's absolute URL required lots of patience and trickery. I first put my cursor in the extreme left-hand corner, right-clicked, and asked to view the background graphic (a gray square). The background image's URL in the browser's URL window is **atyourlibrary.org/sites/default/themes/atyourlibrary/images/bodyBground.png**
>
> I then guessed that the logo's file name might be **logo.png** and I replaced the background file name to obtain what actually turned out to be the logo's **src** absolute URL address:
>
> **<img src="http://atyourlibrary.org/sites/default/them es/atyourlibrary/images/logo.png" />**

Visit **<a href="http://www.atyourlibrary.org">** http://www.atyourlibrary.org **</a>**
for program ideas. Their logo is: **<a href="http://www.atyourlibrary.org"> <img src="http://atyourlibrary.org/sites/default/themes/atyourlibrary/images/logo.png" width="100" alt="The Campaign for America's Libraries" border="0" /></a>**

This image URL is clearly not a short URL and could possibly lead to typos and other errors should the web server location of the graphic change, but unless you want to download it to your web server assets folder, this is the best way to get the logo on your page. To make the logo display better in Figure 05-12 it was placed into an HTML table.

Note that in many HTML files **img** and other empty tags are not closed. Make sure that you add the /> at the end of these empty tags. In the example of Figure 05-12, we have created a hypertext link to **http://www.atyourlibrary.org,** which will not only tell your patrons what the URL is, but also bring them there if they click on that text. Similarly, by surrounding the **img** tag with a hyperlink we can click on the organization's logo to go to the website. Although these were all accomplished with absolute addressing, you can use relative addresses if the images and pages are on your local web space. This is shown where the logo **authorsat.jpg** in your **assets** folder is used as the link to the Author's @ Your Library™ website: **http://www.authorsatyourlibrary.com** using the code in Figure 05-12, section e:

The Author's @ your Library™ program website **(<a href="http://www.authorsatyourlibrary.com">** http://www.authorsatyourlibrary.com **</a>)** is a free online matching service linking publishers and librarians **<a href="http://www.authorsatyourlibrary.com">< img alt="Authors @ your library" src="assets/authorsat.jpg" border="1" /></a>**

With the **border** attribute set to 1 your anchor element automatically adds a 1 pixel border which takes on the default **link, vlink,** and **alink** color scheme for hyperlinks. Of course the better way to accomplish this would be using the CSS techniques of Chapter 6.

Relative Links within a Web Page: The name Attribute

Now is probably a good time to remind you how YOU did not like it when you were surfing the web sometime in the past and clicked "print" on a paragraph you wanted to print out only to have 5, 10, or even 15 pages print out! If you are careful in designing your web pages, they will print one physical page per web page, but even then your page could be too long to fit in one browser screen.

When a web page is very long, at least more than a screen window high, the anchor tag's **name** attribute can be used to navigate between the top, bottom, and other sections of your page.

The anchor opening tag in this instance uses the technique of Figure 05-12 sections g and h to link either text or an image to a location using the **href** attribute and **name** value of the location. The anchor's location variable is preceded by the #sign as in **href="#location"** to link it to the empty anchor tag **<a name="location" /> </a>** (*note there is no # in the* **name** *tag*) which shows the browser where to jump to in the document. Figure 05-12 sections a and h show the **top** and **bottom** target codes, respectively, with Figure 05-12 sections a, g, and h illustrating the hyperlink codes. Figure 05-12 sections a and h also show the use of images, in this case up and down arrows, to navigate to the top and bottom of the page using hypergraphics.

Opening a New Browser Window

When you navigate between web pages and websites, the default anchor tag is **target="_self"** which opens the new page in the same browser window that the current page resides in. This requires the back arrow to be used to return to the original or calling page. The **target** attribute is often used with the value **target="_blank"** to open a new browser window when you link to a new page as in the following example:

<a href="http://www.atyourlibrary.org" target="_blank"> Website**</a>**

Other values for the **target** attribute are utilized when the web page contains frames—a technique where smaller windows divide the browser window into sections. We will NOT be discussing frames in this text as they are a bit more complicated, best left to other texts, and not universally accepted in practice.

Adding Your Email Address to Your Web Page

The last link that we will discuss in this chapter is the **mailto:** variation of the **href** attribute that automatically sends an email to the web master, and so on. The email address is often used with the italics text style to yield the effect shown in Figure 05-13. As always, watch your element tag nesting order.

In Figure 05-13 we have shown not only a typical font style for an email address, but also the use of the anchor element **a** and **href** attribute to create an automatic call to your browser's email program. This action embeds the email address on your web page into an email. Please note that many libraries and other public area systems have email software turned off. If the **mailto:** technique is used on public computers, your patrons may find themselves unable to directly use the public computer's email soft-

Adding an email contact address without hyperlinking:
You can reach me at <i>c.rubenstein@ieee.org</i>
You can reach me at *c.rubenstein@ieee.org*

Adding an email contact address with hyperlinking:
You can reach me at <**a href="mailto:c.rubenstein@ieee.org"**><i>c.rubenstein@ieee.org</i></a>
You can reach me at *c.rubenstein@ieee.org*

Figure 05-13. Using the **mailto:** Hyperlink (**code0513.htm**)

ware. The technique should work fine on your patron's home computers if they have been set up properly.

What's Next?

In this chapter we looked at how HTML is used to include images of various sizes on your web page with the **img** element, how text can be aligned with respect to these images, and how to hyperlink text or graphics using the anchor element.

In Chapter 6 we will look at the basics of stylizing small sections of text using the inline **style** attribute, web page–level document stylization using the internal **style** element, and the website wide **style** files using the technique known as cascading style sheets.

URLs Cited

FREE Clipart without major advertising distractions

http://www.free-clipart-pictures.net

Microsoft® Clipart

http://office.microsoft.com/en-us/images
Royalty-free *clip art,* photos, illustrations, animations, sounds, borders, icons, backgrounds, and more for Microsoft Office products

Flaming Text

http://www.flamingtext.com/start.html
To create logos, download fonts, clipart, buttons, arrows, bullets, and so on

FREE Clipart with software downloading and sponsor offer selection required

Freeze.Com
http://www.freeze.com
No fees, clipart under Home/Office tab. Also offers software, music, video
Uses InstallIQ™ downloading software which includes optional sponsor offers
(be careful to select only the offers you want!)

FREE Clipart with major sponsor and advertising distractions
All Free Clipart

http://www.free-clipart.net
Animated gifs, backgrounds, clipart, and icons
Subscription and fee–based (royalty-free) Clipart URLs

Animation Factory

http://www.animationfactory.com
Animated royalty-free images and templates ($60 to $200/year)

Broderbund

http://www.broderbund.com
CD-ROM Clipart Collections and software (prices vary)

Clipart.Com

http://www.clipart.com
Millions of clipart and photos ($13/week to $140/year)

iStockphoto

http://www.istockphoto.com
Royalty-free stock photos. (with $5 and higher PER PHOTO license fees)

ALA Campaign for Libraries website and logo

http://atyourlibrary.org
http://atyourlibrary.org/sites/default/themes/atyourlibrary/images/logo.png

Chapter 5 Review Exercises

Chapter 5 Fill-In Questions

1. If you download lots of other people's graphic images from the web and put them on your library's web pages you may be ______.
2. The three types of graphics files that your browser should be able to display on your web page are ______, ______, and ______.
3. The default style for a border around an image is _____.
4. The relative addressing scheme is used to create links _____.
5. The **href** attribute is used to _______.

Chapter 5 Multiple-Choice Questions

1. All graphic and media files should be placed inside the _____ folder.

   a) parent b) child c) assets d) images
2. To double the width of an image the value of the width attribute is:

   a) 200% b) 200 c) double d) 2
3. The attribute of an **img** tag needed to include a legend for an image is:

   a) name b) alt c) legend d) text
4. The anchor element attribute that identifies a specific spot in a document is the:

   a) name b) alt c) legend d) text
5. The browser display seen when an image cannot be found is a:

   a) white box with red x in it b) white page

   c) black box for image d) black page

Chapter 5 Design and Discussion Questions

1. Find a small graphic image on the web that is not larger than 100 pixels wide and 200 pixels tall (as this is an educational training exercise, no need to worry about copyright, unless you will be using the image for your library web page). Write the HTML code to create a series of four of these images in a single row.
2. Find a second graphic image that is not larger than 100 pixels wide and 200 pixels tall. Create a four image by four lines (16 images in total) web page that alternates the image of Design Question 1 and the image you found for this exercise.
3. Write the HTML code to create a series of four of these images in a single row where the first and fourth images are twice the size of the second and third.
4. Write the HTML code to create a series of four of these images in a single row where the first and fourth images have a 2 pixel border.
5. Write the HTML code to create a series of four of these images in a single row where the images have a 10 pixel space around them.

6

Cascading Style Sheets and Floating Images

In this chapter you'll discover the use of the **style** markup as either an element or an attribute to easily revise an HTML document's default document type definitions (DTDs) customizing elements, characters in paragraphs, or even whole sections of your web page. The review of the **style** markup begins with its use as an HTML element attribute. Then **style** will be used as an element to redefine the DTD element defaults on a web page. Saving these definitions in a separate file allows us to "call" that file when any page needs that specific styling. This method, called cascading style sheets or CSS, is a convenient way to use collections of style sheet files to create a uniform look-and-feel "template" for each different type of page on your website. Finally, we'll see how to use the **style** techniques inline or in external style sheet files to modify the way images are displayed on a page. This includes the illusion of floating images on a web page. Stylization techniques will be shown in Chapters 7, 8, and 9 on lists, tables, and forms. Enough **style** is covered here so that you can understand how to use **style** to change the display characteristics of the HTML elements already covered in previous chapters. These include adding style one page at a time, changing multiple defaults with **style** on a single page, anchoring link styles, and defining style within elements using classes. *Please note that CSS effects are browser-specific; the Firefox browser is used in this chapter.*

Cascading Style Sheets

Cascading style sheets techniques redefine how a browser displays audio and visual HTML elements. CSS is almost as powerful as a new markup language and it is upward compatible to XHTML, XML, and HTML5. The basic use of the three variations of style sheets—style attributes added inline directly to HTML elements, internal style sheets used to define properties of HTML elements on a single web page, and external style sheets that can be used throughout a website—will be reviewed.

Adding Inline style Attributes to HTML Elements

The **style** attribute can be added to many HTML elements to create inline stylizations of the content the element contains. Sub-attributes of the **style** attribute include text properties (**text-align, text-indent, text-transform, text-decoration, color**), font characteristics (**font-weight, font-color, font-style, font-variant, font-size, font-family**), margins (**margin-left, margin-right, margin-top, margin-bottom**), borders, backgrounds, and padding. For simple stylizations, where you only need to style a few HTML elements on a page, **style** attributes are used to define how your tagged content will be displayed with inline element commands.

Unfortunately, as with any nonstandard method of displaying HTML, not all **style** sub-attribute values display the same way on different browsers. Be sure to check your display results on several browser types as *many* inline **style** attributes do *not* work on all browsers or their older versions. For example, although **font-size** *can* be measured in point sizes, browsers do pretty much everything in terms of pixels with the result that point size text is not always displayed uniformly. So don't fight with your browser trying to use a 12-point type height, use pixels!

As noted in Chapter 4's discussion about the **font** element's **face** attribute, defining a **font-family** can be done with a series of font types, in the order which you want them used. You will not be using the thousands of available fonts and if none of your desired font faces is available on your user's computer, a default generic type face (e.g., sans serif) will be used instead.

CODE:	RESULT:
Default Rule: <hr />	
50% Rule - Left : <hr style="width:50%; text-align:left" />	50% Rule - Left
50% Rule - Right : <hr style="width:50%; text-align:right" />	50% Rule - Right
50% Rule: <hr style="width:50%" />	Width = 50%
50% Rule, height = 16 : <hr style="width:50%; height:16" />	50% Rule - Height=16
50% Rule, color=red: <hr style="width:50%; color:red" />	50% Rule - Color=Red
50% Rule, color=red, height=6: <hr style="width:50%; color:red; height:6" />	Color=Red, Height=6
50% Rule, color=red, height=16: <hr style="width:50%; color:red; height:16" />	Color=Red, Height=16
Width = 50%, noshade : <hr style="width:50%" noshade />	50% Rule - noshade
Height = 16, noshade : <hr style="width:50%; height:16" noshade />	Height=16, noshade
Inset Green Border : <hr style="height:16; border:5 inset green" />	Inset Green Border
Outset Green Border : <hr style="height:16; border:5 outset green" />	Outset Green Border
Solid Green Border : <hr style="height:16; border:5 solid green" />	Solid Green Border
Dotted Blue Border : <hr style="height:16; border:5 dotted blue" />	Dotted Blue Border
Dashed Blue Border : <hr style="height:16; border:5 dashed blue" />	Dashed Blue Border
Double Red Border : <hr style="height:16; border:5 double red" />	Double Red Border
Grooved Red Border : <hr style="height:16; border:5 groove red" />	Grooved Red Border
Ridged Red Border : <hr style="height:16; border:5 ridge red" />	Red Ridge Border

Figure 06-01. Inline Horizontal Line **style** Examples (**code0601.htm**)

Using Border Attributes with Horizontal Rules

We saw in Figure 04-15 that we can modify the **hr** horizontal rule element with **height, width, noshade,** and **align** attributes to make a variety of thicker and width-controlled rule lines.

When inline style attributes are added to rule lines, we have better control of rule line height and width in pixels (**px**) or points (**1pt** to **100pt**) or with words (**thin, medium**—the default, and **thick**). We can define line color in the 16 standard colors (**aqua, black, blue, fuchsia, gray, green, lime, maroon, navy, olive, purple, red, silver,**

teal, white, yellow) or using **#rr gg bb** values. We can also add the **style**'s **border** sub-attribute values **solid, dashed, dotted, groove, ridge, double, inset,** and **outset.**

These stylizations increase the ways you can separate sections of your web page (recall that the horizontal rule behaves much like a heading with implied paragraph tags surrounding it). You can add many other style sheet sub-attributes inline to the **hr** element; for example, adding 5 pixel thick border sub-attributes gives more power to the simple horizontal rule as shown in the examples of Figure 06-01 using the IE browser. NOTE: Firefox does not reproduce these styles.

These same border styles and techniques could be used for creating borders around images and for creating tables.

You have no limit to the creativity you can show using inline **style** attributes. Other styling options for inline **style** attributes include adding spaces between text characters, changing background colors, and even adding image backgrounds behind text. Setting the background color in a single **div** block to the color **#00ff00** can be accomplished using the code:

<div style="background-color:#00ff00">

Defining the font size and adding additional space between all the letters in one paragraph of your text can be accomplished by adding a local **style** attribute inside the **p** opening tag with the following sub-attributes (note that the final sub-attribute value semicolon may be included or not—as is typical, depends on your browser):

> __Good to Know:__ Notice that the **style** attribute values are treated like sub-attributes. They have their own values, and like element attributes there can be more than one inside an opening element tag. Unlike element attributes, the **style** sub-attribute syntax requires that their values begin with a colon and end with a semicolon between sub-attributes:
>
> **<element style="sub-attribute1:value1; sub-attribute 2:value2; ">**
>
> The semicolon after the last sub-attribute, just prior to the final straight quotes, is optional.

<p style="font-size:30px; letter-spacing:25px; ">

This styling ends with the closing paragraph tag. Setting the text size and color of a local italicized section of your text can be accomplished with a **style** attribute inside the **i** opening tag with the following sub-attributes, and ends with the closing tag:

<i style="font-size:18px; color:#00ff00; "> . . . </i>

Internal Cascading Style Sheets

In the previous section we have seen that style sheet concepts can be used, with some good results, as an inline **style** attribute for some HMTL elements. This technique makes for larger files because each time you use an inline attribute you need to repeat it just before the text, division, paragraph, or span you want to stylize.

What if you could standardize the look and feel of your web page with a style list that includes all the **style** definitions at the element level? Then you would have *internal CSS*! The internal CSS "overwrites" the default values your browser uses for any element attributes you redefine. That way you need not use individual inline stylizations, as we saw in the last section, for each and every paragraph to take on the new style. The **style** element defines style characteristics at the document or page level by changing the DTDs of your elements and needs to be placed inside the **head** of an HTML document.

The **style** element, in its simplest form, can modify your page's text properties by aligning the text (**text-align**), indenting it (**text-indent**), and underlining it (**text-decoration**), alter its **color,** one or more **font** characteristics (**font-weight, font-color, font-style, font-size,** and **font-family**). Using **style** you can also modify the page's **border, background, padding,** and its margins (**margin-left, margin-right, margin-top, margin-bottom**).

In Chapter 7, where we discuss creating web page lists, we'll see that style can be used to modify list attributes (**list-style, list-type, list-image, list-position**); in Chapter 8 where we discuss creating web tables we'll review stylizing **table** attributes; and in Chapter 9 where we discuss creating forms, we'll use style to define **form** attributes. These will give you a really good feel for the power of CSS, but in Chapter 11 we take the leap of faith to look at even more creative ways to use this tool.

Adding style—One Page at a Time

The internal **style** element is a listing of the style definitions that will be used on a single web page. This technique avoids the need for declaring individual inline **style** attributes. The **style** element is located just after your **title** description in your web page's **head** area. The internal **style** element opening tag must contain the **type** attribute with its value set to **text/css** as seen here:

<style type="text/css">

The **style** opening tag is followed by each styled element's name with its attribute value(s) definitions separated by semicolons between a pair of *curly braces* (**{ . . . }**); note that just as with an inline style attribute, the final value does not require a semicolon. After all definitions are made, the closing **style** tag completes the page's internal set of style definitions.

This **style** structure or syntax, with the element name and *curly braces* typed inline, is shown in Figure 06-02.

After making any and all **style** changes, you need to close the **head** (**</head>**) of your document before opening the **body.**

The internal style sheet requires a different set of comment tags

<u>Good to Know:</u> In early style sheet designs, the comment tag <!--and --> surrounded the **style** definitions to address the needs of early browsers. Although you may still see comment tags, they are unnecessary. The Internet Explorer browser doesn't care if your CSS values are in quotes. Firefox, on the other hand, doesn't allow quoted values and will not properly display styles if you quote them.

```
<style type="text/css">

element1 { property1:value; property2:value(s); } ← new element1 default(s)
element2 { property1:value; property2:value(s); } ← new element2 default(s)
element3 { property1:value; property2:value(s); } ← new element3 default(s)

</style>
```

Figure 06-02. Inline Style Syntax

than those we have already used for standard HTML comments (<!-- and -->). The comment in a **style** sheet consists of a forward slash followed immediately by an asterisk (/*) opening style comment tag, and a closing style comment tag which reverses the opening tag (*/):

```
/* this is the structure of a style sheet comment */
```

As stated before, your browser ignores extra spaces and tabs. Style definitions can be written to more clearly show the individual element definitions by adding spaces and line breaks. Notice that there are no additional characters between each element redefinition in the following example of an internal generic two element (element1 and element2) style definition set (without final sub-attribute value semicolons):

```
<style type="text/css">
    /* element1 is described in this code */
element1 {
property1: value;
property2: value(s) }
    /* element2 is described in this code */
element2 {
    property1:value;
      property2:value(s)
    }
</style>
```

Style changes can be made for nearly any HTML element. If you want to change the way that the **h1** headline tag is treated, for example, from merely changing its **color** default to **red** and font **family** default to **arial** for an entire web page, the **style** codes, written as single lines, look like:

```
<style type="text/css"> h1 { color:red; font-family:arial; }
```

Note that the attributes of a style sheet are *not* quoted as they are when we use inline techniques. The resulting displayed change in **h1** defaults would look like Figure 06-03.

CODE:

```
<html> <head><title> Changing h1 style Definitions</title> <style type="text/css">
h1 { color:red; font-family:arial; } </style> </head> <body>
<h1>New H1 Default: Red Color, Arial Font</h1> </body></html>
```

RESULTS:

New H1 Default: Red Color, Arial Font

Figure 06-03. Changing **h1** Style Definitions (**code0603.htm**)

Changing Multiple Defaults with style on a Single Page

Of course more than one element can be defined at a time to create a specific look and feel on a single web page using this internal style sheet method. And you can add as many element definitions to the internal style sheet list as you would like using the structure discussed earlier.

Adding more attributes to the element's style definition requires each attribute and its value to be separated by semicolons as seen in Figure 06-03. If you would like to stylize several elements with the same definition rather than re-key the same definition several times, once for each element, here is a solution. You can actually stylize more than one element with the same new default definition by merely separating the element names with commas before the curly bracket definitions:

```
h1, h3, h5 { color:aqua;
font-family:serif; }
h2, h4, h6 { color:green;
font-family:sans-serif; }
b, strong { color:red;
font-size:20px; }
```

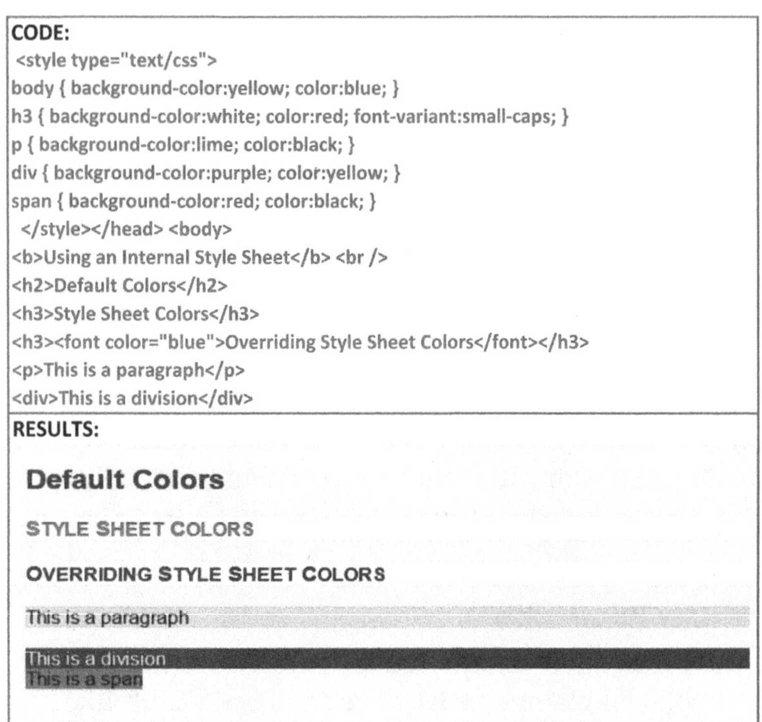

CODE:

```
<style type="text/css">
body { background-color:yellow; color:blue; }
h3 { background-color:white; color:red; font-variant:small-caps; }
p { background-color:lime; color:black; }
div { background-color:purple; color:yellow; }
span { background-color:red; color:black; }
</style></head> <body>
<b>Using an Internal Style Sheet</b> <br />
<h2>Default Colors</h2>
<h3>Style Sheet Colors</h3>
<h3><font color="blue">Overriding Style Sheet Colors</font></h3>
<p>This is a paragraph</p>
<div>This is a division</div>
```

RESULTS:

Figure 06-04. Using an Internal Style Sheet (**code0604.htm**)

Figure 06-04 shows that even when using internal style sheets, the inline **font color="blue"** coding closest to the text "Overriding Style Sheet Colors" overrides the internal style sheet **h3 red** color redefinition just as it would override the **black** default color for **h3** in HTML documents that didn't use style sheets to change the browser's DTD defaults.

Defining style within Elements Using Classes

If you want to have several style variations available to you to select a particular heading or a distinct heading for different areas of the library, using a single style for **h4** would probably require you to remember to add inline styling each time you wanted a different type face or color. That's when your style sheets need to have **class.**

Class is an element selector name used in CSS that provides for a secondary level of **style** descriptions for elements. Using **class** techniques permits you to define more than one type of **style** classification for a given element and then select that particular style in your document at the element level. You can consider classes as nothing more than names given to an element you want to define with more than one set of attributes. Try to make class names semantic; for example, use the **comic sans** font for your children's page calling for that CSS style in the **children** class, and a more formal serif font like **times new roman** for your Board's web pages calling for that CSS style in the **board** class. This will make it easy for you to understand the styles rather than spending time trying to figure out the style effect you wanted.

> **Good to Know:** When you create a style class you give a unique name to a sort-of new element. This is exactly what XML does—more elegantly, but at a much lower level.

Fully Defined Element Class Method

Any element within the **body** of an HTML document can be "classed" in the listing of style definitions inside the **head** of your document. You have two ways to structure the elements and their classes in a style sheet. You can use the "**fully defined element class**" method to define a class that includes the element's name and a class identifier separated by a period:

element.classproperty { property:value; }
EXAMPLE:
h4.red { color:red; }

If you wanted to have the headers all look the same (same **font-family**) except for their **color,** you could completely code each tag:

h1.red { color:red; font-family:Arial; }
h1.green { color:green; font-family:Arial; }

Generic Class Method

Similarly, you can use the "**generic class**" method for those classes that only contain the attribute or other name, preceded by a period.

classproperty { property:value; }
EXAMPLE:
green { color:green; font-family:arial; }

For finer HTML tag control, you could code the headline **font-family** as one style definition and define text-different colors as separate classes giving greater flexibility by defining **red** and **green** as additional classes. Once defined, the color styles can be declared as separate classes in the style sheet set, and they can be used in other elements that require added colorization. Note that if you want to stylize more than one element with the same default, for example declaring all the header elements as **Arial** you merely string them one after the other separated by commas and then define the group:

```
h1, h2, h3, h4, h5, h6 { font-family:Arial; }
.red { color:red; }
.green { color:green; }
```

Notice that although the **fully defined element class** can be used *only* for that particular element, the **generic class** definition can be used to stylize *any* element in the document. Bear in mind that we have only *defined* the **class** in the style sheet. You must "call" it as a **class** attribute by its name within the element surrounding the information you wish to stylize with it on your web page.

With the generic class method you can use the **red** or **green** color classes in any element of your document as if that element had that added attribute. Whenever you want to use one of these colors, you merely "call" them by adding the **class** attribute statement inside of your normal HTML element's opening tag as we'll see in Figure 06-05.

CODE:

```
<html> <head><title> Fully Defined Element and Generic Class Definitions</title>
 <style type="text/css">
h3.red { color:red; } .green { color:green; font-family:arial; } </style> </head>
<body>
<h3> Default h3 Heading</h3>
<h3 class="red">h3.red Stylized h3 Heading</h3>
<h3 class="green">.green Stylized h3 Heading</h3>
</body></html>
```

RESULTS:

Default h3 Heading

h3.red Stylized h3 Heading

.green Stylized h3 Heading

Figure 06-05. Fully Defined Element and Generic Class Definitions (**code0605.htm**)

```
<h1 class="red"> or <h3 class="green">
```

or even elements you have not included in the style set:

```
<p class="green"> or <span class="red">
```

In our next example, the **h3.red** and the **.green** classes in your style sheet are defined:

```
<style>
    h3.red { color:red; }
    .green { color:green; font-family:Arial; }
</style>
```

Once defined, the **h3.red** and the **.green** classes can be used as simply as adding the **class** attribute to an element's code. You must also drop the element's name and class period as appropriate:

```
<h3 class="red">Stylized h3 heading</h3>
<h3 class="green"> Stylized h3 heading</h3>
```

The **h3** element has not been defined with a green class (**h3.green**) in the style sheet. It acquires the **color** and **font-family** definitions from the generic class **green** resulting in Figure 06-05.

Other Class Acts

Classes have only been used with one or two definitions in these examples. Any or all the styles listed at the beginning of the "**Internal Cascading Style Sheets**" section can be used to stylize your elements as well as your classes. The **div** element, for example, can be stylized defining not only how the text will look in terms of **font-size** and **color** but also its alignment. In the following code line the top margin is defined showing where on the web page the **div** section of your document will be placed using the **margin** styles:

```
div { font-size:12px; color:maroon; text-align:center;
    margin-top:100px; }
```

The **margin** attribute can be used in any element in a style sheet to place items exactly where you would like them to be.

Using External Style Sheet Files

Suppose you wanted to use the set of style definitions of Figure 06-04, as they added just the color style you were looking for on a series of pages or even your whole website. This is easier than you might think. Just save the page's **style** components—don't include the style element opening or closing tag—in a plain text file created with notepad or another text editor with the extension "**css**" (e.g., **filename.css**) and store it in the **assets** folder on your web server.

As an example, place the following code in a plain text file called **colors.css:**

```
body { background-color:yellow; color:blue; }
h3 { background-color:white; color:red; }
p { background-color:lime; color:black}
div { background-color:purple; color:yellow; }
span { background-color:red; color:black; }
```

Remember: Do not include the style element opening or closing tags in the file as they are not needed, and *do not* use quotes around your property values.

Then, to use the **colors.css** style sheet definitions on a particular web page, we use the **link** element in the HTML document's **head** instead of the internal **style** sheet element definition list used in the head as shown on the past few pages:

```
<html><head><title>Using External Style Sheets </title>
<link rel="stylesheet" type="text/css" href="assets/colors.css" />
</head>
```

The result would be the same as if you had an internal style sheet definition set with all of those styles placed in the **head** of the HMTL document. If at any time you want to update all the styles on that set of pages, merely revise the **colors.css** file in the **assets** folder and each and every page that refers to it will immediately acquire these changes on viewing the page.

> Good to Know: Although the page is displayed by your browser as if the style sheet was an internal one, the page actually calls the CSS file and overlays the styling it finds there before it renders the page. You can see this by looking at the source code on your browser.

This is called a client-side technique even though the actual files need to be on the server.

If the CSS file has moved or cannot be found, the normal browser defaults will still be there to use. If more than one CSS file is linked to your web page, your browser will cascade or write element changes one on top of the other as appropriate. This is where the term cascading comes from and the stack of element changes is like a stack of pancakes. Changes are stacked one on top of the other and then removed in the order last on, first off. At the bottom of the stack is your browser's default.

Of course you might decide, as your web server is on the web anyway, to use one of the standard template style sheets from an online resource. You can review and test several core W3C web page style templates at:

http://www.w3.org/StyleSheets/Core/preview

As external style sheets are often made for the use of more than one person, it is important that style comments (/* **style comments** */) be included and liberally used for the information of others using them. You might also want to consider making a style sheet test page for each of the CSS you plan on using so you and your technical staff will know which CSS file has the styles you want for any particular page display.

Updating Our Red Rose Library Home Page

To apply some CSS concepts to a sample home page for the Red Rose Library home page, in Figure 06-06, the first step is to decide which styles to incorporate on the page.

This sample home page has nearly every text phrase hyperlinked to another page on the website; therefore, it makes good sense to remove all hyperlink underlining using the **text-decoration:none** attribute with the various hyperlink elements:

```
a:link, a:alink, a:vlink { text-decoration:none; }
```

However, once underlining is removed, the only way to distinguish between text and hypertext is by carefully watching to see if the mouse cursor changes into a

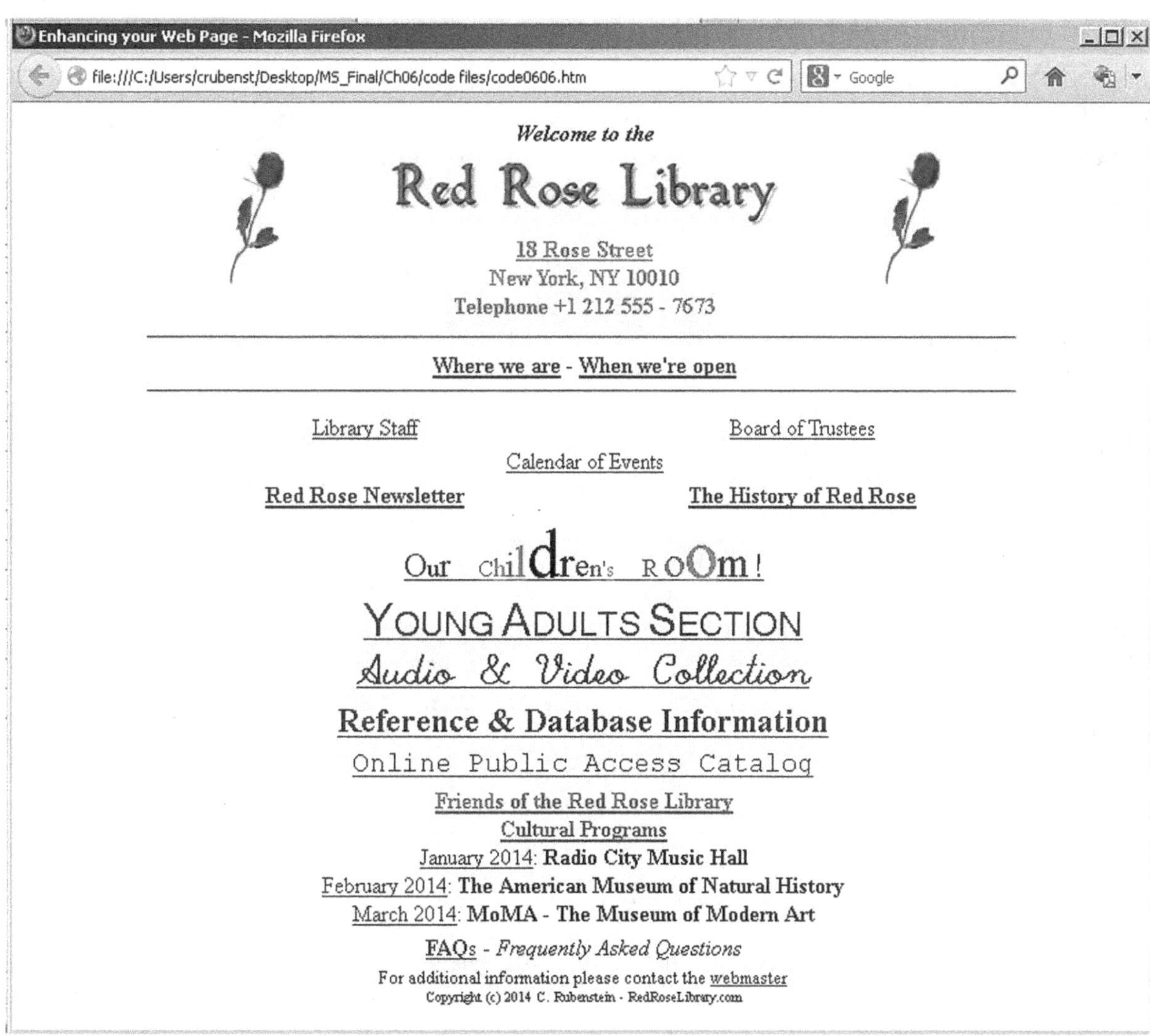

Figure 06-06. Sample Home Page (**code0606.htm**)

hyperlink hand. The actual control for changing the way the text looks when the mouse pointer is over it is called a **mouseover,** and it is changed by defining the anchor elements **hover** sub-element characteristics (**a:hover**). To make sure that your user sees that a hyperlink is available after removing the underlining, you can stylize the hypertext area **mouse over** with a bold, red text that is 25% larger than the surrounding text using the styling attributes **font-weight:bold, color:red** and **font-size:125%:**

```
a:hover { font-weight:bold; color:red; font-size:125%; }
```

If these are the only default changes we are interested in (at this time), and remembering that elements with the same style definition can be stylized in one code line when their names are comma separated, we can easily set up an internal style sheet with the following code:

```
<style>
a:link, a:alink, a:vlink { text-decoration:none; }
```

a:hover { font-weight:bold; color:red; font-size:125%; }
</style>

That same code can be saved as a plain text style sheet file and a link provided to the external style sheet file in your HTML document. The coding for the internal style sheet implementation of Figure 06-07 is **code0607int.htm** with the file set for the external style sheet version being **code0607ext.htm** and **0607style.css** (its required style sheet file which is located in the **image**s folder). Both methods result in the same browser display. The result of removing the hypertext underlining and enhancing the **mouseover** links is demonstrated by hovering over the "History of Red Rose" hyperlink in Figure 06-07.

Please note that hyperlinks that have inline attributes override the style sheet styles (yes, this is also a form of cascading!). Thus the fancy font styles and colors of the Children's Room, Young Adults Section, 18 Rose Street, and Cultural Program phrases are all enlarged, but their font face and color is styled by the local, inline, attributes.

Also note that although this technique will change the response to hypertext when moused over, hypergraphics (images with anchor tags surrounding them) are unable to display the text changes in the **a:hover** stylization. They will display and link with a border (unless **border="0"**) regardless of the **a:hover** style changes.

Be comforted that should you make an error in the coding, your page won't display properly, but no harm will come to your computer. What you will need to do is troubleshoot the coding to correct your error. For this reason it is always best to try out your style changes inline, then elevate them to in page, and finally create the external file and always check the display each time you make a change.

Styling Paragraph Indents and Margins

You can do lots of other tricks with CSS. Examples can be found on the W3Schools website, which also covers more advanced CSS techniques:

http://www.w3schools.com/css

Figure 06-07. Web Page Results from Either Internal or External CSS Techniques

Among these tricks is the styling of paragraphs, made easy with style sheets setting the margin and indentation for whatever style you like for one or more paragraph styles. Assigning paragraph style "one" that has the first letter of the paragraph indented by 35 pixels (about 5–6 character widths) with a 20 pixel margin on the left and a 90 pixel margin on the right could look like:

```
p.one { text-indent:35px; margin-left:20px; margin-right:90px; }
```

To add a few more classes to your document to see how best to structure your page, you could add the following style code class snippets:

```
p.two { text-indent:35px; margin-left:90px; margin-right:20px; }
p.three { text-indent:35px; margin-left:55px; margin-right:55px; }
p.four { text-indent:35px; margin-left:30px; margin-right:60px; }
p.five { text-indent:35px; margin-left:60px; margin-right:30px; }
```

Using the appropriate paragraph opening tags (e.g., **<p class="four">**) around your paragraphs of text will give results something like the first chapter of Genesis from: **http://www.sacred-texts.com/bib/kjv/gen001.htm** shown in Figure 06-08.

Background Images

Background images can also be enhanced by using CSS. By looking at examples that use the internal style sheet, you can use what you have learned to create a more useful external style sheet files with all the styles you want to use on your web pages. In the first chapter, images were inserted on the web page and in Chapter 4, a tiled image background was added using the **body** element opening tag:

```
<body background:"assets/img001.jpg">
```

Create a suitably soft image like the one of Figure 06-09 using Adobe Photoshop or Corel's Paint Shop Pro, or the image might have the effect of making your page unreadable (as was shown in rose tiled background of Figure 04–08).

Using CSS you can create the same effect by styling the **body** element, but using **style** values you can style the page to show a background image that won't tile, a single background image centered on the page, and even add a background color in case the image can't be found, or for those who can't see the image.

Some sample codes for these styles are

Non-tiled Background image:

```
body { background:url(assets/img005.jpg) no-repeat }
```

Centered background image displayed once with yellow background color:

```
body { background:#ffff00 url(assets/img005.jpg) no-repeat center }
```

Genesis – King James Version – Chapter 1 Creation
From: http://www.sacred-texts.com/bib/kjv/gen001.htm

Section 1:1-1:5 Day One (Default Style)
King James Version: Genesis Chapter 1 In the beginning God crested the heaven and the earth. And the earth was without form, and void: and darkness was upon the face of the deep. And the Spirit of God moved upon the face of the waters. And God said. Let there be light: and there was light. And God saw the light, that it was good: and God divided the light from the darkness. And God called the light Day, and the darkness he called Night. And the evening and the morning were the first day.

Section 1:6-1:8 Day Two (Indent 35, Left 20, Right 90)
And God said, Let there be a firmament in the midst of the waters, and let it divide the waters from the waters. And God made the firmament: and divided the waters which were under the fimement from the water which were above the fimament and it was so. And God called the firmament Heaven. And the evening and the morning were the second day.

Section 1:9-1:14 Day Three (Indent 35, Left 90, Right 20)
And god said, Let the waters under the heaven be gathered together unto one place, and let the dry land appear: and it was so. And God called the dry land Earth: and the gathering together of the waters called he Seas: and God saw that it was good. And God said, Let the earth bring forth grass, the herb yielding seed, and the fruit tree yielding fruit after his kind, whose seed is in itself, upon the earth: and it was so. And the earth brought forth grass, and herb yielding seed after his kind, and the tree yielding fruit, whose seed was in itself, after his kind: and God saw that it was good. And the evening and the morning were the third day.

Section 1:14-1:19 Day Four (Indent 35, Left 55, Right 55)
And God said, Let there be lights in the firmament of the heaven to divide the day from the night; and let them be for signs, and for seasons, and for days, and years: And let them be for lights in the firmament of the heaven to give light upon the earth: and it was so. And God made two great lights; the greater light to rule the day, and the lesser light to rule the night: he made the stars also. And God set them in the firmament of the heaven to give light upon the earth. And to rule over the day and over the night, and to divide the light from the darkness: and God saw that it was good. And the evening and the morning were the fourth day.

Section 1:20-1:23 Day Five (Indent 35, Left 30, Right 60)
And God said, Let the waters bring forth abundantly the moving creature that hath life, and fowl that may fly above the earth in the open firmament of heaven. And God created great whales, and every living creature that moveth, which the waters brought forth abundantly, after their kind, and every winged fowl after his kind: and God saw that it was good. And God blessed them, saying, Be fruitful, and multiply, and fill the waters in the seas, and let fowl multiply in the earth. And the evening and the morning were the fifth day.

Section 1:24-1:31 Day Six (Indent 35, Left 60, Right 30)
And God said, Let the earth bring forth the living creature after his kind, cattle, and creeping thing, and beast of the earth after his kind: and it was so. And God made the beast of the earth after his kind, and cattle after their kind, and every thing that creepeth upon the earth after his kind: and God saw that it was good. And God said, Let us make

Figure 06-08. Defining Paragraph Classes (**code0608.htm**)

Centered background image displayed once—no background color (Figure 06-08):

body { background:url(assets/img005.jpg) no-repeat center }

The centered, nonrepeating image method can be used with the first three paragraphs of the Genesis page (Figure 06-08) and the **img005.jpg** watermark graphic to create the style sheet watermarking (Figure 06-10). You will find that, as you change the size of your browser window, the "centered" image repositions as it is positioned relative to the window, not to the content.

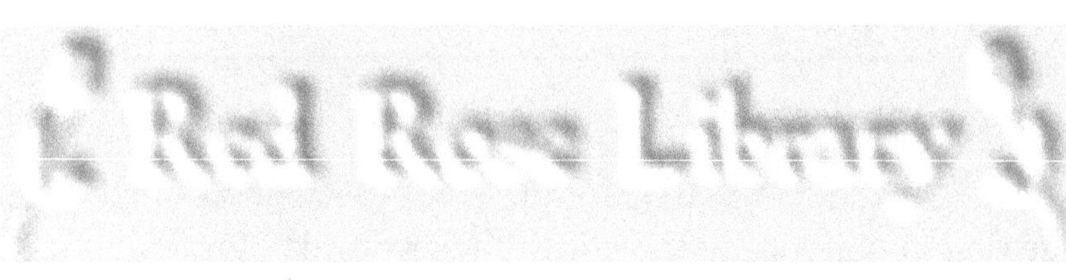

Figure 06-09. Softened Logo for Watermarking Your Page (**img005.jpg**)

Image Borders

As shown previously, simple borders can be placed around your images

Genesis - King James Version - Chapter 1 Creation
From: http://www.sacred-texts.com/bib/kjv/gen001.htm

Section 1:1-1:5 Day One (Default Style)
King James Version: Genesis Chapter 1 In the beginning God created the heaven and the earth. And the earth was without form, and void; and darkness was upon the face of the deep. And the Spirit of God moved upon the face of the waters. And God said, Let there be light: and there was light. And God saw the light, that it was good: and God divided the light from the darkness. And God called the light Day, and the darkness he called Night. And the evening and the morning were the first day.

Section 1:6-1:8 Day Two (Indent 35, Left 20, Right 90)
And God said, Let there be a firmament in the midst of the waters, and let it divide the waters from the waters. And God made the firmament, and divided the waters which were under the firmament from the waters which were above the firmament: and it was so.And God called the firmament Heaven. And the evening and the morning were the second day.

Section 1:9-1:14 Day Three (Indent 35, Left 90, Right 20)
And God said, Let the waters under the heaven be gathered together unto one place, and let the dry land appear: and it was so. And God called the dry land Earth; and the gathering together of the waters called he Seas: and God saw that it was good. And God said, Let the earth bring forth grass, the herb yielding seed, and the fruit tree yielding fruit after his kind, whose seed is in itself, upon the earth: and it was so. And the earth brought forth grass, and herb yielding seed after his kind, and the tree yielding fruit, whose seed was in itself, after his kind: and God saw that it was good. And the evening and the morning were the third day.

Figure 06-10. Style Sheet Watermarking (**code0610.htm**)

because **img** is also an HTML element. We can use style sheets to stylize that border using the border values we saw in Figure 06-01 (**solid, dashed, dotted, groove, ridge, double, inset, outset**) either as inline style attributes or as style sheet coding. In each of the following code sets the **border** default is changed to a **5 pixel** thick, **silver** colored, **dotted** border:

The inline image styling for a single image would look like:

```
<img. src="assets/img004.jpg" width="120" height="83" alt="logo"
style="border:5px dotted silver" />
```

The style sheet code to stylize *all* image borders on a page, or in an external CSS file:

```
img { border:5px dotted silver }
```

We can use this technique to define how a picture is stylized and use it on a staff web page for each of our library staff. The first step would be to have someone with a digital camera take your picture and save it in a file as a **gif** or **jpg** file. Once it is transferred into your computer you can use the **img** element to bring the picture's file into your web page. You don't need to resize the photo as your browser can do the resizing automatically, but if your digital photo is typically 2,600 x 2,000 pixels in size, your **jpg** photo file would be about 1.5 megabytes in size. So let's see. If your patron's browser window is 640 pixels wide and 480 pixels long, your original photo would fill about 16 windows! But even worse is that your patron will need to wait until 1.5 megabytes of data is received by their computer each time your picture is sent to it. Some digital cameras take 5 mega pixel and larger photos. That's a lot of wasted space. Web pages typically use 72 pixels per inch displays. So if we were to crop and reduce the size of the photo to 175–200 pixels on a side, it would become a 6–10 kilobyte file and yield a photo about 2.5 inches square—just enough to make you look great! Figure 06-11 shows a template you can use for your library webpages.

Name: Dr. Charles Rubenstein
Department/Title: Web Page Creator
email: c.rubenstein@ieee.org
Phone Number: +1 516 598-4619

Bio:
Charles P. Rubenstein is a professor in the graduate School of Information and Library Science at Pratt Institute and a visiting professor of engineering in the Institute for Research and Technology Transfer at Farmingdale State University, in New York. He has an engineering doctorate from New York's Polytechnic University and a masters degree in library and information science from Pratt Institute. He has developed web sites for professional societies and educational entities and was creator of the Institute of Electrical and Electronic Engineers, Inc. (IEEE) Region 1 web site and its webmaster for more than a decade. Dr. Rubenstein has been a distinguished lecturer for the IEEE Computer Society and IEEE Engineering Management Society presenting dozens of workshops and tutorials on HTML Web Page Design and Construction in Canada, India, Puerto Rico, and the United States since 1996.

Figure 06-11. Images with Fancy Borders (**code0611.htm = bio.htm**)

Text Boxes and Borders

As shown in Figure 06-01 an inline **style** attribute can be added to horizontal rules that will stylize their type, thickness, and/or color. Style and style sheets can be used to adjust the thickness of any style border around an image. In previous sections a colored background was created behind text and margins and indents were established. In the next section border stylization is added to your text as well as your images.

First create an internal style sheet body definition for the page margins and dotted and dashed border style class (**.dot** and **.dash**). Use the same color scheme for the set of border colors—red (top), lime (right side), blue (bottom), and black (left side) respectively. Add 20 pixels of padding between the text, or image, and the 10 pixel borders. The watermark class style adds a background image behind text in the second paragraph. The styling that will be used to create a History of the Red Rose Library web page is:

```
body { margin-left:100px; margin-right:100px }
.dash { padding:20px; border-color:red lime blue black;
     border-style:dashed; border-width:10px }
.dot { padding:20px; border-color:red lime blue black;
     border-style:dotted; border-width:10px }
.watermark { background-image:url(assets/img005.jpg);
     font-weight:bold }
```

History of the Red Rose Library

The Red Rose Library
18 Rose Street
New York, NY 10010
+1 212 555-7673

The Red Rose Library was established in 1969 at 18 Rose Street in New York City. It has been at this location ever since catering to the patrons and their need for quality audio/visual, children's, young adult, and reference collections.

The Library began its audio collection with cassette tapes and migrated to CD-ROMs as they became popular. In the late 1990's the Library added a video tape collection and has migrated to DVD-ROM titles which account for nearly half the current video titles. Repair facilities for cassette and video tapes as well as for compact discs of all types are present in the technical services area of the library. These services are available for a small fee to our patrons.

We have been fortunate that many online database vendors have seen the benefit to providing our patrons with the use of their resources at reduced cost. As we are in New York State, we also recommend that our patrons apply for and utilize the many reference resources available to them via the New York Public Library system.

Figure 06-12. Styling Text and Image Borders (**code0612.htm = history.htm**)

Dropped Caps

As people of the book, library folks are often enamored by the effect that the use of dropped caps gives to an opening paragraph of a chapter. To create this, you must convince the first letter of a paragraph to act as if it were an inline image located at the left side of the text. You can quadruple the size of this first letter, color it **navy**, and possibly change its **font-family** or other characteristics.

This style may be implemented in several ways. We could set the style as a paragraph, **div, span,** or other text element attribute in a style sheet. In Figure 06-12 the **span** element surrounds the text "Section 1:1" that we want to make into dropped caps. The generic class **.dropcap** is used to stylize "Section 1:6" and **p.cap:first-letter** is used in Section 1:9.

> **Good to Know:** The **first-letter** command is a CSS pseudo-element that defines the styling for only the first letter of text. Other pseudo-elements (**first-line, before,** and **after**) are structured like the anchor pseudo-classes we have already used (e.g., **a:hover**).

After isolating the letter(s) to style the

trick is to use the float attribute **float:"left"** in the style definition. Then the revised element will display as a dropped cap with all other text in the paragraph retaining "normal" styling.

```
span                        { float:left; width:3.2em; font-size:400%;
                                font-family:serif, courier; line-height:80%; }
.dropcap                    { float:left; font-size:400%; color:navy; }
p.dropcap:first-letter      { float:left; font-size:400%; color:navy; }
```

When you want to style a paragraph with a dropped cap, call the **dropcap** class as an attribute for either the paragraph opening tag or the text line, respectively:

```
<p class="dropcap">Your paragraph of text goes here. . </p> or
<b class="dropcap"/>Y</b>our text line goes here . . .
```

Figure 06-13 shows a variety of different ways to define and use dropped caps.

Floating Images for Newsletter Designs

The last CSS trick that we will discuss in this chapter is one that permits you to create a newsletter with images that can be placed on the page using the **float** attribute.

Positioning images to the left or to the right of your text is as easy as defining a style with the **float** attribute. The value **float:right;** displays an image to the right of our text. Add some space between the image and the text by using the **padding-left**

Section 1:1 In the beginning God created the heaven and the earth. And the earth was without form, and void; and darkness was upon the face of the deep. And the Spirit of God moved upon the face of the waters. And God said, Let there be light: and there was light. And God saw the light, that it was good: and God divided the light from the darkness. And God called the light Day, and the darkness he called Night. And the evening and the morning were the first day.

Section 1:6 Day 2 And God said, Let there be a firmament in the midst of the waters, and let it divide the waters from the waters. And God made the firmament, and divided the waters which were under the firmament from the waters which were above the firmament: and it was so.And God called the firmament Heaven. And the evening and the morning were the second day.

Section 1:9 Day Three

And God said, Let the waters under the heaven be gathered together unto one place, and let the dry land appear: and it was so. And God called the dry land Earth; and the gathering together of the waters called he Seas: and God saw that it was good. And God said, Let the earth bring forth grass, the herb yielding seed, and the fruit tree yielding fruit after his kind, whose seed is in itself, upon the earth: and it was so. And the earth brought forth grass, and herb yielding seed after his kind, and the tree yielding fruit, whose seed was in itself, after his kind: and God saw that it was good. And the evening and the morning were the third day.

Figure 06-13. Dropped Caps (**code0613.htm**)

Section 1:1 In the beginning God created the heaven and the earth. And the earth was without form, and void; and darkness was upon the face of the deep. And the Spirit of God moved upon the face of the waters. And God said, Let there be light: and there was light. And God saw the light, that it was good: and God divided the light from the darkness. And God called the light Day, and the darkness he called Night. And the evening and the morning were the first day.

Section 1:6 Day 2 And God said, Let there be a firmament in the midst of the waters, and let it divide the waters from the waters. And God made the firmament, and divided the waters which were under the firmament from the waters which were above the firmament: and it was so.And God called the firmament Heaven. And the evening and the morning were the second day.

Section 1:9 Day Three

And God said, Let the waters under the heaven be gathered together unto one place, and let the dry land appear: and it was so. And God called the dry land Earth; and the gathering together of the waters called he Seas: and God saw that it was good. And God said, Let the earth bring forth grass, the herb yielding seed, and the fruit tree yielding fruit after his kind, whose seed is in itself, upon the earth: and it was so. And the earth brought forth grass, and herb yielding seed after his kind, and the tree yielding fruit, whose seed was in itself, after his kind: and God saw that it was good. And the evening and the morning were the third day.

Figure 06-14. Floating Images (**code0614.htm**)

attribute. Similarly, to have your image displayed to the left of your text, use the padding on the right of it:

```
img.left { float:left; padding-right:50; }
img.right { float:right; padding-left:50; }
```

You already know how to add border styles and colors and to display text with dropped caps. In Figure 06-14 we have used these techniques and the Genesis text with a few rose images to illustrate how images float around the text. We floated a rose image to the right of Section 1:1, floated a second rose image to left of Section 1:6, and a third rose image to the right of Section 1:9.

Additional CSS Resources

In this chapter we have introduced many CSS ideas. Among the dozen CSS websites where you can find additional help in understanding the power of this powerful tool are several listed in the URLs section at the end of this chapter.

What's Next?

Chapter 7 reviews the basic **list** generating HTML elements and then presents how to use CSS to stylize them.

URLs Cited

The CSS Style Sheet test pages

http://www.w3.org/StyleSheets/Core/preview

The CSS Standards

http://www.w3schools.com/css

The King James Bible page

http://www.sacred-texts.com/bib/kjv/gen001.htm

The CSS Reference Sheet

http://www.w3schools.com/cssref

The W3C website

http://www.w3.org/Style/CSS
http://www.webstyleguide.com/type/face.html
http://www.webstyleguide.com/index.html?/pages/font_face.html

Building a web page with CSS

http://www.draac.com/css/css1.html

Chapter 6 Review Exercises

Chapter 6 Fill-In Questions

1. The _______ attribute can be used to change display defaults.
2. The element that is used to create a new set of defaults for your web page is ______.
3. The default width for a horizontal rule is _____.
4. The hr element uses style to create _____.
5. Changing the default font family with a style attribute is an example of an _______.

Chapter 6 Multiple-Choice Questions

1. Using the style element creates an ______ default change.

   a) inline b) internal c) external d) text
2. Using the link element creates an ______ default change.

   a) inline b) internal c) external d) text
3. Using the style attribute creates an ______ default change.

   a) inline b) internal c) external d) text
4. The abbreviation for the style sheet technique is:

   a) SST b) HTML c) CSS d) XHTML
5. Style sheet comments are placed between the */ and _____ delimiters.

   a) // b) /* c) */ d) -->

Chapter 6 Design and Discussion Questions

1. Write the HTML code to set the style sheet background, headline, paragraph and division colors, and font sizes using the **style** element.
2. Design an internal style sheet that creates fully defined classes of paragraphs that are centered, flush left, flush right, have red text, have green text.
3. Describe why you might decide to use an internal style sheet rather than an external one.
4. Describe why you might want to use generic rather than fully defined element classes.
5. Discuss how inline style attributes can change stylization on your page.

7

Lists, Lists, and More Lists

Lists are often used instead of long strings of items in a sentence separated by commas. The list is more readable than the same information in a sentence. Lists come in a wide variety from simple lists with one idea or item on a line and those with numbered, lettered, or "bulleted" sets of items. In this chapter a variety of HTML elements will be used to have items appear in list, or even outline (lists within lists), format on your web page. Then cascading style sheets (CSS) will be added to enhance the style of your web list.

Three Basic Lists

Three HTML list elements, unordered list **ul,** ordered list **ol,** and definition list **dl,** are expected to be used in future HTML versions. Both ordered and the unordered list elements require the list item element **li** to create list displays. List items can be nested to give your web page a traditional outline look and feel, and are block-level elements that create paragraph separations between the list and your other text. They are both easy to use. The definition list works a bit differently and will be described in the section following ordered lists.

Any of the list types can be located within the body of your document, inside a list item **li,** or a block quote, or a **form,** or even other list elements. We will review how to change the list item **type** (**circle** [default], **disc,** or **square** bullet) and **style** list attributes later in this chapter.

Unordered Lists

The **ul, dir,** and **menu** elements are all unordered list elements with nearly the same characteristics in that they all must contain list item elements and can be nested to accomplish a variety of different stylings. The **dir** and **menu** elements yield displays more or less equivalent to that of the unordered list **ul** and have been deprecated. They should not be used as they won't be used in XHTML, XML, or in future versions of HTML.

The unordered list element **ul** defines an unordered list with each list item **li** marked by a bullet symbol rather than the alphanumeric character of the ordered list we will discuss in the next section. The text in list items automatically wraps and indents when displayed by your browser.

The List Item

Both unordered and ordered list elements require the use of list item elements to properly display lists. The **li** can be inside of any list type, and can contain characters and their formatting (**b, i, u**), list elements, hyperlinks, line and paragraph breaks, images, block quotes, preformatted text, and even forms (see Chapter 9). They can be stylized and changed as necessary using bullet **type** and inline **style** attributes as well as using Chapter 6's CSS techniques as will be seen later in this chapter. For unordered lists the bullet **type** values are the **disc** (default), **circle,** and **square.** In the next section we will see that the ordered list **ol** uses Arabic and roman numbers (**1, A, a, I,** or **i**) instead of bullets and can set the starting **value** (**=n**) where the default bullet is **1** and therefore **n=1.**

The syntax for the unordered list with default bullet types is:

```
<ul>
     <li> content for first list item </li>
     <li> content for next list item </li>
     . . .
     <li> content for last list item </li>
</ul>
```

Although you may see the **li** used alone to force a bullet in front of text and the **ul** or **ol** used without the **li** elements to position indented text, these are unreliable solutions and not proper ways to accomplish text styling. Full sets of list elements and items should be used at all times. Figure 07-01 shows the three types of unordered lists, **ul, dir,** and **menu,** side by side for easy comparison.

Depending on your browser, it may only be necessary to learn the **ul** element with list items if you are constructing unordered lists. Also demonstrated in the figure is the use of the **type** attribute in changing the list item bullet shape from **disc** (filled circle) to a filled **square** or an open **circle.**

Ordered Lists

The unordered list element **ul** can be used when there are only a few list items but it does not lend itself well to longer listings or outlines as we'll see in the section on nesting. To deal with these longer lists we will need a bullet that has more content to it, like a letter or number. This is where the ordered list comes into play.

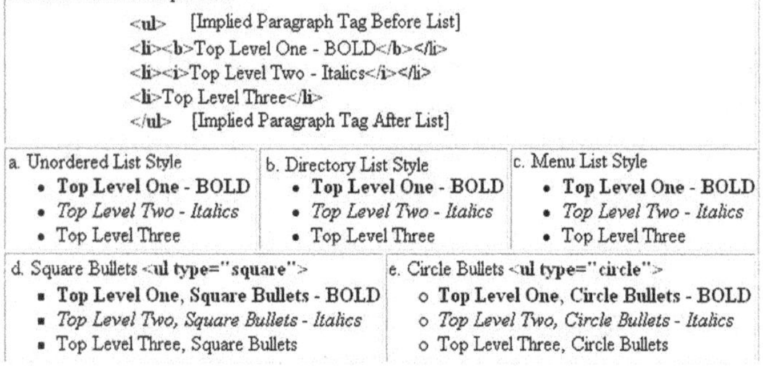

The HTML ordered list element **ol** is used just like the unordered list element **ul** discussed earlier except that it uses numbered lists of items. Just like the unordered list, an ordered list can be used inside of the **body** of the HTML document, block quotes, tables, forms, list items, and

General Code for Simple List:

```
<ul>   [Implied Paragraph Tag Before List]
<li><b>Top Level One - BOLD</b></li>
<li><i>Top Level Two - Italics</i></li>
<li>Top Level Three</li>
</ul>   [Implied Paragraph Tag After List]
```

a. Unordered List Style	b. Directory List Style	c. Menu List Style
• **Top Level One - BOLD**	• **Top Level One - BOLD**	• **Top Level One - BOLD**
• *Top Level Two - Italics*	• *Top Level Two - Italics*	• *Top Level Two - Italics*
• Top Level Three	• Top Level Three	• Top Level Three

d. Square Bullets <ul type="square">	e. Circle Bullets <ul type="circle">
▪ **Top Level One, Square Bullets - BOLD**	o **Top Level One, Circle Bullets - BOLD**
▪ *Top Level Two, Square Bullets - Italics*	o *Top Level Two, Circle Bullets - Italics*
▪ Top Level Three, Square Bullets	o Top Level Three, Circle Bullets

Figure 07-01. The Unordered List Elements (**code0701.htm**)

other lists. Your browser assigns ascending numbers or letters to list items in an ordered list based on the list's bullet **type** attribute (**1, A, a, I,** or **i**) with the Arabic numbering system (**1**) used as a default. The ordered list can also be forced to start at a particular value (**start="5"**), or have a particular **style.**

General Code for Simple List: <ol> <li><b>Top Level One - BOLD</b></li> <li><i>Top Level Two - Italics</i></li> <li>Top Level Three</li> </ol>	a. Default Arabic Numbers Ordered List <**ol type="1"**> 1. **Top Level One - BOLD** 2. *Top Level Two - Italics* 3. Top Level Three
b. Capital Letter Ordered List <**ol type="A"**> A. **Top Level One - BOLD** B. *Top Level Two - Italics* C. Top Level Three	c. Lowercase Letter Ordered List <**ol type="a"**> a. **Top Level One - BOLD** b. *Top Level Two - Italics* c. Top Level Three
d. Capital Roman Numerals Ordered List <**ol type="I"**> I. **Top Level One - BOLD** II. *Top Level Two - Italics* III. Top Level Three	e. Lowercase Roman Numerals Ordered List <**ol type="i"**> i. **Top Level One - BOLD** ii. *Top Level Two - Italics* iii. Top Level Three

Figure 07-02. Ordered Lists (**code0702.htm**)

The syntax for all lists is the same, thus for the ordered list with the default Arabic numbers it is:

```
<ol>
        <li> content for first list item </li>
        <li> content for next list item </li>
        . . .
        <li> content for last list item </li>
</ol>
```

As can be seen in Figure 07-02, letters and roman numerals, either in upper or lowercase, can be set using the **type** attribute in the **ol** opening tag.

Note that list items are automatically sequenced by your browser. The **start** attribute can be used to force the starting character of the series with the remaining items sequencing in an ascending order from that point. In the next section we will see how the ordered and unordered lists can easily nest inside themselves.

Nesting Lists

> **Good to Know:** In outlining long lists on your web page, you would certainly start with Arabic numbers, but the next level down might use lowercase letters with Roman numerals and others to indicate successively lower levels. Varying the ordered list bullet types will go far in helping your patrons understand the outline and sublevels that are not always obvious.

In Figures 07–01 and 07–02 we saw how to display single levels of list items using the ordered and unordered list elements. In Figure 07-03 we see how adding additional levels is accomplished using another **ul** or **ol** element set to nest another list underneath any list item.

Although the unordered list automatically changes the nested items from disc to circle to square, the ordered list keeps the same styles. The **type** attribute can reset the style of bullet as necessary to create more pleasing displays.

CODE: <ol> <li><b>Top Level - BOLD</b></li> <ol> <li><i>Second Level - Italics</i></li> <ol> <li>Third Level </li> </ol> </ol> <li><b>Top Level - BOLD</b></li> </ol>	List Outline Example: 1. **Top Level - BOLD** 1. *Second Level - Italics* 1. Third Level 2. **Top Level - BOLD**

Figure 07-03. Nesting Ordered Lists (**code0703.htm**)

Figure 07-04 shows the nesting results for ordered and unordered lists.

a. Two Level Ordered Lists

1. **Top Level One - BOLD**
2. *Top Level Two - Italics*
    1. **Second Level One - BOLD**
    2. *Second Level Two - Italics*
3. Top Level Three

b. Two Level Unordered Lists

- **Top Level One - BOLD**
- *Top Level Two - Italics*
    - **Second Level One - BOLD**
    - *Second Level Two - Italics*
- Top Level Three

c. Three Level Ordered Lists

1. **Top Level One - BOLD**
2. *Top Level Two - Italics*
    1. **Second Level One - BOLD**
        1. **Third Level One - BOLD**
        2. *Third Level Two - Italics*
    2. *Second Level Two - Italics*
3. Top Level Three

d. Three Level Unordered Lists

- **Top Level One - BOLD**
- *Top Level Two - Italics*
    - **Second Level One - BOLD**
        - **Third Level One - BOLD**
        - *Third Level Two - Italics*
    - *Second Level Two - Italics*
- Top Level Three

e. Four Level Ordered Lists

1. **Top Level One - BOLD**
2. *Top Level Two - Italics*
    1. **Second Level One - BOLD**
        1. **Third Level One - BOLD**
            1. **Fourth Level One - BOLD**
            2. *Fourth Level Two - Italics*
        2. *Third Level Two - Italics*
    2. *Second Level Two - Italics*
3. Top Level Three

f. Four Level Unordered Lists

- **Top Level One - BOLD**
- *Top Level Two - Italics*
    - **Second Level One - BOLD**
        - **Third Level One - BOLD**
            - **Fourth Level One - BOLD**
            - *Fourth Level Two - Italics*
        - *Third Level Two - Italics*
    - *Second Level Two - Italics*
- Top Level Three

Figure 07-04. Nesting Ordered and Unordered Lists (**code0704.htm**)

It is important to remember that a variety of styling techniques for lists can be used. These can be overall list changes that are typically attributes inside the opening tag for the **ol** or **ul** elements. Any style changes made affect the entire list. The styling of our list items themselves can also be used. Figure 07-04 shows how adding color attributes in addition to the bold and italics rendering which were used in Figure 07-03.

Changing the list bullet type defaults is another way to improve your displays. It is easy to see the difference between the various bullet styles in unordered list examples. This is not so easy when looking at the ordered list with default numbering. In the default, all first-level items start with the Arabic number 1.

As image elements can exist inside a list item element, you can create graphical list items! As the anchor element can exist inside the list item, you could create a simple quiz for use on your library's Children's Room pages. A simple example is shown in Figure 07-05.

The answers point to files named **correct.htm** and **wrong.htm** but could be coded to point to more subtle, random, page names if you wanted to. When you check the **code0705.htm** file, you will find that the sample here uses the **table** element. The questions are actually in two separate cells and thus the **start** attribute is required for the second question as it is actually a new list. If the two questions were in a single column, you would not need to use the **start** attribute as these would be two list items of the same list. On the other hand, let's say that the intent was to number the question by the page number on which the answer could be found. You might then use a **start** attribute even with the questions in a single listing.

Figure 07-05. A Children's Room Hypergraphic List Quiz (**code0705.htm, quiz.htm**)

The last list type to be discussed here is the definition list. Often used to render glossary listings, unlike the ordered and unordered lists, the definition list does not exhibit block-level formatting. Ordered and unordered lists (like headings) force a paragraph break before and after their use. They also indent their list items automatically, neither of which the definition does.

Definition Lists

The definition list **dl** does not use the list item element **li** used in ordered and unordered lists, but rather uses the definition term **dt** and the definition description **dd** elements to style list items.

The definition list element **dl** can be used to create lists such as those that would be used for glossaries that contained listings of terms and accompanying descriptions. The definition list can have non-indented **dt** or indented **dd** portions and can be found inside of the **body** of an HTML document or inside of block quotes, other definition lists **dd,** list items **li,** and forms. Definition lists can use the **style** attribute for display stylization.

The non-indented part of a definition list is the definition term element **dt.** Text in definition terms typically consists of only few words.

The indented portion of a definition list is the definition description element **dd.**

Like the definition list itself, content in both definition terms **dt** and definition descriptions **dd** can contain formatting (**b, i, u, pre**), hyperlinking, line breaks, and images. They can also contain block quotes, paragraphs, other lists, and forms.

One example of the syntax for the definition list is:

```
<dl>
    <dt> content for first definition term </dt>
      <dd> content for definition description </dd>
    <dt> content for next definition term </dt>
      <!- - note there is no definition description for this term- ->
    <dt> content for next definition term </dt>
      <dd> content for definition description </dd>
</dl>
```

CODE:

```
<dl>
<dt><b>Activities Calendar</b></dt>
<dt><i> January 2014 - March 2014 </i></dt>
<dt> January 2014</dt>
<dd>Description of event goes here with cost and contact
information.</dd>
<dt>February 2014</dt>
<dd>Description of event goes here with cost and contact
information.</dd>
<dt>March 2014</dt>
<dd>Description of event goes here with cost and contact
information.</dd>
</dl>
```

Activities Calendar
January 2014 - March 2014
January 2014
    Description of event goes here with cost and contact information.
February 2014
    Description of event goes here with cost and contact information.
March 2014
    Description of event goes here with cost and contact information.

Figure 07-06. The Definition List (**code0706.htm**)

Your Red Rose Library Activities Calendar

January 2014–March 2014

January 2014 Program

Radio City Music Hall Stage Door Tour
1260 Avenue of the Americas
New York, New York 10020

The Radio City Stage Door Tour is a one hour, walking tour of the interior of Radio City Music Hall that gives an insider's view of the inner-workings of this legendary showplace.
Click on the Red Rose above for reservations and contact information.

February 2014 Program

American Museum of Natural History
Central Park West at 79th Street
New York, NY 10024-5192

The world of Dinosaurs awaits you at the American Museum of Natural History! As you'll want to spend a relaxing time visiting with these prehistoric earth dwellers, we will meet at the museum for lunch but you are on your own before and after lunch. (The museum is open from 10:00 a.m.–5:45 p.m. and parking is quite expensive - take the bus or train!) Your $30 (Children are only $20) includes admission to the Museum and the Rose Center, a timed entry to the Dinosaurs exhibit, and of course our lunch together.
Click on the Red Rose above for reservations and contact information.

March 2014 Program

The Museum of Modern Art
11 West 53 Street
New York, NY 10019-5497

Your $20 (Children are only $10) includes admission to the Museum and bus transportation.
Click on the Red Rose above for reservations and contact information.

Figure 07-07. A Program Page Template (**code0707.htm, programs.htm**)

The definition description element **dd** can have any number of indented sentences and/or paragraphs in it. One use you may find for the definition list is in listing and describing your library's monthly activities as shown in Figure 07-06.

As you might have additional information for each of these activities, you might want to use anchor elements to hyperlink the months to full-page descriptions of the activities and/or forms to fill out to register for them.

As noted with ordered and unordered lists, definition lists **dl** can also include images. Figure 07-07 shows an "improved" design with hyperlinks to the full description of the event as shown in Figure 07-08 (**1401prog.htm**).

Notice in Figure 07-08 hypertext has been used for the Radio City Music Hall home page and tours page, but an unordered list (at the cursor area) has been imbedded inside of a definition list structure. You could also use a standard page template for each activity, or you might want to vary the look and feel depending on the subject or patron type you are targeting. A visit to the zoo, for example, might be less wordy and have several animal graphics to appeal to children. We'll review the use of web forms in Chapter 9 and show a template you might want to use as an online registration system, presuming you have appropriate web server software.

Your Red Rose Library Activities Calendar

January 2014

Radio City Music Hall Stage Door Tour
1260 Avenue of the Americas
New York, New York 10020

Come join us as we take a trip to New York's famous Radio City Music Hall!
Their web site (http://www.radiocity.com/themusichall_tours.html) notes:
No trip to Radio City is complete without a tour of the legendary theatre.
Reopened after an extensive restoration on October 4, 1999, the Music Hall now reflects its original grandeur of opening night, 1932, sporting behind-the-scenes upgrades and refurbishment. Following the lead of Radio City's experienced tour guides, guests explore: the Great Stage, one of the largest indoor performance stages in the world; the stage's hydraulic system, still in operation since the '30s; the renowned private suite, with 12-feet high gold leaf ceilings and onetime home to Samuel "Roxy" Rothafel. And as an exciting climax to the Stage Door Tour, guests will meet one of the world-famous Radio City Rockettes!
The Radio City "Stage Door Tour" is a one hour, walking tour of the interior of Radio City Music Hall that departs from the Music Hall lobby. Radio City Music Hall is located in the heart of Rockefeller Center at 1260 Avenue of the Americas - 6th Ave and 50th Street.
View the online highlights of the "Stage Door Tour"

- *The Great Stage*
- *Art Deco Design*
- *The Wurlitzer Organ*
- *Samuel Lionel "Roxy" Rothafel*
- *Rockefeller Center*
- *Radio City Avenue Store*

Your Friends of the Red Rose Library have co-sponsored this event.
Admission, round trip bus and one hour to experience the Radio City area after the tour are included for only $25.
Contact the Friends of the Red Rose Library at +1 212 555-7673 to make your reservations. And let us know if you'd be interested in attending a performance at the Radio City Music Hall in the spring...

Figure 07-08. Template for an Event (**code0708.htm, 1401prog.htm**)

List Outline Example:

1. **Top Level - BOLD**
    I. *Second Level Roman Numerals with Italics*
    II. *Second Level Roman Numerals with Italics*
        a. Third Level Lowercase Letters
        b. Third Level Lowercase Letters

Top Level Rose Bullet - BOLD

Second Level Roman Numerals with Italics - doesn't work!

Top Level Rose Bullet - BOLD

I. *Second Level Roman Numerals with Italics after closing list*

Figure 07-09. Lists with Style and Class (**code0709.htm**)

Creating Lists with Style

The list attributes for styling lists are found in Chapter6. To extend these possibilities, you can add several internal and external style sheet properties. As we have seen previously, **style** redefines the inline, on page, or external, **style** characteristics using attributes such as **list-style, list-style-type, list-style-image,** and **list-style-position.**

These style sheet properties can describe which bullet you can use, but more importantly **style** elements or attributes can be used to create and use your own bullet images. Clearly the list style images need to be relatively small with respect to your text, but nonetheless, you can use **style** to create custom image bullets in a list.

The **list-style** property, if your browser supports it, is the easiest to use. With it you can describe the style for your list item's bullet on a line–by-line basis. The types of bullets supported in unordered lists are **disc** (default), **circle, square,** or **none.** The ordered list values are **decimal** (default), **lower-roman, upper-roman, lower-alpha, upper-alpha,** or **none.** But now the idea of bulleted unordered lists can be kicked up a notch by adding images using the format **url (local or web image and location).**

You'll need to be careful about using image list item styles. As you can see in Figure 07-09, even though a bullet change was requested from an image class to a Roman bullet class (at the cursor), the image bullet can be seen in the second line. This is not unusual with nesting complex bullets as they inherit certain characteristics from earlier stylizations. You may have noticed that mixed ordered and unordered list bullets are included inside of an ordered list here. The same display would occur if the list had been defined as unordered. You can use ordered list values in an unordered list, and when you use style sheets the bullet values are incremented in subsequent items just as with an ordered list.

Of course if you want some of your lists to have one style and others to exhibit another, you can always use CSS classes to define several styles such as **li.roman, li.lowalpha,** or **li.red** for list item styles using upper Roman numerals, .

Although Internet Explorer accepts the simple **list-style** property as well as inline style:

li.roman { list-style:upper-roman; } or
li.roman { list-style-type:upper-roman; } and
li.red { list-style:url(assets/img006.jpg); } or
li.red { list-style-image:url(assets/img006.jpg); }

the Mozilla Firefox browser does not seem to like this style sheet method. Using these style sheets in Firefox merely shows the default Arabic number list bullets. Firefox seems to prefer the use of inline **style** attribute coding:

<li style=list-style-type:upper-roman; }
<li style=list-style-image:url(assets/img006.jpg); }

As both major browsers seem to like inline styling, you might want to consider using the **style** element's **list-style-type, list-style-image,** or **list-style-position** properties *inline* instead. You have a nice set of list tools that you can try on your web pages, keep them simple at first, and then add some complexity as you get comfortable with the list elements and their attributes.

What's Next?

Some of the ins and outs of creating web page tables will be shown in Chapter 8. You will also learn the basic use of CSS to style HTML web pages with table-like displays *without* using **table** elements.

No URLs were cited in the chapter on lists, but you can always check out the W3 pages for list elements and CSS for use in lists.

Chapter 7 Review Exercises

Chapter 7 Multiple-Choice Questions

1. The three basic list types are **ul, dl,** and:

   a) **ol** b) **ll** c) **al** d) **ql**

2. The ordered and unordered lists require the use of the list ___ element.

   a) definition b) order c) bullet d) item

3. The default bullet type for top-level unordered lists is the:

   a) bullet b) disc c) circle d) square

4. The default bullet type for top-level ordered lists is a/an ____ character.

   a) Roman b) Alpha c) Arabic d) bullet

5. The **li** element:

   a) must be closed b) is an empty element
   c) is used only with **dl** lists d) cannot be used with **ol** lists

Chapter 7 Design and Discussion Questions

1. Write the HTML code to create a simple outline for use in a table of contents for your library website.
2. When should you consider using an image rather than a standard bullet on a list?
3. Describe why you might decide to use the definition list on a web page.
4. Describe how you can avoid using the list elements and still achieve the look of a bulleted list.
5. Briefly discuss the nesting possibilities of list structures.

8

Tables and Their Creative Uses

At the very beginning of any discussion about web pages that compares them to word-processed pages the reader is told that HTML does NOT display like a word-processed page. That challenge was not lost on early web designers who found that many of the display modes they sought to make a web page look better would be available if they could create rows and columns of information and position that information by using table construction techniques. We already know that tables can be designed to show, or not show, their borders and thus tables can be used to position content to mimic the effect of word processing.

> Good to Know: Alas, HTML table elements have been deprecated and will soon become obsolete. This chapter is intended for the casual web page designer. Cascading style sheet (CSS) techniques are becoming the way to create table-like structures that do not contain tabular material and will continue to do so in the future. *As you should know by now, CSS effects are browser-specific.* Internet Explorer is used in this chapter.

Now let's see how to work that bit of magic.

Building a Table

The HTML **table** element is used for displaying information in a table. It can also be used to force text into looking like the output of a word processor. As some of the table's features and attributes are not supported by all browsers, one way to accomplish table effects is to use CSS techniques to position text and graphics on a web page without using one or more of the five table elements. These are the table, table caption, table header, table row, and table data elements.

The HTML **table** element creates the overall table container. It can be located inside of the HTML document's **body,** quotes, list items, other tables, and forms. It can be stylized using any of these attributes: **background, bgcolor, border, bordercolor, bordercolorlight, bordercolordark, cellspacing, cellpadding, width** and typically contains table captions **caption,** headings **th,** table rows **tr,** and table data **td** elements.

The **caption** element creates table captions. Captions used inside of the **table** can be stylized with **align** and **valign** attributes, and can contain text characters and formatting, hyperlinks, line breaks, and/or images.

All tables are defined by their rows and columns. The table row **tr** element is used inside of the **table** to define a row. It can be stylized with **background, bgcolor, border, bordercolor, bordercolorlight, bordercolordark, width, align,** and **valign** attributes, and contains one or more table data **td** elements.

The table heading **th** and table data **td** elements are both used inside of the **table** container and can be stylized with the attributes: **background, bgcolor, border, bordercolor, align, valign, bordercolorlight, bordercolordark, colspan, rowspan,** and **nowrap.** Table headings and data can contain text characters and formatting, hyperlinks, line breaks, images, and even completely new tables. Table heading **th** and table data **td** must both exist inside of table rows **tr** and create what would be a header or "cell" in a spreadsheet table.

The basic **table** element surrounds the **caption, row, heading,** and **data** (cell) elements to define the construction of a table framework in which text and/or image content can be placed. The **table** element can be inserted anywhere as long as you remember it acts like other block-level formatting elements inserting line breaks around the table itself. The **table** element must have both an opening and a closing tag or else it is possible that the table, and all its content, will "disappear" or become distorted when displayed on your browser. No matter how complex the table, it all begins with a single cell.

A simple single cell table is constructed using just three elements to create a table with one row and one column. Nesting these **table, tr,** and **td** elements results in a block or cell in which the text or image content resides. The cell structure itself cannot be seen (Figure 08-01, code a) without turning the **table** element's **border** attribute "on" by setting it to a non-zero value. This turns a table into an acceptable means for managing text by simulating word-processed output displays. As seen in Figure 08-01, the **color** and thickness of the cell's **border,** as well as the cell's background **color,** can be defined using attributes within the opening tags of these three elements.

If you review how you stylized horizontal rules in Figure 06-01, and text blocks in Figure 06-11, you may now use those same techniques to create a variety of inline style commands to modify the outside borders of a table or cell using border values. Figure 08-02 illustrates a few of the possible single color table border stylizations.

The simple two pixel **cell spacing** default for colored table borders (Figure 08-02, section a) creates the effect of a double line border. As shown in Figure 08-02, section b, the distance between the two colored border lines can be increased by increasing this **cellspacing** value. You may also change the border style from **dotted** to **solid** or **dashed** or another style from Chapter 6 and Figure 06-01.

Using only three core elements, **table, tr,** and **td,** turn on the border (**border="1"**) and the resulting side by side cells will create a single row table with two columns as evidenced in Figure 08-03.

This is the same code included on the left of section a in Figure 08-04, and results in the output on the right side of section a.

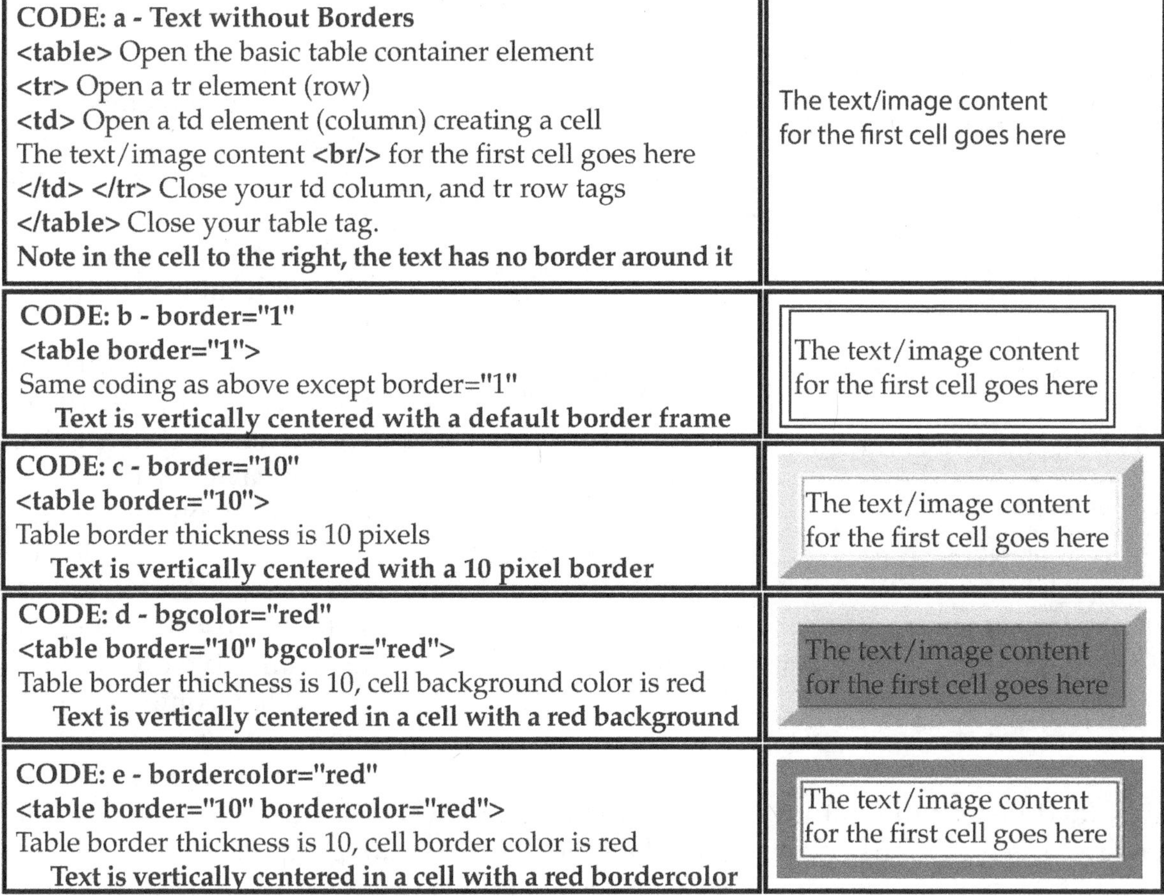

CODE: a - Text without Borders **<table>** Open the basic table container element **<tr>** Open a tr element (row) **<td>** Open a td element (column) creating a cell The text/image content ** ** for the first cell goes here **</td> </tr>** Close your td column, and tr row tags **</table>** Close your table tag. **Note in the cell to the right, the text has no border around it**	The text/image content for the first cell goes here
CODE: b - border="1" **<table border="1">** Same coding as above except border="1" **Text is vertically centered with a default border frame**	The text/image content for the first cell goes here
CODE: c - border="10" **<table border="10">** Table border thickness is 10 pixels **Text is vertically centered with a 10 pixel border**	The text/image content for the first cell goes here
CODE: d - bgcolor="red" **<table border="10" bgcolor="red">** Table border thickness is 10, cell background color is red **Text is vertically centered in a cell with a red background**	The text/image content for the first cell goes here
CODE: e - bordercolor="red" **<table border="10" bordercolor="red">** Table border thickness is 10, cell border color is red **Text is vertically centered in a cell with a red bordercolor**	The text/image content for the first cell goes here

Figure 08-01. One-Cell Tables (**code0801.htm**)

To create a four-cell table, first create a table with one row with two side by side cells (Figure 08-04, section a), then, instead of closing the table, repeat the row design to achieve the results of section c of Figure 08-04.

> **Good to Know:** To create a pair of rows each having a single column you will need to code one cell on top of another. To do this, open a table (**<table border="1">**), then open the row, and open a column (**<tr><td>**). Insert content in this first cell as shown in section b of Figure 08-04. Close the column and the row (**</td></tr>**). Open a second row and a column (**<tr><td>**), and insert content. Then close the column, close the row, and close the table (**</td></tr> </table>**). The result is section b of Figure 08-04.

Although only text was used in these table cell examples, you can include images, hypertext, and even stylize the text and backgrounds of each individual cell.

Any cell can have its contents centered by using the align attribute, and can have blank space surround its contents using the **cellpadding** attribute. Like cell spacing, padding is accomplished by using pixels to enlarge the cell more than usual. The size of

CODE: a - (Centered) Double Red Line Border
<table border="1" bordercolor="red" align="center">
Cell has red border with default 2 pixel cellspacing

CODE: b - 10 pixel Double Red Line Border
The same coding as above with cellspacing="10":
<table border="1" bordercolor="red" align="center" cellspacing="10">
Cell with hollow, 10 pixel wide, red border

CODE: c - Borders with Inline style (dotted, 10px, red)
<table style="border:dotted red 10" align="center">
Using style coding to change the border type,
Color, and border thickness
Cell with a 10 pixel wide red dotted border

CODE: d - bgcolor="red"
<table style="border:dotted red 10" align="center" bgcolor="red">
The same coding as above is used here,
except that the cell background color is red
Text on red background in a red dotted border cell

CODE: e - bgcolor="yellow"
<table style="border:dotted 10 red" align="center" bgcolor="yellow">
Same coding as above, yellow cell background color
Text on yellow background in a red dotted border cell

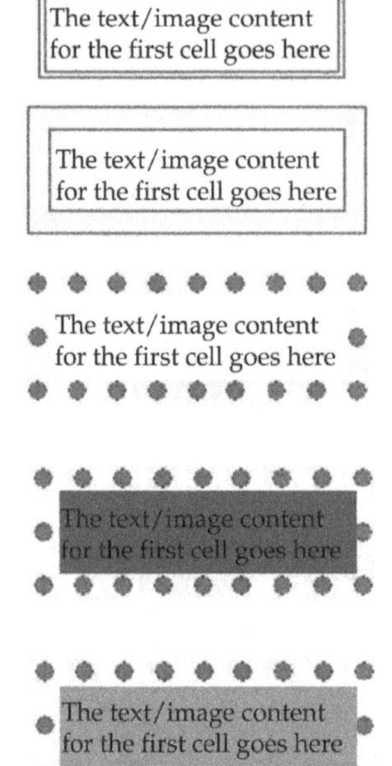

Figure 08-02. Red-Bordered Tables (**code0802.htm**)

tables and cells can also be modified using the width attribute.

Please remember that not all screens are the same size. Although you could opt to use a **width="100%"** attribute and value, and although this technique allows for scalability of the table width regardless of the monitor's screen pixel width, this technique does not always yield the desired cell (column) widths for a table. If you use the 640 pixel table size attribute **width="640"** and center your table on the page, the table's contents will be viewable on all screens in the same size and shape. An added benefit to limiting the table width comes when someone tries to print out the table. A width of 640 pixels is about all most printers can print on an 8.5"×11" piece of paper. However, if you are designing for a mobile device, be aware that they have considerably smaller screen sizes.

Designing a Calendar

Most libraries like to put a monthly calendar on their web pages. This begins with the simple table process described earlier. Then, build a one-week calendar. To de-

```
<table border="1">  ← open a table container
    <tr><td>        ← open the row and open a data cell
    ROW ONE <br/> CELL ONE </td>  ← Insert content, close the first data cell
    <td>            ← open a second data cell
    ROW ONE <br/> CELL TWO </td>  ← Insert content, close the second data cell
    </tr>           ← close the row
</table>            ← close the table
```

Figure 08-03. Basic Table Construction Syntax

sign anything larger than a one-week calendar takes several pages of code, and you may not wish to spend the time this takes. You will also need to use other core table elements, captions and table headings, so these will be shown in the next section. Starting with a one-week calendar, note that this is nothing more than a one row, seven cell table with two more rows if you add day name and headings.

A monthly calendar is a table that has six or seven rows of seven cells each. In Chapter 9 we will see that it can be easier to construct a full-year calendar using **form** elements, but for now, we'll keep the calendars simple. Don't forget that backgrounds, text styles, and borders can have whatever style scheme you can design to accent each cell (date), and that both graphics and hyperlinking can be accomplished inside of individual cells.

Figure 08-05 shows a basic design for a one-row, seven-cell table. In the next section, you'll add a second table heading row and a caption to it.

CODE: **a. Two Side by Side Cells** **<table border="1"><tr>** **<td>** ROW ONE ** ** CELL ONE **</td>** **<td>** ROW ONE ** ** CELL TWO **</td>** **</tr> </table>**	ROW ONE CELL ONE | ROW ONE CELL TWO
CODE: **b. Two Cells One on Top of the Other** **<table border="1"><tr>** **<td>** ROW ONE ** ** CELL ONE **</td>** **</tr> <tr>** **<td>** ROW TWO ** ** CELL ONE **</td>** **</tr> </table>**	ROW ONE CELL ONE ROW TWO CELL ONE
CODE: **c. Four-cell Table (Two by Two)** **<table border="1"><tr>** **<td>** ROW ONE ** ** CELL ONE **</td>** **<td>** ROW ONE ** ** CELL TWO **</td>** **</tr> <tr>** **<td>** ROW TWO ** ** CELL ONE **</td>** **<td>** ROW TWO ** ** CELL TWO **</td>** **</tr> </table>**	ROW ONE CELL ONE | ROW ONE CELL TWO ROW TWO CELL ONE | ROW TWO CELL TWO

Figure 08-04. Two-Cell and Four-Cell Tables (**code0804.htm**)

> Good to Know: One thing to remember is unless you use style sheets to define a special style for the **table, tr,** or **td** elements, or to create classes for them, cells *do not* inherit properties from each other. A cell colored with a red background and green text, when closed, does not pass these styles on to the next cell in its row. For this reason web designers use the powerful CSS techniques to stylize their tables.

> Good to Know: Good practice suggests that web page tables not normally exceed 640 pixels in width so that they will fit on your patron's screen regardless of their monitor type. Two other factors that need to be considered are **screen resolution** (size of the display) and **color quality** (number of bits per pixel—often called color depth).

Adding Table Captions and Headings

To label the one-row, seven-cell structure of Figure 08-05 as a calendar, identification is needed for the month and year for the week. Or you might need to add a title to the table noting that the events are repeated weekly. To do this, the **caption** element creates a caption or title for our table. It is placed inside the **table** element, after the

CODE: Simple One Row, Seven Cell Table

```
<table border="1"><tr>
<td> ROW ONE <br /> CELL ONE </td> <td> ROW ONE <br /> CELL TWO </td>
<td> ROW ONE <br /> CELL THREE </td> <td> ROW ONE <br /> CELL FOUR </td>
<td> ROW ONE <br /> CELL FIVE </td> <td> ROW ONE <br /> CELL SIX </td>
<td> ROW ONE <br /> CELL SEVEN </td>
</tr> </table>
```

ROW ONE CELL ONE	ROW ONE CELL TWO	ROW ONE CELL THREE	ROW ONE CELL FOUR	ROW ONE CELL FIVE	ROW ONE CELL SIX	ROW ONE CELL SEVEN

Figure 08-05. Simple One-Row, Seven-Cell Table (**code0805.htm**)

optional table body element **tbody** and before the first row element **tr.** When your table is displayed in the browser, the **caption** will be centered in its own row. Use the **align** attribute with the **caption** to specify its position. Without using an alignment attribute or using **align="top"** (the default) will have the caption appear above the table like a title. Using **align="bottom"** the caption will display like a photo caption, below the table. As with most table elements, you must surround the **caption** with opening and closing tags such that it will extend across the whole table. The **caption** can use a variety of elements and attributes, and contain hyperlinks. For your example, inside the opening **table** tag use:

```
<caption>
    <font size="+2" color="blue"><b>
    Children's Room Weekly Activities</b></font>
</caption>
```

As you can see in Figure 08-06, the caption does not have any default font style change nor any border. To add day headings to your simple calendar table to identify the days of the week, the table heading element **th** is used inside of the **table** element, before the first row element **tr.** This defines the table's header information. Similar to the **tr** and **td** elements, **th** allows for background and border styling as well as hyperlinking.

The table heading element **th,** unlike the caption, has a border around each of its heading cells like a regular **td** cell within a row. Like the table descriptor, the table heading tags must be contained inside of a table row and surrounded by **tr** tags. Unlike the normal table cell **td,** the table heading element **th** displays its heading information in a bold type face.

With captions and headings included, the code of Figure 08-05 becomes a one-week calendar template. You should be capable of using copy and paste to extract the table elements from the file **code0805.htm** and place it into your own web page without too much difficulty. Merely substitute your text and images in each cell, as appropriate.

This calendar will be used as the basis for a scheduling page for the sample Red Rose Library Children's Room shown in Figure 08-07. The seven head cell names

```
CODE: Simple One Row, Seven Cell Table
<table border="1">
<caption> Title Caption Goes Here </caption>
<th> HEAD ONE </th>  <th> HEAD TWO </th>
<th> HEAD THREE </th>  <th> HEAD FOUR </th>
<th> HEAD FIVE </th>  <th> HEAD SIX </th>
<th> HEAD SEVEN </th>
<tr>
<td> ROW ONE <br /> CELL ONE </td>  <td> ROW ONE <br /> CELL TWO </td>
<td> ROW ONE <br /> CELL THREE </td>  <td> ROW ONE <br /> CELL FOUR </td>
<td> ROW ONE <br /> CELL FIVE </td> <td> ROW ONE <br /> CELL SIX </td>
<td> ROW ONE <br /> CELL SEVEN </td>
</tr> </table>
```

Title Caption Goes Here

HEAD ONE	HEAD TWO	HEAD THREE	HEAD FOUR	HEAD FIVE	HEAD SIX	HEAD SEVEN
ROW ONE CELL ONE	ROW ONE CELL TWO	ROW ONE CELL THREE	ROW ONE CELL FOUR	ROW ONE CELL FIVE	ROW ONE CELL SIX	ROW ONE CELL SEVEN

Figure 08-06. Simple One-Week Calendar Table (**code0806.htm**)

have been replaced with the names of the days of the week. This can be extended to a monthly calendar by merely repeating the number of rows to account for the days in the month and indicating the date in each cell.

A monthly calendar table for the month of September 2014 is demonstrated in Figure 08-08.

Spanning Table Rows and Columns

Perhaps the two most interesting table row and column attributes are **rowspan** and **colspan.** As they imply, if you would like to have a particular table cell to be two rows high or "span two rows," use the **rowspan="2"** attribute. To use more than one column for a particular display of information, perhaps a four-day event spanning four cells, the tag **<td colspan="4">** can be used. The table in Figure 08-08 looks like a two-row table with one three-column row on top of a two-column row. The code file (**code0809.htm**) shows rows styled using the **colspan** attribute as displayed in Figure 08-09.

Each row in this figure is actually four columns

Children's Room WeeklyActivities

Sunday	Monday	Tuesday	Wednesday	Thursday	Friday	Saturday
Time: Event: Contact:	ROW ONE CELL TWO	ROW ONE CELL THREE		ROW ONE CELL FIVE	ROW ONE CELL SIX	ROW ONE CELL SEVEN

Figure 08-07. One-Week Children's Room Activity Calendar (**code0807.htm**)

September 2014						
Sunday	Monday	Tuesday	Wednesday	Thursday	Friday	Saturday
	1	2	3	4	5	6
7	8	9	10	11	12	13
14	15	16	17	18	19	20
21	22	23	24	25	26	27
28	29	30				

Figure 08-08. Simple Calendar for September 2014 (**code0808.htm**)

wide with the first row columns coded **<td>, <td colspan="2">** and **<td>** to yield four columns of data in the row, and with the second row coded **<td colspan="2">** and **<td colspan="2">** to yield four columns of data in that row, give the effect of three columns on top of two columns. The use of advanced table techniques, including spanning, can be seen in Figure 08-10's 12 row by 19-column periodical table of the elements from the website (used by permission) at:

http://www.webelements.com

In addition to the coloring and table cell sizing codes, if you go online to this periodic table website you'll find that most table cells hyperlink to individual page descriptions. This is just one example of the level of complexity that you can design in a table display. As these are sites all about chemistry it is not unexpected that the **sub** (subscript) element is used extensively here to write chemical reactions. Water, for example, is written as **H2O** and rendered H2O.

Once content is in table rows and columns it can be aligned horizontally using the **align** attribute with the values **left, right,** or **center;** or vertically using the **valign** attribute with the values **top, middle, bottom,** or **baseline.**

a. Three Columns on top of Two Columns *An optical illusion!*		
Row One, Cell One	Row One, Cell Two	Row One, Cell Three
Row Two, Cell One	Row Two, Cell Two	

b. Three Columns on Two Columns on Four Columns *What's behind the 'trick'*			
Row One, Cell One Uses <td>	Row One, Cell Two Uses <td colspan="2">		Row One, Cell Three Uses <td>
Row Two, Cell One Uses <td colspan="2">		Row Two, Cell Two Uses <td colspan="2">	
Row Three, Cell One Uses <td>	Row Three, Cell Two Uses <td>	Row Three, Cell Three Uses <td>	Row Three, Cell Four Uses <td>

Figure 08-09. Using **colspan** for Odd and Even Column Rows (**code0809.htm**)

Applying Tables to Red Rose Library Web Pages

To put your knowledge of creating a table look, you will create a simple line drawing map of the local area, such as **img007.gif.** You will place it on a web page with some location information for patrons to use as in Figure 08-11.

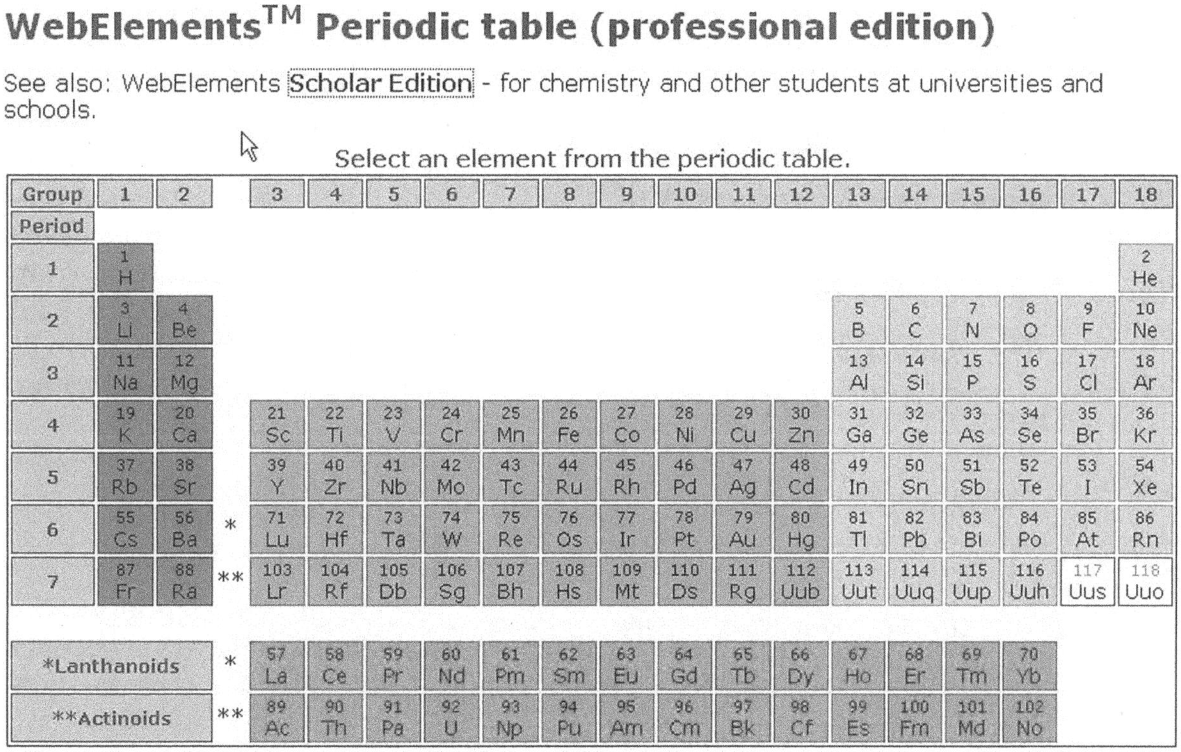

WebElements™ Periodic table (professional edition)

See also: WebElements Scholar Edition - for chemistry and other students at universities and schools.

Select an element from the periodic table.

Group	1	2		3	4	5	6	7	8	9	10	11	12	13	14	15	16	17	18
Period																			
1	1 H																		2 He
2	3 Li	4 Be												5 B	6 C	7 N	8 O	9 F	10 Ne
3	11 Na	12 Mg												13 Al	14 Si	15 P	16 S	17 Cl	18 Ar
4	19 K	20 Ca		21 Sc	22 Ti	23 V	24 Cr	25 Mn	26 Fe	27 Co	28 Ni	29 Cu	30 Zn	31 Ga	32 Ge	33 As	34 Se	35 Br	36 Kr
5	37 Rb	38 Sr		39 Y	40 Zr	41 Nb	42 Mo	43 Tc	44 Ru	45 Rh	46 Pd	47 Ag	48 Cd	49 In	50 Sn	51 Sb	52 Te	53 I	54 Xe
6	55 Cs	56 Ba	*	71 Lu	72 Hf	73 Ta	74 W	75 Re	76 Os	77 Ir	78 Pt	79 Au	80 Hg	81 Tl	82 Pb	83 Bi	84 Po	85 At	86 Rn
7	87 Fr	88 Ra	**	103 Lr	104 Rf	105 Db	106 Sg	107 Bh	108 Hs	109 Mt	110 Ds	111 Rg	112 Uub	113 Uut	114 Uuq	115 Uup	116 Uuh	117 Uus	118 Uuo
*Lanthanoids			*	57 La	58 Ce	59 Pr	60 Nd	61 Pm	62 Sm	63 Eu	64 Gd	65 Tb	66 Dy	67 Ho	68 Er	69 Tm	70 Yb		
**Actinoids			**	89 Ac	90 Th	91 Pa	92 U	93 Np	94 Pu	95 Am	96 Cm	97 Bk	98 Cf	99 Es	100 Fm	101 Md	102 No		

Figure 08-10. Web Page Periodical Table (*Source:* WebElements.com)

The information is all there, but using table elements you can create the more elegant look of Figure 08-12 where all the borders are turned on to see what spacing options are available. Note the wide 10 pixel border around the first table (**cellpadding="10"**) and the fact the widths of the two tables are different.

As shown in Figure 08-13, when you remove all borders and spice the page up with the Red Rose Library Logo (**img008.jpg**), the page becomes the **where.htm** file that we will use on the website.

Earlier you created a single row, seven-column (one-week) calendar display to illustrate your Children's Room schedule of activities in Figure 08-07. When you create a multiple row, double-column, table construction, you can create the one-day event calendar. The first column defines the time of day and the second column tells the activity scheduled. On a very actively updated website this could be used for a daily activity page. In a more realistic situation, it could be the program for a one-day workshop as seen in Figure 08-14.

Clearly, adding additional row and column elements can yield any kind of table for your library's particular needs. For your young adult patrons, for example, you might want to prepare a web page that can be used as a school planner with several rows, a time column, and seven blank columns as in Figure 08-15.

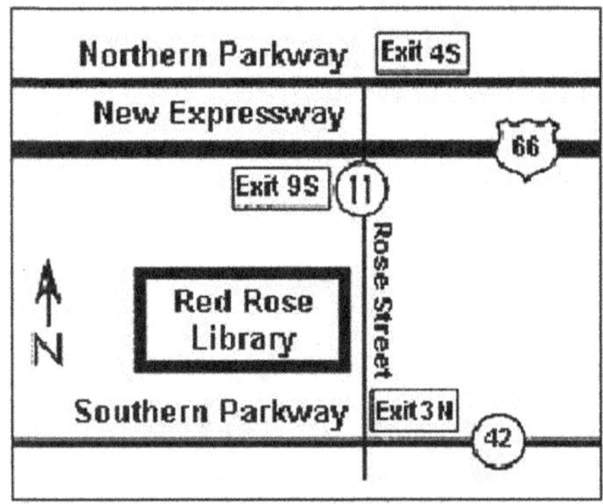

Figure 08-11 Basic Directions Page (**code0811.htm**)

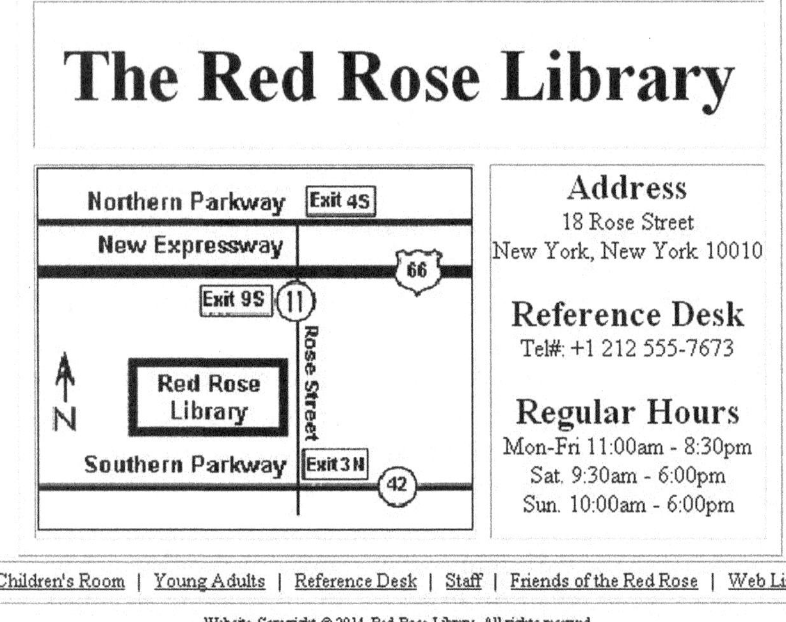

Figure 08-12 Table Directions Page (**code0812.htm**)

In fact, for the Young Adult area, you might want to link to the WebElement's site for student access to the periodic table we saw in Figure 08-10 for their chemistry homework, or even request permission to "mirror" (copy) the table and other files for the periodic table onto your local server.

Using Cascading Style Sheets to Create Tables

If you look inside the code files you will see that to create the calendar type pages discussed earlier we had to repeat **width** and other attributes in each **tr**, **th**, or **td** opening tag. This is quite tedious and adds lots of characters to your file.

You can use CSS, internal or external, to add interesting things to your tables as they have done for other HTML elements as well as to reduce the repetitive style changes in table elements. Additionally, as tables are deprecated, style sheets can be used to create division classes (**div.something**) to control text and image content in a *non-table* element environment. The **div** element classes can be created with style sheets for containers, headers, columns, and footers to match the **table, th, tr,** and **td** elements seen earlier in this chapter.

Style Sheet Table Element Equivalents

```
/* table equivalent (1 pixel solid blue border) */
div.container
  { width:100%; margin:0px; border:1px solid blue; line-height:100%; }
/* table header equivalent (blue colored background) */
div.header
  { color:white; background-color:blue; text-align:center; padding:10px; }
/* table data equivalent (red left side border, 200 pixel margin) */
div.column
  { margin-left:200px; border-left:1px solid red; padding:10px; }
/* table footer equivalent (blue colored background) */
div.footer
  {color:white; background-color:blue; text-align:center; text-size:20px; padding:
5px;}
/* Other common style definitions */
div.left
  { float:left; width:195px; margin:0; padding:10px; }
h1.header
  { padding:0; margin:0; }
a:link, a:alink, a:vlink
  { text-decoration:none; color:red; }
```

These style definitions can be used to construct the table examples of Figures 08–03, 08–05, and 08–06. The internal style coding should be set for the column margins in division class statements as shown earlier rather than by merely adding **tr** and **td** table elements. Using these stylings you can construct the borderless, three row by two column table, as shown in Figure 08-16.

Using these CSS **table** elements, you have all that is needed to stack table rows and add table columns to create a table. The first step in designing a CSS table is to decide on the actual width of each cell in the table and what styling is needed in your design. A maximum screen width of 640 pixels will be used. Because room is needed for

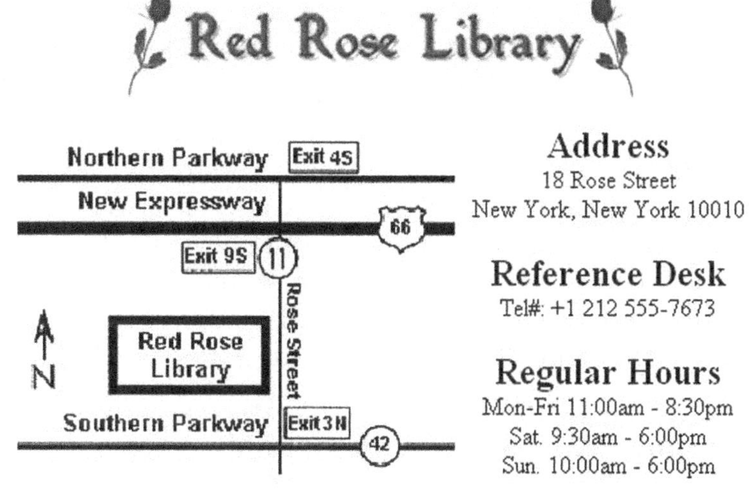

Figure 08-13 Table Directions Page without Border (**code0813.htm=where .htm**)

One Day Workshop

Time	Activity
8:00 - 8:45 am	Welcome and Opening Session
8:45 - 10:15 am	Session 1
10:15 - 10:30 am	Coffee Break
10:30 - 12:00 noon	Session 2
12:00 - 1:00 pm	LUNCH
1:00 - 2:30 pm	Session 3
2:30 - 4:00 pm	Session 4
4:00 - 4:15 pm	Coffee Break
4:15 - 5:45 pm	Session 5
5:45 - 6:00 pm	Closing Ceremony

Figure 08-14. One-Day Calendar Page (**code0814.htm=workshop.htm**)

at least seven columns for a one-week table, you must design each cell to be 90 pixels wide for an overall 630 pixel table width. Your 90 pixel columns will start at 0, 90, 180, 270, 360, 450, and 540. The cells would have to be smaller if you want padding around your content or needed thicker cell borders.

If you want to have a border around the whole table, you can add a 1 pixel, red-colored, border to the left of every cell, except your first cell, and a gray border at the bottom of every cell in all rows except your last row. A borderless design might include column definitions such as:

div.col2 { margin-left:90px; padding:5px; }

Alternatively a fully bordered design could look like:

div.col2

{ margin-left:90px; margin-top:5px; margin-bottom:5px;
border-left:1px solid red; border-bottom:1px solid gray; padding:5px; }

Constructing this style sheet "shell" you need only to add content to the **div** classes to create one-week or one-month table displays without using any **table** elements.

Weekly Planner

Time	Monday	Tuesday	Wednesday	Thursday	Friday	Saturday	Sunday
8:00 - 8:45 am							
8:45 - 10:15 am							
10:15 - 10:30 am							
10:30 - 12:00noon							
12:00 - 1:00 pm							
1:00 - 2:30 pm							
2:30 - 4:00 pm							
4:00 - 4:15 pm							
4:15 - 5:45 pm							
5:45 - 6:00 pm							

Figure 08-15. Weekly School Program Planner (**code0815.htm=program.htm**)

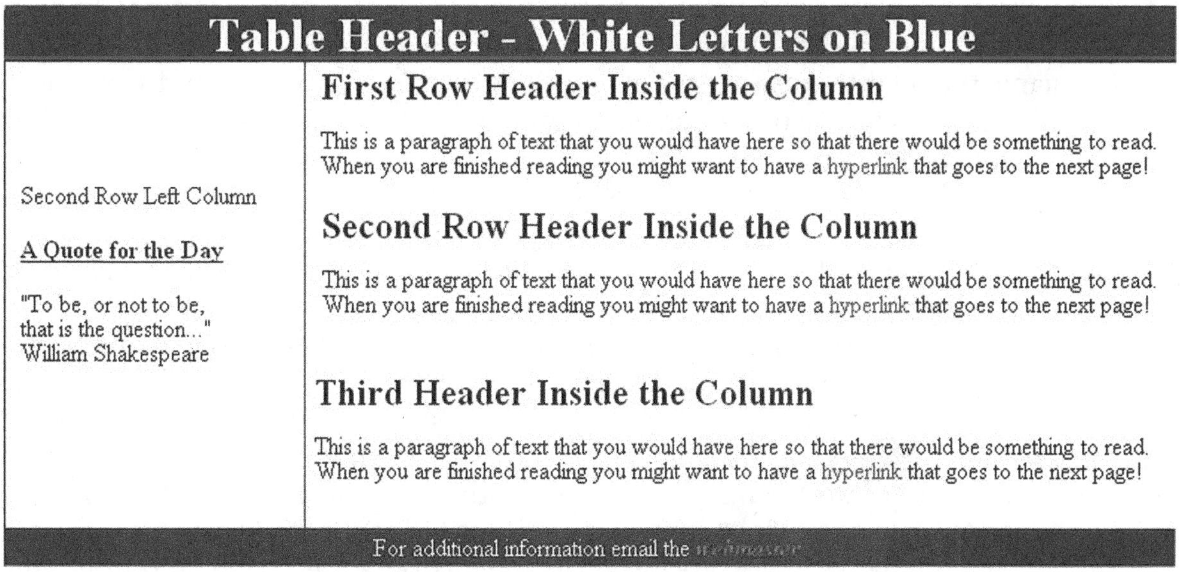

Table Header - White Letters on Blue

Second Row Left Column

A Quote for the Day

"To be, or not to be,
that is the question..."
William Shakespeare

First Row Header Inside the Column

This is a paragraph of text that you would have here so that there would be something to read. When you are finished reading you might want to have a hyperlink that goes to the next page!

Second Row Header Inside the Column

This is a paragraph of text that you would have here so that there would be something to read. When you are finished reading you might want to have a hyperlink that goes to the next page!

Third Header Inside the Column

This is a paragraph of text that you would have here so that there would be something to read. When you are finished reading you might want to have a hyperlink that goes to the next page!

For additional information email the webmaster

Figure 08-16. Style Sheet Table Based on W3 Example (**code0816.htm**)

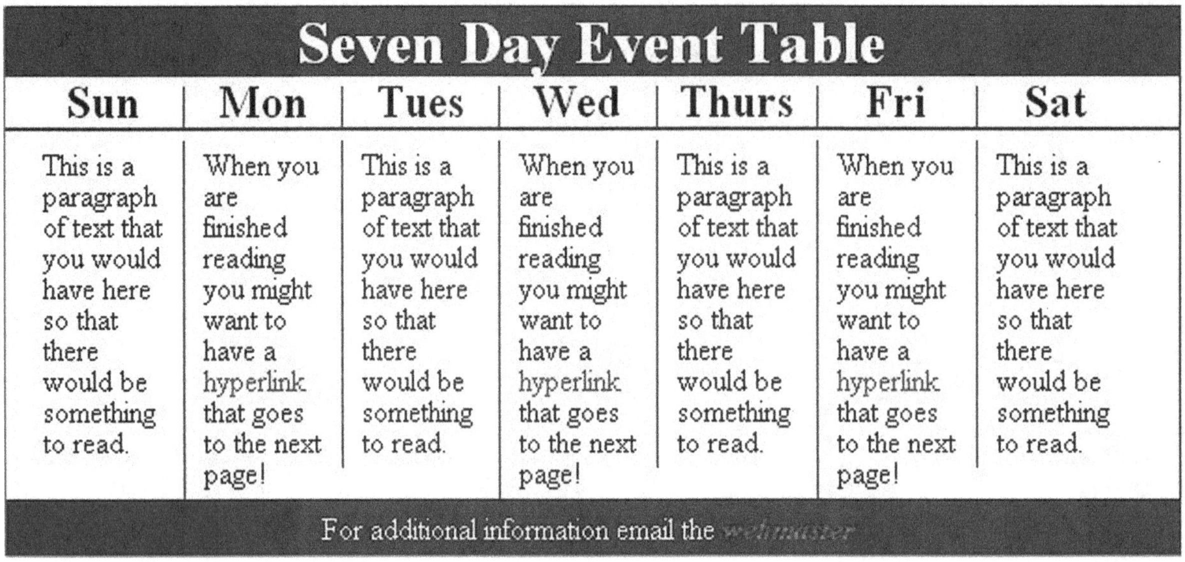

Seven Day Event Table						
Sun	**Mon**	**Tues**	**Wed**	**Thurs**	**Fri**	**Sat**
This is a paragraph of text that you would have here so that there would be something to read.	When you are finished reading you might want to have a hyperlink that goes to the next page!	This is a paragraph of text that you would have here so that there would be something to read.	When you are finished reading you might want to have a hyperlink that goes to the next page!	This is a paragraph of text that you would have here so that there would be something to read.	When you are finished reading you might want to have a hyperlink that goes to the next page!	This is a paragraph of text that you would have here so that there would be something to read.
For additional information email the webmaster						

Figure 08-17. Seven-Column CSS Table (**code0817.htm**)

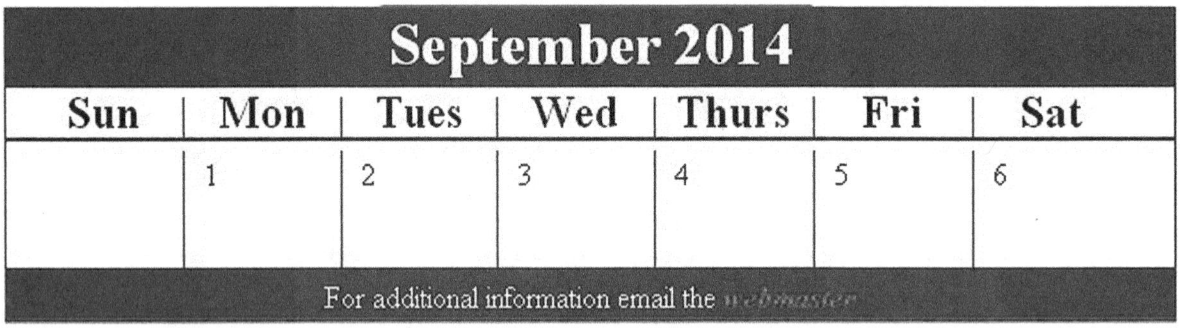

September 2014						
Sun	**Mon**	**Tues**	**Wed**	**Thurs**	**Fri**	**Sat**
	1	2	3	4	5	6
For additional information email the webmaster						

Figure 08-18. CSS One-Week Table Template (**code0818.htm**)

Although these style sheet definition structures could be defined internally on a given page, it is more likely that you would have them as an external style sheet file. You will name them **tables.css** for ease of use all over your website. Extend style sheet principles here to create a two-row, seven-column one-week template as was found in Figure 08-06 and is demonstrated as Figure 08-17.

In much the same way, Figure 08-18 shows a generic one-week calendar using style sheets concepts.

Figure 08-19 extends the one-week table style sheet concept into the design of a one-month calendar.

Continuing with these concepts, any size or shape table can be generated on a web page using style sheets without using any **table** elements.

Tables, either written with the now-deprecated native HTML table elements, or constructed using CSS techniques, give a rigid structure to your web pages. This structure can be used to create tabular displays, or with their borders turned off, mimic word-processed documents. The conclusion of this chapter is that CSS concepts can be used to display simulated word-processed documents on a web page, and although

September 2014						
Sun	**Mon**	**Tues**	**Wed**	**Thurs**	**Fri**	**Sat**
	1	2	3	4	5	6
7	8	9	10	11	12	13
14	15	16	17	18	19	20
21	22	23	24	25	26	27
28	29	30				
For additional information email the webmaster						

Figure 08-19. CSS One-Month Table Template (**code0819.htm**)

they require more effort to do so, they are probably worth it if your library uses similar page structures throughout its website.

What's Next?

In Chapter 9 HTML **form** elements will be added to your répertoire enhancing the way your web pages look, as well as the way your patrons can interact with your web pages.

URL Cited

The Periodic Table of the Elements

http://www.webelements.com

Chapter 8 Review Exercises

Chapter 8 Multiple-Choice Questions

1. The three basic table elements are **table, tr,** and:

   a) **tl** b) **td** c) **tc** d) **cell**

2. Adding the lines around a table requires setting the ___ attribute equal to "1."

   a) line b) edge c) color d) border

3. The default border for a table is:

   a) 1 pixel b) none c) 5 pixels d) gray

4. The default border color for a table is:

   a) none b) red c) black d) gray

5. The **th** element:

   a) is required b) cannot be used with **captions**

   c) is used only within **tr** d) is an empty element

Chapter 8 Design and Discussion Questions

1. Write the HTML code to create a simple monthly calendar for your library website.
2. When should you consider using an image rather than text in a table? Give an example for your library.
3. Discuss reasons why you might decide to use a table, without borders, on your web page.
4. Describe how you can avoid using **style** attributes in the opening tag of your table elements.
5. Briefly discuss the nesting possibilities of table structures.

9

Forms for Patron Interactivity

Not every library needs to use forms on its website. You may not feel you want to create forms or don't need the forms functionality. If you should want to use forms, you might have the option of leaving forms page design to the computer professionals in your community. This chapter will review some simple techniques with which you can create forms and use them.

What Uses Might Your Library Have for Forms?

They might include online requests to reserve a book a patron found on your online public access catalog (OPAC) or for an interlibrary book loan, an "Ask a Librarian" reference service, or to register to attend a library event. After your patrons fill out the online form, they click on a submit button that will send forms data to an e-mail address or database file on a web server. Someone in the library needs to regularly review or retrieve these requests or your patrons will stop making them!

Forms can be used for interrogating your OPAC through your integrated library system software and server, but this interface, too, is best left to computer professionals.

> **Good to Know:** Be aware that not all Internet Service Provider (ISP) web servers will accommodate forms usage. Forms servers typically require special software and hardware configurations. In addition, you may not personally possess the programming ability or technology to create complex forms. There are, however, several vendors that allow you to use their servers and software to manage simple forms processing.

Up until now everything displayed in your browser window was assembled with your browser obtaining additional image files for display but without user input, other than hyperlinking to other web pages or websites. The **form** element creates a container for data input from your patron. Forms can contain buttons (boxes [squares], radios [circles] and text), drop-down lists, and text input fields. In most cases your patron's browser is used solely to collect information for the form which sends this data to a program residing on a web server for further processing. Some simple forms depend on the use of special software programming that may not require software to be installed on your web server.

Creating Web Forms

In this section we'll begin our design and building of a form. Forms and **form** elements can be used on your web page in much the same way as images. Forms can be the only coding on a page, they can exist within blocks of text, or in tables, or they can be surrounded by hyperlinks. The section in your HTML document that deals with each forms processing creates a form container that is between the opening and closing **form** element tags. Much like we can have several lists or tables on a web page, there can be several form sections on a web page, each forwarding the data to a specific Common Gateway Interface (CGI) software program. All active forms contain within them hidden variable names and values that must match the variables in the computer script or program that processes the information your patron's browser sends for processing.

Even if you do not need to use interactive forms, there are several neat displays that form-type button graphic elements to use to create on our web pages. In this chapter you will see how to use **form** elements to create simple forms, use online vendor products to create small survey forms, and use button graphics to create a simple calendar!

The form Element

Even if you do not need to use interactive forms, there are several neat displays that form-type. The various **form** elements and their attributes are listed next, although it is well beyond the scope of this text to cover all aspects of forms creation and usage:

form—Fill-In Forms
Attributes: **method, action, enctype, name**
Can contain: **input, select, textarea, hn, p, hr, dir, dl, menu, ol, ul, address**
Can be inside: **blockquote, body, dd, li, td**
input—Form Field Type
Attributes: **type, name, size, maxlength, value, align, checked, src**
Can be inside: **form, any nonempty element**
textarea—Text Block Input
Attributes: **rows, cols, name**
Can contain: **characters only** Can be inside: **form**
select—Multiple Options
Attributes: **size, multiple, name**
Can contain: **option** Can be inside: **form**
option—Options for select Element
Attributes: **value, selected**
Can contain: **characters only**
Can be inside: **select**

Check box, radio, and text buttons

CODE a: Square 'Check Box' Buttons	
<input type="checkbox" />	☐
<input type="checkbox" name="var1" value="One" />One **<input type="checkbox" name="var1" value="Two" checked />**Two **<input type="checkbox" name="var1" value="Three" />**Three **<input type="checkbox" name="var1" value="Four" />**Four	☐ One ☑ Two ☐ Three ☐ Four
CODE b: Round 'Radio' Buttons	
<input type="radio" />	○
<input type="radio" name="var2" value="One" />One **<input type="radio" name="var2" value="Two" />**Two **<input type="radio" name="var2" value="Three" checked />**Three **<input type="radio" name="var2" value="Four" />**Four	○ One ○ Two ◉ Three ○ Four
CODE c: Text 'Button' Buttons	
<input type="button" />	[ ]
<input type="button" value="18" />	[18]
<input type="button" value="Red Rose Library" />	[Red Rose Library]

Figure 09-01. Check Box, Radio, and Text Buttons (**code0901.htm**)

The input Element

The **input** element is an empty element whose **field-type** attributes specify the type of form field that your patron will see and be able to interact with. The basic code to create a form button is:

<input type="type1" name="name1" value="value1" />

Where the **type** values for **type1** can be **checkbox** (square), **radio** (circle), **text, password, hidden, image, submit,** or **reset,** the **name** attribute values for **name1** must be consistent with those variables described in the web server's software form-processing program so that the **value** can be properly used to process your patron data. Figure 09-01 shows these field-types as graphic elements, without the **form** element surrounding them.

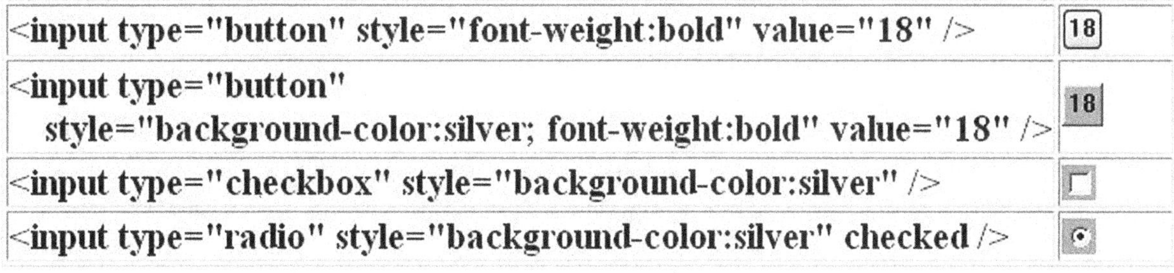

<input type="button" style="font-weight:bold" value="18" />	[18]
<input type="button" style="background-color:silver; font-weight:bold" value="18" />	[18]
<input type="checkbox" style="background-color:silver" />	☐
<input type="radio" style="background-color:silver" checked />	◉

Figure 09-02. Adding Style to Form Buttons (**code0902.htm**)

By now you already know that the default element styles are not always what we need for our web pages. Figure 09-02 shows the result of adding cascading style sheet (CSS) to enhance the look of your buttons.

```
<select name="var3">
<option value="0" selected>
Please make your Selection </option>
<option value="1"> Option One </option>
<option value="2"> Option Two </option>
<option value="3"> Option Three </option>
<option value="4"> Option Four </option>
<option value="5"> Option Five </option>
</select>
```

Please make your Selection
Please make your Selection
Option One
Option Two
Option Three
Option Four
Option Five

Figure 09-03. Adding Drop-Down (**select**) Lists to Your Form (**code0903.htm**)

The select Element

The **select** element can be used to create a menu or drop-down list of items from which your patron can choose. As with all forms elements, the **select**'s variable information used by the form-processing script when it is submitted to the server, is contained in its **name="variablename"** attribute. Other **select** attributes determine the way your choices are displayed. The **size="n"** attribute specifies the length of the list or menu in displayed lines. The default value for the "exposed" list is **size="1"** and most users have this topmost entry as a note that there is a selection possible as shown in Figure 09-03.

The **value** attribute indicates the value to be shown on the form and sent for processing if the particular **option** is selected. In the example, we have given the options a value matching its option number. An **option** may be pre-selected for display on the form by adding the optional **selected** attribute. The **option selected** attribute specifies which entry will be the visible or default selection on the list. Your server's processing program can be designed to check for any **value="0"** selections and respond to a **submit** command with an error message that states all form fields have to be selected, and so on. Be sure to add the closing **</option>** tags, which are optional in HTML but required in XML, for upward compatibility of your web form. I suspect many of you have already figured that this type of selection technique could be used for surveys. Later in this chapter you'll see how to use a line of software code to have the selection of a variable from a drop-down list just like this one to cause your patron to go to another web page or even a website.

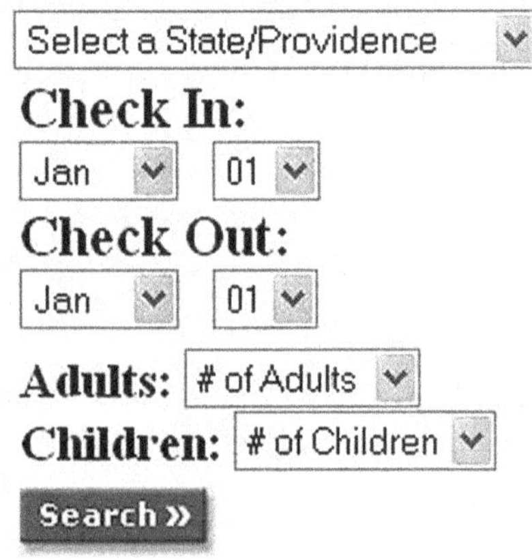

Figure 09-04. Drop-Down Form for Hotel Reservations (**code0904.htm**)

The **select** element is widely used in forms that have address cities and states, days, dates, and years, or other common pre-selectable responses where multiple choices from a set of entries are appropriate. Figure 09-04 shows a portion of a typical online hotel reservation form.

If used in a book search, the title, author, or subject might be selectable andwhen processed, a new drop-down list that includes the various authors or a thesaurus of search terms might be forwarded to the patron. Sometimes you want to allow more than one response for a given question, in that case, the optional **multiple** attribute in the select command to specify that the user can select one or more items from the drop-down list.

The textarea Element

The **textarea** element is a text block input element that extends the **input** element's **text field-type** to allow the creation of multi-line text input fields. It uses three required attributes to identify and provide the size of the text area. The text area's variable information, which is used by form-processing script when it is submitted to the server, is contained in its **name="variablename"** attribute and the **rows="n"** and **cols= "m"** attributes specify the height and the width of the text area in characters as shown in Figure 09-05.

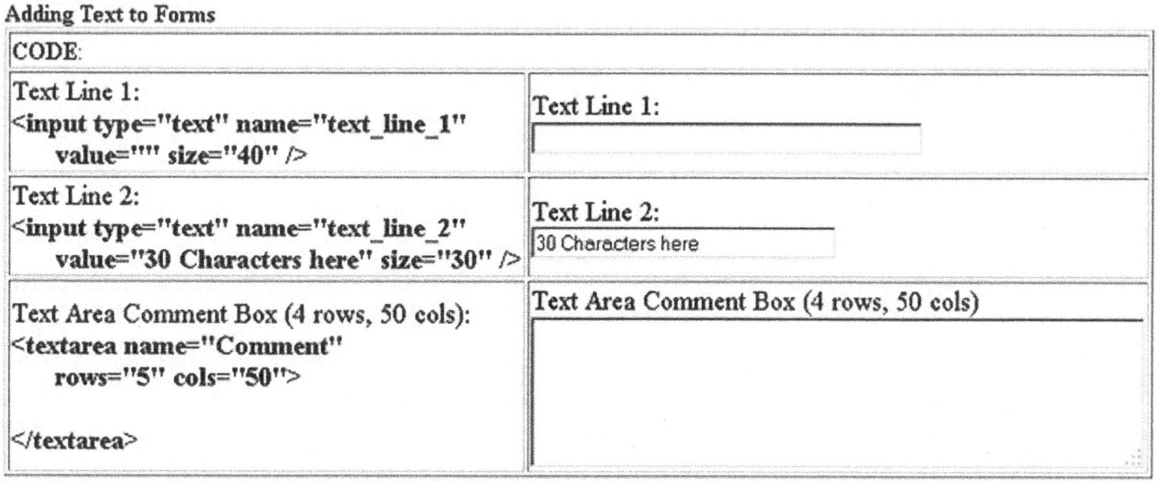

Adding Text to Forms

CODE:	
Text Line 1: **<input type="text" name="text_line_1" value="" size="40" />**	Text Line 1:
Text Line 2: **<input type="text" name="text_line_2" value="30 Characters here" size="30" />**	Text Line 2: 30 Characters here
Text Area Comment Box (4 rows, 50 cols): **<textarea name="Comment" rows="5" cols="50">** **</textarea>**	Text Area Comment Box (4 rows, 50 cols)

Figure 09-05. Adding Text to Your Form (**code0905.htm**)

Adding Color to a textarea Box Form

You can add **color** to the **background** and text of a **textarea** box. Changing the default colors to suit your needs or match your web page colors is a technique sure to spice up your **textarea** boxes.

Figure 09-06 shows the code for a colored **textarea** box with colored text included as a default.

You can also color the scrollbar in just your **textarea** box. If you have a scrollbar on your web page, this will not affect that scrollbar, only the scrollbar in the **textarea** box. CSS codes and can add lot to your web pages. You can also add this colored scrollbar to the **textarea** box with just the colored background. Be sure to close the **textarea** element; otherwise all the remainder of your web page will end up in your **textarea** box as scrollable content. Figure 09-07 shows the code you can use to stylize a **textarea** box with a red colored background, black text, and a multicolored text area scrollbar.

Action Button Types

When used with the attribute **type="submit"** (or **type="reset"),** the **input** element can become an action button that will either submit the data on your form to your e-mail or server for processing, or reset the form back to its defaults (if an error is made).

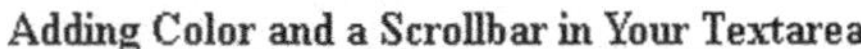
Adding Color and a Scrollbar in Your Textarea

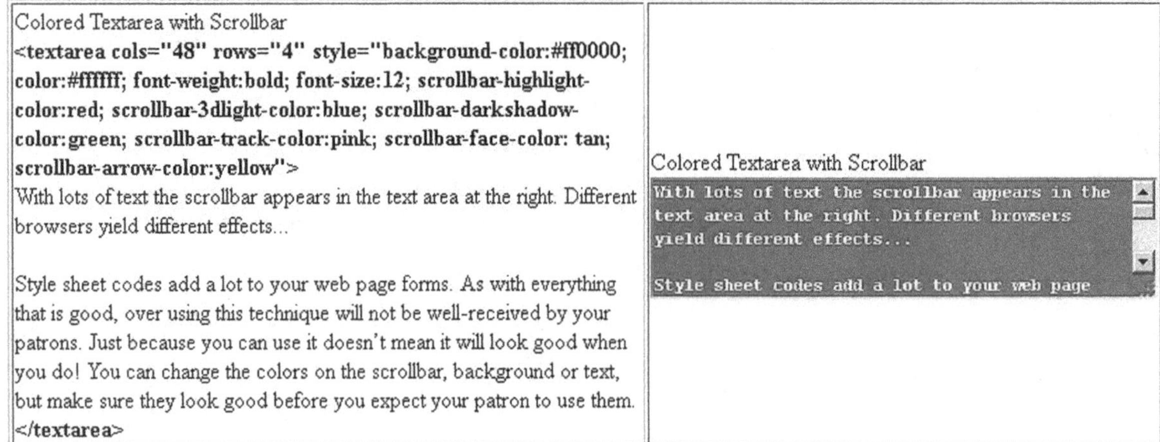
Colored Textarea with Scrollbar
<textarea cols="48" rows="4" style="background-color:#ff0000; color:#ffffff; font-weight:bold; font-size:12; scrollbar-highlight-color:red; scrollbar-3dlight-color:blue; scrollbar-darkshadow-color:green; scrollbar-track-color:pink; scrollbar-face-color: tan; scrollbar-arrow-color:yellow">
With lots of text the scrollbar appears in the text area at the right. Different browsers yield different effects...

Style sheet codes add a lot to your web page forms. As with everything that is good, over using this technique will not be well-received by your patrons. Just because you can use it doesn't mean it will look good when you do! You can change the colors on the scrollbar, background or text, but make sure they look good before you expect your patron to use them.
</textarea>

Figure 09-06. Adding Color to the Textarea (**code0906.htm**)

Figure 09-08 shows several examples of the code needed to add action buttons inside of your form.

Like the examples shown earlier in this chapter, you can use style to create colored action buttons by adding a style attribute for **background-color** and **color** in a **submit** button which you've named **Select Me** as shown in the following code line:

<input style="background-color:#8b008b; color:#ffff00; font-weight:bold; font-size:10px;" type="submit" value="Select Me"; />

As you can see, depending on your application, **submit** and **reset** action buttons do not have to be literal; they can be labeled with any text value or colored without text.

Adding Color and a Scrollbar in Your Textarea

Colored Textarea with Scrollbar
<textarea cols="48" rows="4" style="background-color:#ff0000; color:#ffffff; font-weight:bold; font-size:12; scrollbar-highlight-color:red; scrollbar-3dlight-color:blue; scrollbar-darkshadow-color:green; scrollbar-track-color:pink; scrollbar-face-color: tan; scrollbar-arrow-color:yellow">
With lots of text the scrollbar appears in the text area at the right. Different browsers yield different effects...

Style sheet codes add a lot to your web page forms. As with everything that is good, over using this technique will not be well-received by your patrons. Just because you can use it doesn't mean it will look good when you do! You can change the colors on the scrollbar, background or text, but make sure they look good before you expect your patron to use them.
</textarea>

Colored Textarea with Scrollbar
With lots of text the scrollbar appears in the text area at the right. Different browsers yield different effects...
Style sheet codes add a lot to your web page

Figure 09-07. Adding Color to a Scrollbar in Your Textarea (**code0907.htm**)

CODE:	
<input type="reset" />	Reset
<input type="submit" />	Submit Query
<input type="submit" value="Submit" />	Submit
<input type="submit" value="Send to Red Rose Library" />	Send to Red Rose Library

Figure 09-08. Adding Action Buttons to Your Form (**code0908.htm**)

Server-Side Processing: Making Forms Work with CGI

Most forms rely on a web server to process your input. This server-side processing uses computer programs or scripts in a special **cgi-bin** directory (**cgi-bin** is the abbreviation of Common Gateway Interface binaries). CGI is a standard for interfacing your computer with information or database web servers using external or gateway programs to control data requests. The website at: **http://hoohoo.ncsa.uiuc.edu/cgi** reviews the CGI standard.

> Good to Know: Stored in the server's **cgi-bin** directory are short programs written in C/C++, Fortran, Perl, and other programming and/or scripting languages that are—you guessed it—beyond the scope of our simple text!

Forms designed in this chapter show one of the simplest of **form** applications—an e-mail response generator. But, all is not lost even if you can't program, or even if you can't access your web server's **cgi-bin!** Although without a properly working **cgi-bin** script, a form is just another "static" web page; we can get around the **cgi-bin** requirement for some simple examples using internal JavaScript, so don't skip this section if you do not have **cgi-bin** access.

How the CGI Can Work for You

If you are comfortable in any programming language there are many textbooks that can guide you step by step through "canned" CGI code for forms handling (e.g., *CGI/Perl Cookbook* by Patchett and Wright; Wiley Computer Publishing). But if you just want one or two simple forms codes, they may be available for downloading from web resources that make it possible for you to use, rather than write, processing applications like:

http://www.cgiconnection.com/
http://cgi.resourceindex.com/

The CGI Resource Index website also has links to hundreds of "hosted" CGI form applications. Several of these offer a "free" hosting service. These provide you with the tools to create an interactive form to use with their **cgi-bin** program on their server. You'll need to neither write the forms handling code nor to have your own web server set up to support CGI applications. Bear in mind that merely creating a directory on your website called cgi-bin and saving script files in that directory does not give you the ability to run scripts on your server. The server must be configured by the systems operator to have the software and server linkages that will make a cgi directory work. If the solution is using someone else's server, perhaps one of these will suit your needs:

http://www.response-o-matic.com/
http://www.surveymonkey.com/
http://www.formbuddy.com/
http://www.bfndevelopment.com/
http://freedback.com/

The script on most free sites will send the form information to you by e-mail. Embedded in your web page form code will be a link to that service's **cgi-bin** code that makes it all happen. The code line that goes to the Response-O-Matic service **cgi-bin,** for example, would look like

```
<form action="http://www.response-o-matic.com/cgi-bin/rom.pl"
method="post">
```

where the Perl script that manages your form is in the file **rom.pl** on its server. When sent to this file, your forms' information would be processed and then e-mailed to the address "hidden" in your web page coding. For example the code

```
<input type="hidden" name="your_email_address"
value="your.email@server.com">
```

will send the processed response to your e-mail address: **your.email@server.com.** Code lines using the **type="hidden"** attribute value are hidden from the web page user but must be inside of the **form** code section of your HTML document. The important thing to understand here is that you do not control the cgi-bin script. Response-O-Matic offers this free service for any individual or organization that wants to add forms to their web pages. But you don't get to play with their **cgi-bin** scripts, only to use them.

That's good as there are no copyright issues, but you should still check out their "terms of use" web page if you use their service. If you want to do any other **cgi-bin** program, you will need to find another hosting service. The downside of the service is that you will need to use their template coding to get any results, and when your patron submits a form, they will get a response from the server which, unless you pay a registration fee for the service, includes major advertising. After all, somebody has to pay for the server! Also note that you must use the same variable names (e.g., **name="your_email_address"**) in your form coding that are expected by the script; otherwise your form will not be processed properly.

Online Surveys

If you expect fewer than 100 patrons will respond to a particular survey, SurveyMonkey's resources (**http://www.surveymonkey.com**) can be used to create 10-question online surveys for free and without annoying banner ads. It has an online creation tool that is filled with options to create surveys of the following types:

Choice—One Answer: Vertical, Horizontal, and Menu
Choice—Multiple Answers: Vertical and Horizontal
Matrix—One Answer per Row (Rating Scale)
Matrix—Multiple Answers per Row (and with Menus)
Open Ended: One or More Lines w/Prompt, Essay, Constant Sum, Date, and/or Time
Presentation: Descriptive Text, Image, Spacer

If your surveys are larger, you might consider SurveyMonkey's fee plan. Using the templates or specifications from its hosting service, it takes as little as a half an hour to design, create, and test your forms. Bear in mind that although these services are free, they may not provide you with XML-compliant HTML pages. Some still generate HTML code with uppercase rather than lowercase element and attribute names. You may want to revise the pages to this higher standard. Once that has been done, you can move the files to your website and have your patrons fill them out.

Only one **form** container with eight different **input** types is found in Figure 09-09. This shows some of the power that the **form** element has. Note that the **form** element that created this figure (see **code0909.htm**) does not include a **method** or **action** attribute that links the code to a **cgi-bin** file. Thus although this form seems interactive, pressing either its **submit** or **reset** buttons only results in the **form** page being refreshed and reset to the built-in defaults. No messages will be sent.

Forms Processing Using Simple Email Techniques

The "trick" of creating forms that email their results to you doesn't work well with all browsers. As with all your pages, test them first on all the browsers you expect your patrons to use before they use them and find your solutions don't work! If you include the code line

```
<form action="mailto:your.email@server.com?subject=Email Response"
method="post" enctype="text/plain">
```

in your HTML **form** document, you are asking your browser, when you click on the **submit** button, to send an email message to **your.email@server.com,** which includes the forms data which you wish to be encoded as plain text (**enctype="text/plain"**).

Pressing the **submit** button on the page results in the form data being packaged in an email either as a string of text with the name of each **input** element response followed by an equals (=) sign and then the actual content inserted with plus (+) signs separating any text inputs with the **input** element responses separated by the ampersand sign (&). Other browsers render the data output as a series of data lines with underscores (_) between names and an equals (=) sign before the response.

a. Text Line 1: [ ]
b. Text Line 2: [30 Characters here]

c. Text Area Comment Box (4 rows x 50 cols visible)

d. Vertical Radio Buttons with Button 'Three' Checked
○One
○Two
⊙Three
○Four

e. Horizontal Radio Buttons with Button 'One' Checked
⊙One ○Two ○Three ○Four
f. Horizontal Checkbox Buttons with Button 'Dee' Checked
☐Aye ☐Bee ☐Cee ☑Dee

g. Selection Drop Down Box [Please make your Selection]

h. Select an Action Button: [Submit] [Reset]

Figure 09-09. Email Form Elements (**code0909.htm**)

When I used Internet Explorer as the browser, it gave me a warning:

**"This form was being submitted using email.
Submitting this form will reveal your e-mail address to the recipient,
And will send the form data without encrypting it for privacy.
You may continue or cancel this submission."**

Clicking "OK" automatically opened the Outlook Express email program with the email address and "Email Response" in their correct places; however, the data was not transferred to the email. When sent, the email received was also empty. The same form of Figure 09-09, but with email form coding, **code0909e.htm=email.htm,** opened in Mozilla's Firefox browser was able to correctly send the form information as an email using Microsoft's Outlook Express. (Your patrons must have their email program properly configured to send outgoing mail or this method won't work.) The screenshot of the email window, edited so you could see all the content in the message, showing all of the selected information data is shown in Figure 09-10.

Both the email sending program, Outlook Express, and Netscape's email receiving program actually had the forms data text as a single long line rather than the reproductions here, which show the text wrapped so you can see it all.

The Netscape email message, received seconds after sending it, looked like:

————Original Message————
Subject: Email Response
From: Charles Rubenstein <c.rubenstein@ieee.org>
To: c.rubenstein@ieee.org
text_line_1=text+line+1&text_line_2=30+Characters+here&Comment=comment+box&buttons=Three&alpha=Dee&optnumber=Option+Three&Submit=Submit

Not an elegant solution, but it is enough to do the job. The downside is you will have to figure out how to save the emails and separate the individual data information from the continuous stream of characters. Some browsers send this same data with the data received as single line entries:

text_line_1=text+line+1
text_line_2=30 Characters here
Comment =comment+box
buttons=Three
alpha=Dee
optnumber=Please make your Selection
Submit=Submit

Experimenting a bit with the code may achieve the output set you need. One major problem with simple email-creating form responses is that Outlook Express (and others) opens up and shows your patron the email address and the content of the email it is about to send. If your patrons decides to get clever, they may change the contents before they press send to email it to you.

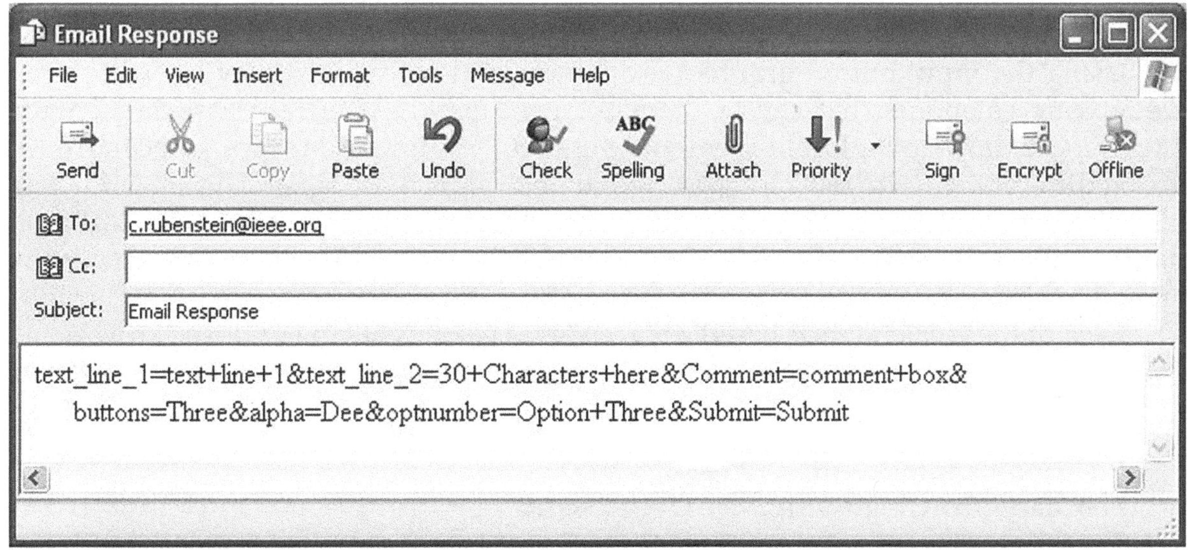

Figure 09-10. Outlook Express Email Generated by Form in FireFox Browser

Making It Work with JavaScript: Client-Side Processing

Alas, not all servers have the software needed to run server-side processing of web forms or will permit your site to access them. What do we do then? There are ways to have some forms processed directly on your computer (client-side processing) through the use of programming scripts. In this section we'll review a few simple ways to avoid the need for a server with **cgi-bin** access by using some JavaScript, a scripting language that can be used inside your web page document—just like we did with internal style sheets.

> Good to Know: JavaScript techniques are covered very briefly here and are well beyond the scope of this text. Lots of prewritten JavaScript code are available online—see www.javascriptsourse.com, in books—search Amazon or other online booksellers, in addition, JavaScript tutorials abound—see: www.w3schools.com/js—which one can use to create forms that are client-side enabled. That is, when we JavaScript enable our form web pages, we may not need to use inelegant email methods nor require a web server to process our requests.

Figure 09-11 is the output from a form using JavaScript which can automatically hyperlink to another web page or even another website. Based on the HTML code in **code0911.htm,** the form and JavaScript are designed to allow a list of URLs to be created and enable your patron to use these for simple website navigation.

As noted earlier in this chapter, JavaScript is a very powerful method for accomplishing a variety of animations on your page, but at the expense of having to learn real programming techniques. If the techniques discussed in this chapter are useful, use them, if not perhaps you'll use the calendar techniques in the next section to create attractive calendar pages for your patrons.

Using Forms Graphics in Calendar Pages

Using the input button graphics is a simple and convenient way to create simple-looking calendars that can be static, or even have hyperlinks associated with one or more dates to highlight them for events or holidays. I am sure you can find a dozen different ways to use calendars to enhance your web pages. The calendar can be a quarterly version such as seen in Figure 09-12 for the first quarter of 2014, or the 4 month by 3 month annual 2015 calendar of Figure 09-13 in landscape print-out mode.

Each of these calendars is based upon creating a series of tables with the rows consisting of empty and numbered or text filled input buttons:

For the month name rows:

```
<tr align="center"><td><big><big><b>
February</b></big></big><br /> </td></tr>
```

For the days of the week table data entries:

```
<td width="14%"><font size="1">MON</font></td>
```

```
<html>
<head><title>
Simple Javascript URL Selection Form</title></head>
<body bgcolor=#ffffff>
<script langage="JavaScript">
<!--
function jumpToPage()
{
 if (document.index.url[document.index.url.selectedIndex])
 {
  location.href = document.index.url[document.index.url.selectedIndex].value;
 }
}
//-->
</script>
<form name="index" method=get action="#">
 <select name="url" onChange="jumpToPage()">
   <option value="#" selected>-- Choose a URL --</option>
   <option value="http://www.redroselibrary.com/">Red Rose Library Web
Page</option>
   <option value="http://www.lu.com/">Libraries Unlimited</option>
   <option value="http://sils.pratt.edu/">Pratt SILS</option>
   <option value="http://www.w3schools.org/">W3 Schools</option>
 </select>
</form>
</body></html>
```

-- Choose a URL --
-- Choose a URL --
Red Rose Library Web Page
Libraries Unlimited
Pratt SILS
W3 Schools

Figure 09-11. Simple JavaScript URL Selection Form (**code0911.htm**)

For the 25th day of the month button:

<td align="center"><input type="button" value="25"></td>

For a "blank" day button to fill in the rows:

<td align="center"><input type="button" value=" "></td>

2014 Calendar - First Quarter

January

SUN	MON	TUE	WED	THU	FRI	SAT
			1	2	3	4
5	6	7	8	9	10	11
12	13	14	15	16	17	18
19	20	21	22	23	24	25
26	27	28	29	30	31	

February

SUN	MON	TUE	WED	THU	FRI	SAT
						1
2	3	4	5	6	7	8
9	10	11	12	13	14	15
16	17	18	19	20	21	22
23	24	25	26	27	28	

March

SUN	MON	TUE	WED	THU	FRI	SAT
						1
2	3	4	5	6	7	8
9	10	11	12	13	14	15
16	17	18	19	20	21	22
23	24	25	26	27	28	29
30	31					

Figure 09-12 First Quarter 2014 Form Calendar (**code0912.htm**)

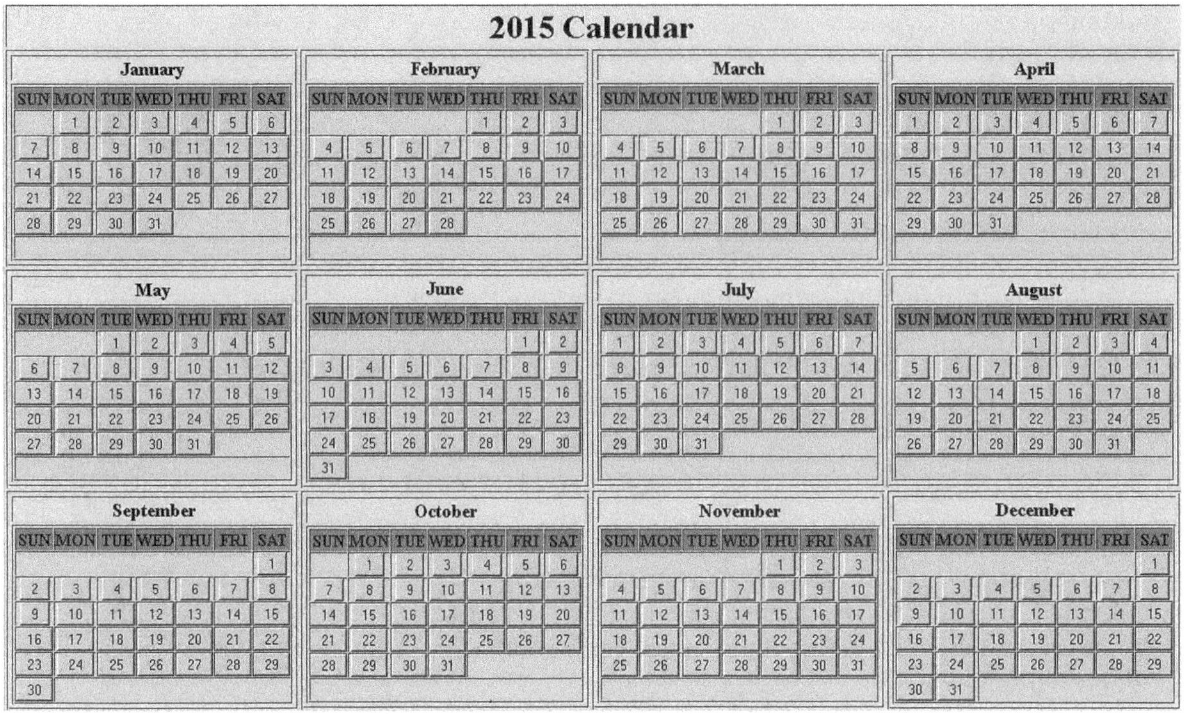

2015 Calendar

January

SUN	MON	TUE	WED	THU	FRI	SAT
	1	2	3	4	5	6
7	8	9	10	11	12	13
14	15	16	17	18	19	20
21	22	23	24	25	26	27
28	29	30	31			

February

SUN	MON	TUE	WED	THU	FRI	SAT
				1	2	3
4	5	6	7	8	9	10
11	12	13	14	15	16	17
18	19	20	21	22	23	24
25	26	27	28			

March

SUN	MON	TUE	WED	THU	FRI	SAT
				1	2	3
4	5	6	7	8	9	10
11	12	13	14	15	16	17
18	19	20	21	22	23	24
25	26	27	28	29	30	31

April

SUN	MON	TUE	WED	THU	FRI	SAT
1	2	3	4	5	6	7
8	9	10	11	12	13	14
15	16	17	18	19	20	21
22	23	24	25	26	27	28
29	30	31				

May

SUN	MON	TUE	WED	THU	FRI	SAT
		1	2	3	4	5
6	7	8	9	10	11	12
13	14	15	16	17	18	19
20	21	22	23	24	25	26
27	28	29	30	31		

June

SUN	MON	TUE	WED	THU	FRI	SAT
					1	2
3	4	5	6	7	8	9
10	11	12	13	14	15	16
17	18	19	20	21	22	23
24	25	26	27	28	29	30
31						

July

SUN	MON	TUE	WED	THU	FRI	SAT
1	2	3	4	5	6	7
8	9	10	11	12	13	14
15	16	17	18	19	20	21
22	23	24	25	26	27	28
29	30	31				

August

SUN	MON	TUE	WED	THU	FRI	SAT
			1	2	3	4
5	6	7	8	9	10	11
12	13	14	15	16	17	18
19	20	21	22	23	24	25
26	27	28	29	30	31	

September

SUN	MON	TUE	WED	THU	FRI	SAT
						1
2	3	4	5	6	7	8
9	10	11	12	13	14	15
16	17	18	19	20	21	22
23	24	25	26	27	28	29
30						

October

SUN	MON	TUE	WED	THU	FRI	SAT
	1	2	3	4	5	6
7	8	9	10	11	12	13
14	15	16	17	18	19	20
21	22	23	24	25	26	27
28	29	30	31			

November

SUN	MON	TUE	WED	THU	FRI	SAT
				1	2	3
4	5	6	7	8	9	10
11	12	13	14	15	16	17
18	19	20	21	22	23	24
25	26	27	28	29	30	31

December

SUN	MON	TUE	WED	THU	FRI	SAT
						1
2	3	4	5	6	7	8
9	10	11	12	13	14	15
16	17	18	19	20	21	22
23	24	25	26	27	28	29
30	31					

Figure 09-13 2015 Annual Calendar—Form in Portrait Mode (**code0913.htm**)

SuDoku Anyone?

Another way to enhance your web pages, especially those in the young adult section, might be to add some sort of SuDoku puzzle. The puzzle is basically a 9 × 9 matrix of numbers configured as nine 3 × 3 matrices. If you don't know how to play it yet, ask any teenager!

You could merely enter the puzzle as a normal 9-row by 9-column table and have your patrons solve them that way (Figure 09-14 on the left) but consider the example of the same figure, on the right, using forms elements to create your puzzle. It will take some effort to work these out, but the codes are all there in the files.

What's Next?

In Chapter 10 we will look at a variety of techniques that you can use to further enhance your web pages. These include using strings of hypertext and image maps for navigation, and how to add marquees and transitions to your pages. We'll also look into a few points on web page accessibility for patrons with limited sight.

URLs Cited

The CGI Standard

http://hoohoo.ncsa.uiuc.edu/cgi.

SuDoku Puzzle – Nested Tables

1	2	3	1	2	3	1	2	3
4	5	6	4	5	6	4	5	6
7	8	9	7	8	9	7	8	9
1	2	3	1	2	3	1	2	3
4	5	6	4	5	6	4	5	6
7	8	9	7	8	9	7	8	9
1	2	3	1	2	3	1	2	3
4	5	6	4	5	6	4	5	6
7	8	9	7	8	9	7	8	9

SuDoKu Puzzle Using Input Buttons

1	2	3	1	2	3	1	2	3
4	5	6	4	5	6	4	5	6
7	8	9	7	8	9	7	8	9
1	2	3	1	2	3	1	2	3
4	5	6	4	5	6	4	5	6
7	8	9	7	8	9	7	8	9
1	2	3	1	2	3	1	2	3
4	5	6	4	5	6	4	5	6
7	8	9	7	8	9	7	8	9

Figure 09-14 SoDuKu Module Using Tables (left, **code0914.htm**) and Using Input Buttons and Color (right, **code0915.htm**)

CGI Scripts for you to use, rather than write

http://www.cgiconnection.com/
http://cgi.resourceindex.com/

Free and fee-based CGI server providers

http://www.response-o-matic.com/
http://www.surveymonkey.com/
http://www.formbuddy.com/
http://www.bfndevelopment.com/
http://freedback.com/

Prewritten JavaScript code resource

www.javascriptsourse.com

JavaScript (and other code) books

www.amazon.com (etc.)

Online JavaScript tutorials

www.w3schools.com/js

Chapter 9 Review Exercises

Chapter 9 Multiple-Choice Questions

1. The three basic form element types are **input, select,** and:

   a) **textarea** b) **output** c) **get** d) **put**

2. The processing of forms requires the use of a ___.

   a) style sheet b) table c) bullet d) special server

3. The various form bullet types can be used for:

   a) tables b) graphics c) hyperlinks d) backgrounds

4. The default **radio** bullet type is a/an ____.

   a) square b) number c) circle d) diamond

5. The **input** element:

   a) must be closed b) is an empty element

   c) is used only with **dl** lists d) cannot be used with **ol** lists

Chapter 9 Design and Discussion Questions

1. Write the HTML code to create a simple email form for your library website.
2. When should you consider using a fee-based online form vendor rather than a simple free service?
3. Describe why you might decide to use forms elements without using a form on a web page.
4. Describe how you can avoid writing forms-processing programs and still achieve the use of a full featured form.
5. Briefly discuss the way forms work.

10

Web Page Navigation, Image Mapping, and Marquees

Much like Chapter 9, the remaining chapters are not for the faint of heart. They attempt to round out your understanding of HTML, CSS, XML, and other topics so you can communicate some of your library's needs to the IT professionals that will probably actually include these techniques on your web pages.

In this chapter we will look at a variety of more complex HTML techniques that you can use to further enhance your web pages. These include adding image maps to create navigation bars and hypergraphics, as well as adding marquees to your pages. We'll also look into a few points on web page accessibility for patrons with limited sight. Many of these techniques require some level of JavaScript computer programming, so you may need to find a local high school student or your IT folks to help you follow these instructions.

Web Page Navigation Techniques

Most web pages have one or more hyperlinks either to other pages on your site or to other websites. Like our Red Rose Library home page, they often have a variety of hypertext links that would be nice to have on all of our web pages to make it easier for your patron to navigate around in your website. This navigation tool can be in a column to the left or right side of the web page, or at the top or bottom of the page. A common problem with setting up a left-side navigation column is that the column takes up room that could be used for content. And when the page is printed, the left-side column prints on the patron's printer, but not the rest of your page!

If you have decided to use a top or bottom navigation tool, there are two solutions to the task. In this section we see one that uses hypertext and in the next section we'll see how to use image map techniques. In each case, clicking on one of the hyperactive areas navigates your patron between the major sections of your website. With the series of code lines in Figure 10-01 at the top and/or bottom of your web page, you will have 11 easy-to-find navigation links on your page in a minimum of space.

Notice that unless you change the link **style** to **text-decoration: none** your hypertext bar will not be as elegant looking as you might like.

CODE:

```
<a href="index.htm" alt="Red Rose Library Home Page"/>Home</a> |
<a href="hours.htm" alt=Hours of operation"/>Hours</a> |
<a href="staff.htm" alt="Library Staff"/>Staff</a> |
<a href="board.htm" alt="Board of Trustees"/>Board</a> |
<a href="archive.htm" alt="Newsletter Archives" target="_blank"/>Newsletter</a> |
<a href="children.htm" alt="Children's Room"/>Children</a> |
<a href="youth.htm" alt="Young Adults" />YA</a> |
<a href="av.htm" alt="Audio/Visual Collection" />AV</a> |
<a href="ref.htm" alt="Reference Desk" target="_blank" />Ref</a> |
<a href="friends.htm" alt="Friends of the Red Rose Library" />Friends</a> |
<a href="faqs.htm" alt="FAQs" target="_blank" />FAQs</a>
```

Resulting Display:

Home | Hours | Staff | Board | Newsletter | Children | YA | AV | Ref | Friends | FAQs

Figure 10-01. Hypertext Navigation Bar (**code1001.htm**)

Surrounding the hypertext codes of Figure 10-01 with horizontal rules (which can also be stylized as **hr style="color:red;"**) and adding some inline **style** attribute code to each anchor element (e.g., **style= " text-decoration: none; color: red; "**) adds a certain quality to your navigation. In the case of the FAQs link, for example, the code

```
<a href="faqs.htm" alt="FAQs" style="text-decoration:none; color:red; "
target="_blank" /> FAQs</a>
```

will remove the default blue color and underline associated with typical hypertext. Add a **font** element to the beginning of the code with a **style** attribute for the full text block to include styling the separating vertical bars and setting the overall font size to 18 pixels

```
<font style="font-size:18px; font-weight:bold; color:red; " >
```

and the result is the hypertext navigation bar seen in Figure 10-02.

You could also add these **style** changes to an internal, or external, style sheet (as well as change the hover style, etc.) as has been discussed previously to create several text navigation bars.

Clicking on any of the text in the navigation bar would take your patron to the appropriate page on your library website. Another way of accomplishing this same action would be to use a graphic and segment the graphic in such a way that each segment works like a single image that exhibits hyperlinking. You could, of course, use individual graphics, but the effect of using a single interactive graphic is quite a bit nicer as we'll see in the next section on image mapping.

Let's return first to the Red Rose Library page of Figure 04–27 (**code0427.htm**). It can be enhanced with the text logo designed in Chapter 5 (Figure 05–04; **img002.jpg**)

Home | Hours | Staff | Board | Newsletter | Children | YA | AV | Ref | Friends | FAQs

Figure 10-02. Stylized Hypertext Navigation Bar (**code1002.htm**)

trimmed to **width="300"** and adding the navigation hypertext code we designed in Figure 10-01 (**code1001.htm**) to the bottom of the HTML page. The result is the creation of the Red Rose Library home page, with navigation, as seen in Figure 10-03.

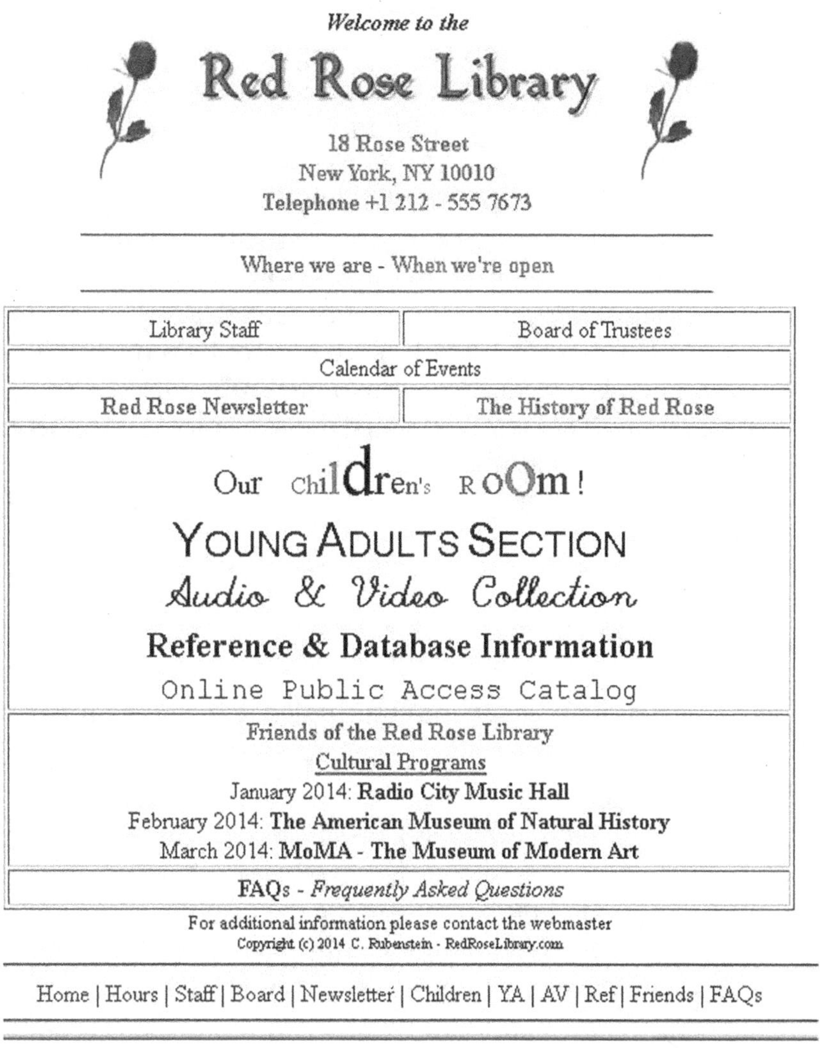

Welcome to the

Red Rose Library

18 Rose Street
New York, NY 10010
Telephone +1 212 - 555 7673

Where we are - When we're open

Library Staff	Board of Trustees
Calendar of Events	
Red Rose Newsletter	The History of Red Rose

Our children's ROOm!
YOUNG ADULTS SECTION
Audio & Video Collection
Reference & Database Information
Online Public Access Catalog

Friends of the Red Rose Library
Cultural Programs
January 2014: **Radio City Music Hall**
February 2014: **The American Museum of Natural History**
March 2014: **MoMA - The Museum of Modern Art**

FAQs - *Frequently Asked Questions*

For additional information please contact the webmaster
Copyright (c) 2014 C. Rubenstein - RedRoseLibrary.com

Home | Hours | Staff | Board | Newsletter | Children | YA | AV | Ref | Friends | FAQs

Figure 10-03. Home Page with Logo and Hypertext Navigation Bar (**code1003.htm**)

Image Maps

An image map is an interactive graphic that the user interacts with by clicking on predefined "hot spots" that result in client-side hypertext jumps. That is, you do not need any information stored in the cgi-bin on a web server. Although we will quickly review the concepts here, please remember that image mapping requires a lot of concentration and typically a software program to create a good quality map. You may have seen one or more examples of this type of web page if you are looking for cellular telephone service areas, or local stores and representatives of a national firm where a map of the United States is shown. It is unlikely that you will have time to become proficient in image mapping, but you might find one of your high school pages with technical experience or a knowledgeable volunteer in the community that would be interested in helping out. The basics will be covered here so that you can create a graphical navigation bar to place at the top and/or bottom of your web page as an example of this technique.

Once only available through web server software using CGI Scripts that required high-level programming ability and access to the cgi-bin directory on your web server, image mapping can be done on your local computer. You'll see how to do it manually here, but client-side mapping software like MapEdit (currently in Version 4.05 for Windows and 2.32 for MacOS X, and available for free evaluation as a fully functional 30-day download at **http://www.boutell.com/mapedit/download.html**) makes the job go faster; a shareware program, you can register it for $10 and get a variety of U.S. and World maps to use on your website.

Perhaps the most common of image maps is the navigation bar. The navigation bar image of Figure 10-04 (**navbar.jpg)** consists of several words in a long rectangle with a fuschia (**#ff00ff**) colored background that users can use to navigate your website.

Unlike standard graphing that starts with the 0,0 origin coordinate in the *lower left-hand corner* of your page, image mapping begins at the *upper left-hand corner* of your graphic. Image mapping relies on the **img** element to identify the image used, but then only cares about the pixel location relative to the upper left-hand corner. Your choice of **gif, jpg,** and even **png** image files can be used.

Image mapping is a powerful method of identifying areas on an image with specific URL links. The empty **map** element's **name** attribute identifies the particular **map** data to match with the **usemap** attribute name of an **img** tag. So we will start with setting up the **img** tag to specify the graphic and the **usemap** attribute name. (This two-part method is similar to the technique used to accomplish relative linking within an HTML document using the anchor tag's **name** attribute.)

Image Map area Attributes

The image map coding for Figure 10-04's 640 pixel width by 26 pixel height **navbar.jpg** image uses the **img** tag with a **usemap** attribute and would look like:

<img src="assets/navbar.jpg" usemap="#navbarmap" />

Note the **#** is used as part of the **usemap="#navbarmap"** attribute value to indicate that the coding for the image map can be found within the current document at the **map name** element's **navbarmap** location. Although the corresponding map element coding can be anywhere inside of your HTML document, map data is typically placed either directly below the **img** tag or at the very end of your document. Image map elements use the same **name** attribute structure used by the anchor tag's **name** attribute (**<a name="internal_hyperlink_name">**). The image map code looks like:

<map name="navbarmap">

This client-side image map coding uses the **area** element to define each individual clickable hot spot **area** in your image. The **area** attributes of **shape** and **coords** are used to specify hot spots.

Valid **shape** attributes that create hyperactive circle, rectangle, or polygon areas are **rect** or **rectangle, circ** or **circle,** and **poly** or **polygon.** The **coords** attribute gives the X, Y coordinates that define these shapes. For a rectangle, these coordinates define the shapes diagonal with two pairs of points: X1, Y1 and X2, Y2. For a circle **shape** the **coords** attribute defines the X, Y center of the circle with a third value giving the circle's radius. The polygon **shape** requires **coords** with three or more pairs of X, Y points to create any other hyperactive shape.

The **href** attribute is used inside the **area** tag for the relative, or absolute, URL link the browser will use to retrieve the file from when the mouse is clicked on that hot

Home | Hours | Staff | Board | Newsletter | Children | YA | AV | Ref | Friends | FAQs

Figure 10-04. The Navigation Bar Image (**navbar.jpg**)

spot. If no link is desired in a particular area, the **nohref** attribute can be used to act as a placeholder for future links.

For our navigation bar example we are quite fortunate that each of the shapes is a rectangle and that they all have the same "Y" top and bottom coordinates—at 0 and 26 pixels. Using any "paint" software program (Paint Shop Pro, Adobe Photoshop, etc.) you can determine the specific starting and ending coordinates for each of our navigation points. You can also add hyperlinks to all the library departments and items on the navigation bar. The correlation between the text on the home page with the files they link to (where bold text is used for the navbar links) is seen in Figure 10-05.

The **Home** rectangular hot spot link, for example, is defined by the upper left-hand coordinate 0,0 and the lower right-hand coordinate at 56,26. The X, Y coordinate sets can be separated by commas, semicolons, or spaces. As you begin setting up the map data for **navbarmap**, you will write the first two entries that **name** the map and begin defining the "hot" **area.** It is important to note that the # is NOT used in the **name** attribute:

```
<map name="navbarmap">
<area shape="rect" coords="0,0 56,26" href="index.htm" />
```

Filename: **code1005.doc**

Text on Page:	File Link to:
18 Rose Street, Where we are	where.htm
When we're open, **Hours**	hours.htm
Library Staff, **Staff**	staff.htm
Library Board of Trustees, **Board**	board.htm
Calendar of Events	calendar.htm
Red Rose Newsletter, **Newsletter**	archive.htm
The History of Red Rose	history.htm
Our Children's Room!, **Children**	children.htm
Simple Online Interactive Quiz	quiz.htm
Young Adults Section, **YA**	youth.htm
Audio & Video Collection, **AV**	av.htm
Reference & Database Information, **Ref**	ref.htm
Online Public Access Catalog	opac.htm
Friends of the Red Rose Library, **Friends** ...	friends.htm
Cultural Programs	programs.htm
January 2014	1401prog.htm
February 2014	1402prog.htm
March 2014	1403prog.htm
FAQs, **FAQs**	faqs.htm
webmaster	mailto:webmaster@ redroselibrary.com
Home Page, **Home**	index.htm

Figure 10-05. Correlation between Hyperlinks and Files (**code1005.doc**)

You would then continue defining the other hyperlink areas with their coordinates and link names to create the full map code of Figure 10-06. The **map** ending tag **</map>** signifies that the map data set is complete.

With the **navbar.jpg** image and this **navbarmap** data set in an HTML document, you will have the navigation aid shown in Figure 10-06.

Other shapes possible for image maps include the **circle** with **coords="X, Y circle center; radius"** whose coding for the Staff mapping would look like:

```
<area shape="circle" coords="141,13; 26" href="staff.htm" alt="Library Staff" />
```

The general polygon shape value **poly** with **coords="X1, Y1; X2, Y1; X2, Y2; X1, Y2"** is used in coding of the rectangle for the Young Adults (YA) link area where **X1, Y1** is the *upper left corner,* **X2, Y1** is the *lower left corner,* **X2, Y2** is the *upper right corner,* and finally **X1, Y2** is the *lower right corner* as illustrated here:

```
<area shape="poly" coords="402,0; 436,0; 436,26; 402,26" href="youth.htm"
alt="Young Adults" />
```

Since the image map technique does not care where the map data is with respect to the image, navigation bar image tags can be repeated more than once inside an HMTL document (e.g., at the top and bottom of the page). Note, too, that you can use **alt** attributes inside the **area** elements so that when the mouse hovers over the image map area additional information can appear. Hovering over the **Ref** area, for example, makes three changes in the browser display. You see the cursor become a hand, you see the drop-down **alt** tag value "Reference Desk" and at the bottom of the browser screen you see the file name and location that this hot spot is linked to (**ref.htm**). We used relative URLs in this example but could just as easily have used absolute addressing

```
<img src="assets/navbar.jpg" usemap="#navbarmap" />
... other web page stuff goes here ...
... hidden map data can be placed anywhere ...
<map name="navbarmap">
<area shape="rect" coords="0,0 56,26" href="index.htm" alt="Red Rose Library Home Page" />
<area shape="rect" coords="56,0 116,26" href="hours.htm" alt="Hours of operation" />
<area shape="rect" coords="116,0 166,26" href="staff.htm" alt="Library Staff" />
<area shape="rect" coords="166,0 228,26" href="board.htm" alt="Board of Trustees" />
<area shape="rect" coords="228,0 322,26" href="archive.htm" alt="Newsletters" target="_blank" />
<area shape="rect" coords="322,0 402,26" href="children.htm" alt="Children's Room" />
<area shape="rect" coords="402,0 436,26" href="youth.htm" alt="Young Adults" />
<area shape="rect" coords="436,0 472,26" href="av.htm" alt="Audio/Visual Collection" />
<area shape="rect" coords="472,0 512,26" href="ref.htm" alt="Reference Desk" target="_blank" />
<area shape="rect" coords="512,0 584,26" href="friends.htm" alt="Friends of the Red Rose Library" />
<area shape="rect" coords="584,0 640,26" href="faqs.htm" alt="FAQs" target="_blank" />
</map>
```

... other web page stuff goes here ...
... hidden map data can be placed anywhere ...

Home | Hours | Staff | Board | Newsletter | Children | YA | AV | Ref | Friends | FAQs

Figure 10-06. Image Mapping a Navigation Bar (**code1006.htm**)

with full URLs. As discussed earlier in this chapter, the **target** attribute can be used to load the linked page or image either into the current window (default is **target="_self"**) or into a new browser window (**target="_blank"**) as we illustrated for the newsletters, reference desk, and FAQs links in this example.

Adding Navigation to the Red Rose Library Page

The home page with image map navigation is shown in Figure 10-07.

Where we are - When we're open

Library Staff	Board of Trustees
Calendar of Events	
Red Rose Newsletter	The History of Red Rose

Our children's RoOm!

YOUNG ADULTS SECTION

Audio & Video Collection

Reference & Database Information

Online Public Access Catalog

Friends of the Red Rose Library

Cultural Programs

January 2014: **Radio City Music Hall**

February 2014: **The American Museum of Natural History**

March 2014: **MoMA - The Museum of Modern Art**

FAQs - *Frequently Asked Questions*

For additional information please contact the webmaster

Copyright (c) 2014 C. Rubenstein - RedRoseLibrary.com

Home | Hours | Staff | Board | Newsletter | Children | YA | AV | Ref | Friends | FAQs

Figure 10-07. Adding Navigation to the Red Rose Library Page (**code1007.htm**)

You cannot resize the 640 pixel wide navigation bar as the image map does not scale to a resized image. We would have to redesign the navbar image and the image map data set if we wanted to size it to the text above it. The other option is to resize the original web page. Figure 10-08 resizes the original web page to fit the 640 pixel navigation bar. And since you know how to create hyperlinks, you can supply all navbar links with real file names.

As you did with the hypertext version of this code, you can turn off the navbar's **Home** link to this home page using the **nohref** attribute instead of the **href** attribute in its line of code:

<area shape="rect" coords="0,0 56,26" nohref alt="Red Rose Library Home Page" />

Figure 10-08 shows the effect of setting the bottom table's **border** to **0** to improve the overall look of the web page.

Another trick you can use to enhance the look of this home page is to control the color of text hyperlinks (normally blue with blue underlines) by surrounding the text inside the anchor tag using **font** elements with **color** attributes. This is seen in the text of lines "18 Rose Street," "Our Children's Room," "Friends of the Red Rose Library," and "Cultural Programs." Figure 10-09 shows a finished page where this stylization has resulted in each case with the underline also takes on the text's font color.

Figure 10-08. Adding Hyperlinks and Real File Names (**code1008.htm**)

Marquees

You can use the **marquee** element to create a horizontal area in your document that contains scrolling text or characters and is called a marquee. The **marquee** attributes include **align, behavior, bgcolor, direction, height, hspace, loop, scrollamount, scrolldelay, vspace,** and **width.**

The **align** attribute specifies the alignment of the marquee with respect to the surrounding text. Where the **left, center,** and **right** attributes create marquees that are independent of the surrounding text, the **top, middle,** and **bottom** attributes include the marquee as part of it.

The **behavior** attribute default is **behavior="scroll".** The text starts at one side of the document, scrolls across it, and scrolls off the other side, and repeats. Other variations are **behavior="slide"** where the text starts at one side, scrolls across, and stops at the opposite margin staying there, and **behavior="alternate"** where the text starts at one side, scrolls across, and bounces off the opposite margin. This repeats with the text traveling back and forth across the page. Treating the text as an image, the **width="n"** or **height="m"** attributes size the marquee. The value of **n** or **m** here can be a number of pixels (**width="450"**) or a percentage of the screen (**width="75%"**). The **scrolldelay="n"** attribute sets the delay (milliseconds) between each series of scrolling text in the display. These simple marquee codes

Figure 10-09. Restyled Hyperlinks for a "Finished" Look (**code1009.htm**)

```
<marquee behavior="alternate" width="450px" scrollDelay="100"
style="color:#ff0000; font-weight:bold; font-size:25px; font-style:italic; ">
Welcome </marquee>

<marquee behavior="slide" width="450px" scrollDelay="100"
style="color:#ff0000; font-weight:bold; font-size:25px; font-style:italic; ">
to our </marquee>

<marquee behavior="scroll" width="450px" scrollDelay="100"
style="color:#ff0000; font-weight:bold; font-size:25px; font-style:italic; ">
Website </marquee>
```

result in the three line scrolling display of Figure 10-10.

Other attributes add a variety of other stylings to the marquee. These include determining the **direction** in which the text scrolls with the default being **left,** that is, the text begins at the right and scrolls left. This attribute can also have the value: **direction="right"**

"Welcome" Marquee

Welcome

to our

Web Site

Figure 10-10. Adding Marquees to Your Page (**code1010.htm**)

which reverses the direction of text movement. Much like an image, the marquee uses the **hspace="n"** and **vspace="m"** attributes to provide left and right or top and bottom margins around the marquee.

The scrolled text can be further modified using **scrollamount="n"** to set the space (**pixels**) between each series of scrolling text or the **loop="n"** attribute can be used to set the number of times the text scrolls through the marquee. For infinite scrolling, use **loop="-1"** or **loop="infinite".** Marquees can also be generated using JavaScript, but that requires programming.

Section 508

Federal regulation Section 508 (of the Rehabilitation Act of 1973, as amended [29 U.S.C. 794d]) defines 16 accessibility requirements to which government websites must comply to be accessible to people with disabilities. If your library is included in this group or if you are concerned about the accessibility of your web pages to your patrons, you need to be aware of the Section 508 guidelines and standards at:

http://www.section508.gov

You can learn more about this important topic at:

http://www.netmechanic.com/accessibility.htm

The pages you designed in this text are pretty much all in compliance with the accessibility guidelines, but the rules should be reviewed before you post your specific pages.

What's Next?

From image maps to marquees to accessibility, this chapter has provided some guidance and examples that should prove helpful. In Chapter 11, More Fun with CSS, we continue our leap of faith in web design knowing that we may not be doing these techniques, but it is good to understand the geek talk so we can communicate what we want on our pages to the IT folks who may be doing the actual coding. We'll start with an overall view of what CSS does and how, cover some additional CSS concepts, and then go on in Chapter 12 to see how the combination of HTML and CSS becomes the basis for the extended markup language—XML, and finally see how content management systems use these higher-order markup techniques to create interactive web pages that select "answers" to patron queries from relational databases.

URLs Cited

The MapEdit Image mapping software

http://www.boutell.com/mapedit/download.html

Accessibility concepts and standards

http://www.section508.gov
http://www.netmechanic.com/accessibility.htm

Chapter 10 Review Exercises

Chapter 10 Multiple-Choice Questions

1. The three basic hyperlink techniques are by **image mapping, graphic linking,** and:

   a) text links b) mapping c) graphing d) tagging

2. It is best to add the optional ______________ attribute to all hyperlinks.

   a) **hl** b) **hr** c) **img** d) **alt**

3. The image map element is the:

   a) **imgmap** **b) map** **c) usemap** **d) mapname**

4. The default style for hypertext is ______________ characters.

   a) blue b) red c) blue, underlined d) red, underlined

5. The **target** attribute:

   a) can open a new window b) is an empty element

   c) can open a new tab d) cannot be used with **href**

Chapter 10 Design and Discussion Questions

1. Write the HTML code to create a simple hyperlink navigation bar for your library website.
2. When should you consider using image mapping rather than a text navigation bar?
3. Describe why you might decide to use navigation bars at the top *and* bottom of a web page.
4. Describe why it is important to make sure that your website complies with Section 508.
5. Briefly discuss what a marquee is and how you might use it on your web page(s).

11

More Fun with CSS

In the past few chapters we have introduced lists, tables, and form elements, and used basic cascading style sheet (CSS) concepts to fine-tune the styles you desired on your web pages. Before getting deeper into the use of CSS, let's try to better understand the concepts of document type definitions (DTD).

HTML Doctypes

The HTML document structure is dependent on 90 or so basic elements defined by the DTD in your browser. But what if you want to change that DTD? Using the browser-optional, but as far as we are concerned required, doctype declaration, you can tell your patron's browser exactly which version of which markup language to use. The first line of your HTML document contains the doctype DTD reference as well as both a formal public identifier (FPI) and a formal system identifier (FSI):

<!DOCTYPE html PUBLIC "FPI" "FSI">

For the HTML 4.01 strict specification, this would look like:

**<!DOCTYPE html PUBLIC "-//W3C//DTD HTML 4.01//EN"
"http://www.w3.org/TR/html4/strict.dtd">**

Note that unlike our normal HTML elements and names, the doctype declaration is a system command and requires the uppercase latters shown in this example. Recall that there are three different HTML vocabulary types: Strict, Transitional (or loose), and Frameset. Your browser will evaluate your doctype declaration for completeness and correctness. This is known as doctype sniffing or doctype switching. The website at **http://hsivonen.iki.fi/doctype** has lots more information on this checking process and what happens if your browser doesn't understand what it finds in your **DOCTYPE** statement.

We can group the element types into those that surround content with opening and closing tags, or those that are empty in as much as they are *replacement elements.* The action of empty, one-sided, or replacement elements is to replace the HTML code with an image (**img**), form input (**input**), rule (**hr**), external file (**link**), or a line break (**br**). This type of element needs to be written in lowercase and self-closing to be consistent with our desire for future upgrading to XML or HTML5. All other elements are deemed *nonreplaced* or double-sided and naturally require the proper nesting of opening and closing tags to establish proper containers for their content.

About the CSS Specification

Both replaced and nonreplaced elements can be styled using CSS. The creation of CSS specifications began in 1994. In 1996 CSS1 was released and in 1998 CSS2 became the standard. In 2012 "Cascading Style Sheets, Level 2 Revision 1" —CSS2.1 for short, became the CSS specification standard. The CSS 2.1 specification is available at:

http://www.w3.org/TR/CSS21

We use the CSS2.1 specification of June 2011 throughout this text. Quoting from the specification's abstract:

> CSS 2.1 is a style sheet language that allows authors and users to attach style (e.g., fonts and spacing) to structural elements (e.g., HTML documents and XML applications). By separating the presentation style of documents from the content of documents, CSS 2.1 simplifies Web authoring and site maintenance. . . . It also supports content positioning, table layout . . ."

The nearly 500-page CSS2.1 specification can be viewed or downloaded from

http://www.w3.org/TR/2011/REC-CSS2–20110607

Due to the large number of groups working on the individual sections of the CSS specification, and in an attempt to permit updates to be approved and used more quickly than could be done with a 500-page document, the latest Level 3 CSS specification processing is a bit different from these earlier versions. Rather than a single specification for CSS3, new revisions are made on segments of the specification called modules. The more than a dozen CSS3 modules include ones for color level, namespaces, media queries, and selectors. Identified as "css3-modulename" the **css3-selector** module at **http://www.w3.org/TR/css3-selectors,** for example, defines how style properties can be bound to elements in HTML and XML documents. Included in this smaller, 28-page, document are the latest technical definitions, syntax, and examples for the CSS pseudo-classes and pseudo-elements we discussed in Chapter 6 as well as many selector issues and topics we did not cover. Many of the CSS3 module standards are already included in the latest browsers, but, as they are not yet standard, we won't be discussing them here.

The status of the various CSS Level 3 modules can be accessed at **http://www.w3.org/TR/#tr_CSS** as well as at **http://www.w3.org/Style/CSS/current-work.**

CSS Rules

CSS "commands" are often called CSS rules. The parts of a CSS rule include the CSS Selector, which is the specific element and/or class name that is to be styled, followed by a declaration block. The declaration block includes one or more CSS property-value pairs. Each CSS property in the block is followed by a colon with the CSS property's value followed by a semicolon.

> **Good to Know:** Although the last property-value pair does not require the semicolon to separate it from another property-value pair, it is a best practice to include the semicolon—just in case you want to add another pair at a later date.

Much as we saw in dealing with HTML documents in general, all browsers ignore extra spaces, tabs, new lines, and so on, placed in your document. CSS likewise permits you to create rules that are compact, or include lots of whitespace. The syntax for CSS rules identifies a CSS selector as an element, class, or ID whose style is changed by putting one or more CSS property-value pairs *declaration blocks* inside of curly braces. Each CSS property is separated from its style value by a colon, with the style value ending in a semicolon:

CSS Rule: **selector {declaration block1; CSSproperty2:value; . . . }**

The code for **h1**, a **blue** text on a **fuscia** background heading style 1, would be as seen in Figure 11-01 in either the compact or expanded format.

Compact Format:

```
h1      { color:blue; background:fuscia; }
```

Expanded, Whitespace, Format:

```
h1
{
color:blue;
background:fuscia;
}
```

Figure 11-01. Example of CSS Rule Syntax

Block-Level and Inline-Level HTML Element Types

The CSS2.1 Standard differentiates between block-level and inline-level HTML element types. Block-level elements include the body (**body**), paragraph (**p**), division (**div**), and even list item (**li**) elements that create a break before and after the element's content creating a sort of box look. Inline-level elements, on the other hand, create a container for content without adding line breaks before and after the changes.

The italics/emphasis (**i, em**), bold/strong (**b, strong**), span (**span**), and even the anchor element (**a**) are examples of inline-level elements. It is most common to have inline-level elements inside of block-level elements, as long as the inline elements are all properly nested.

Dozens of CSS style guides are available for your review on the Internet. Notable among these are:

The Google HTML/CSS Style Guide

http://google-styleguide.googlecode.com/svn/trunk/htmlcssguide.xml

CSS Wizardry (Harry Robert's CSS Style)

http://csswizardry.com/2012/04/my-html-css-coding-style

The Github Style

http://github.com/styleguide/css

The CSS-Tricks code snippet website

http://css-tricks.com

Default Element Styles

We know that each browser's software has an area where the 90 or so "official" HTML elements and their attributes are fully defined as to their *initial* default DTD values. We can think of these DTD values as existing in a table, or even visualize them as a stack of pancakes with the initial default as the bottom-most pancake. This area with all the default DTDs that describe how each element will initially be interpreted might look something like Figure 11-02.

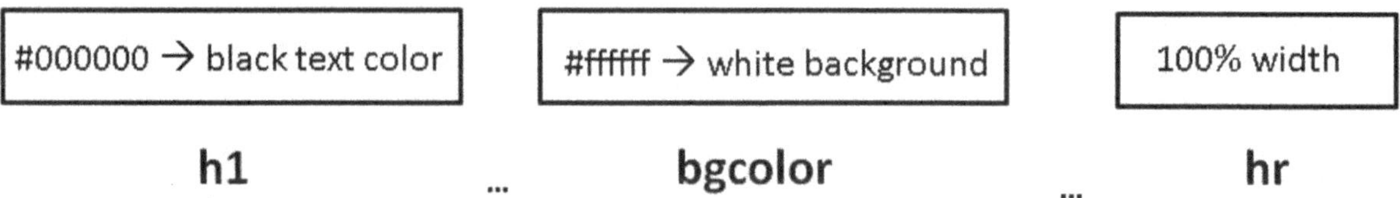

Figure 11-02. Example of a Default DTD Table

On top of each of these DTD attribute defaults are layered, one by one, any CSS changes saved in external files with **css** extensions, internal changes identified in the document's head, and inline (and **class**) style changes in the opening tag of the specific element for the content being styled. These changes create a "look and feel" styling at the website, page, and even container level.

External Style Sheets and the link Element

The empty or single-ended **link** element opening tag

```
<link rel="stylesheet" type="text/css" href="assets/style.css" />
```

is placed inside the head area of your HTML document. The preceding code shows the default set of attributes that define the style sheet relationship (**rel="stylesheet"**), the file type (**type="text/css"**), and a call to retrieve an external style sheet file, either on your website in the assets folder as shown here (**href="assets/style.css"**) or on another website altogether (**href= "http://www.anyserver.com/stylefile.css"**). Most **link** tags will look like the above, but on some more complex web pages the **link** tag will include the powerful **media** attribute, which we will discuss in a later section.

> **Good to Know:** There can be more than one **link** element request for external CSS files. The overall library stylization would be linked first, then the department CSS and possibly even a specific function or collection CSS could be added.

When the browser opens your HTML document, it looks for any style sheet commands within the head of the document that will change how you would like your elements displayed. You can divide your *external* style sheets into one you want to use for the entire site and others for your individual department or website sections.

Figure 11-03 shows what the **head** area of your document might look like if you used the external CSS technique with several **link** elements for the video page of the children's department of your library.

```
<head><tittle>REd Rose Library Home Page></title>
<link rel="stylessheet" type="text/css"href="assets/site.css"/>
<link rel="stylessheet" type="text/css"href="assets/children.css"/>
<link rel="stylessheet" type="text/css"href="assets/video.css"/>
...
</head>
```

Figure 11-03. Using Multiple Style Sheets in the Head of an HTML Document

Each of the style changes in these files is placed on top of the element defaults in the order in which they are presented. Thus any **site.css** changes are stacked on top of the browser's DTD defaults, the **children.css** changes on top of that, and the "changes on top of all of those changes.

If we could look at the **bgcolor** attribute portion of the **body** element inside the DTD Table we would see a stack of defaults for each element with the **bgcolor** default being **white** (#ffffff) on top of which has been placed

> **Good to Know:** If an element is changed in more than one style sheet file, each change will be placed on the top of the element's style in the DTD table. Thus even though the entire site might have a style standard for a particular element, you can change that for this particular web page by adding the department's standard to overwrite the site standard. One practical use would be to style the background of general pages with one color and possibly use other colors to code your department pages. The last change, at the top of the stack, will be seen by the browser as the current default.

the **site.css** default color being **blue** (#0000ff) and the **children.css** default color being **lime** (#00ff00) and, finally the topmost **bgcolor** default, the **video.css** color, being **blue** (#0000ff). Note that this is hardly a use of pale, light, soothing, pleasing, web page compatible background colors—this is just an extreme example! But if you did create these style changes, when the browser opened your page the background at this point would be blue, the top of the stack style, as seen in the DTD table representation of Figure 11-04 where the top part shows a stacking of styles one on top of another, and the bottom left shows a cascading view of the same effect.

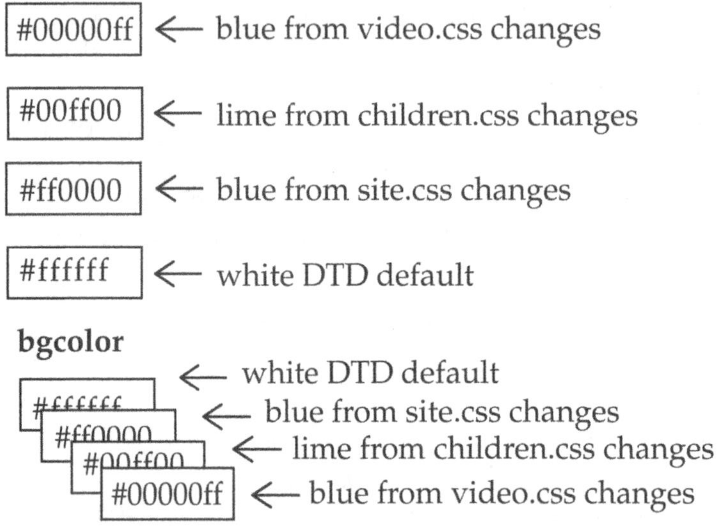

Figure 11-04. Effect of External CSS Changes on the Body Background Color

Media Attributes

It was a simpler time in the 1990s when mostly anyone who had access to the Internet did so on either a desktop or tower computer with a 640 pixel wide by 480 pixel high, color TV–screen like monitor. Jump-forward to today and your patron's interface with the Internet can have pixel per inch (ppi) resolutions of 132 through 326 ppi and higher, and be via their web-enabled smartphone (960 × 640 to 1136 × 640 or larger!), a 5-inch or larger tablet computer or one of the iPad® versions (typically 800 × 480 or 1024 × 768), a laptop computer, a full-size monitor, or even a web-enabled television!

"We've come a long way baby!" It is definitely a time where one web page size does not fit all your patron's possible output displays.

So how can we design our page for one display without having our patrons complain that the view on their screen was too small, or too large? How can we design a single web page compatible with all the previous resolutions and screen size formats? Can you say CSS?

The basic **link** element reviewed in the last section has an additional attribute that is used to query the browser's display default. Enter the **media** attribute. Using Boolean algebraic constraints (***AND, NOT,*** and ***OR***) your browser can tell the web server which of several link declarations to use based on the media the browser is displaying on. Thus a single web page can be used with these several specific link declarations to select from different style sheets that create your page in a variety of different output formats. The **media** attribute can be used not only in the **link** but also in **style** elements, the media descriptor portion of an **@import** declaration, or, as we'll see in the next section as a stand-alone **@media** declaration in a media block.

Good to Know: JavaScript coding can also be used to query the patron's browser type, but the media method is much simpler. Later in this chapter we will use the **if** and **endif** queries to adjust the CSS versions used on web pages when opened by an Internet Explorer browser.

When no **media** attribute is included in any of the these declarations on your web page, if your browser supports media types, the media default is "all" (**media="all"**) meaning that the style sheet called for in **link** (etc.) declarations should be used with all presentation media displays. When the **media** attribute *is used and is supported by the browser,* one or more specific style sheets can be identified for different media types as will be reviewed later. The intent is to define the display output based on the patron's device browser selecting a specific set of styles.

Good to Know: Current browsers do NOT support most media types. Those that do, typically support "all," "screen," "print," and "projection." And of course mobile-device browsers support the "handheld" media type. The CSS2.1 specification describes many **media** options; aural (for speech synthesizers, and screen readers), braille (for use with Braille devices), embossed (used with Braille printers), handheld (for PDAs and web-enabled cell phones), print (standard printers and print preview use), projection (with LCD projectors), screen (for desktop monitors), tty (for teletype printers), and TV (for presentation on a television). However, as noted, most of these media types are *not* supported by any browsers at this time.

The **media** descriptor's task is to provide your patron's browser with a query that matches the type of output to the style sheet(s) that will be selected. The **media** query can be further enhanced using logic terms between media values. Several **media** features can be linked to allow for selecting among different output devices. To make sure a specific style sheet is viewed when the display is **color** *AND* in **landscape mode** *AND* is **800 pixels wide,** we enclose each condition in parentheses using the logical *AND* to combine them as shown here:

```
<link rel="stylesheet" type="text/css" href="css/800.css"
media="(color) and (orientation:landscape) and (min-device-width:
800 px)" />
```

If all criteria are met, the style changes of the **800.css** file stored in the **css** folder on your website are loaded onto the CSS stack. If even one of the criteria fails, the browser will ignore the call to place the style sheet file on the CSS stack.

In the event that a particular style file should *not* be used for a particular display, use the logical NOT for conditions that the file should not be used with. The ***NOT*** logic selector *must* be used only with the very first condition in your query as seen here:

```
<link rel="stylesheet" type="text/css" href= "css/not.css"
media="not (color) and (orientation:landscape) and
(min-device-width:800px)" />
```

This more complex query requires the **not.css** style sheet to be used *except* when the output display is **color** in **landscape mode** and is **800 pixels wide.** Interestingly, the current specification does not permit the direct use of the logical ***OR.*** Instead, to accept ***OR*** logic criteria, conditions need to be separated only by a comma. In the following link tag, the **color800.css** file style sheet changes are used anytime the media is **color** and if it is *either* in **landscape mode** or **at least 800 pixels wide:**

```
<link rel="stylesheet" type="text/css" href="css/color800.css"
media="(color) and (orientation:landscape), (min-device-width:800px)" />
```

Finally, to maintain compatibility with older browsers, "only" can be used in front of the first condition to check. When seen by older browsers, the **print.css** style sheet is ignored altogether:

```
<link rel="stylesheet" type="text/css" href="css/print.css"
media="only print" />
```

The syntax for using media queries with **style** and **@input** declarations is the same as noted earlier for the **link** element. Thus it is possible to see the following coding lines on a web page using embedded style sheets:

```
<style type="text/css" media="(query here)" >
    h1 { color:green; }
    . . .
    </style>
```

Or even:

```
<style type="text/css">
    @import <media="print" url(css/print.css) />
    h1 { color:red; }
    . . .
    </style>
```

The **media** declaration has lots of options with descriptors with values in *pixels* that can be used which include:

width, min-width, max-width
device-width, min-device-width, max-device-width
height, min-height, max-height
device-height, min-device-height, max-device-height

The **media** descriptors with values in *width-to-height* (e.g., 2/1) values include:

aspect-ratio, min-aspect-ratio, max-aspect-ratio
device-aspect-ratio, min-device-aspect-ratio, max-device-aspect-ratio

The **media** descriptors with *integer* values that can be used include:

color, min-color, max-color
color-index, min-color-index, max-color-index
monochrome, min-monochrome, max-monochrome

Other **media** descriptors that can be used include **resolution, min-resolution, max-resolution** (dpi), **orientation** (portrait or landscape), **scan** (progressive or interlace) for use with TV outputs, or even **grid** (0 or 1) where the value 1 is used with teletypes.

The **media** query is, as should be clear at this time, a great future method for customizing output web pages based on specific style sheets for each individual display type that might be standardized. Also obvious is that a very fine level of style granulation can be based on a wide variety of criteria and descriptors as noted in the examples earlier.

Media Blocks

We saw how we can use the **media** query in embedded or internal style declaration and with the **@import** declaration. If you want to limit internal style sheet changes based solely on media, in addition to or instead of the **@import**, an **@media** declaration can be used in the style element area of your head, just as we defined the **@import** declaration in the previous section. This technique, called using a media block, as seen later, will apply all the CSS rules *only to print output media.* When the browser output is not to a printer, the **h1** "12 point text" style is ignored. Figure 11-05 shows a representative code example.

> Good to Know: Be careful of the order of where your media block is placed. In the preceding example, the **h1 font-size** style for the page is set to 14-point text. Whenever the media block query is true, the **font-size** would be changed to 12-point text overriding the 14-point **body** style before printing. Should you *incorrectly* place the media block *before* the embedded changes, the **h1** font style for the main page would override the media block resulting in 14-point text even when being printed. To be safe, always place the media block after any embedded changes.

Avoid Using title Attributes in the link Tag

A **link** attribute that is problematic, and should ***not*** be used at this time, is the **title** attribute inside of the **link** element that can be used if your browser allows selecting alternative style sheets. Only Firefox currently allows your browser to select among several style sheets using the **link title** attribute. The **title** attribute adds a name to one or more different style sheets. However, your patron must select the specific set of alternative style sheets to use! So, for now, ***don't*** use the link's **title** attribute!

```
        ...
        <style type="text/css">
        ...
        .newclass { parameter1:value1; parameter2:value2; }
        p.newclass { parameter1:value1; parameter2: value2; }
        #content { parameter1:value1; parameter2:value2; }
        div#contents {parameter1:value; parameter2:value2; }
        <style>
        ... </head>
<body>
        <div class=newclass>
                ...
                <div class=newclass> ... </p> </div>
        <div ID=contents>
                ...
                <p ID=content> ... </p> </div>
</dody><html>
```

Figure 11-05. Embedded Style Codes Including Media Block

Without the **title** attribute, linked external style sheets will be viewed as *persistent* style sheets:

```
<link rel="stylesheet" type="text/css" href="css/style.css" />
```

With the **title** attribute there could be one or more *preferred* **title="Default"** default style sheets

```
<link rel="stylesheet" type="text/css" href="css/default.css" title="Default" />
```

in addition to the **title="alt"** alternative style sheets:

```
<link rel="alternate stylesheet" type="text/css" href="css/alt1.css" title="alt" />
<link rel="alternate stylesheet" type="text/css" href="css/alt2.css" title="alt" />
<link rel="alternate stylesheet" type="text/css" href="css/alt3.css" title="alt" />
```

You should *NOT* use the **title** technique, but in the future you might see sets of **link** tags like:

```
<link rel="stylesheet" type="text/css" href="css/default.css" title="Default" />
<link rel="alternate stylesheet" type="text/css" href="css/alt1.css" title="alt" />
<link rel="alternate stylesheet" type="text/css" href="css/alt2.css" title="alt" />
<link rel="alternate stylesheet" type="text/css" href="css/alt3.css" title="alt" />
```

Why should you NOT include **title** default and alternate style sheets in your designs? If you do, your patron must not only be *aware* that an alternate style sheet set can be selected, but your patron must also *know* how they can change the style set. Thus using the **title** requires more technical knowledge on your user's part as to how to make the change.

A Firefox screen shot of a really good example of how several alternative style sheets can be used is "Eric Meyer's Complex Spiral Demo" (**http://meyerweb.com/eric/css/edge/complexspiral/demo.html**) as shown in Figure 11-06.

Internal Style Sheets and Inline Styling

Of course *external* CSS is not the only way you can stylize your web pages. You can add even finer, more granular control of a specific page within your website by adding *internal* style commands inside the head of your HTML document, and then even finer granular control in the opening tag of the specific element surrounding the content you wish to style. These techniques were discussed in Chapter 6 and should be reviewed as necessary, but the overall concept is that the style change *closest* to the actual content will be used to stylize your content. Depending on the reference work you are using for CSS, this set of style changes, most typically inside the HTML document's head area, is called the *document style sheet*, or the *embedded style sheet*. As it is usually placed after the external style sheet **link** elements, the style element's stylizations "sit" on top of the external styles. Interesting to note is that another form of external file link, the **@import** can also be used to call external files from the internal style element section. All **link** and **@import** commands must appear *first* in the **style** section. Adding the **newstyle.css** file's style sheet (stored in the **css** folder) changes inside the style element (again, refer to Chapter 6 to refresh your memory of how internal style works) looks like:

```
<style type="text/css">
    @import url(css/newstyle.css);
    element1 { parameter1: value1; parameter2: value2; }
    element2 { parameter1: value1; parameter2: value2; }
<style>
```

Figure 11-06. Screen Shot of Alternate Style Sheets (Eric Meyer's Complex Spiral Demo) **http://meyer web.com/eric/css/edge/complexspiral/demo.html**

> **Good to Know:** Once the inline styled element closes, the "new" attribute style value is removed from the stack and whatever property value is now at the top becomes the default for that element attribute the next time it is used.

If the change is an *inline* one, at the element opening tag level, the change will revert to the next lower style once your browser reads the element's closing tag. Thinking of these style changes as a pancake on a stack of pancakes is often a good idea with the closing tag "eating" your last style change and uncovers the next lower style.

The individual web page can also have style changes based on additional stylizations created using the **style** element within the head of the document. These changes, as long as they occur after the linked external CSS files, go on top of those external style changes.

Finally, each HTML element within your webpage can acquire an even finer granulation of stylization using the inline style attributes at the division, span, paragraph, or even character level. Figure 11-06 illustrates the way DTD space inside your browser might look after these three techniques have all been used to change the way a particular element is displayed. Note that external and internal stylizations are fixed for a particular page and *only* inline style changes to the DTD stack are removable after the element that added them closes. For this reason the **class** concept is used to create, as already shown in Chapter 6, styles that are defined in external and internal CSS but "called" or only *activated* using the inline **class** attribute for specific elements. Using the **class** attribute means that all the "look and feel" we want for a specific page in a particular department of your library will be there when we want it, but will allow other styles to the rest of the page.

Figure 11-07 shows the DTD stack after several CSS changes, much like Figure 11-04 did earlier.

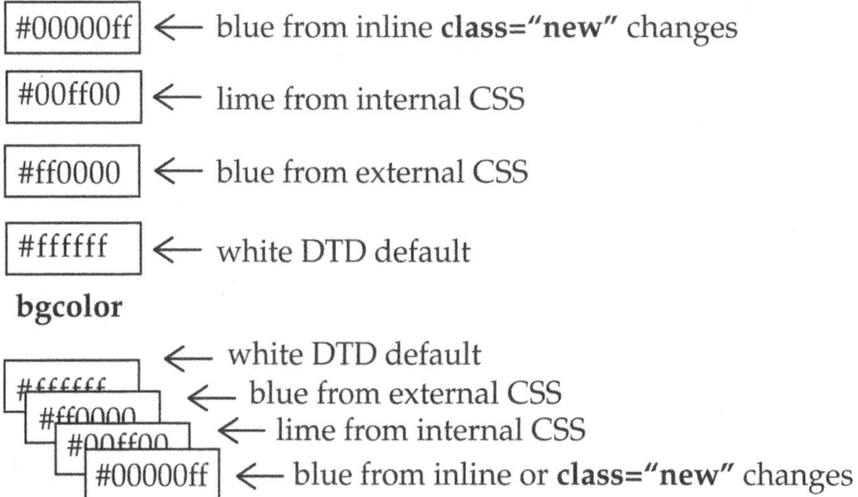

Figure 11-07. Inline or **class** Attributes and the DTD Stack

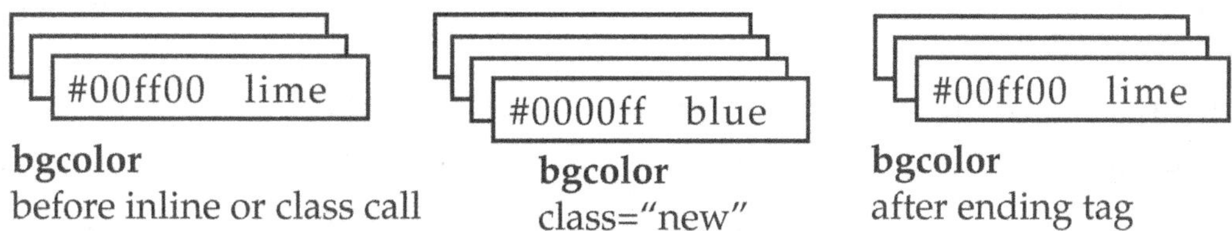

Figure 11-08. Stripping Inline or **class** Attributes from the DTD Stack

Figure 11-08 illustrates the effect on the DTD stack of either an inline style or **class** change on the DTD before the particular opening tag (left most stack), during its use (center stack), and after the closing tag (right most stack). This cascading method makes CSS changes consistent, but does not force a page "look and feel" if not needed.

ID Selectors

In addition to the generic or fully defined **class** selectors (**.newstyle** or **p.newstyle**) reviewed in Chapter 6, style sheets can include ID selectors, typically a generic or fully defined often called dependent stylizations typically used in the divisions (**div**) of your HTML document. Within your style sheet definitions, the ID selector is defined as a number sign preceding a lowercase alphanumeric name that may not have any spaces and must not begin with a number (e.g., **#contents** or **div#contents**). Like classes, the ID is used in the opening tag where desired (**<div ID ="#contents">**; unlike classes, a specific ID selector can be used only once on any particular web page. There is really no need for us to use the ID on our relatively simple web pages, but it is good to know that one more level of stylizations is possible. The CSS setup and use of ID selectors, as shown in Figure 11-09, is identical to that of classes. In the head of your document place the style changes desired, and call for their use in an elements' opening tag.

```
          ...
          <style type="text/css">
          ...
          .newclass { parameter1:value1; parameter2:value2; }
          p.newclass { parameter1:value1; parameter2: value2; }
          #content { parameter1:value1; parameter2:value2; }
          div#contents {parameter1:value; parameter2:value2; }
          <style>
          ... </head>
<body>
          <div class=newclass>
                    ...
                    <div class=newclass> ... </p> </div>
          <div ID=contents>
                    ...
                    <p ID=content> ... </p> </div>
</dody><html>
```

Figure 11-09. Example Using **class** and **ID** Selectors

Note that the IDs in this example are named **content** and **contents** respectively.

Checking for IE Browser Type: Conditional Comments

We now have lots of style possibilities available for use in designing web pages. But what if the particular style you want to use does not render properly by your patron's Internet Explorer browser? Turns out that IE, and only IE, allows you to use what are called conditional comments in the style area that permit fixing what is an Internet Explorer–specific set of style challenges. Unlike normal HTML comments, conditional comments are found only in the **head** of the HTML document and begin with the "less than" symbol followed by the exclamation point, two dashes, a space, and the query **if IE #.#** inside square brackets (*where #.# is the optional IE version number*) followed by the "greater than" symbol as the conditional comment opening tag. The style changes for that version of IE are then presented, typically as a link to an external CSS file. Then the special closing tag containing the "less than" symbol followed by the exclamation point and **endif** inside square brackets followed by the "greater than" symbol as seen in Figure 11-10.

If the specific version of IE (several queries can exist in a single page) is found, that particular set of CSS style fixes are loaded onto the DTD stack. The browser ignores any queries whose result is "false."

Boxes and Borders

As, alas, tables are being deprecated for future HTML documents, it is important to understand a bit about how your web page can be viewed as a set of boxes for your content. The general definition of the box that the window your browser presents is defined as shown in Figure 11-08.

If all we are interested in is a single content container as noted here, we only need to style the margins and paddings and we are done. However, what if we want a more complication structure?

Box Margin Shorthand

The units for our borders and margins are **px** for pixels, **em** for the width of an "m" in the font, or **ex**, the height of an "x" in the font in use. If we want our CSS box to contain all possible elements in our HTML document we can use the CSS Selector "*"

```
<head> ...
        <!-- [ if IE ]>      ← Conditional Comments opening tag
        <link rel="stylesheet" type="text/css" href="css/iefix.css" /> ← CSS adjustments
        <![ endif ]>     ← Conditional Comments closing tag
        ...
</head>
```

Figure 11-10. Using Conditional Comments to Adjust for Different IE Versions

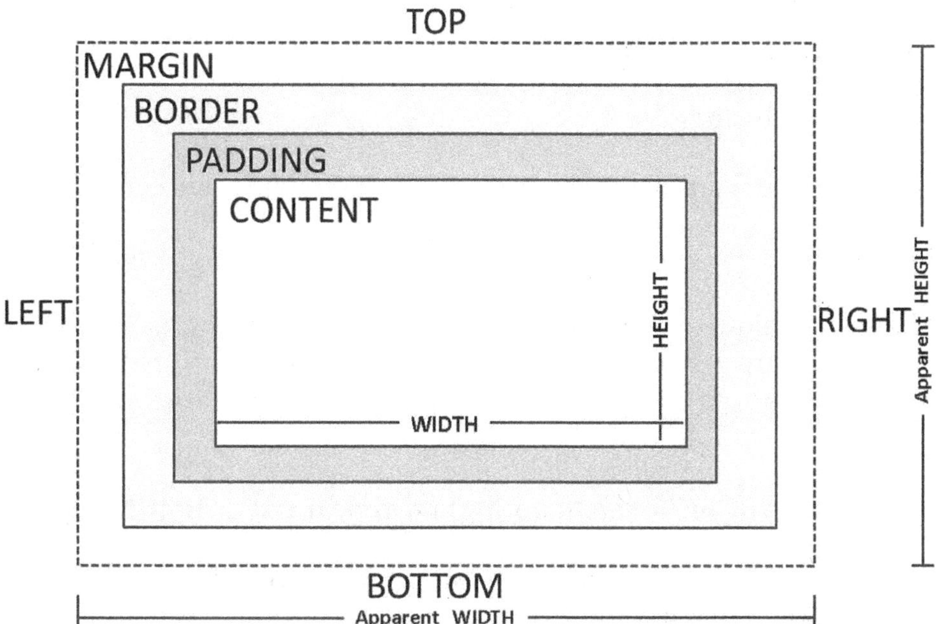

Figure 11-11. Browser Window Box Definitions (from "CSS, DHTML & Ajax," fourth edition by Jason Teague, Peachpit Press; Figure 6.1, page 160)

and describe the declaration blocks for the top, right, bottom, and left margins appropriately, in that order, using the margin attributes.

```
* { margin-top:5em; margin-right:10em; margin-bottom:25em
margin-left:5em; }
```

This string of style changes could also be written:

```
* { margin-top:5em;
  margin-right:10em;
  margin-bottom:25em;
  margin-left:5em;
}
```

Although the order of property-value style changes in declaration blocks is normally arbitrary, if we want to write the margin in shortcut form, we need to observe the top, right, bottom, and left style order:

```
* { margin 5em 10em 25em 5em; }
```

But what if we want the right and left margins to be the same, **10em** wide? We can write:

```
* { margin 5em 10em 25em; }
```

Similarly, if we want both the top and bottom margins to be **5em** wide with the right and left margins both **10em** wide, we can write:

*** { margin 5em 10em; }**

And finally, if we want both all margins to be **5em** wide, we can write:

*** { margin 5em; }**

Shorthand techniques are also available for use in calling background graphics and other common structures. The shorthand call for a white-colored background with the image (assets/logo.jpg) to be only placed on the page one time and fixed to the top right of the page, the coding would look like:

*** { background #fff url(assets/logo.jpg) no-repeat fixed right-top; }**

If only the graphic is noted, then the background color is presumed transparent, the graphic repeated across and then down the page, scrolling as it goes, with the position starting at the top left:

*** { background url(assets/logo.jpg); }**

Good to Know: Unfortunately, the adage "beware the browser" is even more evident when trying to create boxes of content and boxes within the content area. A lot of compatibility problems in current versions make one yearn for the use of tables. Clearly, should you want to fully use CSS to create boxes and other more complex displays using only CSS, you need to refer to one of the many texts out there covering the finer details of CSS. Among these reference works are several O'Reilly texts—too numerous to list—as well as:

"CSS, DHTML & Ajax," fourth edition, © 2007 by Jason Cranford Teague, Peachpit Press ISBN: 0-321-44325-X

"The Ultimate CSS Reference" Tommy Olsson and Paul O'Brien, © 2008 SitePoint Pty. LTD.

ISBN: 978-0-9802858-5-7

What's Next?

In this chapter we extended the basic CSS methods that you can use to create the specific "look and feel" and stylization that you need to make your pages give your patrons a consistent presentation as we saw in Chapter 6. We went deep into the DTD and came back with an appreciation of how CSS changes and how you can use queries and shorthand to create a variety of useful stylizations for your web page. Next we'll look at the next leap of faith in markup languages, XML, the extensible markup language that permits you, YES YOU! to create your own special element vocabularies to simplify your library's web page needs, as well as to incorporate data searches into your web pages. Chapter 12 will also review some of what the result of adding HTML 4.01, CSS 2.1, and CSS3, and XML together in a great big cauldron coming soon called HTML5.

URLs Cited

The HTML 4.01 strict specification

http://www.w3.org/TR/html4/strict.dtd

Information on doctype sniffing or doctype switching

http://hsivonen.iki.fi/doctype

The CSS Standard CSS2.1

http://www.w3.org/TR/CSS21

The latest (June 2011) CSS Standard CSS2.1 (500-page document!)

http://www.w3.org/TR/2011/REC-CSS2–20110607

The CSS3 Selector Specification "**css3-selector** module"

http://www.w3.org/TR/css3-selectors

The status of the various CSS3 modules

http://www.w3.org/TR/#tr_CSS
http://www.w3.org/Style/CSS/current-work

The Google HTML/CSS Style Guide

http://google-styleguide.googlecode.com/svn/trunk/htmlcssguide.xml

CSS Wizardry (Harry Robert's CSS Style)

http://csswizardry.com/2012/04/my-html-css-coding-style

The Github Style

http://github.com/styleguide/css

The CSS-Tricks code snippet website

http://css-tricks.com

Screenshot of alternate style sheets (Eric Meyer's Complex Spiral Demo)

http://meyerweb.com/eric/css/edge/complexspiral/demo.html

Chapter 11 Review Exercises

Chapter 11 Multiple-Choice Questions

1. There are three types of HTML doctype declarations, frameset, transitional or loose, and

   a) tight b) complete c) complex d) strict

2. The most complete version of the CSS specification is:

   a) CSS 2.1 b) CSS 1.0 c) CSS 3 d) CSS 4

3. The CSS declaration block includes a property separated by a colon from its:

   a) bullet b) element c) value d) style

4. The two basic HTML element types are the inline-level and the:

   a) bullet-level b) value-level c) block-level d) outline-level

5. The DTD stack shows the default element:

   a) on top b) at the bottom c) in the middle d) outside the stack altogether

Chapter 11 Design and Discussion Questions

1. Write the CSS code to create a library website which has two external style sheets. One which is website-wide called **site.css** and the other which is specific to the young adults section called **ya.css** which are found in the **css** folder on your website.
2. When should you consider using a media query rather than just a single set of external style sheets?
3. Describe why you might use the **@media** instead of the **@import** techniques.
4. Describe how and why you would use the CSS ID selector method to achieve the "look and feel" of a newsletter.
5. Briefly discuss the creation of CSS box structures and the shorthand for creating them.

12

XML

Just as entire textbooks have been written dedicated solely to unlocking, one by one, the many secrets and tricks of cascading style sheets (CSS), many texts have been written on the magic of Extensible Markup Language (XML). It would be foolish to think that we can put *every* detail about XML even leaving out the higher-level style sheeting, transformation, and other topics in a single chapter.

Instead, as we did with CSS in Chapters 6 and 11, we will try to unravel *some* of the many mysteries of XML so you may see how it can be used to enhance your library's web page designs and understand how Encoded Archival Description Language (EAD) and other XML applications or vocabularies are created and used. Our goal, then, is to outline how XML works and its applications. After reading this chapter you might decide to go further with XML by obtaining one of the many available references, or may find what is here is more than you need for your library's website. Either way, in Chapter 13 we'll give you a bit of a heads up on what to expect when HTML 4.01, CSS, and XML converge as the HTML5 specification of the future.

After some preliminary information on XML, this chapter will be split into two sections. The first is what I will call XML-lite, a method of describing new elements using style sheets; and the second shows the process of creating XML elements by writing document type definitions (DTDs) thus creating new DTD entries. As noted earlier, what we will not cover are the many, many more complex XML topics such as XML transformations, namespaces, and other "high-end" tools that are really a part of using XML to query databases and create output files. We will mention these, but only in passing.

This is a long, intense, chapter and, as noted once before, perhaps not for everyone. You might review some of the beginning sections to get an overview of XML and then pass over to the HTMLs chapter if/when you find your eyes glazing over.

What Is XML?

Like HTML and XHTML, XML, the Extensible Markup Language is a member of the family of standard generalized markup language document processing standards that have revolutionized the way content is presented via the Internet. HTML is a cross-platform, software and hardware independent tool used to format and display information that was designed to display data and focus on *how your data looks.* XML is a cross-platform, software and hardware independent tool for transmitting information that was designed to describe data and focus on *what your data is.* XML is much more than merely a markup language in that it allows anyone to create and format documents using customized elements in a new XML application or XML vocabulary. This establishes an unlimited number of semantically or cryptically named elements that a browser can interpret *in addition to* the 90 or so HTML 4.01 set of elements. The XML document can thus be defined by unique DTDs or schemas that specify how elements can be combined and what they can or must contain. As we will see later in this chapter, like CSS a simple DTD can be embedded into the XML document. A *schema* cannot be embedded in the XML document and has an extension of **.xsd** where external DTD files normally use the **.dtd** extension. As should be anticipated by now, you can find the 35-page XML 1.0 specification in its fifth edition on the W3 website at:

http://www.w3.org/TR/xml

But, we also said that XML is more than merely a markup language. XML can store data in files and databases for subsequent retrieval! That means that using higher levels of XML documents you could enter recipes into an online cookbook or add appointments to an online calendar. Or delete them. Or repackage them. All without hardcoding a single HTML document. Alas, many of these options are not available using our simple introduction to XML. You'll have to first understand the basics here, and then go off on your own, young web-savvy library page in hand, to master those techniques!

XML Applications or Vocabularies

The creation of specialized applications or vocabularies of semantic elements is a major outcome of the XML. We have already noted that although we have been calling it HTML, we have been actually using HTML written as an XML application, that is, XHTML. Among the dozens of other XML-based applications, chemists developed the Chemical Markup Language (CML), mathematician's created the Mathematical Markup Language (MathML), musicians the Musical Markup Language (MML), and newspapers came up with a way to distribute the news of the day via Really Simple Syndication (RSS). A list of these and other XML vocabularies for science and math applications and their namespace URLs can be found at the end of this chapter.

These efforts have not been lost on the library field where, in addition to RSS, our archivists have established the Encoded Archival Description Language (EAD) for finding aids, academics have created the Text Encoding Initiative (TEI), and librarians even created XML versions of the Dublin Core Metadata Element Set (DCMES).

Basic Web Document Requirements

Building on the HTML document requirements summarized in Figure 12-01, we have been designing our HTML web pages with a document declaration (**DOCTYPE**) followed by the root element (**html**), a **head** element container including the **title,** CSS and other content, then a **body** element container with the page content, and ending with the **html** root element closing tag.

Basic HTML Document Requirements

- include a **doctype** declaration
- use **html** as the document's root element
- use a **head** element container for **title**, **style**, etc.
- use a **body** element container for page content
- use lower case for ***all*** elements, attributes, values
- have all values enclosed in straight quotes [**"value"**]
- obey the element rules:

  non empty elements - must have an ending tag **[<p>...</p>]**

  empty elements - must be terminated **[
 ]**
- have no overlapping elements (***well-formedness***)
- use an **html** root element closing tag

Figure 12-01. Basic HTML Document Requirements

We have used only lowercase elements, attributes, and values; we've been "quoting" our values, terminating empty elements and being careful to avoid element overlapping.

Our HTML document files are ready to upgrade to become XML documents!

The XML Document

XML documents consist of three parts. The first is a four-part *prolog;* the second is the XML *document body* containing the document's hierarchical tree structure. The last is the optional XML *epilog* containing final comments and processing instructions.

The XML Prolog

The XML prolog consists of *four parts* in the following order:

1. An XML declaration
2. Miscellaneous statements and/or comments
3. XML processing instructions
4. An XML DTD

The XML declaration is always the first line of code in an XML document. It is a special type of processing instruction and thus, as with all processing instructions, must begin with a "less than" symbol followed by a question mark and end with a question mark followed by the "greater than" symbol. In general, then, an XML processing instruction follows the syntax:

```
<?target attribute="value" . . . ?>
```

The target for an XML declaration is **xml**—naturally all lowercase. This processing statement tells the processor that the document that follows is written using XML. The instruction can also provide any information about how the parser should interpret the code as attributes. The complete syntax of the required, generic, XML declaration is:

<xml version="*version number*" encoding="*encoding type*" standalone="*yes | no*" ?>

A typical XML declaration in an XML document would look like

<xml version="1.0" encoding="UTF-8" standalone="yes" ?>

or even merely:

<xml version="1.0" ?>

Notice that after the XML declaration **version** attribute (the default version is **"1.0"**) is the optional **encoding** attribute followed by the **standalone** attribute. But what do these attributes and their values mean?

Encoding: The Unicode Transformation Format

The default XML **encoding** attribute value is **"UTF-8"** with UTF-8 being a standard representing the Unicode Transformation Format that since 2010 has become the dominant character set on the web. **UTF-8** is an 8-bit version of the variable-width UTF character encoding that can represent every character in the Unicode character set. It was designed for backward compatibility with the American Standard Code for Information Interchange (ASCII) and pronounced As-key, which is the character set universally used in the beginning of computer messaging. UTF-8 Version 6.2 is the current standard that includes character sets for many different languages. Additional information on the ASCII Code and the various UTF standards, including character set tables, can be found at the following websites:

The ASCII Code

http://www.asciitable.com/

The Unicode Character Database

http://www.unicode.org/ucd/

The Unicode Transformation Format 8-bit Encoding website

http://www.utf-8.com/

One could, of course, use another encoding standard—typically **ISO-8859-1,** the Latin-1 character set which includes characters from non-English Western European languages. In either event please note that the **encoding** value *may* include uppercase letters, but the attributes themselves are *all* lowercase.

The last part of the XML declaration is the optional **standalone** attribute that allows the author to indicate whether the XML document includes links to external files. The pipe symbol (|) in the syntax structure example discussed earlier indicates that either "yes" *or* "no" is the value for the XML declaration's **standalone** attribute. If the XML declaration has either no **standalone** attribute or **standalone="no"** it implies the default value which indicates that there *are* external DTD files that your browser will need to use to parse or decode the document's XML elements. Answering **standalone="yes"** indicates that your XML document is self-contained although it may have DTDs embedded; and no external DTD files are required to be called nor are any needed to decode the document.

XML Comments and Style Sheets

XML comments or miscellaneous statements may appear anywhere in the document after the declarations and have the same syntax used in HTML:

<! - - comment text - - >

We also place our links to external style sheets in the prolog of our XML document. One or more links from the XML document to a style sheet can be created using an XML processing statement noted earlier using the general **<? . . . ?>** structure. A style sheet **processing instruction** is a command that gives instructions to the XML parser to link style sheets to the XML documents. Linking an XML document to a style sheet formats the XML document. The XML processor combines the style sheet with the XML document and applies any formatting codes defined in the style sheet to display a formatted document in your browser window.

Two main style sheet languages are used with XML: cascading style sheets (CSS) and Extensible Style Sheets (XSL). By separating content from format, you can concentrate on the appearance of the document. As we saw in our HTML documents, different style sheets can be applied to the same XML document. If we were creating an online public access catalog, we might include style sheets that would produce the equivalent of a subject card, title card, author card, and so on.

As may be expected, any style sheet changes will be automatically reflected in any web page based upon the particular external style sheet. We will review how to use both types of style sheets in XML later in this chapter.

Doctypes and DTDs

After we have informed the browser that it is looking at an XML document, we need to provide it with some doctype information. The XML document type declaration or DTD unlike that for an HTML document is *not* already saved inside your browser. The HTML 4.01 (etc.) DTD was there when you opened an HTML document; but with XML, your browser must be linked to whatever new elements, attributes, and others, are in a customized set of document display rules, the XML DTD. Even if you are using a "standard" XML Vocabulary DTD like EAD, TEI, and so on, *those* DTDs are *not* in your browser and thus must be included as internal subsets or have their external vocabulary file(s) linked to your document before it can be displayed properly.

In Chapter 11 we saw that the first line of our HTML documents contains the doctype DTD reference as well as both an external formal public identifier (FPI) and an external formal system identifier (FSI):

<!DOCTYPE html PUBLIC "FPI" "FSI">

In this example, the *document type name* **html** is by default the root or top-level element. Two external identifier keywords can be found immediately after this root

The HTML Doctype Declaration

<!DOCTYPE html PUBLIC "-//W3C//DTD HTML 4.01//EN" ← **PUBLIC identifier**

"http://www.w3.org/TR/html4/strict.dtd"> ← **SYSTEM identifier**

Figure 12-02. The HTML **DOCTYPE** Declaration

element, PUBLIC, the public identifier, and SYSTEM, the system identifier. In the HTML 4.01 strict specification doctype, we saw it contained a public identifier followed by a system identifier of Figure 12-02.

Note that when both a public and a system identifier are included in the doctype, only PUBLIC is declared. The system identifier uses a fully defined, absolute addressed external URL. If you create or have a local DTD file, in a **dtd** folder, it could be used using relative addressing (e.g., **dtd/root.dtd**).

The required XML doctype declaration is constructed in much the same way as that for HTML, but note that it does not indicate **xml** as the root element, but rather **root.** That is due to all XML documents being root element containers, described by the root element DTD.

```
<!DOCTYPE root_elementName SYSTEM | PUBLIC "name" "URL" >
```

Note the pipe symbol between SYSTEM and PUBLIC. It denotes the fact that the DTD can be either already built-in to your browser (PUBLIC) or if it is an external file called an external subset, it can be downloaded into your browser using the SYSTEM command. So what is the XML DTD? We will find most XML documents link to a customized DTD resident on their website:

```
<!DOCTYPE root SYSTEM "dtd/root.dtd" >
```

The reason is simply that there is no standard XML DTD, and thus no public version that could possibly be included in any browser.

The best we can do for a PUBLIC external XML DTD is to use the XHTML 1.0 DTD:

```
<!DOCTYPE html PUBLIC "-//W3C//DTD XHTML 1.0 Strict//EN"
        SYSTEM "http://www.w3.org/TR/xhtml1/DTD/xhtml1-strict.dtd" >
```

OK, OK, I know what you are thinking, that's not an XML DTD! You're right.

EAD, TEI, and Other Library-Oriented Vocabularies

There are several XML vocabularies that *are* available and *do* have public identifiers and are used by subsets of our library and information science profession. Perhaps the most popular of these is the archivist's friend, the EAD, which defines the markup and rules for encoding archival finding aides.

The prolog of all (XML) EAD-encoded documents must begin with the following document type declaration:

```
<!DOCTYPE ead PUBLIC "-//Society of American Archivists//DTD
        ead.dtd (Encoded Archival Description (EAD) Version 1.0)//EN">
```

Notice that this declaration defines the **ead** root element and does not have a system identifier as it uses the Society of American Archivists (SAA) EAD version 1.0 DTD directly. Another common public EAD identifier links to the EAD DTD version 2002:

<!DOCTYPE ead PUBLIC "+//ISBN 1-931666-00-8//DTD ead.dtd (Encoded Archival Description (EAD) Version 2002)//EN">

Lots of additional support information is available online from either the SAA, the Library of Congress, or by doing a web search on EAD:

The Society of American Archivists EAD Standard

http://www2.archivists.org/groups/technical-subcommittee-on-encoded-archival-description-ead/encoded-archival-description-ead

The EAD Tag Library (Version 2002)

http://www2.archivists.org/sites/all/files/EAD_TagLibrary_2002.pdf

The LOC Official EAD Website

http://www.loc.gov/ead

EAD Application Guidelines for Version 1.0

http://www.loc.gov/ead/ag/

Another library-relevant XML vocabulary is the TEI designed for the scholarly analysis of texts. According to its website, TEI is a consortium that collectively develops and maintains a set of guidelines, which specify encoding methods for machine-readable texts, chiefly in the humanities, social sciences, and linguistics. Although I have not personally used TEI, and TEI does not seem to have a public identifier, the TEI Consortium website has tutorials on how to utilize the general XML structure to capture and encode text. TEI defines concepts to represent a much wider array of textual phenomena, amounting to a total of 503 elements and 210 attributes. These are organized into 21 modules, grouping related elements and attributes.

A *namespace* for TEI can be invoked as the first line of a TEI document, that is, an XML document with a TEI root element:

<TEI xmlns="http://www.tei-c.org/ns/1.0" xml:lang="en">

A namespace declaration permits us to obtain a DTD from an external s, the declaration begins with the TEI declaration, TEI, followed by **xmlns**—the abbreviation for XML Namespace whose URL is in quotes. The URL is followed by the declaration that English **xml:lang="en"** is the language in use. Academic librarians may well wish to investigate this vocabulary further!

The Text Encoding Initiative Consortium (TEI-C) has TEI information at:

http://www.tei-c.org

Another LOC XML vocabulary that may be of interest to catalogers is the LOC's initiative for XML encoding of Machine Readable Cataloging (MARC) records of books and others. LOC has downloadable DTD files as well as XML schema. The Lane Medical Library at Stanford University Medical Center created a software program XMLMARC that converts MARC records into XML and MARCUTL (the MARC Update and Transformation Language) which is a mapping language that converts MARC into XML or MARC into "updated MARC" based on the instructions in a MARCUTL file but it seems they may have abandoned the project after September 2002. The U.S. National Library of Medicine on the other hand seems to have created a Journal Article Tag Suite, which includes an Archiving and Interchange Tag Set, a Journal Publishing Tag Set, an Article Authoring Tag Set, and an NCBI Book Tag Set:

MARC in XML from LOC

http://www.loc.gov/marc/marcxml.html

Medlane XMLMARC at Stanford University

http://xmlmarc.stanford.edu

National Center for Biotechnology Information NISO Journal Article Tag Suite

http://dtd.nlm.nih.gov/

Although the Dublin Core, DC, is an HTML **meta** element, and not really an XML application, it is often used in XML documents. Later in this chapter we will view take a look at the Dublin Core Metadata Element Set (DCMES) of 15 elements we normally see as **meta** element **name** attributes (contributor, coverage, creator, date, description, format, identifier, language, publisher, relation, rights, source, subject, title, and type). The DCMES standard file is stored as a resource description framework **RDF** file. We won't be discussing the RDF data model here, but that doesn't mean you could not use this link and point to the namespace to use the DMCES. We will see how the Dublin Core DTD was developed later in this chapter.

Dublin Core Metadata Initiative

http://dublincore.org/

Dublin Core Metadata Element Set Namespace (RDF File)

http://purl.org/dc/elements/1.1/

The Open Archives Initiative (OAI) is a project headquartered at Cornell University that develops and promotes interoperability standards that aim to facilitate the efficient dissemination of content. The OAI has its roots in an effort to enhance access to e-print archives as a means of increasing the availability of scholarly communication. It does this primarily by sharing XML-encoded (DC) metadata between its member institutions.

Open Archives Initiative

http://www.openarchives.org/

Internal DTD Subsets

In addition to external subsets of DTDs we can link to, we can have an internal subset of embedded document type definitions in our XML document. That is we can use both as long as the two DTDs do not use the *same* element names as that *would confuse our browser,* and we *don't* want to do that!

The general doctype declaration for the root element **root** is defined in the **root.dtd** file on our website in the **dtd** folder, and expanded by an internal subset of additional element, attribute and entity references would look like:

```
<!DOCTYPE root SYSTEM "dtd/root.dtd"
[
    <!-- internal subset document type definitions -->
]>
```

We will see what those internal subset document type definitions look like for elements, attributes, and entity references and how to create them later in this chapter under the heading Creating XML Documents using DTDs. In the prolog of our XML document we would also see one or more calls for special external files. These would include XML namespaces discussed earlier when we reviewed the TEI namespace and style sheets.

The XML Body

Any overview of the **body** section of an XML document, except for the XML-specific declarations and doctypes, would show a pretty typical HTML-like document. We would notice that the root or document element was not **html,** and we would see some "strange" element names; we did after all just create them <grin>—but the overall, well-formed element container structure would be there and be relatively easy to follow and understand. The document ends with the closing of the root or document element as we saw with the **</html>** closing tag of our HTML document and as we'll see in Figure 12-03.

The XML Epilog

The last part of an XML document is the optional and seldom-used epilog that can include processing instructions and any final comments. Regrettably, there is very little said about the epilog in the various texts and online. If present, the epilog appears after the closing element tag. Fortunately the browser's parser doesn't read these anyway, so you can put lots of notes for others to follow about how your document was created, or even what you plan on doing if you ever get a chance to revise the document.

According to Robert Richards in his text *Pro PHP XML and Web Services* © 2006, a Google e-Book published by Apress (**http://www.apress.com**) with ISBN13: 978–1-59059–633–3, the epilog section of an XML document refers to the markup *after* the close of the XML document **body** and "is the equivalent to the **MISC*** portion of the

Basic XML Document Structure

```
<?xml version="1.0" encoding="UTF-8" standalone="yes" ?>
<!DOCTYPE root SYSTEM"dtd/root.dtd"
        [
                <! - - internal sub set document type definitions - ->
        ]>
<root>
        <body>
          <element1>...</element1>
          <element2>...</element2>
          <! - - other Web Page Content using HTML, XML elements, etc. - - >
          <element3>...</element3>
          <element4>...</element4>
        </body>
</root>
```

Figure 12-03. Basic XML Document Structure

document definition as defined using the Extended Backus-Naur Form (EBNF) notation." His example is

Document ::* prolog element MISC*

Putting all the XML prolog pieces together, *not including the optional epilog*, yields a document like Figure 12-03.

Creating XML Documents without Using DTDs

Later in this chapter we'll see that we can create either an internal subset of DTD declarations or an external file with customized declarations in it. For now, we'll look at an easier way to produce an XML document method that I will call ***XML-like*** which relies not on document type declarations, but on already familiar style sheet techniques to describe how a particular element should look. Finally, you'll get to see some code!

A CSS-Structured XML Cookbook

So here is our scenario, your Friends of the Red Rose Library decide to collect recipes from local professional chiefs, your staff, and your other patrons as a fund-raising project. Of course *you* will have to figure out how to assemble them as a cookbook and sell them <grin>. It is also decided to have the contents available in a web accessible format for access within the library.

They envision the cookbook to have one or more recipes. You suggest that it should also have a table of contents and index. Each recipe would include a recipe category (e.g., beef, lamb, fish, eggs, vegetarian); the recipe's title and author(s); a recipe summary which includes the difficulty level, preparation time, cooking time, and yield for the recipe; a list of ingredients with the amount and kind of ingredients; the recipe instruction steps; and, finally, any notes deemed necessary or appropriate, for example, who the author is or where the recipe came from.

The basic hierarchical structure for a cookbook with table of contents (contents), three recipes (**recipe**) and an index, might look like Figure 12-04.

```
cookbook
        contents
        recipe
                category
                title
                author
                summary
                        level
                        preptime
                        cooktime
                        yield
                ingredients
                        amount, kind
                        ...
                directions
                        steps
                        ...
                notes
        recipe
        ...
        recipe
        ...
        index
```

Figure 12-04. Basic Hierarchical Structure for a Cookbook

We could, of course, go about creating an HTML document that would probably incorporate CSS to produce a recipe web page using standard HTML elements. That document might be similar to Figure 12-05.

Note that a formal HTML doctype declaration *is* in the actual **code1205.htm** file, but not included here as has been our norm. When displayed in a browser, the recipe could look like Figure 12-06.

Well this is a pretty simple, but decent-looking recipe display. The presentation is fine and the code is good, so why would we want to change it?

What if we could define each of the types of content not by simple division, paragraphs, and the like, but by meaningful element names, like the way we have the structure laid out in Figure 12-04 with words like recipe, yield, and so on? What if those element names could be selected by the web page document to be displayed in different ways for say tables of contents, related recipes, and so on? What if we could put the content of all our recipes into a database and then call the specific content out when we want it rather than having a prewritten web page for each and every recipe? We can, using XML.

XML Document Construction

All XML and HTML elements must be nested within a single **document** or **root element.** There can be only **one** root element. The HTML root element is **html.** An **open** or **empty** element is an element that contains no content. They can be used to mark sections of the document for the XML parser and are single-ended, self-closing elements. Their syntax is:

<empty_element_name />

```
<html>
        <head><title>Friends of The Red Rose Library Cookbook: EGGS</title>

        <style ...>
        </style>

        </head>
<body>
        <h1>All About Eggs</h1>
        <h2>Hard Boiled Eggs</h2>
        <h4>Anonymous</h4>
<div class="summary">
        Level: Beginner <br />
        Preparation Time: None <br />
        Cooking Time: 3 to 5 minutes <br />
        Yield: One egg per person <br />
        </div>
<div class="ingredients">
        <ul>
        <li> One per person:  Egg </li>
        </ul>
</div>
<div class="directions">
        <ol>
        <li> Put egg(s) into pot covering them with 1 inch of water. </li>
        <li> Heat water to a brisk, rolling boil.</li>
        <li> After 3-5 minutes remove from heat.</li>
        <li> Drain water and allow to cool.</li>
        <li> Remove shell and eat.</li>
        </ol>
</div>
<div class="notes">
        Make sure to wait until the egg(s) cools down before removing
        the shell or you might burn your fingers!
        </div>
</body></html>
```

Figure 12-05. Basic HTML Recipe for a Cookbook (**code1205.htm**)

Closed or double-ended XML elements also have the same syntax as we saw for HTML elements:

<element_name>Content</element_name>

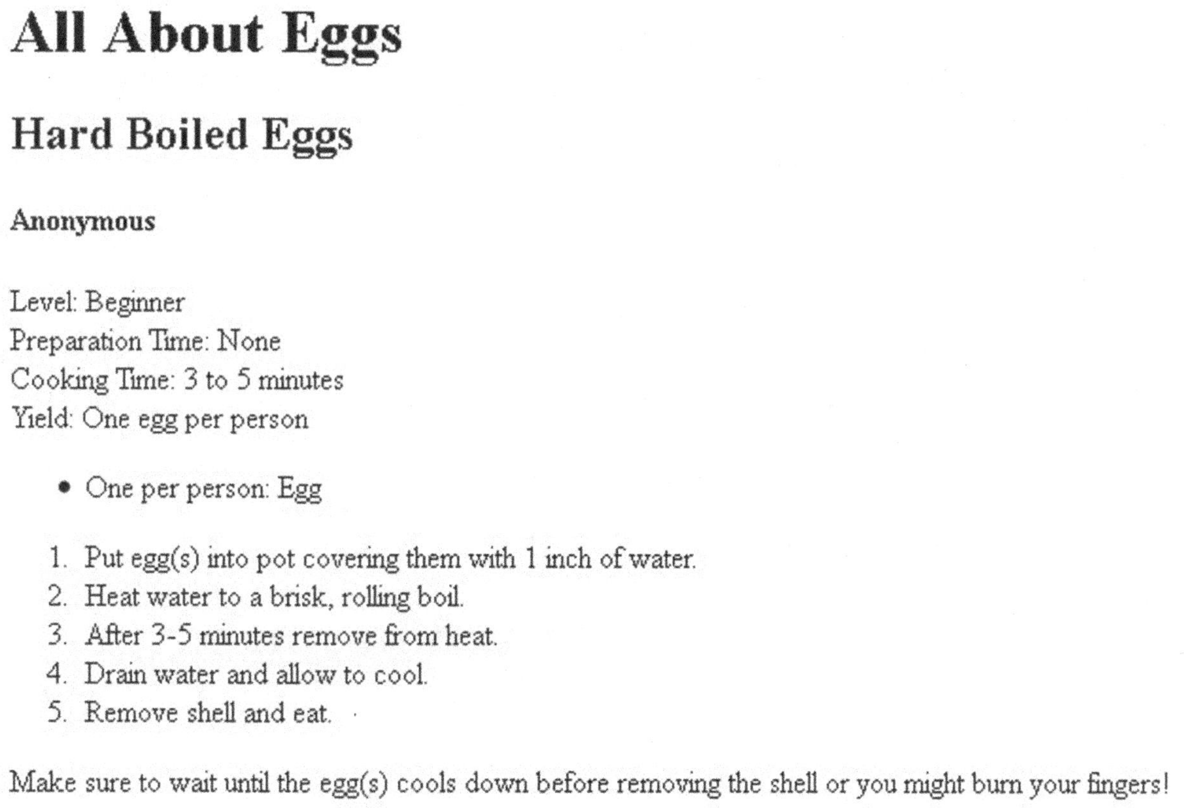

All About Eggs

Hard Boiled Eggs

Anonymous

Level: Beginner
Preparation Time: None
Cooking Time: 3 to 5 minutes
Yield: One egg per person

- One per person: Egg

1. Put egg(s) into pot covering them with 1 inch of water.
2. Heat water to a brisk, rolling boil.
3. After 3-5 minutes remove from heat.
4. Drain water and allow to cool.
5. Remove shell and eat.

Make sure to wait until the egg(s) cools down before removing the shell or you might burn your fingers!

Figure 12-06. HTML Recipe Browser Display (**code1205.htm**)

Good to Know: Unlike HTML elements, ***All XML element names are case sensitive.*** Simply speaking, the element named **recipe** will *NOT* match the elements Recipe, reCipe, and so on, and thus the opening tag **<recipe>** will result in a syntax error when your browser finds **</reCipe>** which is not a matching ending tag.

As we observed with HTML documents, elements must be nested correctly per Figure 12-07.

These nested elements are often called child elements. Child element containers must be enclosed within their parent element containers.

Creating an *XML-Like* Document

If we merge the semantic structure names of Figure 12-04 with the HTML document of Figure 12-05, we will get a new document that semantically describes each of the element containers of the document—Figure 12-08.

Wow, that looks great in the text editor. But what does it look like when the browser opens the file thinking it is an HTML document? Figure 12-09 shows that the browser has no way of knowing what these strange element names are. So in true browser fashion, it ignores all the tags and treats our file as if it were a simple text file.

```
<directions>                                                          ← Parent Opening tag
<steps> 1. Put Egg in pot, cover with an inch of cold water </steps>  ← Child container
<steps> 2. Heat the water to a rolling boil. </steps>                 ← Child container
</directions>                                                         ← Parent Opening tag
```

Figure 12-07. Element Nesting for Well-Formedness

```
<cookbook>
        <contents>The table of contents info goes here</contents>
        <recipe>
                <category>All About Eggs</category>
                <title>Hard Boiled Eggs</title>
                <author>Anonymous</author>
                <summary>
                        <level>Beginner</level>
                        <preptime>None</preptime>
                        <cooktime>3 to 5 minutes</cooktime>
                        <yield>One per person</yield>
                </summary>
                <ingredients>
                        <amount>One per person</amount>
                        <kind>Egg</kind>
                </ingredients>
                <directions>
                        <steps>
                Put egg(s) into pot covering them with inch of water</steps>
                        <steps>Heat water to a brisk, rolling boil</steps>
                </directions>
                <notes>
                Make sure to wait until the egg(s) cools down before removing
                the shell or you might burn your fingers!
                </notes>
        </recipe>
        (repeat for additional recipes ... )
        <index>your index of all the recipes goes here</index>
</cookbook>
```

Figure 12-08. Semantic Recipe Elements (**code1208.htm**)

Well that doesn't look very good at all. We have all the content, but none of the styling. Now what? Perhaps if we were able to add some style to these new elements the browser could be "tricked" into thinking that they were legitimate element names and would display them in a nicer way? Well, let's see if that can work.

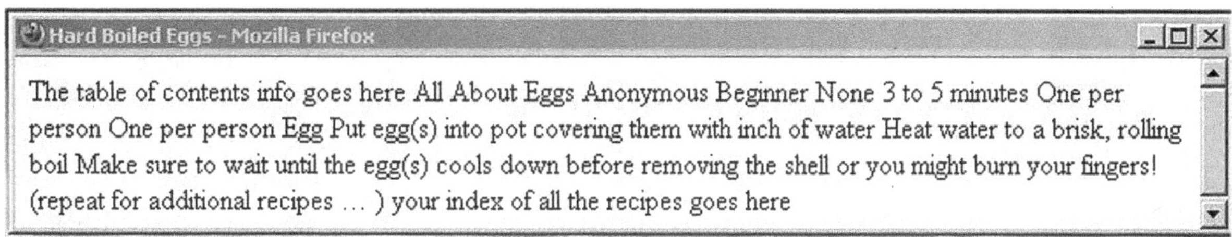

Figure 12-09. Browser View of Semantic Recipe Elements (**code1208.htm**)

The XML Document Tree

Since we will be looking only at its style characteristics, we really don't need to verify the structure of this new document at this time. But this is a good point in our discussion to bring up the concept of visualizing a document's hierarchical structure using tree diagramming. We will have to make some definitions for how the individual elements can be described. Elements are described relative to where they are in the structure. The topmost or root element is considered the overall *parent element* in the document. Each element inside the parent container is considered a *child element.* A child element can also be a parent element if it, too, has child elements in its container. We will have to presume that we can have situations where we would only have a single element, others where we could have one or more and repeatable elements, and so on, as shown in Figure 12-10.

These rules are summarized, and put into a tree diagram model for possibilities of elements for a library in Figure 12-11 where the library **collection** parent may have zero or more **book** children, with each **book** having **title, author(s)**, and possibly **chapter** child elements.

Character — Meaning(s) / **(Example)**
(none): — ***must*** have only one child element
(element_name)
*** Asterisk:** — ***zero or more*** child elements (*optional, repeatable*)
(element_name)* *or* **(element_name*)**
+ Plus: — ***one or more*** child elements (*occurs at least once*)
(element_name)+ *or* **(element_name+)**
? Question Mark: — ***at most one*** child element (*zero or one occurrence*)
(element_name)? *or* **(element_name?)**
, Comma (AND/sequence): ***must*** *contain 1, 2, and 3* ***in that order***
(element_name1, element_name2, element_name3)
| Pipe (OR/choice): ***may*** *contain elements 1, 2, and 3*
(*either/or/all, optional, repeatable; zero or more*)
(element_name1 | element_name2 | element_name3)

Figure 12-10. Establishing Tree Structure Rules

If we were to combine all four sub-diagrams of Figure 12-11 together, we could create a tree diagram such as Figure 12-12 where the library **collection** parent may have zero or more (*) **book** child elements, with each **book** child being the parent to one **title** element, one or more (+) **author** elements, one or more (+) **chapter** child elements who might or might not be a parent element to **figures** child elements.

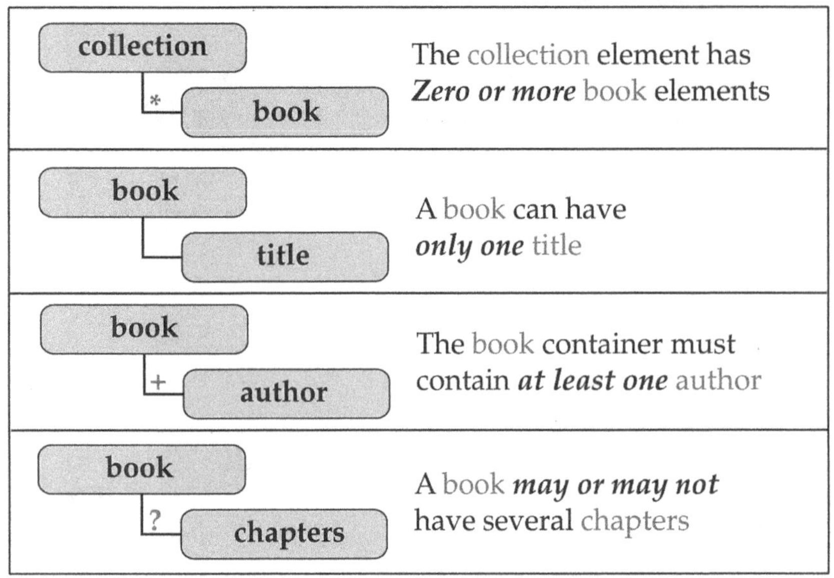

collection
*
book
The collection element has
Zero or more book elements
book
title
A book can have
only one title
book
+
author
The book container must
contain at least one author
book
?
chapters
A book may or may not
have several chapters

Figure 12-11. Tree Diagram Modules with Structure Rules

Referring back to Figure 12-04, we can create a tree diagram for a **cookbook** that contains a table of contents, one or more recipes, and one index as noted in Figure 12-13. The topmost or root element for the XML document would be **cookbook.** Decoding the cookbook element according to these tree diagram rules shows that a **cookbook** can have one **contents,** at least one (+) **recipe** and one **index.**

The **recipe** element tree of Figure 12-14, although quite a bit more complicated, is also based upon the hierarchical cookbook structure of Figure 12-04. You would have one **recipe** structure for each recipe in the XML **cookbook** root document. The **recipe** in this diagram does not a represent a root element, even though it appears to be the topmost element in this figure. This is due to it actually being a child element inside the **cookbook** parent element container of Figure 12-13. Decoding the **recipe** element tree diagram of Figure 12-14, a **recipe** can have one **category,** one **title,** at least one (+) **author,** one **summary** with one **level,** one **preptime,** one **cooktime,** and one **yield,** with a set of **ingredients** with at least one (+) **amount** and **kind,** a set of **directions** with at least one (+) **step,** and zero or one **notes** element for every **recipe** element (in the **cookbook** document).

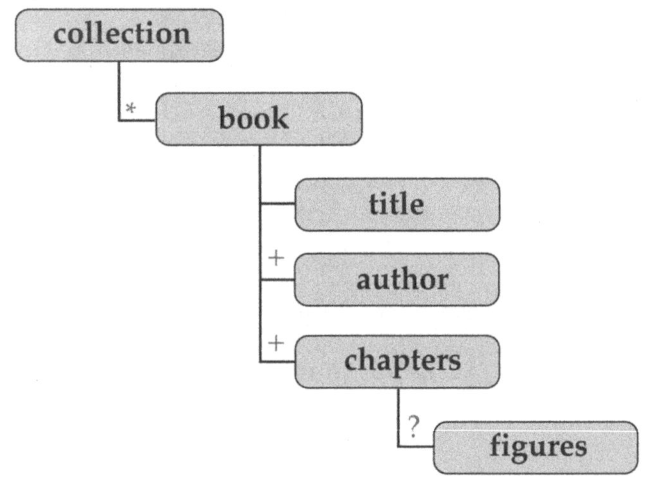

collection
*
book
title
+
author
+
chapters
?
figures

Figure 12-12. Basic **books** Tree Diagram

We can create additional tree diagram structures to illustrate how an XML **play** document might look in Figure 12-15, where a **play** can have one **title,** one **abstract,** at least one (+) **act,** with one **act_number** and zero or more (*) **scenes**, with a **scene_number** and **location** and at least one (+) **actor** for each **scene** element.

We can also create a tree diagram structure to illustrate how a record collection document might look. In Figure 12-16, the topmost or root element **records** can have zero or more (*) **albums.** Each **album** *must* have one **title,** at least one (+) **artist,** may or may not have (?) **tracks,** but if they do exist, there must be at least one (+) **track.**

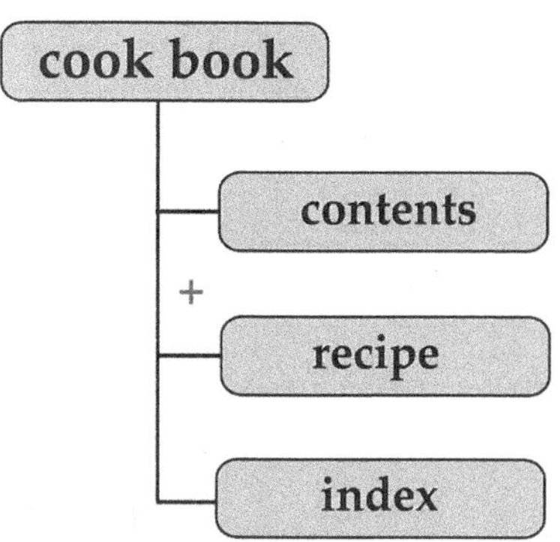

Figure 12-13. Basic **cookbook** Tree Diagram

XML Namespaces

You develop a DTD and share it with your colleagues. They add a bit and you all agree on several modifications. Now everyone in your library system wants to use the same DTD for their web portfolios. They could each place a copy of this new DTD on their individual websites or DTD folder to use. BUT, what if you and your group members want to use that DTD as a standard?

Namespaces were designed to fix a single instance of a DTD for ease in use and maintainability at a single website using a Uniform Resource Identifier (URI), just another name for a URL, where the group's resources are stored. So let's say you were part of the Dublin Core Metadata Element Set (**DCMES**) group. After creating your DTD, you might store the file at:

http://purl.org/dc/xmlns/2008/09/01/dc-ds-xml/

The resource there, **dcelements.rdf,** is a Resource Description Framework **RDF** file. The RDF data model is a modeling approach based upon the idea of making statements about web resources, in the form of subject-predicate-object expressions known as *RDF triples.* The RDF *subject* denotes the resource, and the *RDF predicate* denotes traits or aspects of the resource and expresses a relationship between the subject and the *RDF object.* For example: "*The sky* has the color blue."

The RDF triple for "The sky has the color blue" is "the sky" as the subject, "has the color" as a predicate, and "blue" is an object. More information on RDF can be found at the W3 Consortium website at:

http:// www.w3.org/RDF

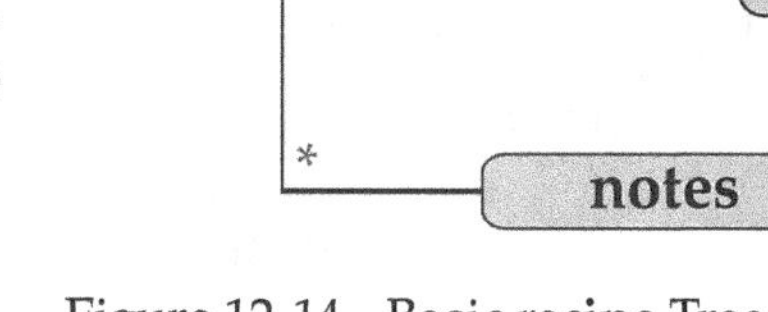

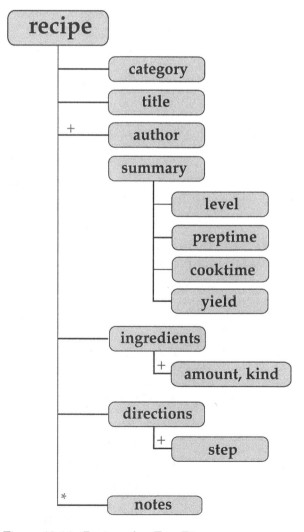

Figure 12-14. Basic **recipe** Tree Diagram

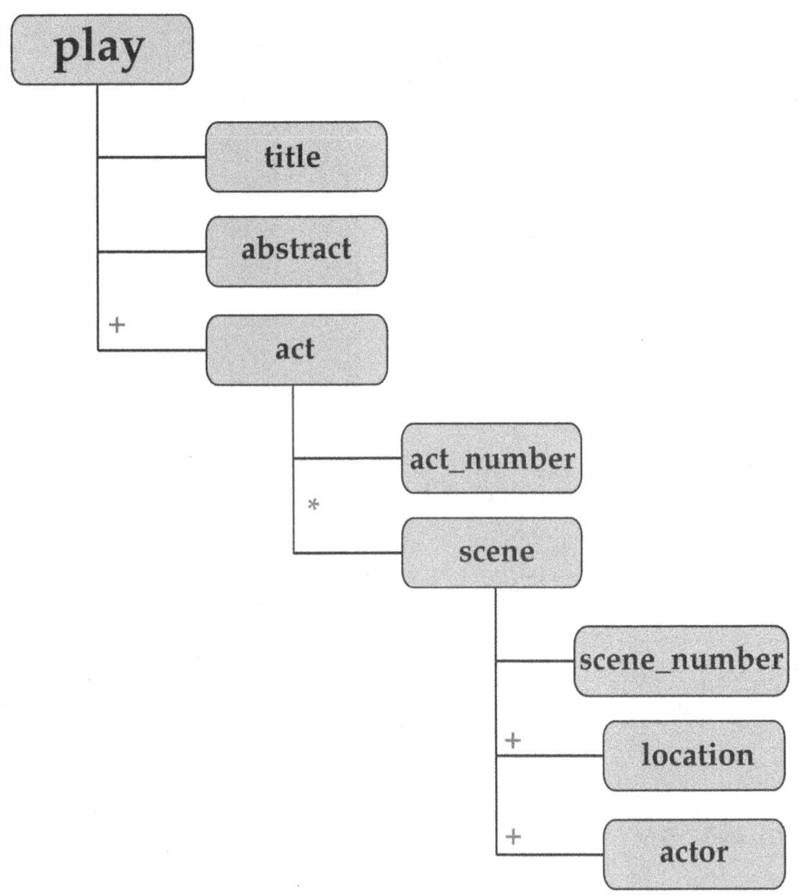

Figure 12-15. Basic **play** Tree Diagram

XML Dublin Core Metadata Set (DCMES) Tree Diagrams

We can use tree diagrams to illustrate how the 15-element XML Dublin Core Metadata Set (**DCMES**) **Collection** document might look. In Figure 12-17, the **Collection** can have zero or more (*) **records**. Each **record** *must* have one **title,** at least one (+) **creator,** at least one (+) **subject,** one **description, publisher, contributor,** and **date,** at least one (+) **type,** one **format, identifier, source,** and **language,** at least one (+) **relation,** may or may not have (?) **coverage** and one **rights** Dublin Core element.

Clearly there are lots and lots of other documents we use all the time that have hierarchical structures and thus could be visualized as tree diagrams. Once these are diagrammed, that diagram can be used to create either an *XML-like* or *full XML* (with DTD) document.

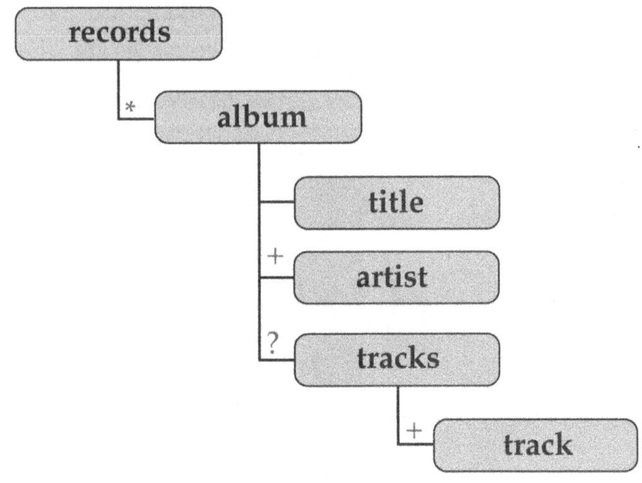

Figure 12-16. Basic **records** Tree Diagram

XML-Like Presentations: Using CSS to Create an XML Document

As we saw earlier, in Figure 12-08 (**code1208.htm**), we can create a document using the elements that we previously created; but as we saw in Figure 12-09, our browser, as it has no default style information on these "unknown" elements, will render the page as if they did not exist. We end up with an XML document that is displayed, without style, just like a basic, unstyled, plain text HTML document. Our **cookbook, contents, rec-**

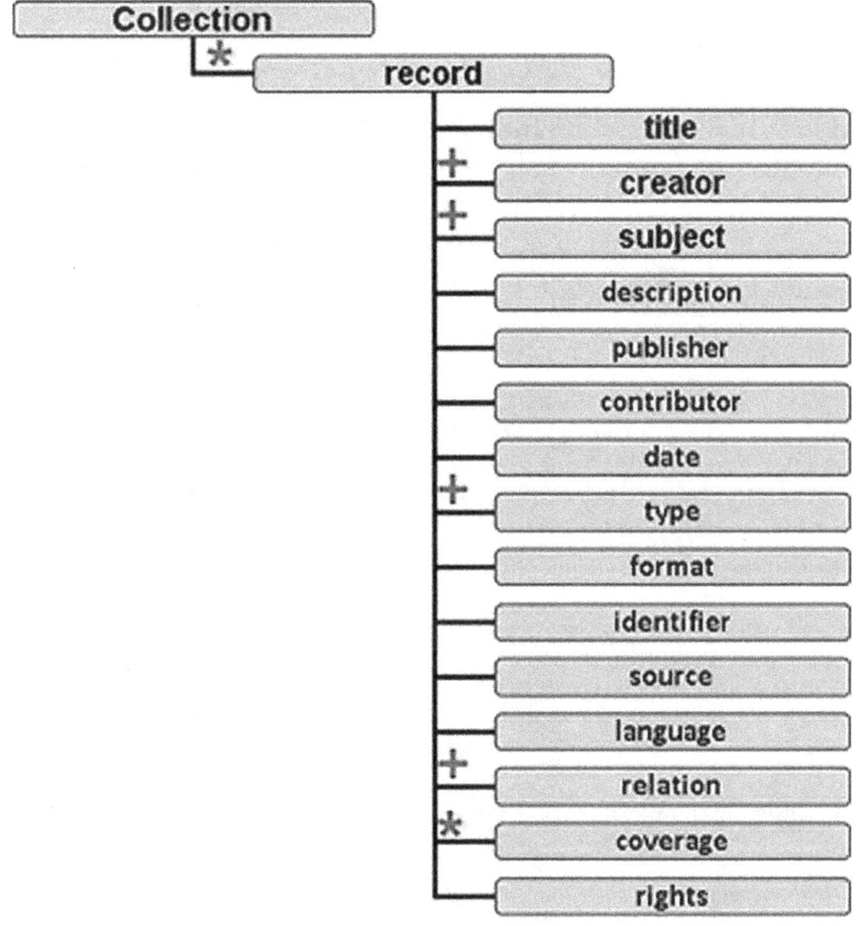

Figure 12-17. Basic **Dublin Core Metadata Set** (DCMES) Tree Diagram

ipe (and all its children), and **index** elements have no match to the HTML elements in our browser's DTD tables.

Let's recall that using style sheet techniques, per Chapters 6 and 11, we can change the style defaults for HTML elements in our browser DTD stack by merely including internal or external CSS declarations. Going back to **code1208.htm,** let's add inline **style** declarations to the **con-**

Good to Know: Had we defined any new elements that had the same names as the HTML 4.01 DTD element set stored in our browser (e.g., the **title** for our **recipe** element, as we did here), we would expect to see those elements interpreted properly by the browser. Thus, we would expect to see "Hard-Boiled Eggs"—the **title** of the **code1208.htm** file—shown as the **title** in the browser rather than the file name: **code1208.htm.** Indeed, referring back to Figure 12-08, we see that the browser *has* found the **title** element and correctly decoded it (even though we did not use the HTML root) and displayed the HTML title at the top of its display.

tents element that will give it bold, centered, and blue 20 point high Arial text inside of a solid blue-bordered ivory box with a 10 pixel margin and 15 pixels of padding using the opening tag of Figure 12-18

```
<contents style="color:blue; font-weight:bold; text-align:center:
font-size:20pt; font-family:Arial, Helvetica, sans-serif; border:3px solid blue;
background-color:ivory; margin:10px; padding:15px;">
```

and see what, if anything, happens to our browser's output. Figure 12-18 shows the addition of these inline stylizations.

```
<cookbook>
    <contents style="color:blue; font-weight:bold; text-align:center;
            font-size:20pt; font-family: Arial, Helvetica, sans-serif;
            border:3px solid blue; background-color: ivory;
            margin: 10 px; padding: 15px; ">
The table of contents info goes here </contents>
  <recipe>
        <category>All About Eggs</category>
        <title>Hard Boiled Eggs</title>
        <author>Anonymous</author>
...
</cookbook>
```

Figure 12-18. Adding Inline Style Code to the **cookbook** Document (**code1218.htm**)

Note that at this time we are not declaring any document type, and there may be a browser error in some cases. Please also note that the remainder of the **code1208.htm** document code is removed from the figure except for **cookbook** closing tag to simplify the figure. Figure 12-19 shows how the browser, once again, only styles or displays properly those elements already in its DTD or that have been styled in the document itself. Note that as we did not center the contents block nor did we create any spacing using either HTML or style, the remaining text flows inside and all around the contents styling.

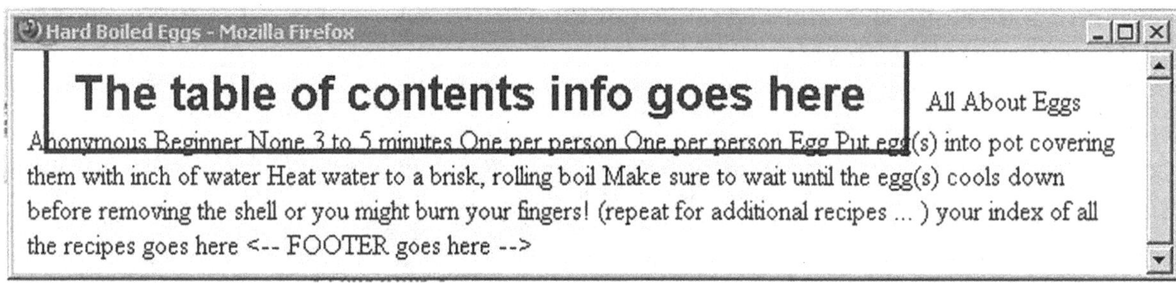

Figure 12-19. The **cookbook** Document with Inline CSS Styling (**code1218.htm**)

Adding the style **display:block;** to this file results in the display of Figure 12-20, which looks more pleasing as well as more like what we might want to see in our browser display. The block creates the needed directions that declare this to be a standalone block of content that should be separated from the remaining text.

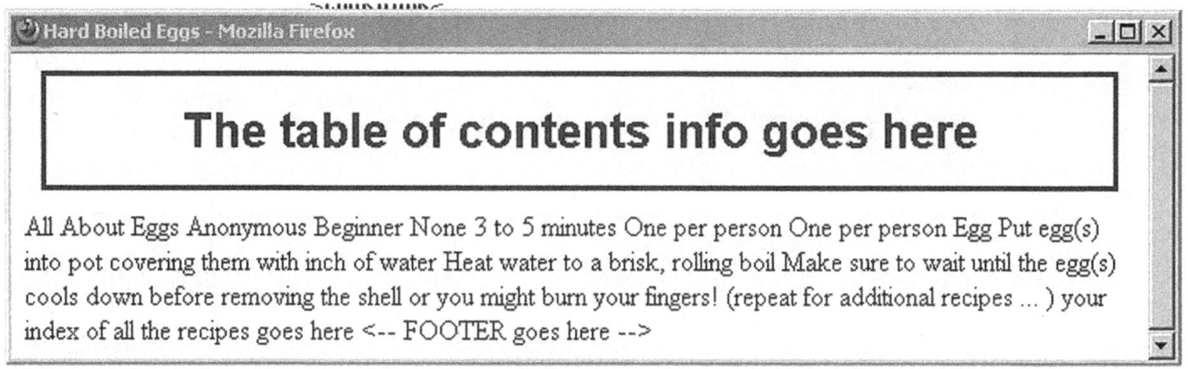

Figure 12-20. The **cookbook** Document with CSS Block Style (**code1220.htm**)

Clearly, you should realize that if this result can be had by merely adding inline style to the new element names, we could create a quality display using internal, or even external CSS style declarations. Our next step, if we want to replicate the HTML recipe display of Figure 12-06, would be to match our new element names with the HTML elements used to present the Hard-Boiled Egg recipe. Looking at Figures 12-05 and 12-08 we find that if we were to create **h1, h2,** and **h4** headlines as well as an unordered and ordered list, we would receive the result we are looking for. The concordance between these two files is shown in Figure 12-21.

Our task then is to create styles for **h1, h2, h4, ul, li, ol,** and the general **body** elements, remove the inline styling of the **contents** element, and include it and the styles for our other elements as internal **style** commands placing them after the opening **cookbook** element. We can use the same style for the index as the contents element, but bear in mind that normally we would not want the browser display to exceed the length and width of a printed piece of paper. You might actually only link to those two pages and not have them "frame" the recipe and might well want to include a banner for the cookbook instead.

Figure 12-05	Figure 12-08
h1	category
h2	title
h4	author
ul	ingredients
li	amount, steps
ol	directions
(body)	level, preptime, cooktime, yield, notes

Figure 12-21. Equating HTML and **recipe** Document Elements

Creating HTML Element Styles in CSS

Although we could meticulously look up the HTML DTDs for the elements we want to create by examining the existing HTML 4.01 specification or another vocabulary, and their default attributes and styles, note that the three headlines required here are all "blocks" of content in that they have a paragraph-like structure with spaces before/after them.

Good to Know: The CSS2.1 specification indicates the standard *style* for an **h1** element is:

> **h1 {font-weight:bold; font-size:12pt; line-height:14pt; font-family:Helvetica; font-variant:normal; font-style:normal}**

We should recall that unlike our *XML-like* method of using CSS to create element structures, the HTML **h1** element already has a DTD and thus the CSS is not concerned with the structural aspects of its definition.

As the only difference between headline elements is their size, we'll use 18 point, 14 point, and 10 point, bold, with some color (red) and with the text 20 pixels from the margin. We could have used the **line-height** or other styles of the typical h1 element, but the idea here is to create a display of our styling. Thus, we can let the browser decide on what font-family to display, which will probably be the serifed Times New Roman. For the **category** element headline this styling looks like:

category {display:block; font-size:18pt; font-weight:bold; color:red; margin:20px;}

Good to Know: Lest we forget, the margin, as well as padding, and so on, whitespace styles have the ability to define an all-around spacing of 20 pixels using, as shown here, **margin:20px;** or can be broken down into the individual **margin-left, margin-right, margin-top,** and/or **margin-bottom** definitions.

We want to display plain text as the browser's defaults with a new line formed each time for our **level, preptime, cooktime,** and **yield** elements, as well as our **kind** element, currently a child element of **ingredients.** When we create the DTD later in this chapter, we will use **kind** as an attribute of **amount** rather than as a new element. We'll color the first four elements green to make sure we can identify them for future reference. Each element needs to be 20 pixels from the left margin. By adding **margin-bottom:10px;** to the **yield** element's style we gain a separation between this block of elements and the ingredients.

Our plain text **notes** element needs to be in a block format, black text, perhaps in italics and a bit smaller than the regular text to make the display a bit more pleasing:

```
level, preptime, cooktime {display:block; color:green; margin-left:20px;}
yield {display:block; color:green; margin-left:20px; margin-bottom:10px;}
notes {display:block; font-size:10pt; color:black; font-style:italic;
       margin:20px;}
```

The CSS style definition of unordered and ordered lists (**ul** and **ol**) is a bit more interesting, not to mention difficult. Let's ignore the unordered **amount** and **kind** list for the single ingredient of this recipe and create it as text displayed as an inline block with the **display:inline;** declaration and set it a bit deeper into our display by increasing the **amount** element's left margin to 35 pixels. As the **kind** element is intended to be on the *same line* and as an attribute of the **amount,** we'll just color it red to remind us it is not the same element. The result is as shown here:

```
amount {display:inline; margin-left:35px;}
kind {color:red;}
```

We will define our **steps** element's *ordered list* using the **display:list-item;** declaration, whose default bullet is a filled circle even though the bullets in the HTML display of Figure 12-06 were decimal numbers. To make the list even more easily recognizable, we can reduce the font size to 10 pixels as well as add some color and a font change to the **steps** element stylization. To make the steps easier to read, we can include a top margin of 3 pixels between steps and also increase the left margin to 50 pixels so the steps are nestled nicely under the ingredients listing:

```
steps {display:list-item; font-size:10pt; color:green;
font-family:Arial, Helvetica, sans-serif; margin-left:50px; margin-top:3px;}
```

As noted earlier, the contents and index element styling is identical to show where header banners and footer elements might go on a recipe page. The resulting internal CSS styling of our *XML-like* document is shown in Figure 12-22. The full document is included in the **code1221.htm** file; note that there is no doctype declaration in that file as this is not a standard HTML or XML document.

Note that only the new declarations shown in Figure 12-22 create the display of Figure 12-23, illustrating the results of adding internal CSS stylization to our new element names. Interestingly enough, although the **title** element is interpreted properly as an HTML element as noted in the browser calling the "web page" Hard-Boiled Eggs, the new **title** element also acquires its new role with CSS styling. *Note: Some spacing has been removed to make the figure fit better on this page.*

```
    <style>
contents, index {display:block; width:600px; color:blue; text-align:center;
    font-size:20pt; font-family:Arial, Helvetica, sans-serif;
    border:3px solid blue; background-color:ivory; margin:10px; padding:15px;}
category {display:block; font-size:18pt; font-weight:bold; color:red; margin:20px;}
title  {display:block; font-size:14pt; font-weight:bold; color:red; margin:20px;}
author  {display:block; font-size:10pt; font-weight:bold; color:red; margin:20px;}
level, preptime, cooktime {display:block; color:green; margin-left:20px;}
yield  {display:block; color:green; margin-left:20px; margin-bottom:10px;}
amount        {display:inline; margin-left:35px;}
kind  {color:red;}
steps {display:list-item; font-size:10pt; color:green;
    font-family:Arial, Helvetica, sans-serif; margin-left:50px; margin-top:3px;}
notes  {display:block; font-size:10pt; color:black; font-style:italic; margin:20px;}
    </style>
```

Figure 12-22. Internal CSS Style Declarations (**code1222.htm**, also **xmlstyle.css**)

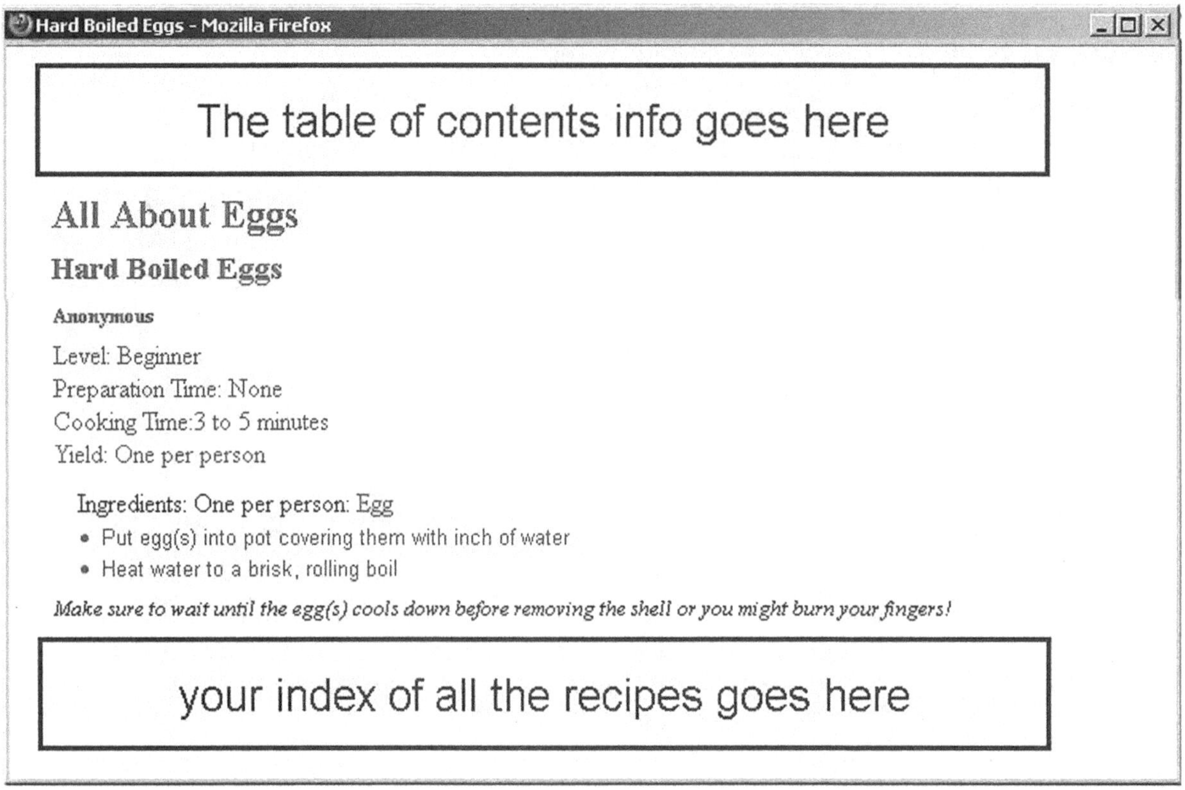

Hard Boiled Eggs - Mozilla Firefox

The table of contents info goes here

All About Eggs

Hard Boiled Eggs

Anonymous

Level: Beginner
Preparation Time: None
Cooking Time:3 to 5 minutes
Yield: One per person

Ingredients: One per person: Egg

- Put egg(s) into pot covering them with inch of water
- Heat water to a brisk, rolling boil

Make sure to wait until the egg(s) cools down before removing the shell or you might burn your fingers!

your index of all the recipes goes here

Figure 12-23. Results of Internal CSS Style Declarations (**code1222.htm**)

Wow, and to think it looked like a string of characters just a few pages ago! As these CSS style declarations did more than merely style an element, they effectively created the document type declaration for these new elements, which we often call them *rules*. We have, therefore, been creating **contents** rules, **category** rules, and so on, that govern the display of our new elements. We have demonstrated here that we can use inline and internal or embedded style rules to create defaults for the new elements. Although this is not yet an XML file, it seems like we're getting close! What about creating an external style rule file? How do we do that?

External CSS Style Processing in *XML-Like* Documents

When we reviewed the XML document's prolog requirements at the start of this chapter, we were introduced, albeit hastily, to the XML processing statement:

<?target type="value" href="value" ?>

We were told that we could use this method to add style sheet files to our XML document and that the syntax for a style sheet processing instruction looked like:

<?xml-stylesheet type="style" href="sheet" ?>

In this instruction, the value of the **target** is **xml-stylesheet,** the **type** attribute value **"style"** with **"sheet"** as the **href** attribute value. You may recall that in HTML **style** element declarations the **type** attribute default style **text/css** describes what the file content looked like rather than its functionality. The value **"sheet"** is replaced with the absolute or relative address location and file name (e.g., **css/xmlstyle.css**) of your external style sheet file.

If we were to save the style declaration rules of Figure 12-21 as a plain text external style sheet file named **xmlstyle.css** in the **css** folder of our website, we would have a way to use these new elements in more than one XML-like document, as if we were using a document type declaration or DTD. We need not repeat the style portion of Figure 12-21, but we will extract those rules and save them as the **xmlstyle.css** file. It is important to remember that although it could have one, the prolog of this non-XML document does not include an XML language doctype as there is none for these particular elements; but it does include the **xml-stylesheet** processing statement calling the external file followed the contents of **code1221.htm** containing all our new element names, and so on, except the style section and rules which have been saved in the **xmlstyle.css** file as seen in Figure 12-24.

```
<?xml-stylesheet type="text/css" href="css/xmlstyle.css" ?>
<cookbook>
        <contents>
        The table of contents info goes here </contents>
        <recipe>
                        <category>All About Eggs</category>
                        <title>Hard Boiled Eggs</title>
                        <author>Anonymous</author>
                <summary>
                                <level>Level: Beginner</level>
                                <preptime>Preparation Time: None</preptime>
                                <cooktime>Cooking Time:3 to 5 minutes</cooktime>
                                <yield>Yield: One per person</yield>
                </summary>
                        <ingredients>
                                <amount>Ingredients:  One per person:</amount>
                                <kind> Egg </kind>
                        </ingredients>
                <directions>
                                <steps>
                        Put egg(s) into pot covering them with inch of water </steps>
                                <steps> Heat water to a brisk, rolling boil</steps>
                        </directions>
                <notes>
                        Make sure to wait until the egg(s) cools down before removing
                        the shell or you might burn your fingers!
                        </notes>
                </recipe>
                                /* repeat for additional recipes */
        <index>
        your index of all the recipes goes here </index>
</cookbook>
```

Figure 12-24. Linking to External CSS Style Files (**code1224.htm, code1224.xml**)

This pairing of external CSS with the new elements in our document should result in exactly the same display that we saw in Figure 12-24. But, alas, now that we have invoked an XML processing instruction, the file is no longer looked at as an HTML document by our now-confused browser that displays the text without any stylizations, but in the tree outline view much as we saw previously in Figure 12-09.

Which to Use: .htm or .xml Extensions?

Thus, before we add XML process instructions to bring external style sheets into our document, we'll need to see what the effect of changing our file extension from **.htm** to **.xml** might be. Merely making the change, using **code1224.xml,** without adding a doctype declaration, will create the more pleasing *XML-like* display of Figure 12-23!

If there are no style sheet rules or DTD, the browser will, in the absence of clear instructions, display the tree structure it finds for the document and also see if there are any major syntax errors that would stop it from rendering the document properly. Now that we have what we want, let's play a bit with this code.

Browser XML Tree Displays

Figure 12-25 shows how the display of our now-**.xml** extension file would look if we commented out our style sheet by placing "**<!--**" in front of the **xml-stylesheet** declaration, and "**-->**" immediately after it.

Notice in both of these tree diagrams, the "–" denotes an expanded parent element and its child elements. The "+" denotes a collapsed element set. Removing the "com-

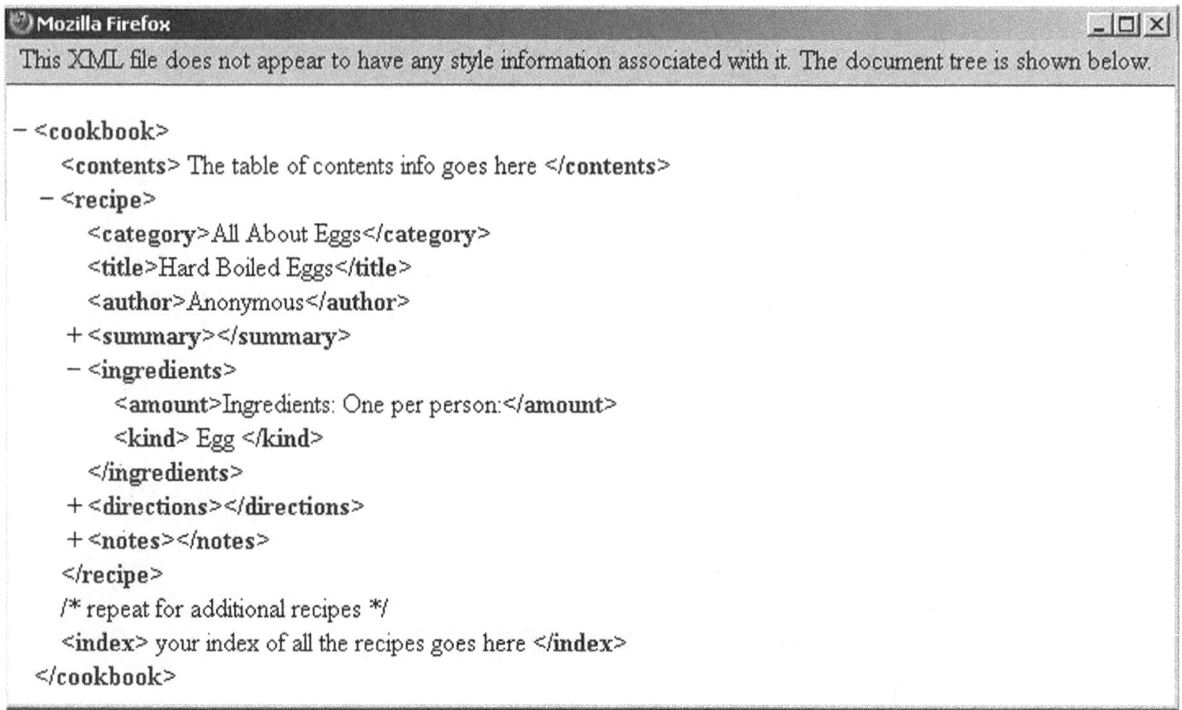

Figure 12-25. The **.xml** Extension and Browser Tree Structure (**code1225.xml**)

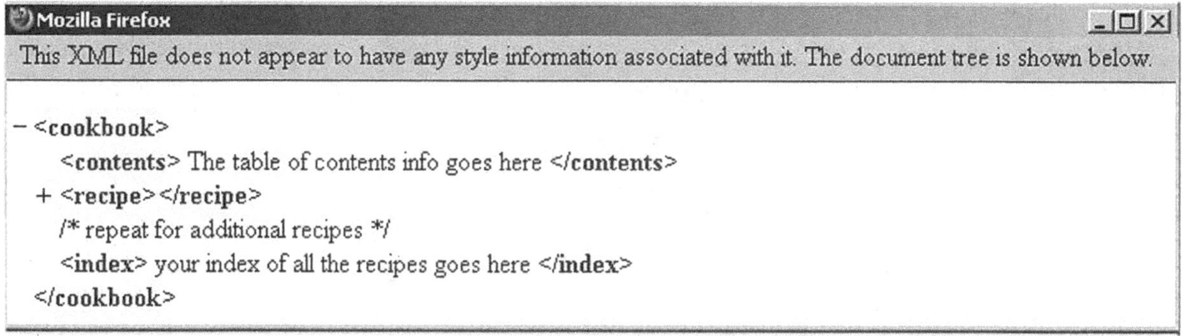

Figure 12-26. Collapsing the Browser's Tree Display (**code1225.xml**)

ment" brackets from the processing instruction restores our style sheet and results, again, in Figure 12-26.

So that's all there is to creating an *XML-like* document that can have inline and internal style sheets as well as use the XML processing instruction and **.xml** extension to create a document that can acquire external style sheets. All three options allow us to create new elements and style them without the need to understand how to create an actual document type definition vocabulary.

Creating XML Document Type Definition Vocabularies

If you made it thus far in this chapter, congratulations! This next part is a bit more detailed as with these techniques you will be creating the actual document type definitions for the new elements you have been using. Although mistakes creating document type definitions have never caused a computer or server to melt down, they can be frustrating, *very* frustrating. I often suggest that modifying *any* web page is a five-minute job that can take all weekend. Simply speaking an error in creating the DTD declaration may not be any more obvious than leaving out a closing tag in an HTML table construction (see Chapter 8); that is, you will either get a nonreproducible lovely display, a horrible one, or possibly nothing at all.

As seen in previous sections of this chapter, XML documents *can* be created using simple CSS techniques to uniquely identify hitherto *unknown* elements. This is a technique much like using the preformat element in HTML documents. It works, but is not as elegant, nor as easy to use as if we had actually created a new vocabulary of elements. We are also hampered using the *XML-lite* method as we cannot define new attributes for these new elements, nor can we establish new entity character references using CSS style sheets.

In the sections that follow we'll see how to create DTD declarations for elements, attributes, and entity references as well as how to use them either as an internal subset of embedded DTD declarations or as an external file using those declarations. We'll start by examining how elements are used in markup language documents.

To create a document type definition requires understanding the element, what other elements you might or might not want to appear or contain within it, what attributes you might or might not think would be important to further describe the element, and what default styling you would like to see for the element. Then you can create an appropriate document type definition set for the browser to use to parse future XML documents using your new vocabulary.

XML Element Declarations

If we want to create a DTD vocabulary, we need to start with an understanding of the basic element syntax used in the DTD:

<!ELEMENT element_name content-specifications> or
<!ELEMENT elementName (elementContentModel)>

In this structure the **!ELEMENT** declaration, like our **!DOCTYPE** declaration is an instruction for the browser. The **element_name** or **elementName** is whatever we want to call our new element. Of course there are element name rules. Elements can begin with a letter or underscore only. There is no length limit, but the name cannot start with xml or a number. It may not have any spaces or @ characters in it, and can only have colons if specifying namespaces. Bear in mind that it is best NOT to use names that are the same as HTML DTD element names or the browser will not know which element you have in mind to use. If the same names are used in a single document, the two elements are said to collide. While there are ways around this challenge using namespaces, and so on, let's just avoid using them and not worry!

The last part of the element declaration is its rules or **content-specifications.** The four types of XML DTD rules or content specifications are **ALL, EMPTY, children,** and **mixed. ALL** denotes no specific constraints for the elements; **EMPTY** is used for elements like the open-ended HTML **img** element; **children** lists the elements allowed in the container, and **mixed** lists **cdata** and/or elements allowed in the container. In use these rules are enclosed in parentheses.

All and Empty Element Specifications

The **ALL** element content specification or element content model is used for double-ended elements that have no specific required children or other constraints. The syntax is:

<!ELEMENT element_name ALL>

An example here might possibly be the HTML division **div** that may contain any type of content including other div elements:

<!ELEMENT div ALL>

Conversely, the **EMPTY** content specification is used for single-ended elements like the HTML **img, br, hr,** and others, where there is no content contained in the element:

<!ELEMENT element_name EMPTY>

Our HTML DTD for the break **br** might therefore look something like:

<!ELEMENT br EMPTY>

Children and Mixed Element Specifications

Most double-ended element rules or content specifications include a listing of the various *child elements* that the parent element may, or must, contain. The mixed content element specification lists character data **cdata** and/or parsed character data **pcdata** and/or whichever elements allowed in the container:

<!ELEMENT element_name (children)> or
<!ELEMENT element_name (mixed)>

We'll see lots of examples of these most common types of element in the next section where we convert the tree diagram of our cookbook into a series of element declarations.

Content Specification Element Occurrence Rules

Just as we saw when we were creating the tree diagrams earlier in this chapter, there are straightforward rules that govern the way elements can be defined in the element declaration.

These are based on the symbol, or lack thereof, placed after the content specification or rule. As noted earlier, all rules are enclosed in parentheses with one or more **element_name** inside them. Note that the occurrence symbols can be inside or outside of the parentheses depending on the intent of the rules as shown here in Figure 12-27. It is useful to note that *more than one* **element_name** is possible inside of a single content specification.

(element_name)
(no characters): *must* have only one child element

(element_name)* or (element_name*)
Asterisk:** ***zero or more child elements (*optional, repeatable*)

(element_name)+ or (element_name+)
+Plus: ***one or more*** child elements (*occurs at least once*)

(element_name)? or (element_name?)
?Question Mark: ***at most one*** child element (*zero or one occurrence*)

(element_namel, element_name2, element_name3)
, Comma (AND/sequence): ***must*** *contain 1, 2, and 3* ***in that order***

(element_namel | element_name2 | element_name3)
| Pipe (OR/choice): ***may*** *contain elements 1, 2, and 3*
(either/or/all, optional, repeatable; zero or more)

Figure 12-27. Content Specification Occurrence Rules

The Cookbook DTD Element Set

Although we haven't discovered yet where to put the element declarations inside our document, or if they can be placed in an external file, the first step in creating the DTD is to list the elements and their rules so we can create the element declarations.

According to the tree diagram of Figure 12-13, a **cookbook** can have one **contents,** at least one (+) **recipe,** and one **index.** The cookbook element declaration would therefore look like:

<!ELEMENT cookbook (contents, recipe+, index)>

Similarly, the **recipe** element tree of Figure 12-14 is actually a child element inside the **cookbook** parent element container of Figure 12-13. Decoding the **recipe** element tree diagram, a **recipe** can have one **category,** one **title,** at least one (+) **author,** one **summary** with one **level,** one **preptime,** one **cooktime,** and one **yield,** with a set of **ingredients** with at least one (+) **amount** and **kind,** a set of **directions** with at least one (+) **step,** and zero or one **notes** element for every **recipe** element (in the **cookbook** document). Note that as is typical for HTML documents, spacing is ignored so we can put the rules on the same line or as seen here, on two lines:

<!ELEMENT recipe
(category, title, author+, summary, ingredients, directions, notes?)>

But several elements seem missing! These missing elements are the child elements of the **summary, ingredients,** and **directions** elements. We can define these other elements based on the **summary** having one **level,** one **preptime,** one **cooktime,** and one **yield;** with the **ingredients** having at least one (+) **amount** and **kind;** and the **directions** element having at least one (+) **step.**

<!ELEMENT summary (level, preptime, cooktime, yield)>
<!ELEMENT ingredients (amount, kind)+>
<!ELEMENT directions (step+)>

We will also need to define each and every individual *child* element, as to the type of content it expects. But first we will need to learn a bit about the kinds of character data that can be used to describe our elements.

Parsed and Non-Parsed Character Data

We will pause here in our discussion of creating an XML DTD to review the data content options for XML elements, **PCDATA** and **CDATA.**

Parsed character data **PCDATA** consists of all those characters that XML treats as parts of the code of XML document; the XML declaration, the opening and closing tags of an element, empty element tags, character or entity references, and comments.

Character data **CDATA,** on the other hand, can exist alone in an XML document as a large block of text the XML processor will **interpret only as text**. Thus any elements or instructions included inside the CDATA block will be ignored and treated and displayed as plain text. The syntax to create a **CDATA** section is:

```
<! [CDATA [
    Content Block that will be read as simple Text and NOT decoded . . .
] ]>
```

The **CDATA** section that follows stores several HTML tags within an element named **htmlcode** that are *not* interpreted as tags, but displayed as is:

```
<htmlcode>
<![CDATA[
    <h1>The Friends of the Red Rose Library</h1>
    <h2>Your Resource for Improving Your Library</h2>
] ]>
</htmlcode>
```

In an XML attribute declaration **CDATA** signifies that the data is not to be parsed; that is, it is not intended that the element include any sub elements in its element container.

Typically we define most elements such that they may contain parsed character data—text as well as any decodable content—denoted as **#PCDATA:**

Child elements of **summary:**

```
<!ELEMENT level (#PCDATA)>
<!ELEMENT preptime (#PCDATA)>
<!ELEMENT cooktime (#PCDATA)>
<!ELEMENT yield (#PCDATA)>
```

Child elements of **ingredients:**

```
<!ELEMENT amount (#PCDATA)>
<!ELEMENT kind (#PCDATA)>
```

Child element of **directions:**

```
<!ELEMENT steps (#PCDATA)>
```

Note that the parent elements of our root **cookbook** (as well as the **recipe, summary, ingredients,** and **directions** elements) do not need to be further defined as they all contain defined child elements.

Creating an Internal XML DTD

Using our definitions of these new elements as if they were normal document type definitions, we incorporate them as an internal DTD in the first DOCTYPE line of the XML Document's prolog with the following general syntax:

```
<!DOCTYPE root_element
[
<!ELEMENT element_name1 contentSpecifications >
  . . .
<!ENTITY entity_nameN contentSpecifications >
] >
```

Figure 12-28 shows the complete internal DTD for the root element cookbook. The tabs shown in the figure are only an attempt to illustrate the parent/child element relationships, and are not required in the XML document.

Placing this set of coding as the first lines of our **cookbook** document before the root **cookbook** element creates the DTD for our elements therein. We do *not* need to have a CSS file to create the overall structure, *nor* do we need to rename our extension to **.xml!** However, the display, using the **.htm** extension, is merely a plain text string. If we do change the file to the **.xml** extension creating a new file **code1228.xml** the browser will "complain" that we don't have any style information, but *will* show us the tree structure of the document.

If we add the XML processing instruction seen earlier right after this doctype declaration to link the **xmlstyle.css** external style sheet to this document (**code1227CSS.xml**), the result is the display we hoped for, as seen previously in Figure 12-23.

```
<!DOCTYPE cookbook
 [
<!ELEMENT cookbook (contents, recipe+, index)>
        <!ELEMENT recipe
(category, title, author+, summary, ingredients, directions, notes?)>
                <!ELEMENT category (#PCDATA)>
                <!ELEMENT title (#PCDATA)>
                <!ELEMENT author (#PCDATA)>
                <!ELEMENT summary (level, preptime, cooktime, yield)>
                        <!ELEMENT level (#PCDATA)>
                        <!ELEMENT preptime (#PCDATA)>
                        <!ELEMENT cooktime (#PCDATA)>
                        <!ELEMENT yield (#PCDATA)>
                <!ELEMENT ingredients (amount, kind)+>
                        <!ELEMENT amount (#PCDATA)>
                        <!ELEMENT kind (#PCDATA)>
                <!ELEMENT directions (step+)>
                        <!ELEMENT steps (#PCDATA)>
                <!ELEMENT notes (#PCDATA)>
```

Figure 12-28. Basic **cookbook** Internal DTD (**code1228.htm**)

Creating an Unordered List Document Type Definition

So maybe this was a bit too much creativity, too complex, and too fast.

The simple unordered list element, built into our HTML DTD, allows us to create a simple bulleted list using a simple construction like:

```
<ul>
    <li>one</li>
    <li>two</li>
</ul>
```

What if there were no elements for an unordered list? How would we go about creating one?

We would first need to define the element name(s) and what the presentation structure would look like. We could say that we want each "**un**" list to have one or more (+) "**line**" entries. We would then need to consider what the characteristics of each **line** child element would be. Do we want only plain text or character data? That is, do we want to include hyperlinks, font changes, and so on—parsed character data? To make the list as general as possible let's let each of our newly defined **line** elements include any content just as the regular HTML list item element, **li,** does.

Our new **un** list element could be defined as

```
<!ELEMENT un (line+)>
<!ELEMENT line (#PCDATA)>
```

denoting that one or more **line** child element is permitted in each **un** parent element container, and the **line** might be defined such that as *any* elements are permitted inside the **line** the line element's contents must be parsed to detect the existence of other elements that might need to be decoded. In general we would create an XML structure a bit more complex with the outermost container being the root element and having the new **un** element as one of many options available. But if we just wanted a simple unordered list, the XML document could have the root **un.** The list is all that will display. The general internal DTD element definition syntax is shown in Figure 12-29.

```
<!DOCTYPE root_elementName
  [
    <!ELEMENT root_elementName (content specifications)>  ← Root element definition
    <!ELEMENT elementName (content specifications)>       ← other element definition
    ...
  ]>
```

Figure 12-29. Internal DTD Subset Syntax

Attributes and even special entity relationships could be defined in the internal DTD as we will see in the next sections of this chapter. Note, too, that there can be several DTDs linked to a particular XML document. The challenge of multiple DTDs is that elements do not cascade and thus there must *not* be overlapping element names; we don't want to confuse the browser, do we? But for now we only have one DTD statement, so the internal definition and use of our new unordered list and line elements might look something like the XML document of Figure 12-30.

Of course we can also embed style sheets in our XML document. These would go right after we defined our new DTD elements.

```
<?xml version="1.0"?>                  ← XML declaration
<!DOCTYPE un [                         ← Internal DTD rules for un Root
<!ELEMENT un (line+)>
<!ELEMENT line (#PCDATA)>
  ]>                                   ← End of Internal DTD Rules
      <un>                             ← un Root element opening tag
            <line>milk</line>          ← line element container
            <line>bread</line>         ← line element container
      <un>                             ← line element container
```

Figure 12-30. XML Document with Internal DTD (**code1230.xml**)

External XML DTDs

Rather than waiting until we fully define our document type definitions with element attributes and optional entity references, which we cover later in this chapter, we can see what would be needed to save these declarations as an external DTD as well as how to call them into our XML documents.

In the same way we removed internal CSS styles and put them into a callable external file, we can remove customized internal DTDs and store them in an external file. We typically store our DTDs in a **dtd** folder. One other difference is that the syntax for our external DTD file, with the extension **.dtd,** *requires that we add the XML declaration to the external file,* even if one did not exist in the XML document:

```
<xml version="1.0" encoding="UTF-8" ?>
<!ELEMENT root_element_name contentSpecifications>
. . .
<!ELEMENT element_name contentSpecifications>
```

For our unordered list example, if we stored the new DTD declarations in an external file called **unlist.dtd** in our **dtd** website folder, we could refer to it anytime we want. The contents of the **unlist.dtd** file would be:

```
<?xml version="1.0" ?>
<!ELEMENT un (line+)>
<!ELEMENT line (#PCDATA)>
```

The **unlist.dtd** file is brought into our browser by the XML document's doctype declaration. This external file method is a bit different from the **link** element command used for our CSS files in HTML as a DTD is a *system* file that must be linked using a *system call* in our doctype declaration. The syntax requires that we begin the doctype command and then enter the root of the resulting XML document, the command SYSTEM, and then the location of the DTD file

```
<!DOCTYPE root_element SYSTEM "URL.dtd">
```

where the **SYSTEM** call opens the absolute or relatively addressed DTD file **URL.dtd** which is brought into the browser.

In this case, the first line of the XML document (**uncode.xml**) is the root **un** that uses an external DTD file called **unlist.dtd** in the **dtd** folder that includes the unordered list content we saw in Figure 12-30:

```
<!DOCTYPE un SYSTEM "dtd/unlist.dtd">
<un>
    <line>milk</line>
    <line>bread</line>
</un>
```

We can easily imagine what the list would look like and the overall structure of this simple XML document. Naturally if we looked at this document without any style we would only see its structure in the browser. Hopefully this document is easier to comprehend than the more usable, but a more bit complex, **cookbook** document.

The Dublin Core DTD

A much more general **DCMES** tree diagram than the one we developed earlier in Figure 12-17 would be one where a **Collection** can have zero or more (*) **records** with *each* **record** having zero or more (*) of any of the 15 typical Dublin Core metadata elements: **title, creator, subject, description, publisher, contributor, date, type, format, identifier, source, langu-age, relation, coverage,** and **rights** as shown in Fig-ure 12-31.

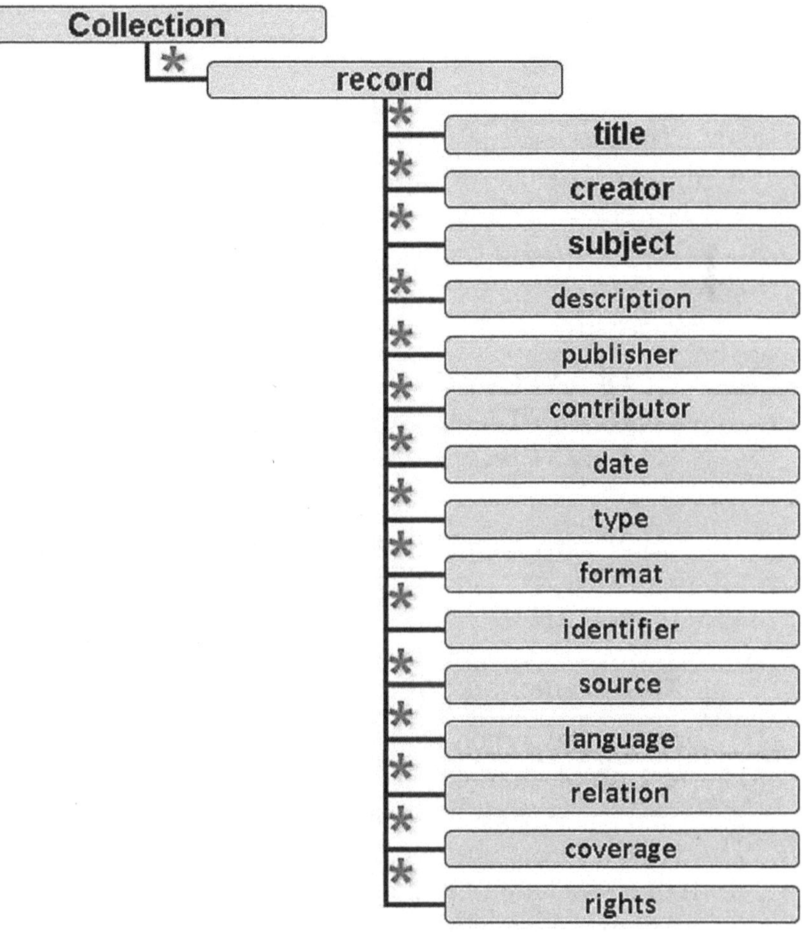

Figure 12-31. General **Dublin Core Metadata Set (DCMES)** Tree Diagram

The *external* DTD coding for this basic Dublin Core **record** that may contain *zero or more* (*) of *any* (|) of the 15 DC elements would look like Figure 12-32. Recall that an external DTD file *must* include an XML declaration.

To take advantage of the standardization of the Dublin Core that is managed by the Dublin Core Metadata Initiative

```
<?xmlversion="1.0" encoding="UTF-8"?>
<!ELEMENT record (title | creator | subject | description | publisher | contributor | date |
type | format | identifier | source | language | relation | coverage | rights)*>
<!ELEMENT title (#PCDATA)>
<!ELEMENT creator (#PCDATA)>
<!ELEMENT subject (#PCDATA)>
<!ELEMENT description (#PCDATA)>
<!ELEMENT publisher (# PCDATA)>
<!ELEMENT contributor (# PCDATA)>
<!ELEMENT date (#PCDATA)>
<!ELEMENT type (#PCDATA)>
<!ELEMENT format (#PCDATA)>
<!ELEMENT identifier (#PCDATA)>
<!ELEMENT source (#PCDATA)>
<!ELEMENT language (#PCDATA)>
<!ELEMENT relation (#PCDATA)>
<!ELEMENT coverage (#PCDATA)>
<!ELEMENT rights (#PCDATA)>
```

Figure 12-32. External DTD Coding Basic Dublin Core **record (dc.dtd)**

(DCMI), it is recommended that all DCMES records use *namespaces.* For our purposes here, a namespace is simply a web accessible file where the most current specifications are stored for use in your documents.

We'll develop the method of creating attributes in our next section, but for now suffice it to say that we can add an attribute to our record element. The overall header portion of our Dublin Core XML document would look like:

```
<!DOCTYPE Collection SYSTEM "dtd/dc.dtd" [
<!ELEMENT Collection (record)>
<!ATTLIST record xmlns CDATA #FIXED "http://purl.org/dc/elements/1.1/">
]>
```

Don't worry, we'll find out shortly what the syntax of attributes is and what this all means.

XML Element Attributes

As we saw when we were working with predefined HMTL elements, an **attribute** is a feature or characteristic of an element that defines its structure in the absence of style sheets as well as creates value pairs for the browser to use as default values. Having defined a specific element, we can now see how to define the list of attributes for that new element and establish their defaults.

Attributes are normally text strings and must be placed in single or double quotes; we always use the double quote. The XML attribute syntax is the same as for HTML attributes where one or more attribute/value pair is in the opening tag and only the element name appears in the closing tag that contains the element's content:

<element_name attribute="value"> . . . </element_name>

Creating an XML **element** and **attribute** name follows the general element naming standards we saw previously where attributes *may* contain an underscore (_), hyphen (-), period (.), or colon (:); *may NOT* start with XML or xml (etc.); *may NOT* include blank spaces, tabs, and so on; and *may NOT* start with a number, hyphen, or period.

XML Attribute Declaration Syntax

Any markup element can have zero or more attributes associated with it. This gives rise to the *attribute list* declaration **ATTLIST,** which has the generic syntax:

<!ATTLIST element_name
attribute_name attribute-type attribute-default
. . .
attribute_name attribute-type attribute-default
>

The ATTLIST declaration includes the **element_name** with which the attributes are associated with; one or more sets of **attribute_name,** the name assigned to the attribute using standard XML naming rules; the **attribute-type,** the kind of values the attribute can take which can be either **string, enumerated,** or **tokenized;** and an **attribute-default** which allows the default attribute setting to be either **#REQUIRED, #FIXED,** or **#IMPLIED.** As suggested earlier, there can be more than one attribute for a particular element resulting in several name/type/default definitions. In the following examples we will define attributes that might exist in our cookbook example. Let's first look at the **attribute-default** definitions.

Required, Fixed, and Implied Attribute Defaults

Whenever an attribute is *not* required to be present when its element is in use, we will use the **attribute-default #IMPLIED** definition which denotes that the attribute is optional. **#IMPLIED** is used when not all attribute "fields" have data in them. An HTML example would be for the **style** or the **class** attribute. Neither the **style** nor the **class** attribute *must* be in any of the various HTML elements that use them, but *could* be included if desired.

Conversely, whenever an attribute is required to be present when its element is in use, we will use the **#REQUIRED** default. An example would be the definition of the source **src** attribute of the HTML image element **img.** The **attribute-default #REQUIRED** definition does *not* provide an actual value for the default.

Lastly, whenever a specific attribute value is required to be present when its element is in use, we will use the **#FIXED** default. The **attribute-default #FIXED** definition *does* require and provide an actual value for the default as a straight-quoted value (e.g., **#FIXED "Fall 2014"**). All fixed defaults are *required* defaults. If that value is not part of the opening tag, the browser will supply it automatically. I'm not sure that

I have seen the use of this in HTML documents, but we'll see an example of the **#FIXED** default in the next section.

String, Enumerated, and Tokenized Attribute Types

A **string** attribute type allows an arbitrary string of characters **CDATA** as its value. Our **record** element might *require* a **date** attribute in the **record**'s opening tag:

<!ATTLIST record date CDATA #REQUIRED >

Alternatively, we might want to *fix* the required value of the record date as fall 2014 in which case we could use a **#FIXED** attribute default:

<!ATTLIST record date CDATA #FIXED "Fall 2014" >

Often we want to only use specific or *enumerated* attribute values from a list supplied by our DTD. These values are enclosed in parentheses and separated by vertical pipes:

<!ATTLIST subject terms (DDC | LCC | LCSH | UDC | MESH) #REQUIRED >

In the previous section when we looked at the internal DTD for a Dublin Core document we saw the record element had an attribute defined as:

<!ATTLIST record xmlns CDATA #FIXED "http://purl.org/dc/elements/1.1/">

We can now fully decode this as the record element has a default, required, fixed value of **http://purl.org/dc/elements/1.1/** for its XML namespace. This will provide all the other elements and attributes for the Dublin Core vocabulary. Note: *See section on namespaces after we discuss entities.*

The two most common *tokenized* attribute types are **ID** and **IDREF.** The value of the **ID** type attribute must be unique to the document, must be named according to the XML specification, and must be *required.* The attribute name **recNum** can be used to assign an identification code for each unique record. Like the **ID,** the value of the **IDREF** tokenized attribute must also be unique to the document, must be named according to the XML specification, and must be *required.*

Definitions for these attributes would be that the **record** element requires a **recNum** attribute with an ID, and the **item** element requires an **itemNum** attribute with an **IDREF:**

<!ATTLIST record recNum ID #REQUIRED >
<!ATTLIST item itemNum IDREF #REQUIRED>

XML Character and Entity References

As we saw in earlier discussions, there are special characters, as seen in Appendix B, that have a character reference number, for example, **©** many of which also have an entity reference short name, for example, © which can be used in HTML documents to place otherwise non-keyboard characters in a document. *Note that not all special characters have short name entity references.* The syntax for these special characters requires that they begin with the ampersand "**&**" and end with a semicolon "**;**" after the entity reference name: **&entityname;** or character reference number: **&#entitynumber;.** Common predefined entity names and their corresponding character numbers include those in Figure 12-33.

In addition to these *predefined* character and entity references with XML you can create your own *customized* entity references; it is after all XML! So what would you create? You might want to create a special entity reference short name that, whenever seen in your XML document, will replace the short name entity reference (e.g., **&fred;**) with a longer string of characters such as "Friends of the **Red Rose Library.**" We'll see how to create these in the next section on XML Entity Declarations.

		Entity Reference	Character Reference
Symbol	Name	EntityName	EntityNumber
&	ampersand	**&**	**&**
©	copyright symbol	**©**	**©**
™	trademark symbol		**™**
®	registered symbol		**®**
<	less than symbol	**<**	**<**
>	greater than symbol	**>**	**>**
‘	apostrophe	**'**	****
"	double straight quote	**"e;**	****
“	left double quotes		**“**
”	right double quotes		**”**
£	British Pound sign		**£**
€	Euro sign		**€**

Figure 12-33. Some Predefined Entity and Character References

XML Entity Declarations

XML is often considered a collection of storage container units called entities. The three major types of entities are the familiar **character entity,** the **general entity,** and the **parameter entity.** The first, the **character entity,** *represents math symbols and special characters by* either character reference numbers or entity reference names. See Appendix B. The **general entity** is used to *replace references inside of a document element* as described in this section and, as we'll see in the next section. The **parameter entity** is a very useful tool with which we can gather like characteristics for attributes of "families" of elements and use a single entity to *replace references inside of a DTD* that includes links to other document type definitions.

The syntax for defining general entities in a DTD requires that they begin with the ENTITY declaration followed by the **entityName** which must be a valid XML name assigned to the entity and then the **entityContentModel** or content for replacement:

<!ENTITY entityName (entityContentModel)>

The entity declaration can exist anywhere in your DTD; however, they are typically placed at the end of the declarations after all elements and attributes have been defined. As noted earlier, perhaps we want to create the short name entity reference **&fred;** that would be replaced with the longer string of characters "Friends of the Red Rose Library" when our document was displayed. In this case we would define the entity:

<!ENTITY fred "Friends of the Red Rose Library">

and inside our document would include **&fred;** whenever we wanted "Friends of the Red Rose Library" to appear. So the paragraph *in your document* might look like

> The **&fred;** provided a retirement party for the Library Associate Director last Tuesday. Sam Jones, the President of the **&fred;** told the crowd that Shirley had brought lots of good will to the Library during her 25 years of service and had been very good to the **&fred;** by assisting them in their many fundraising efforts.

with the browser display looking like you typed "Friends of the Red Rose Library" three times:

> The Friends of the Red Rose Library provided a retirement party for the Library Associate Director last Tuesday. Sam Jones, the President of the Friends of the Red Rose Library told the crowd that Shirley had brought lots of good will to the Library during her 25 years of service and had been very good to the Friends of the Red Rose Library by assisting them in their many fundraising efforts.

DTD Parameter Entity Syntax

As noted earlier, the *parameter entity* is used to replace references *inside of a DTD.* Parameter entities can *only* be used with DTD files; this technique *does not* work in internal DTDs. The parameter entity allows a shorthand version of what would otherwise be a more complicated-looking external DTD:

```
<?xml version="1.0" ?>
............
<!ELEMENT vocational (school, program)*>
<!ELEMENT twoyear (school, program)*>
<!ELEMENT fouryear (school, program)*>
```

The parameter entity permits substitution of a child element repeated several times in the DTD without repeating the content string. The parameter entity declaration syntax is:

```
<!ENTITY % name "replacement_text">
```

In an external DTD element's declaration the parameter entities are called in a similar manner to general entities, but with the format **%name;** instead of **&name;.** If we wanted to simplify the preceding DTD, we could create a parameter entity for the elements school and program as shown here:

```
<?xml version="1.0" ?>
............
<!ENTITY % type "school, program">
<!ELEMENT vocational (%type;)*>
<!ELEMENT twoyear (%type;)*>
<!ELEMENT fouryear (%type;)*>
```

Wherever in the document the character string **%type;** is found, the browser substitutes the quoted information: **school, program** into the individual element declaration.

External Entity File Syntax

Just as with external DTD files, external entity files are declared with a generic SYSTEM call

<!ENTITY name SYSTEM "location_of_file" >

where **location_of_file** is either an absolute or relative URL for the external file in which the entity substitution materials are found. These are loaded into the document by the browser when called. It is not necessary to have an external DTD or style sheet to have an external entity file.

Internal cookbook DTD

Putting together elements, attributes, and entity declaration for the "**cookbook**" set of semantic elements might look like Figure 12-34. You should be able to "read"

```
<!DOCTYPE cookbook
[
<!ELEMENT cookbook (contents, recipe+, index)>
<!ELEMENT contents (#PCDATA)>
<!ELEMENT recipe (category, title, author, summary, ingredients, instructions, notes)>
<!ELEMENT category (#PCDATA)>
<!ELEMENT title (#PCDATA)>
<!ELEMENT author (#PCDATA)>
<!ELEMENT summary (level, preptime, cooktime, yield)>
<!ELEMENT level (#PCDATA)>
<!ELEMENT preptime (#PCDATA)>
<!ELEMENT cooktime (#PCDATA)>
<!ELEMENT yield (#PCDATA)>
<!ELEMENT ingredients (amount, kind+)>
<!ELEMENT amount (#PCDATA)>
<!ELEMENT kind (#PCDATA)>
<!ELEMENT directions (steps+)>
<!ELEMENT steps (#PCDATA)>
<!ELEMENT notes (#PCDATA)>
<!ELEMENT index (#PCDATA)>

<!ATTLIST recipe author CDATA #REQUIRED>
<!ATTLIST recipe date CDATA #IMPLIED>

<!ENTITY cookbook "The Red Rose Library Cookbook">
<!ENTITY editor "Friends of The Red Rose Library">
<!ENTITY publisher "The Red Rose Cookbook Press">
<!ENTITY copyright "Copyright 2013 Red Rose Cookbook Press">
]>
```

Figure 12-34. Basic Internal Subset DTD Structure for a Cookbook

```
<!DOCTYPE cookbook SYSTEM "dtd/cb.dtd">
<?xml-stylesheet type="text/css" href="css/xmlstyle.css" ?>
<cookbook>
        <contents> The table of contents info goes here  </contents>
        <recipe>
                <category>All About Eggs</category>
                <title>Hard Boiled Eggs</title>
                <author>Anonymous</author>
                <summary>
                        <level>Level: Beginner</level>
                        <preptime>Preparation Time: None</preptime>
                        <cooktime>Cooking Time:3 to 5 minutes</cooktime>
                        <yield>Yield: One per person</yield>
                </summary>
                <ingredients>
                        <amount>Ingredients:  One per person: </amount>
                        <kind> Egg </kind>
                </ingredients>
                <directions>
                        <steps>
                Put egg(s) into pot covering them with inch of water </steps>
                        <steps> Heat water to a brisk, rolling boil </steps>
                </directions>
                <notes>
                Make sure to wait until the egg(s) cools down before removing
                the shell or you might burn your fingers!
                </notes>
        </recipe>
/* repeat for additional recipes ... */
<index> your index of all the recipes goes here </index>
</cookbook>
```

Figure 12-35. Possible XML Cookbook Document **(cb.dtd, code1235.xml)**

this internal DTD and make some sense of it! If so, you have figured out how you can use the XML constructs to create your *own* DTD vocabulary.

The next step in viewing our cookbook as an XML web page is to add the content inside of the new element containers our DTD just specified, the recipe for making a Hard-Boiled Egg, add the **.xml** extension, and then we can view the document's tree structure of Figure 12-35.

Note that the first "two" lines of the XML document, its prolog, inform the browser that this is an XML document and provide the DOCTYPE declarations for your DTD.

If we add a "third" line—the style sheet request for a CSS called "**xmlstyle.css**" stored in the **css** folder on the same website as this file:

```
<?xml-stylesheet type="text/css" href="css/xmlstyle.css" ?>
```

the result we are presented with, Figure 12-36, in Internet Explorer, reminds us that we can create and style our own XML document type definitions, BRAVO!

Using Multiple DTDs

So you can now create an XML DTD. Recall that the XML vocabulary for the Dublin Core is composed of the DCMES XML document elements: collection, record, **title,** creator, subject, description, publisher, contributor, date, type, format, identifier, source, language, relation, coverage, and rights. But suppose we wanted to use these DC elements and also include the elements in our cookbook vocabulary: cookbook, contents, recipe, category, **title,** author, summary, level, preptime, cooktime, yield, ingredients, amount, kind, directions, steps, notes. We can certainly use more than one DTD file; we don't see any reason why we can't, or can we?

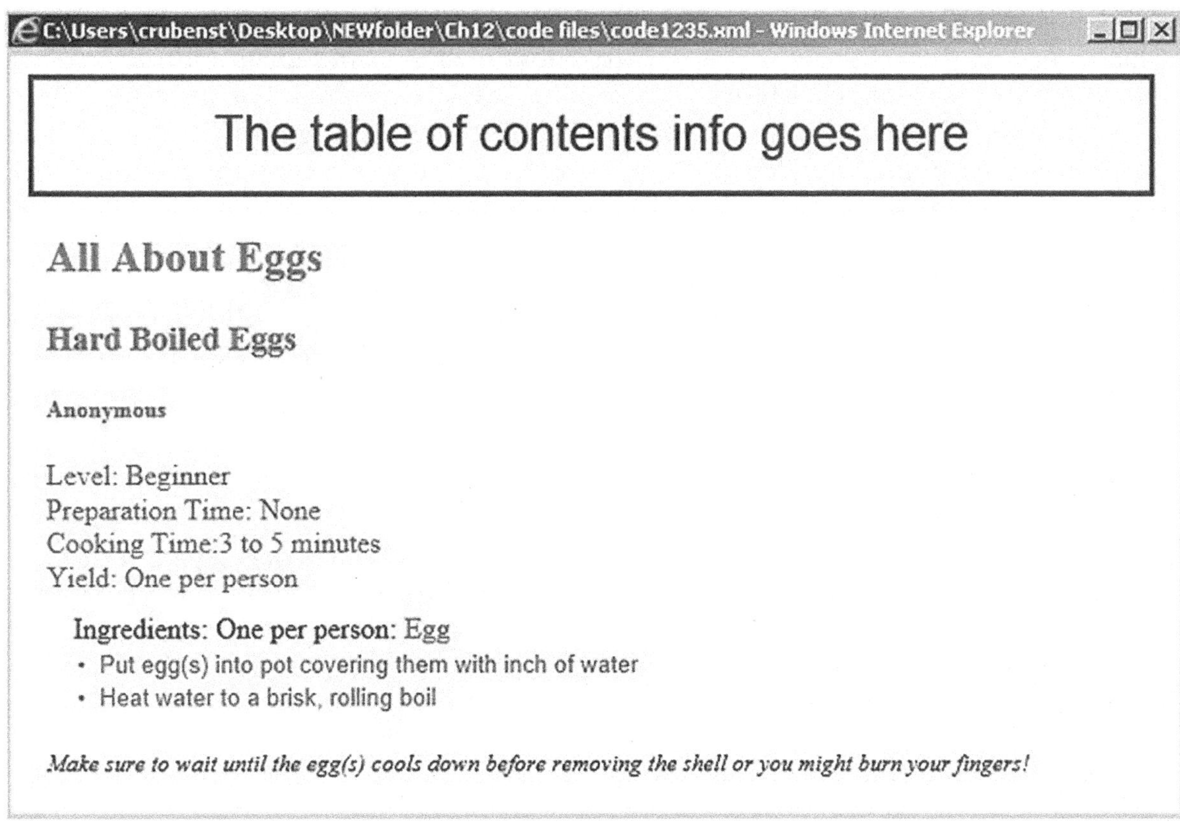

Figure 12-36. XML Cookbook Document IE Display **(code1235.xml, cb.dtd, xmlstyle.css)**

Take another look at the last paragraph and note that although we normally put all element names in bold, only the DC **title** and cookbook **title** elements are bold. That is to point out that the same element name, for example, **title** is used in more than one DTD. (Yes, there is also an HTML **title** element, but once we declare the use of XML the browser knows this not to be a problem and defaults to the XML **title** element as we saw earlier.)

With two or more document type definitions of the **title** element, your browser will not know which DTD to use when it tries to decode a **title** element. Indeed, should you add a style file, it, too, would be uncertain as to which **title** is which.

To make matters even worse, there are hundreds of markup language vocabularies already available and standardized for our use. Wikipedia, the Free Encyclopedia, on the Internet lists 221 XML markup variations, some of which are no longer being used, along with links to their Wikipedia pages at:

http://en.wikipedia.org/wiki/List_of_XML_markup_languages

The Massachusetts Institute of Technology (MIT) on its Physical Markup Language, an XML vocabulary for describing physical objects for use in monitoring and control of a physical environment, website at:

http://web.mit.edu/mecheng/pml/standards.htm

hosts a web page which lists more than 440, mostly XML vocabulary, standards! Interesting to note is that as these DTDs are typically developed independently from each other there are many vocabularies that use the same acronyms. For example, there are six different "AML" listings covering abstracts, advertising, animation, annotations, astronomy, and avatars! Use these lists carefully to make sure you are using the standard(s) you need.

We have been and will be addressing several of the library-specific XML vocabularies like Dublin Core **DCMES,** Text Encoding Initiative **TEI,** and Encoded Archival Description **EAD,** in this text, but some of the science, math, and XML standards that might be of interest to you or your patrons include those vocabularies listed in at the end of this chapter.

Why Use Namespaces?

ATTENTION: Rough Road Ahead! Whenever we see **xmlns** in a markup language file it means that the author is declaring some external DTD as a *namespace* so it may be used as a common DTD standard on their web pages. You may well have noticed calls to namespaces in HTML documents as well to define your HTML document as one obeying the XHTwML vocabulary and rules. Recalling the structure of the doctype declaration

```
<!DOCTYPE rule type "id" "url">
```

the XHTML 1.1 specification doctype would look like:

```
<!DOCTYPE html PUBLIC "-//W3C//DTD XHTML 1.1//EN"
      "http://www.w3.org/TR/xhtml11/DTD/xhtml11.dtd">
```

To set XHTML as the default namespace for an HTML document you need only to use:

```
<html xmlns="http://www.w3.org/1999/xhtml">
```

Besides defining where a common DTD specification exists, namespaces also allow us to resolve the "colliding elements" challenge that can occur when using multiple DTDs. If you are sure that you will not be using more than one DTD, you need not worry about this section.

When we use more than one DTD, declaring namespaces is a technique that can define each DTD's elements uniquely so the DTDs can use the same element name (e.g., **title**) and the browser will know exactly how you want it to decode that element. Namespaces are declared by adding the **xmlns** *attribute* to an element in your document:

```
xmlns:prefix="uri"
```

Where the abbreviation for "XML namespace" **xmlns** is separated from a unique namespace prefix **prefix** and **uri** is the relative or absolute URI for where the namespace is located.

As an example of the use of the namespace technique to avoid element collisions, let's consider a namespace DTD stored at the location **uriMA.com** which will

> **Good to Know:** Although namespaces could be any of the vocabularies found at the end of this chapter, for example, the Dublin Core vocabulary, or from the MIT or Wikipedia lists where no standard vocabulary exists, you can create your own URI even if it does not really exist!

use the prefix **ma** and a second DTD stored at the location **uriPA.com** which will use the prefix **pa.** In general the namespace will be declared in the XML document with the overall root element, in this case from the **ma** DTD and then the two namespaces as shown here:

```
<ma:root xmlns:ma="uriMA.com" xmlns:pa="uriPA.com">
```

The document would then continue with all XML selectors (elements) referenced to their specific namespaces:

```
<ma:selector1>content<ma:selector1>
<ma:selector2>content<ma:selector2>
    <pa:root>
        <pa:selector1>content</pa:selector1>
        <pa:selector2>content</pa:selector2>
    </pa:root>
</ma:root>
```

Note that for this example we had the **pa** DTD as a child of the **ma** parent positioned after a few **ma** elements and thus we see the call to the **pa** root element **pa:root,** its elements (**pa:selector1** and **pa:selector2**), and then the closing tag for the **pa** root. We could have additional **ma** elements after the closing of the **pa** container and then, lastly, the **ma** root closing tag.

Unfortunately, even though there is only one duplicate element name (**title**) in the DC DTD and our cookbook DTD, all elements of both DTDs would have to have their respective namespace prefixes to avoid confusing the browser. In the example shown earlier, the DC DTD (**dc**) would be used as the **ma** namespace, as it is used first in any XML document that includes Dublin Core declarations, and the **cookbook** DTD (**cb**) would be treated as the **pa** namespace was as it resides inside of the overall DC container. The first few lines of the Cookbook XML Document with the Dublin Core DTD stored as **dtd/dc.dtd** and the cookbook DTD stored as **dtd/cb.dtd** would be:

```
<?xml version="1.0" encoding="UTF-8">
<dc:record xmlns:dc="dtd/dc.dtd" xmlns:cb="dtd/cb.dtd">
    <dc:title>The Friends of Red Rose Library Cookbook</dc:title>
    <dc:publisher>Red Rose Library</dc:publisher>
        <cb:cookbook>
            <cb:contents>Table of Contents</cb:contents>
            . . .
            <cb:title>Hard-Boiled Eggs</cb:title>
        </cb:cookbook>
    </dc:record>
```

Alas, we need to extend this prefixing over to any style files so they, too, need not worry about colliding element names. We won't go into the fine details here, but as you can imagine the CSS namespace syntax is browser dependent, and for multi-browser use the CSS style file(s) must contain multiple syntax sets. For Firefox the namespace CSS syntax is:

```
@namespace ma url(uriMA.com);
ma | selector1 { attribute1:value1; attribute2:value2 }
ma | selector2 {attribute1:value1; attribute2:value2 }
```

For IE the namespace escape CSS styles syntax is:

```
ma\:selector1 {attribute1:value1; attribute2:value2 }
ma\:selector2 {attribute1:value1; attribute2:value2 }
```

Figure 12-37 illustrates a style file used in his text with an XML document "model. xml" that contains both Firefox and IE namespace styles used by Carey Ng, in his *New Perspectives on XML* tutorial 2.

Figure 12-38 demonstrates a few CSS style examples of the differences between Firefox and IE coding for namespace styles.

At this point you really have a good general understanding of the basics behind the creation of an XML document, actually more than enough to get into some really interesting designs. BUT, please note, this is only the surface of XML. We have not covered how XML can search and retrieve content from a flat or database file and display it, on demand, to create, from general collection catalog information, the data to display subject-like card, author-like card, and other displays. The XML files can be pre-coded to seek all the texts in a particular area or topic from a database that may be updated regularly and display the results in unique ways; but we have already spent a great deal of time on XML. These other areas would require several more chapters. I strongly advise those interested in a more thorough treatment of XML obtain a copy of Carey Ng's

```
/* Filename: model.css
  New Perspectives on XML: Tutorial 2 - Tutorial Case
  This file contains styles used in the model.xml file */
/* CSS FireFox namespace styles here */
@namespace mod url(models);
mod|model {font-family:Arial, Helvetica, sans-serif; font-size:12pt}
mod|title, mod|description, mod|type, mod|ordered
    {display:block; padding:2px; margin:5px; color:blue;
     border:1px solid black; background-color:ivory}
mod|title        {width: 150px}
mod|description {width: 250px}
mod|type         {width: 150px}
mod|ordered      {width: 50px}

/* CSS IE namespace escape styles start here */
mod\:model
    {font-family:Arial, Helvetica, sans-serif; font-size:12pt}
mod\:title, mod\:description, mod\:type, mod\:ordered
    {display:block; padding:2px; margin:5px; color:blue;
     border:1px solid black; background-color:ivory}
mod\:title        {width:150px}
mod\:description  {width:250px}
mod\:type         {width:150px}
mod\:ordered      {width:50px}
```

Figure 12-37. Combined Firefox and IE Namespace Styles **(model.css)**

New Perspectives on XML, which includes library examples, one of Patrick Carey's XML texts: *Creating Web Pages with HTML, XHTML, and XML* or *XML* both in their second edition (Thomson Course Technology), or one of the many O'Reilly texts.

```
Special cases – Firefox                 IE (escape styles):
        ma|title {width:150px}          ma\:title {width:150px}
applies width styling to all title elements in ma
        ma|* {width: 150px}             ma\:* {width:150px}
applies width styling to all elements in ma
        *|title {width: 150px}          *\:title {width:150px}
or      title {width: 150px}            title {width: 150px}
applies width styling to title elements in any namespace in the document
```

Figure 12-38. Firefox and IE Namespace Style Coding

HTML 5—The Future Is Near!

We're not done. "Coming soon to a browser you will use" is the convergence of HTML, CSS, and XML in one package, HTML 5. Although still a W3 candidate recommendation, HTML 5 has been gathering steam as the next big thing in markup since 2004 and is already being partially supported by today's browsers. HTML 5 will allow better control over page layout adding new elements like **article, section, nav, header,** and **footer,** and adds about 40 more elements to HTML 4.1's roughly 70 elements, several of which are now deprecated, and creates a dozen element groupings like section, text-level semantics, embedded, tabular data, forms, and interactive. Notably missing in the new specification are frame constructs (which I never liked anyway <grin>) as well as the font, center, and underline elements. HTML 5 will include better forms handling that will not require complex coding; better handling of audio, video, and visual media; elements like **canvas** which will allow patrons to render two-dimensional objects and enumerated attributes like **contenteditable** that will allow wiki-style editing of your library's web pages of the future.

The 29 April 2014 HTML 5 Candidate Recommendation is online at the W3 Consortium website:

http://www.w3.org/TR/html5

Another location with lots of materials on the HTML 5 specification is:

http://www.whatwg.org/specs/web-apps/current-work/multipage/

The "new" **canvas** element is already usable in current versions of Firefox; however, it uses JavaScript to create pieces of code that will do the painting in the web "canvas." Information on its use, including tutorials and code snippets, is available on the Mozilla Developer pages at:

https://developer.mozilla.org/en/HTML/Canvas

One important requirement of HTML 5 is that all HTML files must begin with a doctype declaration. Unlike previous versions of HTML which we saw required a link to the DTD, the HTML 5 DTD is presumed already in your browser and the overall HTML 5 document looks like:

```
<!DOCTYPE html>
    <html>
    . . .
    </html>
```

When web designers finally get the official HTML 5 to work with, there will be lots of excitement; but suffice it to say, that by combining the best of XHTML, CSS, and XML, the new specification will be awesome.

What's Next?

You should now have a good general understanding of the basics behind the creation of an XML document. We covered how to trick your HTML document into accepting new, customized, original element names using CSS to describe the new elements, and then saw how to create new elements, attributes, and entity characters using XML document type definitions by either embedding the new definitions in the XML file, or by using external DTD files. We topped off our XML overview with HTML 5, the convergence between HTML, CSS, and XML.

In Chapter 14, we'll review the concepts of content management systems and overview a bit of social media, QR codes, and adding them to your website.

URLs Cited

The XML specification

http://www.w3.org/TR/xml

The ASCII Code for text

http://www.asciitable.com/

The Unicode Character Database

http://www.unicode.org/ucd/

The **U**nicode **T**ransformation **F**ormat **8**-bit Encoding website

http://www.utf-8.com/

The Society of American Archivists EAD Standards

http://www2.archivists.org/groups/technical-subcommittee-on-encoded-archival-description-ead/encoded-archival-description-ead

The EAD Tag Library (Version 2002)

http://www2.archivists.org/sites/all/files/EAD_TagLibrary_2002.pdf

The EAD Application Guidelines for Version 1.0

http://www.loc.gov/ead/ag/

The Library of Congress Official EAD website

http://www.loc.gov/ead

The Text Encoding Initiative Consortium

http://www.tei-c.org

MARC Records in XML from Library of Congress

http://www.loc.gov/marc/marcxml.html

Medlane XMLMARC at Stanford University

http://xmlmarc.stanford.edu

National Center for Biotechnology Information NISO Journal Article Tag Suite

http://dtd.nlm.nih.gov/

The Dublin Core Metadata Initiative

http://dublincore.org/

The Dublin Core Metadata Element Set Namespace (RDF File)

http://purl.org/dc/elements/1.1/

The Open Archives Initiative

http://www.openarchives.org/

HTML 5: 29 April 2014 Candidate Recommendation

http://www.w3.org/TR/html5

More on the HTML 5 Specification

http://www.whatwg.org/specs/web-apps/current-work/multipage/

The HTML 5 **canvas** element

https://developer.mozilla.org/en/HTML/Canvas

Some XML Vocabulary Namespaces for Science and Math

Vocabulary	Name/Namespace URL
BioPAX	Biological Pathways Exchange Analysis of biological pathway data **http://www.biopax.org**
CML	Chemical Markup Language Codes chemical compounds, reactions, and molecular information **http://www.cml-xml.org**

GML Geography Markup Language (ISO 19136)
Expresses geographical features
http://www.opengeospatial.org/standards/gml

MathML Math Markup Language
Mathematical equations and operations
http://www.w3.org/TR/MathML2

MML Musical Markup Language
Music and sound notation and lyrics
http://www.musicmarkup.info

RSS Real or Really Simple Syndication
(also called Rich Site Summary or RDF Site Summary)
News headline and columns delivery
http://purl.org/rss

SBML Systems Biology Markup Language
Models metabolism, cell signaling, and so on
http://www.sbml.org

SMIL Synchronized Multimedia Markup Language
Authoring of interactive streaming audiovisual presentations
http://www.w3.org/AudioVideo/

SVG Scalable Vector Graphics Markup Language
Describes two-dimensional graphics in XML
http://www.w3.org/Graphics/SVG/Overview.html

VoiceXML Voice Markup Language
Creates audio dialogs featuring synthesized speech and recognition
http://www.voicexml.org/

XLink XML Linking Language
Creates and describes links between resources
http://www.w3.org/XLink

XML Schema Extensible Markup Language Schema
Defines the structure, content, and semantics of XML documents
http://www.w3.org/XML

XSLT Extensible Style Sheet Language Transformations
Expresses style sheets
http://www.w3.org/TR/xslt

Chapter 12 Review Exercises

Chapter 12 Multiple-Choice Questions

1. The target of the XML declaration for an XML Document is:

   a) **XML** b) **HTML** c) **html** d) **xml**

2. UTF is an abbreviation for Uniform Transformation:

   a) Formula b) Format c) Function d) Figure

3. The XML vocabulary or application used by archivists is called:

   a) TEI b) EAD c) ARC d) REC

4. The Tree Diagram symbol for "zero or more" is:

   a) – b) + c) * d) **?**

5. In a markup language document the first-named element is the __ element.

   a) topmost b) child c) root d) namespace

Chapter 12 Design and Discussion Questions

1. Write the basic XML element document type definitions to create a **records** DTD consistent with the structure of Figure 12–15.
2. When should you consider using a predefined DTD or namespace rather than developing your own DTD standard?
3. Describe why you might decide to use the *XML-like* techniques on your web page.
4. Create an XML document, using an internal XML DTD, for an ordered list of items "one" and "two."

13

Content Management Systems, Mobile Applications, and Things That Go Bump in the Night

Well you are nearing the finish line. This, our last chapter, much like the last few, is not recommended for the faint of heart. In this chapter we will look at some aspects of web page design you might not normally expect. Specifically we will overview the concepts of content management systems, CMS, used with interactive web portals, take a glance at the variety of social media "Web 2.0" tools, discuss web page usability, learn a bit about using mobile applications, and see how to add a QR code, a fancy bar code, to your printed materials that will allow your patron to directly access your web page(s) from their smart phone or tablet.

Many of these techniques require some level of higher-level computer programming, but we will just be touching the surface of their use so you have enough information to reach out to commercial vendors or programmers to use these in your library or information center.

Content Management Systems

Although you will not find as many unique CMS in use as there are XML vocabularies, a great many are used by libraries and information centers. Among the most popular of commercially available CMS that libraries use are OCLC's industry-strength CONTENTdm product—a full-featured online digital library tool being used in CMS courses in many library schools to illustrate turn-key Digital Collection Management Software tools, and the free or very low-cost Drupal, Joomla!, and WordPress applications designed to allow full user-defined websites (of course that requires a bit more IT knowledge than the turn-key systems like CONTENTdm). These will be reviewed in a later section.

Is it worthwhile using a CMS? Website design is an expensive project, but programming and other "page fixes" cost money as well:

Annual Savings = (Time Saved in hours)(#New Pages/yr)($fully loaded IT cost)

So let's say that a CMS might save 10 minutes (1/6 hours) for each page update, and you change 100 pages per week or 5,200 pages/year and that the fully loaded IT staff salaries were *only* $40 per hour—what a bargain! Using a CMS would provide annual savings of **$34,666** (1/6 hour × 5,200 pages × $40 per hour)!

The CMS process is always the same: acquire or create content, manage the content, publish the content, present the content. Perhaps you are getting the picture: a CMS is all about the content of your project whether it be a baseball or postcard collection, a collection of VHS tapes and DVDs, your vertical files, or the whole library's collection.

Now that we have demonstrated that there may be money to be saved using CMS, and that librarians should have more than enough applications to justify using a CMS, are libraries and information centers the only place to find CMS? Of course not. Step Two Designs has excellent information on CMS in general as well as a page of vendor lists broken down by specific markets, commercial and open-source vendors, on its website at:

http://www.steptwo.com.au/resources/cms-lists

Using a CMS typically involves documenting your content, for example, information that might be in a card catalog or perhaps a recipe book, creating scenarios of how your patrons might be needing to use your content, for example, title, author, subject cards, or individual recipes. It also involves overviewing of requirements (space in gigabytes for your data, etc.), creation and management of your content (creation, editing, storing), publishing (approving the content), and then presentation (web, smartphone, print). As you see, it's *all* about your content. Indeed some CMS are designed for different content types.

The first generation of CMS was based on a flat file database, a plain text and often comma-separated value file (**.csv**), derived from spreadsheets and queried using XML and CSS techniques. Due to space limitations, we were unable to expand Chapter 12 to include any XML query techniques. These CMS applications created "publish on demand" web pages of search results but often had very little search capability or taxonomy built into them. They were typically one-offs created for a single purpose and proprietary in nature. Few commercial applications were available.

The second-generation CMS were database enabled. CONTENTdm was an early adopter of this technology. In most cases data is stored in a structured query language (SQL) relational database like Microsoft Access. Content was stored with metadata fields that include information on when to "show" the information and "date-expire" fields that let the CMS know when to stop showing the content. The key here is that rather than extracting the content as was required in the first-generation spreadsheet to **csv** conversions, the content remains untouched in the database for reuse and/or modification and maintenance. Web pages were still created by XML, JavaScript, and others, "on-the-fly," but now only the most current content is available using metadata and XML/CSS sorting techniques.

> **<u>Good to Know:</u>** You may not be aware of the magic of relational databases, for example, Microsoft Access. Typically these databases provide four basic actions: creation of individual tables wherein content is stored with specific fields along with key fields and overlapping field names; creation of forms to insert metadata into the tables without the user realizing he or she may be inserting into several individual tables; selection of primary (etc.) "keys" with which the various individual tables are linked together, relations; and creation of new results "tables" by queries across the database and generation of reports and/or web pages to display them.

These CMS are database-driven and use the full power of XML with templates that have a uniform *"look and feel"* and navigation. The CMS creates forms for content insertion into page templates allowing the addition of metadata, tags, and other options. There are also options for indexing the database to speed up content displays.

Figure 13-01 shows the tables that a full "Book" database might include.

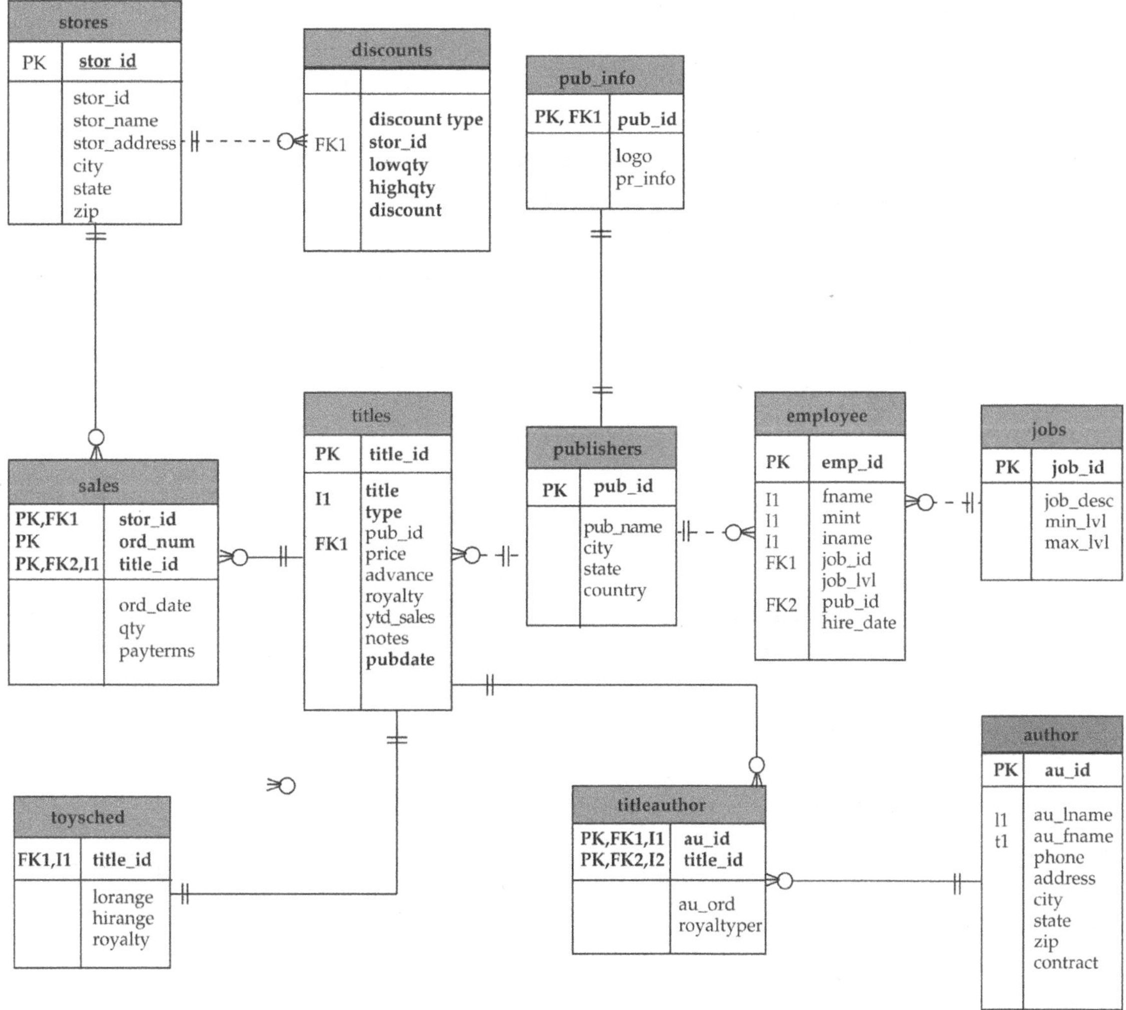

Figure 13-01. "Book" Database Tables for a Microsoft Access Relational Database

Figure 13-02 shows an enlarged section that Book database illustrating several PK or primary key field names and their linkages for the **titles, publishers, title author,** and **authortables.**

The third generation of CMS was marked by the addition of web team enabling. These are typically enterprise-level, large, customized, CMS projects requiring programmers and code creators, user interface experts, information architects, editors, and content managers, often worldwide. Examples include customer service portals and eCommerce transaction applications. This level of CMS is typically *VERY expensive,* requires substantial IT maintenance, and is *not* compatible with the majority of library and information center budgets.

The fourth-generation CMS were collaboration enabled. But here, in order to reduce the overall expense for a web team noted earlier, library systems and/or consortia often teamed together to collaborate on their needs and share the overall CMS development and maintenance costs. The result was a more general CMS that needed less individual tweaking and has one joint IT group instead of several handling requests for updates, and so on. So although third-generation systems were expensive, the market found a work around that produced library-friendly, actually small business-friendly, systems.

The fifth-generation CMS are much more user friendly and cost-effective. Focusing on "Personalization, Portals, and Dashboards" user content is now aggregated on shared servers with vendors charging based on actual use and amount of content stored. The Dream Host–shared server CMS examples later in this chapter show that despite their power, using shared resources, these relatively easily customizable CMS are available even for small libraries. With them non-IT librarians and information specialists are able to design their own pages using templates that provide

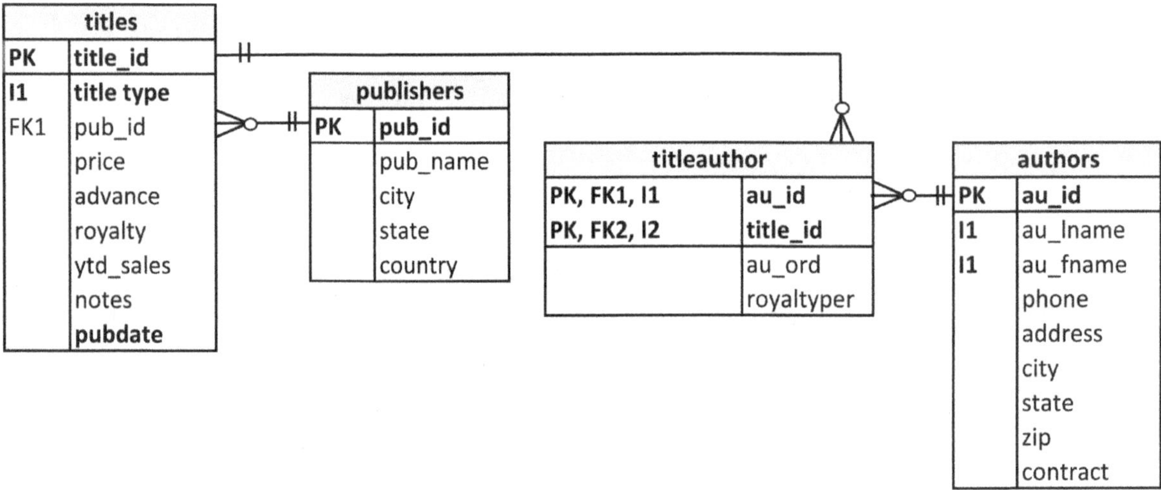

Figure 13-02. Title/Author/Publisher Links for a Microsoft Access Relational Database

a consistent look and feel while using otherwise IT-intensive solutions to managing content on a website and providing databases and other tools for rapid design and deployment.

One needs to have in mind there are many characteristics and services when one is seeking to purchase space on a shared hosted server. These include "24-7-365" technical support via phone/email; a dedicated, secure, DNS-enabled *server* URL (e.g., **https://server.domain.com**) with lots of storage dedicated to projects; access to a SQL or other programmable database with easy installation and maintenance of server software (e.g., programming languages, CMS); and the ability to archive directory and software backups.

What Is Content?

Static desktop and web page publishing uses a word processing application, for example, Word, to create word-processed document content. Similarly, a graphics application, for example, Adobe Photoshop, creates and/or modifies graphic image content. This content is integrated in a publishing application, for example, Word or Microsoft Publisher, or one of the Adobe Creative suite applications, and then stored for later presentation, for example, via a web browser on your patron's device. Documents can be printed or used to create camera-ready pages. Saving the "print" content portions with gif/jpg/png graphics on a website results in a set of HTML and other files that your browser can display. Capturing the web pages results in presentations that can become printed, for example, pdf, publications.

> **Good to Know:** One aspect often overlooked in creating a CMS is that in order to find something in the CMS, it must be there in a way that the application can find and retrieve it. The many commonly used databases, for example, DIALOG, have sets of database fields included in their standard searches that have the title field but do not have the author field. As a result searching for an author will only find their name in the title of an article. For example searching "Albert Einstein" will not reveal anything written by him, but likely many articles written either about him or his works. Be sure that you figure out what searches your patron will want to do and then construct your database around those fields. More fields, no problem; fewer fields, can't be searched.

Basic Content Management Process

From content creation through presentation, there needs to be management and process control to assure quality of search and retrieval. Issues to consider in content creation include WYSIWYG document consideration, whether authoring is in word processing or web page design. Bear in mind that the content should be designed for reuse, cross-platform, and multiple languages. Although there can be additional groupings of elements, perhaps the three simplest "blocks" of a CMS include (1) the content creation and storage, a document repository; the control and maintenance of the database of the content, (2) records management and integration with external systems;

and (3) the retrieval, publishing, style sheets, page templates, publishing models with a focus on presentation, usability, accessibility, human-readable URLs, and valid HTML/XML coding of the content.

The Step Two Designs **Intranet Roadmap,** shown as Figure 13-03, from their web page at: **http://www.steptwo.com.au/products/roadmap** describes all the activities required to develop or redevelop an intranet. An intranet is a local network or workgroup that typically is not part of the Internet. The Roadmap's recently released second edition covers a holistic approach to the management of an intranet project with activities in five key streams: strategy, design, content, change and communications, and technology. It illustrates what activities need to be conducted, showing the sequence of activities required, and the techniques that will help at every stage of the project.

The Step Two Designs Roadmap also highlights which activities, such as usability testing, affinity diagramming, personas and collaborative design, can be used to support individual activities.

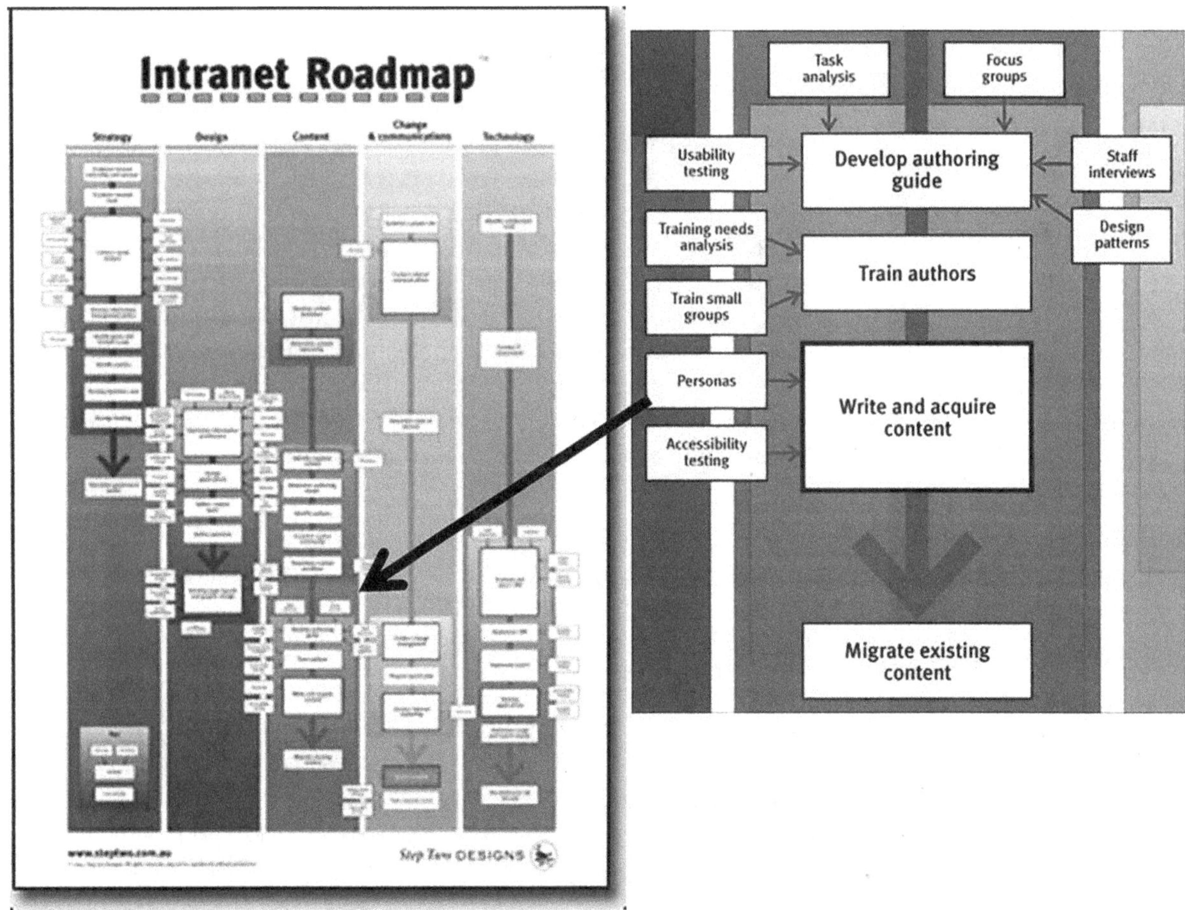

Figure 13-03. Intranet Roadmap with Highlighted Section (from **http://www.steptwo.com.au/products/roadmap**)

CMS Web Design Methodology

How can we implement a web-based CMS? We need to do a lot of work before we can jump in and set up any of the CMS applications mentioned earlier. In general this task *could* be broken into the following segments:

- Inventory your content
- Understand how users (think they) want to access your content
- Develop, test, and refine site structure
- Finalize site structure
- Develop, test, and refine page designs
- Finalize page design
- Create home page
- Implement and publish the website

The core technologies for building web pages have, for the most part, already been covered in the previous chapters. They include **HTML** or **XML**, the language of ***page structure***, and **CSS** which separates content from presentation by providing ***style for page layout***. By now you should be comfortable enough to realize that HTML/XML can be used to publish online documents with headings, text, tables, lists, photos, and so on. HTML/XML also uses forms for conducting transactions with remote services, searching for information, making reservations, ordering products, and so on. (NOTE: There may well be a need for a dedicated or special transaction server to accomplish these, but you have the basic tools to use.) HTML/XML allows inclusion of spreadsheets, video clips, sound clips, and other applications directly in their documents and can retrieve online information via hypertext links.

CSS, on the other hand, can be used to stylize web page colors, layout, and fonts; can be used to configure your page's display for different types of devices, for example, laptops, smart phones or printers; and works with HTML, XML, HTML5 as well as most scripting and programming languages. We have seen how external CSS style sheet files can be shared across pages and websites to configure pages to different internal departments as well as output devices.

CONTENTdm Digital Collection Management Software

CONTENTdm is a single software solution that handles the storage, management, and delivery of your library's digital collections to the web for use by patrons with a variety of browsers. CONTENTdm Project Client uses spreadsheet tools in a robust

Windows-based, digital collection tool where data and digital items can be prepared in large batches for uploading to your server or an OCLC-hosted server where the data and images are stored and can be edited.

The system also permits uploading and editing single collection metadata and images directly through a web portal using non-Windows systems. Editing and approving items in a collection can also be accomplished directly over the Internet using a web-based discovery interface.

Many libraries and information centers require uploading their digital content to WorldCat. The CONTENTdm Digital Collection Gateway is a self-service tool for uploading the collection's metadata. As one of OCLC's products, it is natural that it can be integrated with other OCLC products for building collections with cataloging workflows, harvesting from websites and adding long-term preservation.

How CONTENTdm Works

Your CONTENTdm digital collections reside on either a local or OCLC-hosted web server containing CONTENTdm server software which produces web pages that look like the one shown in Figure 13-04.

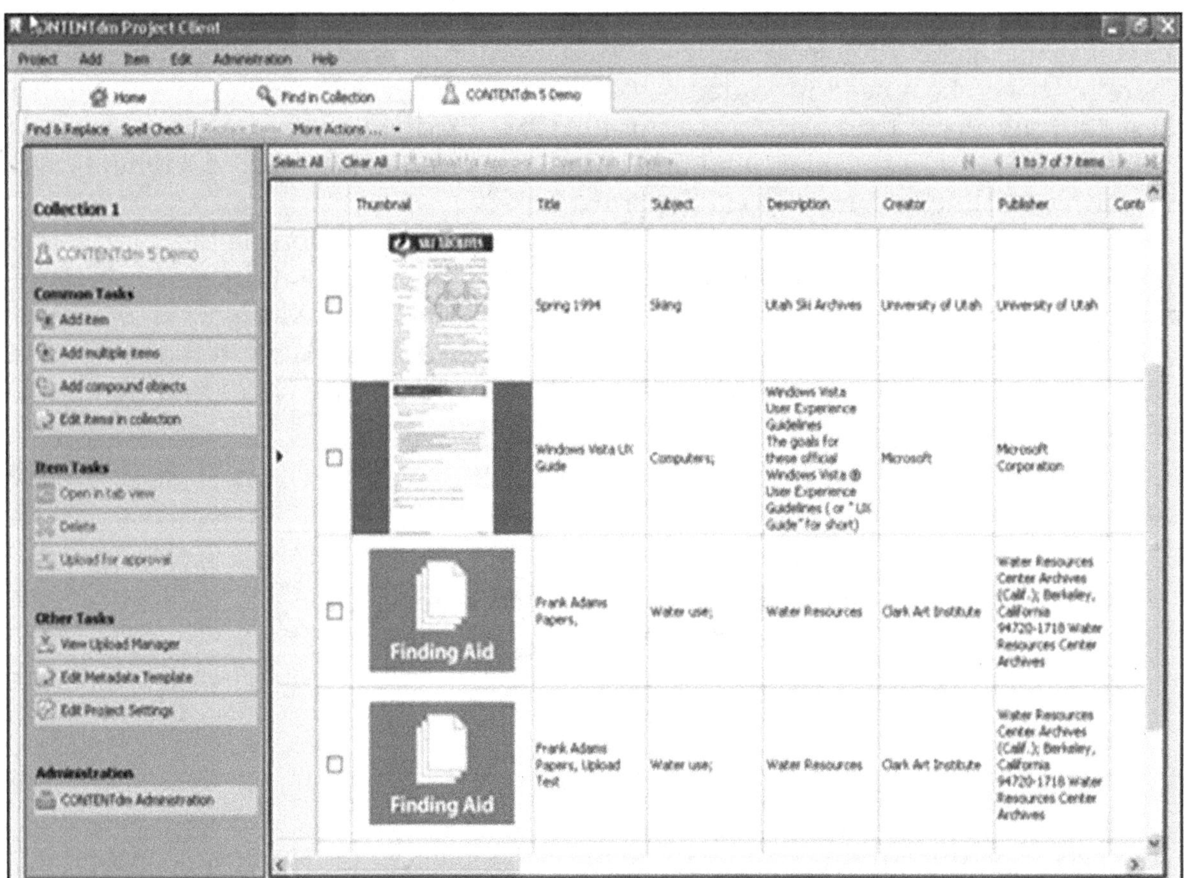

Figure 13-04. The CONTENTdm Windows-Based Project Client Interface (Spreadsheet View)

Digital items can be added from anywhere using the CONTENTdm Project Client seen in Figure 13-05, which can be used by staff and collaborating partners, the Connexion client tool using Connexion digital import, a web browser using a simple web form, the CONTENTdm Flex Loader tool for newspapers, or the CONTENTdm Catcher web service used for batch editing metadata.

Once uploaded, edited, and approved, unless you choose to restrict access during collection development when only staff can see what is in the collection, your digital collections can be searched via the web using standard web browsers by any number of patrons. With its ability to handle any file type, CONTENTdm can serve as a repository to bring a variety of collections together into a cohesive and accessible web-based environment.

The CONTENTdm Content Management System

The first step in creating a CONTENTdm website for the collection, management, and display of an online digital collection is for the website administrator, typically an IT person, to use his or her login and password to gain access to the overall website design and construction web-accessible CONTENTdm Server Administrator Website Configuration Tools. The administrator has a wide variety of tools at his or her disposal to customize the appearance, searching and browsing, user interface (UI widgets), image viewer, navigation, page types, tools, custom pages/scripts, global website settings, and individual collection settings.

As you will typically receive an email or phone call stating that the library has installed or licensed hosting of a CMS system and that you will *not* be the administrator of the system, we will not dwell on the use of these tools here, but we will show you what is available so you may interact with the system administrator to better serve your collection's need. The CONTENTdm defaults would typically be used for your initial collection and customization of the collection's screens considered later on.

The CONTENTdm Web Browser Administration tools include three tabs for administration of the Server, the Collections, and individual Items.

The Server tab includes tabs for Collections, Harvesting, Website, Users, Reports, About, and Help as seen in Figure 13-05. This tab is normally "greyed out" for all but the actual server administrator who will configure the various directories for item and metadata storage as well as customize the website for your collection.

Once the server is configured defining the directories where the collection will be stored, and so on, we need to "tell" CONTENTdm what the name of our collection will be and what fields we will need in the database your patrons will be searching when they access your collection. Either the website administrator or the collection's authorized administrator/editor can customize the collection by creating the Collection's Database Fields. Although the Dublin Core is the default "out of the box" database configuration, other collection types are also available and custom database fields can be created that map into the Dublin Core filed types.

The Collections tab includes tabs for Profile, Fields, Website, Reports, Export, View Collection, and Help. Clicking on "fields" brings us to the display of the default Dublin

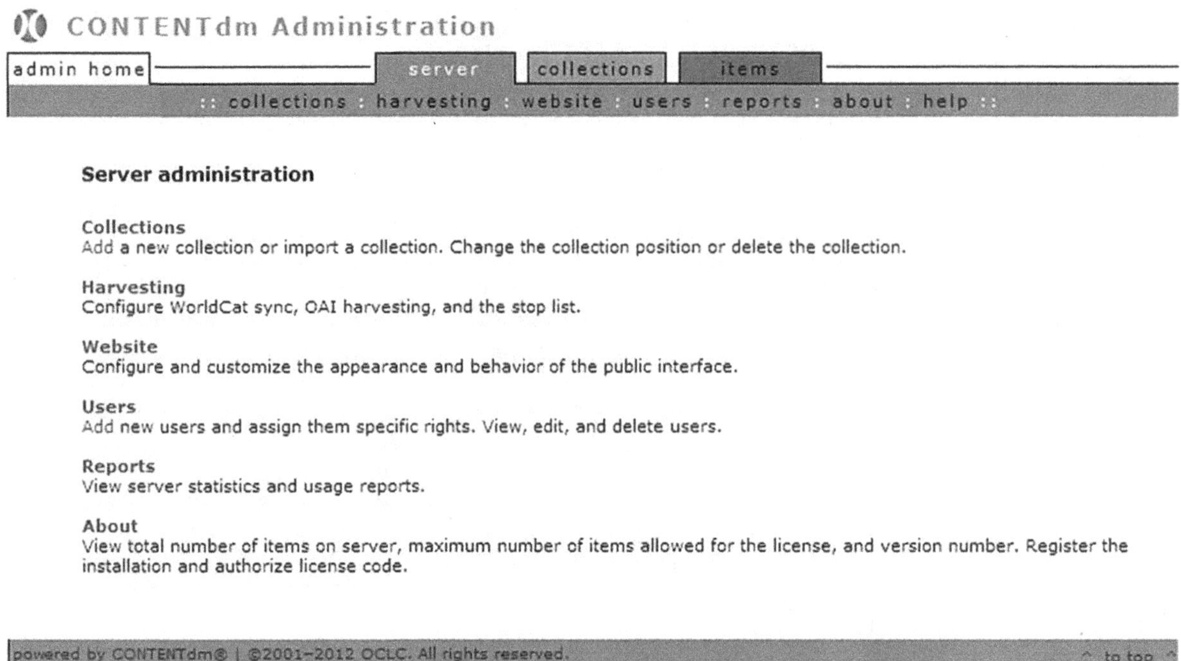

Figure 13-05. CONTENTdm Web Browser Administration Interface, Server Tab

Core metadata fields as seen in Figure 13-06. Note that all these fields are not typically displayed in one browser window.

Other metadata sets are also available, and using the Fields tab your collection administrator can define the specific fields of the collection and describe if these fields can be mapped to the Dublin Core fields, are text or other data type, whether they will be displayed in a large, multiline field space or not, if they are hidden from patron view, are required or the item will not be displayed, and finally, if they have a controlled vocabulary associated with terms in that field in the database.

If a controlled vocabulary, your collection administrator will be able to determine what thesaurus or custom vocabulary the field's "values" are restricted to. In the event a term in a controlled vocabulary field is *not* in the controlled vocabulary for that field, CONTENTdm will ask the editor/administrator if that new term should be added to your vocabulary or if you want to change the field contents to another term. Remember if what your patron is searching for is not in your database, for example, missing fields, unauthorized controlled vocabulary terms, they will not find what they are looking for.

After server administration, and the collection's database definitions are set up (Step 1: Create the Collection's Database Fields), the process by which a digital collection goes from being a set of images, CONTENTdm's *items,* and isolated metadata into a content managed collection is shown in Figure 13-07. Please note that after each step there are opportunities and/or requirements built into the system for editing and approving the changes made. These approvals can be assigned to the collection administrator or another staff member as needed.

The tasks of acquiring and editing, finding and replacing items and metadata, as well as uploading these items and metadata to the server can be authorized at the

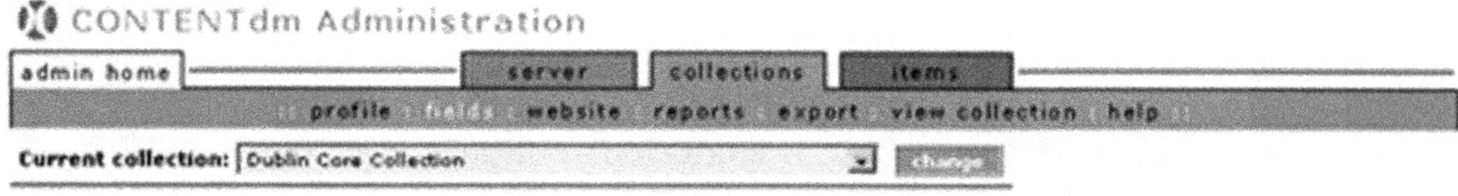

Metadata fields

View and configure collection and administrative fields.

Collection field properties

View, add, edit and delete fields. Enable full text searching and controlled vocabulary. After you have added, changed, or deleted fields, index the collection to update changes.

	Field name	DC map	Data type	Large	Search	Hide	Required	Vocab		add field
1	Title	Title	Text	No	Yes	No	Yes	No	move to	edit | delete
2	Subject	Subject	Text	No	Yes	No	No	No	move to	edit | delete
3	Description	Description	Text	Yes	Yes	No	No	No	move to	edit | delete
4	Creator	Creator	Text	No	No	No	No	No	move to	edit | delete
5	Publisher	Publisher	Text	No	No	No	No	No	move to	edit | delete
6	Contributors	Contributors	Text	No	No	No	No	No	move to	edit | delete
7	Date	Date	Text	No	No	No	No	No	move to	edit | delete
8	Type	Type	Text	No	No	No	No	No	move to	edit | delete
9	Format	Format	Text	No	No	No	No	No	move to	edit | delete
10	Identifier	Identifier	Text	No	No	No	No	No	move to	edit | delete
11	Source	Source	Text	No	No	No	No	No	move to	edit | delete
12	Language	Language	Text	No	No	No	No	No	move to	edit | delete
14	Coverage	Coverage	Text	No	No	No	No	No	move to	edit | delete
15	Rights	Rights	Text	No	No	No	No	No	move to	edit | delete
16	Audience	Audience	Text	No	No	No	No	No	move to	edit | delete
	Field name	DC map	Data type	Large	Search	Hide	Required	Vocab		add field

Administrative fields

View and edit administrative fields (some field properties are system-defined and cannot be edited). Index the collection to update changes.

Field name	DC map	Data type	Search	Hide	
Archival file	None	Text	No	Yes	edit
OCLC number	None	Text	No	Yes	edit
Date created	None	Date	No	Yes	edit
Date modified	None	Date	No	Yes	edit
CONTENTdm number	None	Text	No	Yes	edit
CONTENTdm file name	None	Text	No	Yes	edit

Figure 13-06. CONTENTdm Web Browser Administration Interface, Collections Tab

- **Create the Collection's Database Fields**
  – *Edit and approve as needed*
- **Acquire Items & Metadata**
  – *Edit and approve as needed*
- **Upload Items & Metadata to Server**
  – *Edit and approve as needed*
- **Index the Collection**
  – *Edit and approve as needed*
- **View the Collection**
  – *Review and recommend revisions as needed*

Figure 13-07. CONTENTdm Digital Collection Process

general level of library or information science professional or delegated to specific individuals using CONTENTdm Web Client Tools, either from the CONTENTdm Project Client or directly through the browser. Either your collection administrator or another staff member would then "approve" items in the pending queue and then "index" the collection's searchable fields.

At this point in the process it is not unusual for only the library staff to have access to reviewing the collection information. Only after all these steps, including indexing, are accomplished and the restrictions are placed on what users can access the "in progress" materials will your Collection be visible online to the world. Ofcourse in some instances *you* are the administrator, item scanner, metadata provider, AND the editor.

Finally, to make it easy for staff to add, edit, and otherwise maintain your items and their metadata, there is an Items tab. The Items tab allows administration of item Approve, Index, Add, Edit, Find & Replace, Lock Administration, View Collection, and Help as shown in Figure 13-08. Also seen in Figure 13-08 is an overlay of the Edit tab.

Sometimes you don't need a full-featured, online collection tool such as CONTENTdm. Presuming that you have personal IT background or an eager IT person who is a friend of your library or information center, you can create your own CMS using some of the following available CMS tools.

DreamHost and Common CMS Systems

In the absence of a dedicated server on which to mount their CMS librarians often turn either to a commercial CMS vendor that provides hosting or to one of the general sites like DreamHost (**http://www.dreamhost.com**) that offers hosting for a small monthly fee, but allows several different options for your website's CMS. Perhaps the most common of all CMS applications is WordPress which has been used by individuals, not-for-profits, and enterprises for web logs and websites for many years. Also available with "one-click" installation are CMS applications by Drupal, Omeka, Joomla!, Get Simple, ComisCMS, Moodle, and MediaWiki to name a few. One key reason for using this type of shared server is that you can select one of several CMS types to highlight the specific type of collection you have, and all the tools are there, including a database and eCommerce, for a relatively small monthly fee. You have two basic phases for creating your CMS on DreamHost. Phase 1 uses the quick install to initialize your selected CMS, and phase 2 allows you to customize the setup a bit as shown in Figure 13-09.

One of the most popular DreamHost CMS selections is WordPress. As we will see in the next section, WordPress is available via shared servers such as DreamHost, on the WordPress server itself, or can be on your library's server.

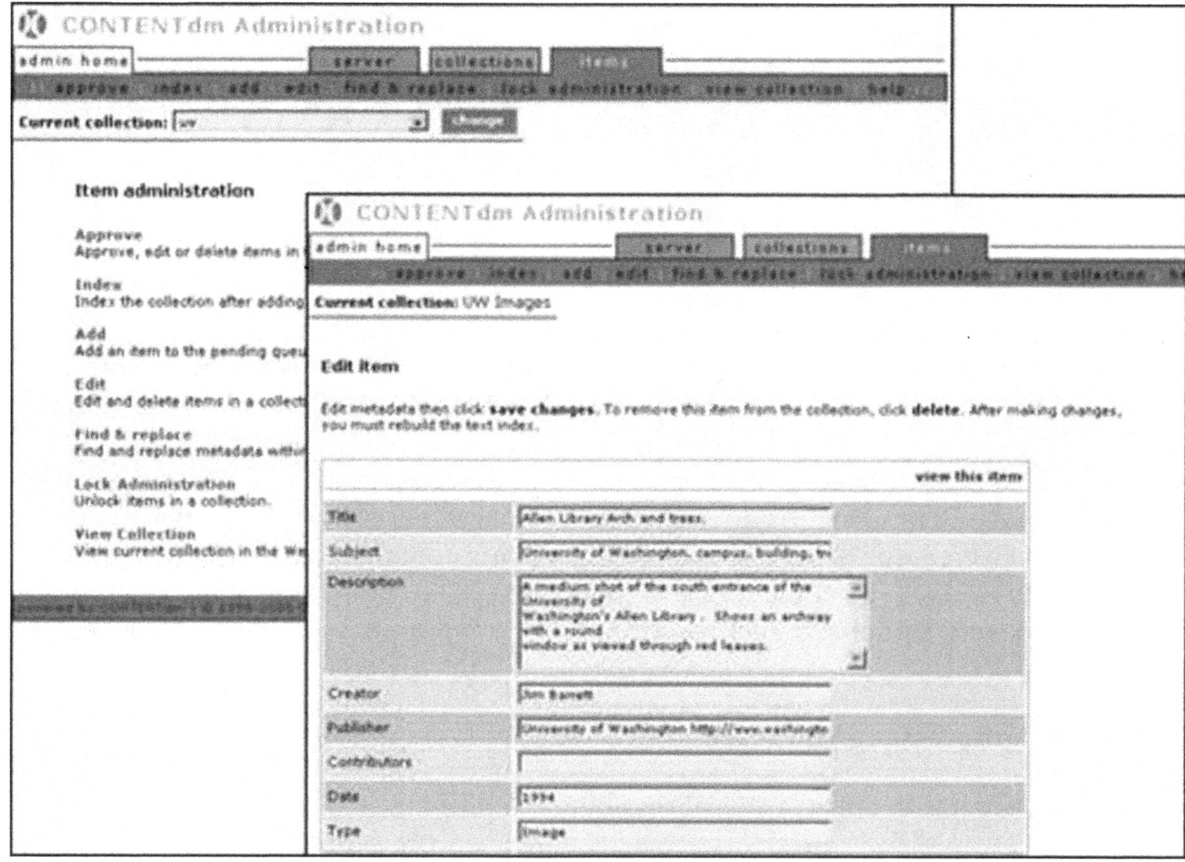

Figure 13-08. CONTENTdm Web Browser Administration Interface, Items Tab

DreamHost Phase I (*From Quick Install Setup*)

- *Create 'sysop' account*
- *Print out empty database fields*
- *Print out defaults screens, etc.*
- *Create database metafields (e.g., APA Style for bibliography): Print result*
- *Load bibliocite metadata, PDFs*
- *Display bibliocite in default CMS style: Print results*

Note anything interesting/unusual...

DreamHost Phase I (*From Quick Install Setup*)

- *Stylize your CMS*
    - *or at least note what you can/can not do and 'how'*
- *Create a stylized CMS 'landing page'*
- *Print out Search screen*
- *Print out results of a search*
- *Create a "shoot-out" Addendum for your CMS*

Note anything interesting/unusual...

Figure 13-09. Two Phases of DreamHost CMS Setup

WordPress: The Popular Blog and Bibliography Collection CMS

WordPress is an open source content management system, often used as a blog, web-log, interactive publishing application. It is powered by the PHP programming language and the MySQL (my-SEQUEL) structured query language database. It has many features, including a plug-in architecture and a template system. Used by over 12% of the 1,000,000 biggest websites, WordPress is one of the most popular CMS in use today. On your server, DreamHost or another vendor shared server, or even on WordPress servers you can create a WordPress blog or design and construct a library and/or information center website-level content management system complete with eCommerce online purchasing options. Checkout some of the featured WordPress websites for ideas

http://wordpress.org/showcase

or see how easy it is to create a WordPress blog (FREE!) at:

https://signup.wordpress.com/signup/

Why WordPress? It's **free.** Working with WordPress will cost you nothing except your time or that of your IT professional. So it is probably already in your budget! WordPress is licensed under a **GPL** or General Public License. The GPL allows developers the freedom to modify and redistribute the software, as long as they provide others the same freedoms. WordPress is known for its incredibly simple 5-minute install through the quick start web page illustrated in Figure 13-10 currently at **https://signup.wordpress.com/signup.**

WordPress has been around for about 10 years and it is still actively developed. Thus there are an enormous number of WordPress resources available on the web both on the two WordPress sites and on other sites. These include free themes and a large number of both written and video tutorials. The WordPress team oversees the WordPress documentation called the Codex5 and organizes community meetups, as well as conferences called WordCamps. To learn more about these efforts, visit:

http://central.wordcamp.org

Should You Use WordPress.com or WordPress.org?

The pros and cons of the many differences between the creation of a WordPress site on **WordPress.com** and **WordPress.org** are shown in Figure 13-11.

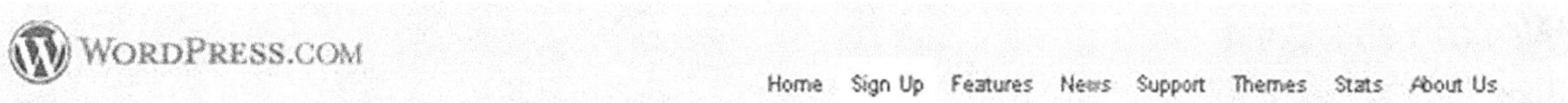

Get your own WordPress.com account in seconds

Fill out this one-step form and you'll be blogging seconds later!

Blog Address

.wordpress.com Free

Choose an address for your blog. Don't worry, you can change this later.

If you don't want a blog you can signup for just a username.

Username

Your username should be a minimum of four characters and can only include lowercase letters and numbers.

Password

Great passwords use upper and lower case characters, numbers and symbols like !"£$%^&(.

Password Strength

Confirm

E-mail Address

We'll send you an email to activate your blog, so please triple-check that you've typed it correctly.

Follow our blog to learn about new themes, features, and other news.

Figure 13-10. WordPress Quick Setup at **https://signup.wordpress.com/signup**

WordPress is based upon web page templates called themes. Themes are essentially divided into three components: presentation, content, and logic. Your WordPress theme's *presentation* is governed by a file called **style.css** that contains all the style rules that will be applied to it. The template files describe what *content* should be output on each of WordPress' pages: lists of posts, single posts, search results, and so on. Finally, a file called **functions.php** contains any additional *logic* your theme needs in order to, well, function. This is where plugin-like functionality is included in your theme: new custom widgets, or perhaps a theme-specific administration panel for customizing the color scheme and layout. This logic file is immediately loaded during WordPress' initialization, but it can be modified to define common functions that are used throughout your theme.

You can download WordPress from:

http://wordpress.org/download/

WordPress.com

Pros

- hosted and managed for ***free***
- hosted on hundreds of servers, resulting in virtually 99% uptime
- set up, comment spam, and database back ups performed automatically for free

Cons

- limited access to themes (around 100), and custom themes not permitted
- unable to modify underlying PHP code
- custom plug-ins can't be implemented
- listed as **mysite.wordpress.com** - a sub-domain of **wordpress.com**
- (it is possible to map your own domain address to this URL)

WordPress.org

Pros

- access to thousands of custom themes
- use of custom widgets and plug-ins
- retention of 100% control over the markup
- access to the ***MySQL*** database, should you need to make revisions or create new tables
- *can be installed either on your **desktop computer**, web server, or virtual machine*

Cons

- responsible for acquiring your own hosting, ***at a cost***
- manual installation of software required
- download required of necessary plug-ins to prevent spam (e.g., ***Akismet plugin***)

Figure 13-11. Differences between Websites on WordPress Sites

To install it review the information at:

http://codex.wordpress.org/Installing_WordPress

You will be presented with the base framework, and a page with the default theme "Twenty Ten" as illustrated in Figure 13-12.

Your site's theme administration page (from the Dashboard, click Appearance, then Themes) will show you a selection of all the themes you've installed, default shown. WordPress includes drag and drop interfaces that allow authors to simply configure the different types of content that should be shown in each sidebar of Figure 13-13.

Planning Your WordPress Theme

What do you start with? Figure out what you want your pages to look like. Will you have patrons able to make posts, or only have pages with media and links? What custom fields, categories and tags, comments, widgets, and menus do you want on your page? Deciding these in advance allows you to select the template that gives you the best fit for your website.

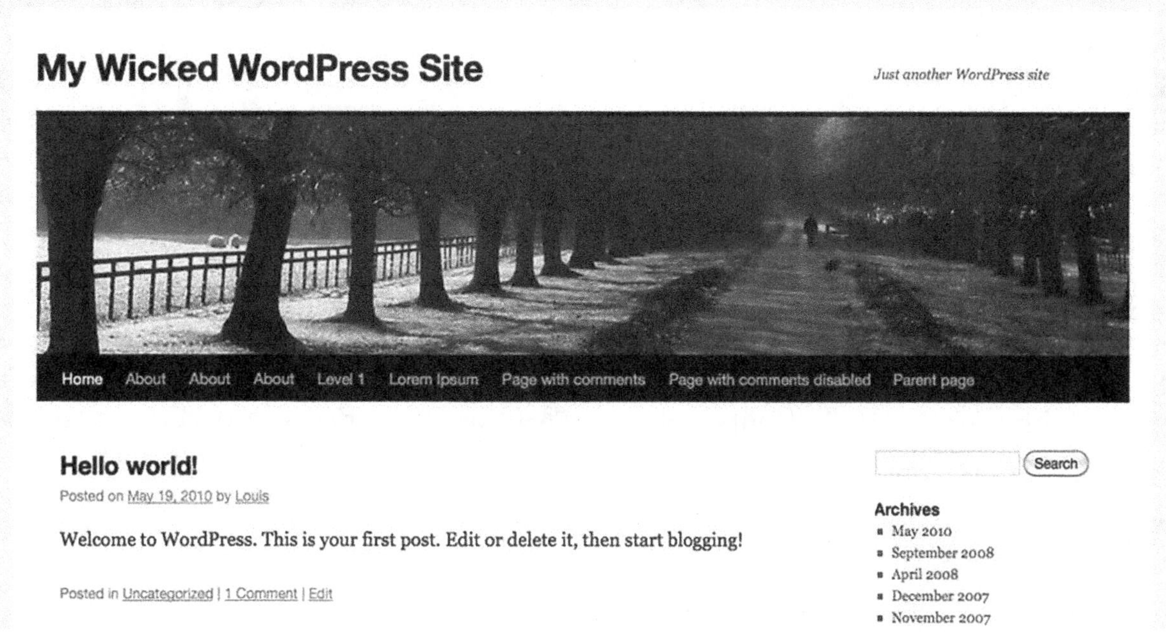

Figure 13-12. WordPress "Twenty Ten" Default Template

WordPress success involves letting your content lead your design. Be sure to spend sufficient time researching CMS websites created/customized by others *before* designing and creating/customizing your own by researching themes, plug-ins available, programming scripts your IT folks might suggest and most assuredly what similar library and information centers are using. Also important in this stage is planning for your patrons, what do they need? Planning for the web publication and planning for your website organization and its hierarchy so you can develop a sitemap for your website.

If you have decided on WordPress to be your CMS, you will need to use tutorials on its website or others that cover the principles of WordPress theme design, not necessarily so you can create your own customized template, but more so you can understand how to modify someone else's.

Basics of color, page branding, and consistent typography are available to create a visual style, but also, bear in mind evaluation of the page's layout and composition. The anatomy of a WordPress theme is shown in Figure 13-14.

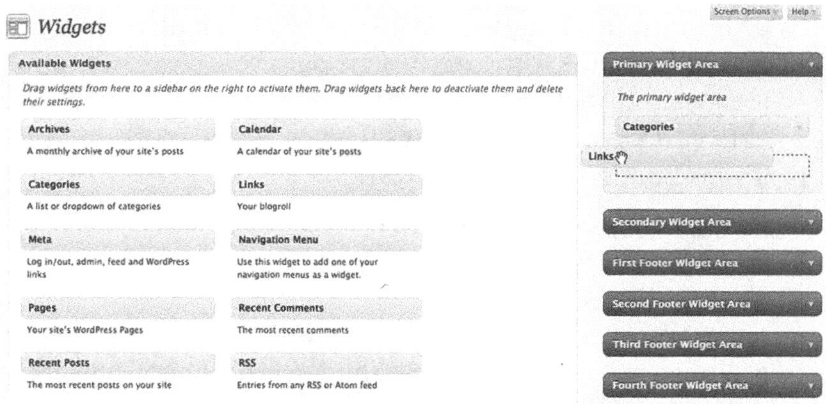

Figure 13-13. WordPress Widgets Administration Page

Another WordPress technique uses theme frameworks which, just like themes in general, can

The Header
The Navigation Menu
The Loop
Pagination
Comments
Sidebars and Widgets
The Footer
The Home Page
The Standard Page / Single Post Template
The Archive, Author, Category, and Tag Page Templates
The Search Results Page; The 404 (file not found) Error Page
Standard Styling for HTML Elements and Extra Features

Figure 13-14. Anatomy of a WordPress Theme

be free or fee-based and can have sub-themes, for example, Child Themes. As you may not use WordPress, there is enough here to get you started and then use one of the tutorials or texts to go further.

Some resources for CMS in general and WordPress in particular are included at the end of the chapter.

Other DreamHost CMS Options

Other CMS are available on DreamHost as well as other vendor shared server sites. Among these are the Drupal, Joomla!, Omeka, GetSimple, ComicCMS, MediaWiki, and Moodle:

Drupal, http://drupal.org

Use Drupal to build everything from personal blogs to enterprise applications. Thousands of add-on modules and designs let you build any site you can imagine. Drupal is free, flexible, robust, and constantly being improved by hundreds of thousands of passionate people from all over the world.

Joomla!, http://www.joomla.org

Joomla! is a popular open source CMS written in the PHP programming language. It uses object-oriented programming (OOP) techniques and software design patterns, stores data in a MySQL database, and includes features such as page caching, RSS feeds, printable versions of pages, news flashes, blogs, polls, search, and support for language internationalization.

Omeka, http://omeka.org

Omeka is a free, flexible, and open source web-publishing platform for the display of library, museum, archives, and scholarly collections and exhibitions. Omeka falls at a crossroads of web content management, collections management, and archival digital collections systems.

Omeka is designed with non-IT specialists in mind, allowing users to focus on content and interpretation rather than programming. It brings Web 2.0 technologies and approaches to academic and cultural websites to foster user interaction and participation. It makes top-shelf design easy with a simple and flexible templating system. Its robust open-source developer and user communities underwrite Omeka's stability and sustainability. Until now, scholars and cultural heritage professionals looking to publish collections-based research and online exhibitions required either extensive technical skills or considerable funding for outside vendors. By making standards based, serious online publishing easy, Omeka puts the power and reach of the web in the hands of academics and cultural professionals themselves. *Omeka is funded by the Institute of Museum and Library Services (IMLS), Alfred P. Sloan Foundation, and Samuel H. Kress Foundation.*

***GetSimple,* http://get-simple.info**

GetSimple is an XML-based lite content management system. To go along with its best-in-class user interface, we have loaded it with features that every website needs, but with nothing it doesn't. GetSimple is truly the simplest way to manage a small business website.

***ComicCMS,* http://comiccms.com**

ComicCMS can be installed on your website to easily create a webcomic site. It will then create and manage all the pages your site needs effectively and efficiently. By using ComicCMS's easy, online admin panel you can add/edit your comics and manage everything your site needs in one place, giving you full flexibility of your site's design without the need to know any PHP.

***MediaWiki,* http://www.mediawiki**

Turn your website into a collaborative knowledge base! MediaWiki is most well known for being the software behind Wikipedia. It is now used by several other projects of the non-profit Wikimedia Foundation, such as Wikipedia, Wiktionary, and Wikinews, as well as on many other Wiki websites worldwide.

Moodle, **http://moodle.org**

Moodle is a free software e-learning platform designed to help educators create online courses with opportunities for rich interaction. Moodle can be used in many types of environments such as in education, training and development, and business settings.

Social Media and "Web 2.0"

The notion of a "Web 2.0" is intended to signify that your website uses technologies that go beyond merely posting static pages. Web 2.0 doesn't truly use new ideas and technologies as much as it signifies a maturity of these in use in page designs on the web and the greater use of servers to create and store data. Figure 13-15 shows the seven key features of Web 2.0 according to WebAppRater (**http://webapprater.com/general/7-key-features-of-web-2–0.html**).

Thus, your WordPress page may permit users to create blogs, web logs, of user-generated content or may direct patrons to a dedicated virtual community web page. The variety of social networking tools, like Wikis, Facebook, Twitter, Flickr, YouTube, **del.icio.us,** and LinkedIn, are considered Web 2.0 as they use server-based applications, CMS, and interactivity usually presumed to exist only in software applications such as a word processing program directly on a local computer. As an indication of the popularity of these social media tools, consider Twitter. In January 2008 there were about 300,000 tweets per day. This rose to 2 million a day in 2009, 32 million a day in 2010, 200 million a day in 2011, and in October 2012 there were 400 million tweets per day. By June 2014 the number of Tweets grew to 500 million per day (**https://about.twitter.com/company**). According to the "By the Numbers: 164 Amazing Twitter Statistics web page, which has been updated to June 2014, Twitter registered users grew to about one billion (yes, with a B!) with 77% of these outside the U.S.' 53 million users. In the UK there are about 10 million and 35.5 million in China, and Twitter supports over 35 languages (**http://expandedramblings.com/index.php/march-2013-by-the-numbers-a-few-amazing-twitter-stats/#.U5SzrXaiXcg**). These social media tools all permit interaction between you and your patron via these web server–enabled systems.

Lastly, Web 2.0, rather than using a taxonomy or pre-defined classification framework with categories and subcategories, uses a folksonomy which provides a user-created framework with a free classification and arrangement of information also known as social tagging.

1. **Folksonomy : Free Classification of Information**
2. **Rich User Experience**
3. **User as a Contributor**
4. **Long Tail**
5. **User Participation**
6. **Basic Trust**
7. **Dispersion**

Figure 13-15. The Seven Key Features of Web 2.0 (from **http://webapprater.com/general/7-key-features-of-web-2-0.html**)

Web 2.0 and its social networks harness the much greater computing power of a server's operating system. Instead of your smartphone, tablet, or laptop having to have lots of storage space for special software and data, the web becomes a computing platform with links between multiple software, database, and transaction servers. Indeed, most iPhone, iPad, and Mac laptops can communicate seamlessly with each other sharing contacts, calendars, and other content through a virtual iCloud environment created when they are connected to the same wireless access point! Cloud computing, using Internet servers, is an attractive way to expand your storage capabilities; but beware that *you* do not control the access to and maintenance of these depositories and therefore *you* need to have backups of any materials you deposit there. Also privacy issues may need to be taken into consideration before storing patron information in remote storage areas. The use of Dropbox and other like services needs to be carefully reviewed by your legal advisors.

For most library and information centers, creating social media accounts will permit their patrons another level of interactivity for requesting information and so on. It is very common to include links to any of the library's social media presence using one or more of the logos of Figure 13-16 as hypergraphics on your web pages. First step, of course, is to find a staff member or volunteer that is adept in these, as a social networking presence that is not moderated is not a professional way to put your library's best face forward.

Figure 13-16. Popular Social Network Logos and URLs

As more and more mobile applications (apps) are created, it is likely that there will be one created to interconnect your library to patrons for updating their requests for interlibrary loan materials, AV already in circulation, forwarding ready reference queries to your staff, and even to remind them of collection material due dates and overdue notices.

Web Page Usability

Perhaps one of the most popular series of easy-to-read and understand texts on web usability is by Steve Krug. *Don't Make Me Think: A Common Sense Approach to Web Usability* (2005. New Riders, ISBN: 0-321-34475-8) and its how-to companion *Rocket Surgery Made Easy: The Do-It-Yourself Guide to Finding and Fixing Usability Problems* (2010. New Riders, ISBN: 0-321-65729-2) both now in their second editions are a great way to begin to understand that what is obvious to the designer and library professional on our web pages may not be as crystal clear to our patrons and trustees. On his website at

http://www.sensible.com

Krug also posts tools such as a usability test script, recording consent form, instructions for observers, dialog that you can use as a usability facilitator, a demo test video, "Usability Testing Checklists," and even excerpts from his texts.

Remote usability study software approaches to usability testing are available to walk participants through a variety of requested tasks during which their click paths are recorded. Examples, from a good review of usability testing at **http://www.measuringusability.com/blog/method-comparison.php** are:

UserZoom

http://www.userzoom.com

Loop11

http://www.loop11.com

Webnographer

http://www.webnographer.com

The extension of usability concepts has created UX, user experience (also known as UXD, user experience design). Keeping UX in mind helps you design web pages and interfaces that attract and keep patrons coming to your website by coupling usability testing with the page design process in a true human-computer interaction (HCI). By addressing the needs of users the hope is that your patrons will work with you to maximize their use of your website. It forces us all to remember that our websites are not just for use by library and information science professionals <grin>. A set of 50 user experience best practices is available as an e-Book by *The Above the Fold Team*" (**www.abovethefolddesign.com**) from User Experience Designs at:

http://www.userexperiencedesigns.com/assets/pdf/50-UX-Best-Practices.pdf

Mobile Applications

With the proliferation of smartphones, and Wi-Fi accessible iPads, Kindles, NetBooks, other tablet computers, and other devices, what once was an 8.5″ ×11″ (14″ diagonal) 640 × 480 pixel desktop monitor display format is now crammed onto a 2″ × 3″ or smaller mobile phone screen. These smart devices, like their Internet-connected desktop counterparts, have interactive capabilities that make them ideal candidates for accessing your web pages. We reviewed some of the ways we can accommodate these device displays in our previous chapters, but bear in mind that getting a large screen readable page to be also readable on a smart device is often a losing battle. They are just too small! You will need to develop a mobile-sized version of your pages if you want to view pages using mobile apps. The first step would be to look at how other libraries and commercial sites have reorganized their content for the ultra-small screen. Then decide if your content is compatible with the size limitations, and finally make sure that you use the usability testing concepts and tools to assure yourself that *your patrons* want to do what you are providing for them to do on their mobile device.

The Ubiquitous QR Code

Imagine if there was a way to get your customer/patron directly to your website in seconds without their having to type in a dozen or more letters of a website address. If they have a smartphone and other mobile device with a built-in cameras (e.g., a tablet or iPod)—that is exactly what is possible using a Quick Response or QR code.

Patented and trademarked by Toyota's Denso Wave subsidiary to keep track of vehicles during manufacture, QR codes are basically two-dimensional bar codes whose technical specifications are described in the ISO-18004 standard. QR codes can contain text information but are typically used to direct the user to a URL. The largest standard QR code is a Version 40 symbol that is 177 × 177 modules in size and holds up 4,296 characters of alphanumeric data compared to 25 characters for a Version 1 QR Code. Although they can be as large as 3,000 × 3,000 pixels, they are typically 100 × 100 pixel smart device readable graphics that have content and even error-correction control built into the graphic as can be seen in Figure 13-17, the main figure on the concept of QR codes from the U.S. patent cited earlier, US Patent #5726435 "Optically readable two-dimensional code and method and apparatus using the same/"

The patent claims note that the QR code is

> A two-dimensional code **1** consists of three positioning symbols **2,** a data region **3,** timing cells **4** and an apex detecting cell **5**. The shape of the whole code **1** is a square having the same number of vertical and lateral cells. A scanning

> line passing through the center of each positioning symbols **2** always gives a constant frequency component ratio-dark:light:dark:light:dark = 1:1:3:1:1, irrespective of the scanning direction. For this reason, even if a rotational angle of the two-dimensional code is not certain, the specific frequency component ratio of each positioning symbol **2** can be easily detected by executing only one scanning operation in a predetermined direction. Hence, the coordinates of the center of each positioning symbols **2** can be easily found. Thus, the position of the two-dimensional code **1** is quickly identified.

More complete information on the history, creation, and use of QR codes is available on the Denso Wave Incorporated at:

http://www.qrcode.com or **http://www.denso-wave.com/en/**

QR codes have two basic types, static and dynamic. Static QR codes have a URL which is embedded into the code that cannot be changed. Dynamic QR codes point to a "permalink" or redirect space on a vendor's website that allows you to change the target URL without changing the code itself. But QR codes are not just for URLs. They can contain calls to App stores for downloading apps, or even accomplish Wi-Fi ser-

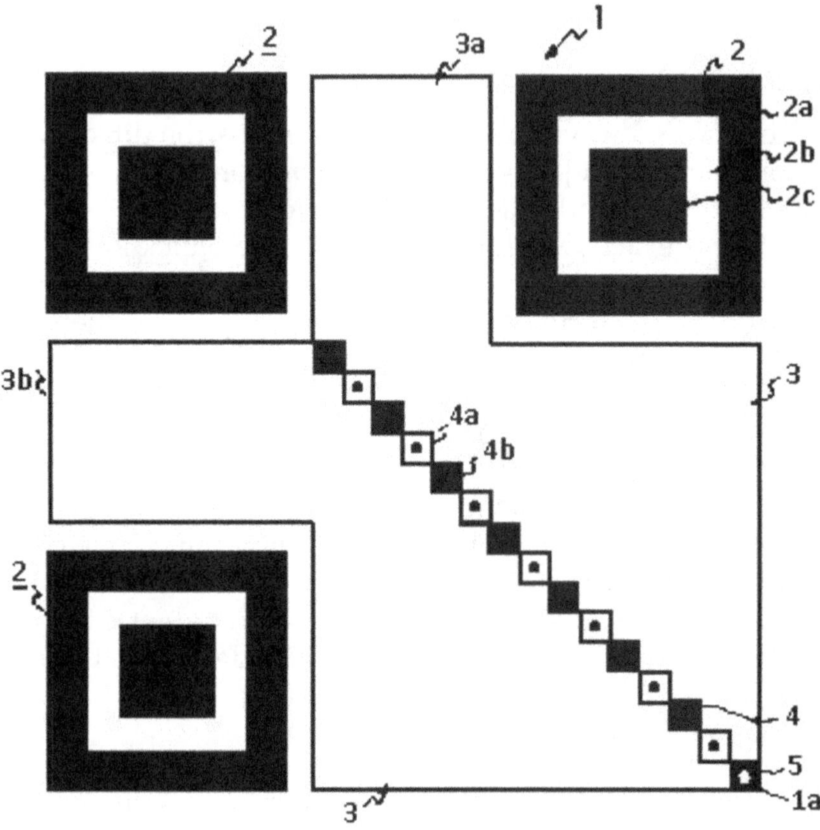

Figure 13-17. Anatomy of a QR Code (from **U.S. Patent # 5726435**)

vice logins. Most airlines now permit you to check-in to your flight by having a QR code scanned at the gate. Even SMS-encoded messages can be contained in QR codes (160 character limit on these) that contain the message and a mobile phone number. You can even put customized QR codes for each patron's library card that includes about 250 characters of pertinent information about them. In general, once the code is created, the graphic is placed on printed materials, posters, or even business cards.

Although QR code generating software is available for downloading and creating QR codes locally on Windows-based systems at the Denso Wave websites, the codes can be easily generated using one of the many free online services such as:

QR Stuff

http://www.qrstuff.com

Go QR

http://goqr.me

Google Chart Tools for QR Codes

http://createqrcode.appspot.com/

KAYWA

http://qrcode.kaywa.com

To read the codes you will need a mobile or smart device that has a camera and one of the many free QR code scanning software applications downloaded to it from your device's app store.

Scan on the QR code that follows as Figure 13-18 to go directly to the Red Rose Library website.

In simple readers, the information from the scan, presuming it is a URL, will cause the smart device to go to that URL. Some more advanced apps also permit you to collect information from the QR code that could be used in making future circulation services possible.

Figure 13-18. 150 × 150 pixel QR Code for the Red Rose Library Website **(http://www.redroselibrary.com)**

Up and Coming Buzz Words to Consider

We are almost at the end, but before you finish I wanted to review a few of the up and coming topics and buzz words you may be hearing about. Back in Chapter 11 we discussed CSS techniques that you can use to match your web page design to the output it is displayed upon. Responsive web design instills a sense of matching mobile devices to page design. Often this is as easy as replacing discrete pixel heights and widths with screen percentages, e.g., 20% rather than 200 pixels. This adds scalability to your web page but scalability is only one way to address the challenges of responsive web design for varying screen resolutions and aspect ratios.

Although already mentioned few times here as being beyond the scope of this text, JavaScript is at the heart of most interactive designs. JavaScript and JQuery which is JavaScript for forms and database designs, PHP and MySQL, a commonly available programming language and simple structured query language database tool, are among the tools computer programmers and IT professionals use to yield increasingly interactive web pages that folks want to return to. The term PHP currently stands for "PHP: Hypertext Preprocessor," which is a server-side scripting language that is a powerful tool for making dynamic and interactive Web pages. This set of tools permits building database-driven full-featured websites. Many of the content management systems discussed earlier in this chapter are created with these powerful programming tools.

We Covered a Lot of Things, but Not Everything

Many other techniques can be used to dress up your web page. Pop-up windows can be created for emergency announcements. Again, like transitions, they can be abused, and you can embed music and videos and special programming scripts in your web page.

All of these are well beyond what you need to set up a good library web page. The challenge is usually to keep the page up to date with current information. Remember, the key to information is content. The most beautiful page doesn't help your library if the content on it is a year old! You need to begin a process of having someone on the staff or a volunteer, possibly the newsletter editor, review materials as they become available and have these materials forwarded to you for posting. You have enough work without having to do the web page editing, too!

One thing you need to know is that you need to find personal gratification in seeing your web page go live after all your hard work and testing. True enough, the time you put into the design of your website will increase your patrons efficiency to use it. Not many will appreciate the effort. Don't despair. After all, you designed the published web page. Perhaps you've tested its usability, and now, you've finished the book!

Congratulations!

URLs Cited

Step Two designs

http://www.steptwo.com.au/products/designing-intranets/sample-pages
http://www.steptwo.com.au/products/roadmap

Checkout future WordPress website ideas

http://wordpress.org/showcase

Create a FREE WordPress Blog

http://www.wordpress.com/setup

The Drupal Content Management Site

http://drupal.org

The Omeka

http://omeka.org

The Joomla!

http://www.joomla.org

The GetSimple

http://get-simple.info

The ComicCMS

http://comiccms.com

The MediaWiki

http://www.mediawiki

The Moodle

http://moodle.org

The WordPress.com and WordPress.org

http://central.wordcamp.org
http://wordpress.org/download/
http://codex.wordpress.org/Installing_WordPress

Web references and resources
All web standards

www.w3.org

Sophisticated web development

Interwoven: www.interwoven.com
BroadVision: www.broadvision.com

Content characterization

Lucidmedia: www.lucidmedia.com
Autonomy: www.autonomy.com
Multicosm: www.multicosm.com

Web-based collaborative authoring

WebDev: www.webdev.org

CMS Library URLs (from Eden text, see below)

www.carolinelibrary.org
library.rpi.edu
www.lib.umn.edu

Facebook

https://www.facebook.com

Twitter

https://twitter.com

Twitter Statistics

https://about.twitter.com/company

By The Numbers: Amazing Twitter stats

http://expandedramblings.com/index.php/march-2013-by-the-numbers-a-few-amazing-twitter-stats/#.U5SzrXaiXcgFlickr
http://www.flickr.com

YouTube

http://www.youtube.com

Delicious (del.icio.us)

https://delicious.com

LinkedIn

http://www.linkedin.com

Dropbox

https://www.dropbox.com

Web Page Usability
Steve Krug's Website

http://www.sensible.com

Usability Testing

http://www.measuringusability.com/blog/method-comparison.php

User Zoom

http://www.userzoom.com

Loop

http://www.loop11.com

Webnographer

http://www.webnographer.com

Usability Best Practices

http://abovethefolddesign.com
http://www.userexperiencedesigns.com/assetts/pdf/50-UX-Best-Practices.pdf

QR code history, creation, and use

http://www.qrcode.com or **http://www.denso-wave.com/en/**

Free online QR code services
QR Stuff

http://www.qrstuff.com

Go QR

http://goqr.me

Google Chart Tools for QR Codes

http://createqrcode.appspot.com/

KAYWA

http://qrcode.kaywa.com

Web 2.0 article on WebAppRater

http://www.webapprater.com/general/7-key-features-of-web-2-0.html

Textbooks

CMS in Libraries

Eden, Bradford L., Ed. 2008. *Content Management Systems in Libraries: Case Studies.* Scarecrow Press. Washington, D.C. ISBN: 978–0-8108–5692–9.

Usability

Krug, Steve. 2005. *Don't Make Me Think! A Common Sense Approach to Web Usability.* New Riders. San Francisco, CA. ISBN: 0–321–34475–8.
Krug, Steve. 2010. *Rocket Surgery Made Easy: The Do-It-Yourself Guide to Finding and Fixing Usability Problems.* New Riders. San Francisco, CA. ISBN: 978–0-321–65729–9.

PHP

Shafik, Davey, Lorna Mitchell, and Matthew Turland. 2011. *PHP Master: Write Cutting Edge Code.* SitePoint.com. Collingwood, Australia ISBN: 978–0-9870908–7-4.
Any one of the dozens of HTML, CSS, XML, web design, and coding texts by a variety of publishers, for example:

SitePoint Pty. (www.sitepoint.com),
O'Reilly & Assoc. (www.oreilly.com),
Packt Publishing (www.packtpub.com)

Chapter 13 Review Exercises

Chapter 13 Multiple-Choice Questions

1. The extension for comma separated value database files is:

   a) **.csv** b) **.xls** c) **.com** d) **.cms**

2. A ___ database is used to store data in a CMS.

   a) definition b) relational c) flat file d) CSV

3. The metadata of a database contains the content of individual:

   a) tables b) pages c) fields d) DC values

4. The default field set in CONTENTdm is based on the:

   a) CSV b) VRA c) LOC d) Dublin Core

5. The DreamHost shared server uses quick install techniques and is linked to the following database:

   a) Access b) AnySQL c) DreamBase d) MySQL

Chapter 13 Design and Discussion Questions

1. What would determine why you would select a WordPress site on WordPress.com versus WordPress.org?
2. When should you consider using a customized rather than a standard WordPress template?
3. Review the DreamHost CMS options in this chapter and discuss how they can be used in libraries and information centers.
4. Briefly describe how you interpret what "Web 2.0" is.
5. Briefly discuss the need for usability testing and how that can be accomplished on site or remotely.

Appendix A
HTML Element Syntax

All HTML pages should begin with a DOCTYPE command immediately followed by the **html** element. This informs the browser that the contents in the file are tagged with HTML elements. As with most HTML elements, the html element requires a closing tag at the end of the document creating a "container" that includes all the markup elements of your document.

As we saw in Chapter 1, opening tags contain the name of the element and may also include one or more optional "attributes" that can further stylize the way your element's marked-up content is displayed. The element's closing tags only contain a slash that precedes the element name.

The Standard HTML Element Tag Set Syntax is:

<element attribute1="value" attribute2="value"> content to be styled
</element>
In the syntax statements below we will represent this as:
<element> . . . </element>

The approximately 90 standard HTML elements can be broken into several groupings. *Please note that we have not included ANY of the HTML Frameset elements here. Should you have interest in HTML frames, please visit the W3C website at:* www.w3.org.

DOCTYPE in HTML Document Files

Although optional, the DOCTYPE command is the recommended first line of code in any HTML document. For HTML files the **DOCTYPE** command is <**!DOCTYPE html**> a document's declaration that it is an HTML (etc.) document.

This appendix is subdivided into two parts. Part 1 is titled **HTML Document Structure, Paragraphs, and Headings**. It illustrates the elements that can be used to create a layout of the structure of HTML documents. A listing of the new HTML5 elements is also provided. Part 2 is a **Chart of HTML Elements and Syntax with Selected Examples** which the user may find helpful in deciding which elements to use and how to use them.

In these appendices, ellipses (. . .) are used to denote content surrounded by an HTML element container. Where practical, or important, we have included deprecated elements or attributes in this chart denoted by the **(D*)** mark. A deprecated element or attribute is one that is being phased out and therefore will, eventually, not be supported by common browsers. That said, note that some very commonly used elements (e.g., b, i, center, and even tables) are among those listed as being deprecated. The reason for this is the shift to using cascading style sheets to stylize the content on web pages.

Comments in HTML Document Files

Whenever we want to provide design notes or comments, we use the following set of opening and closing tags:

<!-- . . . -->

These are not listed as one of our HTML elements, but it is important to note that when updating existing documents, we can "remove" older marked-up content by placing it inside of the comment "tags" as the browser ignores anything in the comment container.

Part 1: HTML Document Structure, Paragraphs, and Headings

The elements in this grouping are used to provide a structure to the HTML document. All elements except for the DOCTYPE command are contained inside of the HTML root element container. Several of the elements are contained inside of the **head** of an HTML document. The rest reside within the **body** container.

The list that follows is not expected to be complete, but includes most HTML 4.01 elements.

Note that we are using XHTML style for singleton or empty tags, HTML5 is reverting to not requiring self-termination (e.g., **
** rather than **
). Note, too, that many of these element names, although still "decoded" by most browsers, are deprecated (shown by "(D*)**" notation) and should be avoided where possible in creating new web pages. Additional information on HTML, XHTML, XML and HTML5 can be found on the website of the World Wide Web Consortium (W3C), an international community that develops open standards to ensure the long-term growth of the Web. The dozens of web standards include HTML, XHTML, XML, and others, see:

www.w3.org/TR/tr-technology-stds

HTML Elements

<html> Document root element is HTML
<!-- . . . --> used for comments
<head> Document head opening tag
  <base . . . /> Base URL (empty element)
  <basefont . . . /> Base font styles **(D*)** (empty element)
  <isindex . . . /> Searchable document (empty element)
  <link . . . /> Relationship(s) to other document(s) (empty element)
  <meta . . . /> Adds document meta-information (empty element)
  <script> . . . </script> Defines JavaScript or other programming language scripts
  <style> . . . </style> Defines cascading style sheet "internal" commands
  <title> . . . </title> Adds a document title to the browser display
</head> Document head closing tag
<body> Document body opening tag
  All other HTML Document content is placed here
</body> Document body closing tag
</html> Ending root element tag for HTML document

HTML Elements that can be contained within the **body** Element

Layout Elements

<h#> . . . </h#> Heading style (level # ; #=1–6)
<pre> . . . </pre> Identifies preformatted text
<p> . . . </p> Paragraph container
<div> . . . </div> Division container
<span> . . . </span> Span container (inline)
<center> . . . </center> Center text **(D*)**
<address> . . . </address> Address information
<blockquote> . . . </blockquote> Block text quotation
<br . . . /> Forced line break (empty element)
<hr . . . /> Horizontal rule (empty element)

Graphics Elements

<img . . . /> Inline image (empty element)

Hyperlink Elements

<a> . . . </a> Hypertext anchor

Form Elements

<form> . . . </form> Fill-in form
- **<input . . . />** General input element (empty element)
- **<button> . . . </button>** Creates a clickable push button
- **<select> . . . </select>** Selectable list of items
- **<option> . . . </option>** Item in list
- **<textarea> . . . </textarea>** Text input area

List Elements

<dl> . . . </dl> Description or directory list (for glossaries, etc.)
<dt> . . . </dt> Description term
<dd> . . . </dd> Description descriptor
<ol> . . . </ol> Defines an ordered or numbered list
<ul> . . . </ul> Defines an unordered or bulleted list
<dir> . . . </dir> Defines a directory list (**(D*)** see **ul**)
<menu> . . . </menu> Defines a list/menu of commands
<dfn> . . . </dfn> Defines a definition term
<li> . . . </li> Defines a list item for **ol** and **ul** lists

Table Elements

<table> . . . </table> Table **(D*)**

<caption> . . . </caption> Defines a table caption
<col . . . /> Creates a group of table column properties (empty element)
<colgroup> . . . </colgroup> Creates a specific column group of **table** columns
<tbody> . . . </tbody> Table body
<td> . . . </td> Table data
<tfooter> . . . </tfooter>Table footer
<thead> . . . </thead> Table header
<th> . . . </th> Table header cell
<tr> . . . </tr> Table row

TEXT CONTROLS: Physical Phrase Markup

Physical Phrase markup elements can contain text, character-level elements, other phrase markup elements, and hypertext anchors.

<b> . . . </b> Bold text (**(D*)** see Strong)
<big> . . . </big> Increases text by one size greater than the default **(D*)**
<del> . . . </del> Indicates deleted text with "strikethrough"
<i> . . . </i> Italic text (**(D*)** see Emphasis)
<ins> . . . </ins> Indicate inserted text with underlining
<nobr> . . . </nobr> Text displayed without break
<small> . . . </small> Decreases text by one size less than the default **(D*)**
_{. . .} Text displayed as subscript
^{. . .} Text displayed as superscript
<tt> . . . </tt> Teletype, fixed width, text (**(D*)** use CSS)
<u> . . . </u> Underlined text

TEXT CONTROLS: Logical Phrase Markup

Logical Phrase markup elements can contain text, character-level elements, other phrase markup elements, and hypertext anchors

<cite> . . . </cite> Citation text
<code> . . . </code> Typed code
<em> . . . </em> Emphasized text (italicized)
<kbd> . . . </kbd> Keyboard input
<samp> . . . </samp> Sample text
<strong> . . . </strong> Strongly emphasized
<var> . . . </var> Text style for a variable

Other HTML Elements

<abbr> . . . </abbr> Identifies abbreviated text
<acronym> . . . </acronym> Identifies acronyms (**(D*)** use **abbr**)
<area> . . . </area> Defines hot spot areas inside an image-map (see **map**)
<bdo> . . . </bdo> Overrides the current text direction
<del> . . . </del> Deleted text (**(D*)** use **del**)
<font> . . . </font> Identifies font size, color, family, and others (**(D*)** use CSS)
<map> . . . </map> Identifies client-side image-maps
<strike> . . . </strike> Identifies deleted text (**(D*)** use **del**)
<q> . . . </q> Quoted text

New HTML5 Elements

As HMTL browsers are updated to the new HTML5—a combination of the best of HTML, XML and CSS, several of the common HTML (from: **www.w3schools.com/tags***) elements and additional standard elements will be defined and older ones deprecated.*

<article> . . . </article> Defines an article
<aside> . . . </aside> Defines content aside from the page content
<audio> . . . </audio> Defines sound content
<bdi> . . . </bdi> Isolates text to be formatted in a different direction from other text
<canvas> . . . </canvas> Draws graphics, on the fly, via scripting (usually JavaScript)
<command> . . . </command> Defines a command button
<datalist> . . . </datalist> Specifies predefined list of options for drop-down list
<details> . . . </details> Defines details of an element user can view or hide
<dialog> . . . </dialog> Defines dialog box or window
<embed> . . . </embed> Defines a container for an external (non-HTML) application
<figcaption> . . . </figcaption> Defines a caption for a **<figure>** element
<figure . . . /> Specifies self-contained content
<footer> . . . </footer> Defines a footer for a document or section
<header> . . . </header> Defines a header for a document or section
<keygen> . . . </keygen> Defines a key-pair generator field (for forms)
<mark> . . . </mark> Defines marked/highlighted text
<meter> . . . </meter> Defines a scalar measurement within a known range (a gauge)
<nav> . . . </nav> Defines navigation links
<output> . . . </output> Defines the result of a calculation
<progress> . . . </progress> Represents the progress of a task
<section> . . . </section> Defines a section in a document
<source> . . . </source> Defines multi-media resources for elements **video** and **audio**
<summary> . . . </summary> Defines a visible heading for a <details> element
<time> . . . </time> Defines a date/time
<track> . . . </track> Defines text tracks for media elements **video** and **audio**
<video> . . . <video> . . . </video> Defines a video or movie
<wbr . . . /> Defines a possible line-break

Part 2: Chart of HTML Elements and Syntax with Selected Examples

General Structure of HTML Elements

Element Function	Syntax	Description
Typical Element	**<tag> . . . </tag>**	Elements define HTML tags
Empty Element	**<tag . . . />**	Singleton/self-closing HTML element tags

Overall Elements for HTML Document Definition and Structure

Element Function	Syntax	Description
Document Type	**<!DOCTYPE html>**	Document's declaration of what it is (optional)
HTML	**<html> . . . </html>**	Identifies the document root element as HTML
Language Attribute	**lang="name"**	Identifies the language in HTML tag
Bidirectional Algorithm	**<bdo> . . . </bdo>**	Overrides the language character directionality
Head	**<head> . . . </head>**	Creates a head container
Body	**<body> . . . </body>**	Creates the body container
Comments	**<!-- . . . -->**	Creates comment areas with the document
Content	. . .	Indicates content within the document tag

Elements within the HEAD Container of an HTML Document

Element Function	Syntax	Description
Add browser page title	**<title> . . . </title>**	Document title
Add page-specific CSS	**<style> . . . </style>**	Cascading style sheet "internal" commands
Metadata	**<meta . . . />**	Adds document meta-information
Provide base URL	**<base . . . />**	Identifies a base URL by **href** and **target**
Enable Search	**<isindex . . . />**	Allows for document searches
Link to other items	**<link . . . />**	Links to other document(s), e.g., CSS files
Add programming	**<script> . . . </script>**	JavaScript/other programming scripts

(*Continued*)

Elements Within the HEAD Container of an HTML Document (*Continued*)

Element Function	Syntax	Description
Alternate Script	**<noscript> . . . </noscript>**	Alternate content for browsers not supporting client-side scripts
Object	**<object> . . . </object>**	Identifies a generic embedded object
Parameter	**<param . . . />**	Set of values required by an object at run-time
Default Font Size	**<basefont size="x" />**	Identifies a base font color; name, size (1 to 7)

Layout Elements within the Body Container of an HTML Document

Element Function	Syntax	Description
Heading—Level 1	**<hl> . . . </h1>**	Identifies first-level heading
Heading—Level 2	**<h2> . . . </h2>**	Identifies second-level heading
Heading—Level 3	**<h3> . . . </h3>**	Identifies third-level heading
Heading—Level 4	**<h4> . . . </h4>**	Identifies fourth-level heading
Heading—Level 5	**<h5> . . . </h5>**	Identifies fifth-level heading
Heading—Level 6	**<h6> . . . </h6>**	Identifies sixth-level heading
Use preformatted text	**<pre> . . . </pre>**	Identifies preformatted text (default width=80)
Paragraphs	**<p> . . . </p>**	Paragraph container; surrounded by blank line
Content Division	**<div> . . . </div>**	Division container; surrounded by blank line
Text Spans	**<span> . . . </span>**	Span container; inline text changes

Element Function	Syntax	Description
Font	**<font> . . . </font>**	Modifies font appearance. **(D*)** **size**, **color**, **family** are common attributes
Center Content	**<center> . . . </center>**	Center enclosed text **(D*)**
Address Information	**<address> . . . </address>**	Add address to footer area
Block Quote	**<blockquote> . . . </blockquote>**	Block text quotation
Line Break	** **	Forces clear line break (empty tag)
Line Separation	**<hr />**	Horizontal rule (empty element)
Fieldset	**<fieldset> . . . </fieldset>**	Groups together related controls
Label	**<label>**	New HTML 5 Element
Legend	**<legend>**	New HTML 5 Element
Spacer	**<spacer />**	New HTML 5 Element

(*Continued*)

Graphics and Images within the Body Area of an HTML Document

Element Function	Syntax	Description
Embed an image	**<img src="graphic" alt="text"/>**	Embeds an inline image on web page, when mouse is over image "text" appears
Align an image	**<img align="?" src="graphic" />**	Embeds an image on web page aligned. "?" equals: top, middle, or bottom Other attributes: border="x," width="x," height="x",
Map an image	**<img src="graphic" ISMAP />**	Embeds an image on web page which is coupled to a map
Map	**<map> . . . </map>**	Identifies a client-side image map
Area	**<area> . . . </area>**	Defines hot spots (client-side image, see maps)

Anchors and Hyperlinks within the Body Area of an HTML Document

Element Function	Syntax	Description
Link to an Anchor	**<a name="anchor name"> . . . </a>**	Creates hyperlink to anchor on a web page
Internal text link to document, same window	**<a href="filename"> clickable text </a>**	Creates text hyperlink to a document named "filename" in current web server directory
Internal text link to document, in a new browser window	**<a href="filename" target="_blank"> clickable text </a>**	Creates text hyperlink to a document named "filename" in current web server directory, in a new browser window
External text link to document, same window	**<a href="URL/filename"> clickable text </a>**	Creates text hyperlink to a document named "filename" in current web server directory (URL= http://www.server.com)
Internal image hypergraphic Link	**<a href="filename"> <img src="graphic" /> </a>**	Creates graphic hyperlink to a document named "filename" current website (See **img** element)
External image hypergraphic Link	**<a href="URL/file"> <img src="graphic" /> </a>**	Creates graphic hyperlink to a document named "filename" at URL website (See **img** element)
Email link	**<a href="mailto:me@me.com"> . . . </a>**	Opens an email application on client side

(*Continued*)

Form Elements within the Body Area of an HTML Document

Element Function	Syntax	Description
Form Structure	**<form action="mailto: me@myaddress.com" method="post"> . . . </form>**	Opens typical fill-in form container. Attributes are **action, method,** etc., Container can include **input, select, textarea, p, hr, dir, dl, menu, ol, ul,** and **address** elements
Input	**<input />**	General input element. Attributes: **src, type, name, size, maxlength, value, align, checked**
Select from list	**<select> . . . </select>**	Selectable list of items. Attributes: **multiple, size, name.**
Selection List name	**<select name="name"> </select>**	Creates and names a drop-down list of options for selection
Selection List option	**<option** [selected]**> . . . </option>**	Creates options for selection Attributes: **value, selected**
Create a text input	**<textarea> . . . </textarea>**	Text input area
Opt Group	**<optgroup> . . . </optgroup>**	Creates a logical group of options in a form
Text Area	**<textarea name="response" rows="5" cols="25"> </textarea>**	Create a Text Input area. Attributes: **rows, cols, name**
Button, Image	**<input type="image" src="graphic" name="name" value="value" />**	Creates push button on a form
Button, Password field	**<input type="password" size="15" />**	Creates a password field button
Button, Radio	**<input type="radio" name="name" value="value" checked />**	Creates radio button on a form. Adding "checked" displays that button as checked
Button, Reset	**<input type="reset" value="clear" />**	Creates reset button that resets all form changes to initial defaults
Button, Submit	**<input type="submit" value="submit" />**	Submits all form values
Check Box	**<input type="checkbox" name="name" value="value"** [checked] **/>**	Creates checkbox on a form. Adding "checked" displays that box checked on the form
Scrolling List—pull-down menu	**select name="pulldown" size="3"> <option value="firstitem"> First Item</option> <option value="seconditem" selected> Second Item </option> <option value="thirditem"> Third Item</option> <option value="fourth"> fourth Item</option> </select>**	Creates text input area

(Continued)

Table Elements within the Body Area of an HTML Document

Element Function	Syntax	Description
Create a Table	**<table> . . . </table>**	Table container **(D*)**
Caption	**<caption> . . . </caption>**	Adds a table caption
Body of Table	**<tbody> . . . </tbody>**	Table body
Header of Table	**<thead> . . . </thead>**	Table header
Footer of Table	**<tfooter> . . . </tfooter>**	Table footer
"Cell" of Header	**<th> . . . </th>**	Table header cell
Table Rows	**<tr> . . . </tr>**	Table row (encloses **td**)
"Cell" Contents	**<td> . . . </td>**	Table data or descriptor
Columns	**<col />**	Creates a group of table column attributes
Column Groupings	**<colgroup> . . . </colgroup>**	Creates a specific column group

List Elements within the Body Area of an HTML Document

Element Function	Syntax	Description
Definitions	**<dd> . . . </dd>**	Glossary or definition list definition
Definition List	**<dl> . . . </dl>**	Glossary list
Definition Terms	**<dt> . . . </dt>**	Glossary list terms
Numbered List	**<ol type="?"> . . . </ol>**	Ordered list (uses **li**), default is type="1" capital Roman numerals ("i"= lowercase Roman numerals, "A"= capitals, "a"= lower case)
Bulleted List	**<ul type="?"> . . . </ul>**	Unordered list (uses **li**), default is type="disc" : "square" = solid square, "circle" = open circle
List Item	**<li> . . . </li>**	List item (used with **ol** and **ul**)
Directory	**<dir> . . . </dir>**	Directory list
Menu	**<menu> . . . </menu>**	Menu list

Text Controls: Physical Phrase Markup within an HTML Document

Physical Phrase markup elements can contain text, character-level elements, other phrase markup elements, and hypertext anchors.

Element Function	Syntax	Description
Bold Text	**<b> . . . </b>**	Boldface text (**(D*)** use Strong)
Increase Text Size	**<big> . . . </big>**	Increases text by one size greater than the default
Blink Text	**<blink> . . . </blink>**	Blinking text
Deleted Text	**<del> . . . </del>**	Indicates deleted text with strikethrough

(*Continued*)

Text Controls: Physical Phrase Markup within an HTML Document (*Continued*)

Element Function	Syntax	Description
Italics	**<i> . . . </i>**	Italicizes text (**(D*)** use Emphasis)
Inserted Text	**<ins> . . . </ins>**	Indicates inserted text with underlining
No Line Breaks	**<nobr> . . . </nobr>**	Text displayed without break
Decrease Text Size	**<small> . . . </small>**	Decreases text by one size less than the default
Subscripts	**_{. . .}**	Text displayed as subscript
Superscripts	**^{. . .}**	Text displayed as superscript
Teletype Text	**<tt> . . . </tt>**	Teletype, fixed width, monospaced text
Underline Text	**<u> . . . </u>**	Underlined text
Preformatted Text	**<pre> . . . </pre>**	Overrides HTML's text formatting
Quoted Text	**<q> . . . </q>**	Identifies a short inline quotation

Text Controls: Logical Phrase Markup within an HTML Document

Logical Phrase markup elements can contain text, character-level elements, other phrase markup elements, and hypertext anchors.

Element Function	Syntax	Description
Cite Text Style	**<cite> . . . </cite>**	Indicates a citation or source reference
Code Text Style	**<code> . . . </code>**	Indicates a computer code fragment
Emphasis/Italicized Text	**<em> . . . </em>**	Indicates emphasis usually displays in italics
Keyboard Style	**<kbd> . . . </kbd>**	Keyboard input
Sample Text Style	**<samp> . . . </samp>**	Sample text
Strong/Bold, Text	**<strong> . . . </strong>**	Strongly emphasized
Variable Text Style	**<var> . . . </var>**	Text style for a variable

Other HTML Elements within an HTML Document

Element Function	Syntax	Description
Abbreviations	**<abbr> . . . </abbr>**	Identifies abbreviated text
Acronym	**<acronym> . . . </acronym>**	Identifies acronyms
Definition	**<dfn> . . . </dfn>**	Definition of a term

Common CSS Style Attributes for Most HTML Body Elements

Element Function	Syntax	Description
ID	**id="name"**	CSS Document-wide identifier
Class	**class="name"**	CSS classes

Appendix B

HTML Entity Relationship Characters

HTML Entity Relationships—The ISO 8859 Latin 1 Character Set

We have all seen them in text and on the web, but how can you include special characters on your web pages? The characters are defined in the **ISO 8859 Latin 1 Character Set**—an 8-bit ASCII-based standard for character encoding. You probably know that in a word-processing program, to input the copyright symbol, you can do a shortcut by typing: **(**"then the "**c**" and then the"**)** and your word processor probably converts that automatically to the ©. A more consistent way to invoke this character is to place your cursor where you want the symbol to be inserted, hold down the **Alt** key, using the numeric key pad, type the symbols numeric code from the tables here: **0169,** and then release the **Alt** key.

Character entities in an HTML or XML document are definable (see Chapter 12), case-sensitive combinations of letters and/or numbers that represent a specific character, letter, or symbol. The Character Entity Syntax is relatively straight forward:

- They are case-sensitive.
- They must begin with an ampersand (&).
- Numeric entitles must have a hash mark or pound sign (#) before the entity number.
- They must end with a semicolon (;).

Every character in the **ISO 8859 Latin 1 Character Set** has a numeric reference like **®** but not all characters have equivalent semantic character reference like ®—either of these two entities directs the web page to insert the registered trademark symbol ® at that spot. The numeric or semantic values can be used interchangeably, and even mixed in the same web document. The five *reserved* characters in the following table must be inserted using a numeric or semantic character entities as they are used to create HTML and XML tagging commands:

Symbol	Semantic	Numeric	Name
"	"	"	Straight quote
'	'	'	Straight apos-trophe
&	&	&	Ampersand symbol
<	<	<	Less than symbol
>	>	>	Greater than symbol

All characters have a code associated with as may be seen on the following tables broken into:

1. Letters and numbers
2. Miscellaneous
3. Punctuation, symbols, and special characters
4. Math symbols
5. Currency
6. Language symbols: letters with *accent grave; accent acute; accent tilde; accent circumflex; accent umlaut and* letters with other language symbols

There are many additional characters in the **ISO 8859 Latin 1 Character Set** as can be seen on the W3C web pages beginning at:

http://www.w3schools.com/tags/ref_charactersets.asp

1. Letters and Numbers

Capital Letter	Code	Lowercase Letter	Code	Number	Code
A	A	a	a	0	0
B	B	b	b	1	'
C	C	c	c	2	2
D	D	d	d	3	3
E	E	e	e	4	4
F	F	f	f	5	5
G	G	g	g	6	6
H	H	h	h	7	7
I	I	i	i	8	8

(Continued)

(*Continued*)

Capital Letter	Code	Lowercase Letter	Code	Number	Code
J	J	j	j	9	9
K	K	k	k		
L	L	l	l		
M	M	m	m		
N	N	n	n		
O	O	o	o		
P	P	p	p		
Q	Q	q	q		
R	R	r	r		
S	S	s	s		
T	T	t	t		
U	U	u	u		
V	V	v	v		
W	W	w	w		
X	X	x	x		
Y	Y	y	y		
Z	Z	z	z		

2. Miscellaneous

Symbol	Semantic	Numeric	Name
			Soft hyphen
¶	¶	¶	Paragraph sign
¸	¸	¸	Cedilla
»	»	»	Right angle quote
←	←	←	Left arrow
↑	↑	↑	Up arrow
→	→	→	Right arrow
↓	↓	↓	Down arrow
↔	↔	↔	Horizontal arrow
♠	♠	♠	Spade suit
♣	♣	♣	Club suit
♥	♥	♥	Heart suit
♦	♦	♦	Diamond suit

3. Punctuation, Symbols, and Special Characters

Symbol	Semantic	Numeric	Name
©	©	©	Copyright symbol
®	®	®	Registered trademark symbol
			Blank space character (non-breaking space)
			Normal space
!		!	Exclamation point
(		(	Parenthesis (left)
)		):	Parenthesis (right)
*		*	Asterisk
,		,	Comma
.		.:	Period
/		/	Slash
:		:	Colon
;		;	Semicolon
?		?	Question mark
@		@	Commercial "at" sign
]		[	Square bracket (right)
\		\	Backslash
[		]	Square bracket (left)
^		^	Caret
_		_	Underscore
{		{	Curly brace (left)
|				Vertical bar
}		}	Curly brace (right)
¦	¦	¦	Broken vertical bar
§	§	§	Section sign
«	«	«	Left angle quote
•	•	•	Bullet
§	§	§	Section symbol
†	†	†	Dagger
‡	‡	‡	Double dagger
–	–	–	en-dash
—	—	—	em-dash
¶	¶	¶	Paragraph symbol
¡	¡	¡	Inverted exclamation mark
¿	¿	¿	Inverted question mark

4. Math Symbols (see also: http://www.w3schools.com/tags/ref_symbols.asp)

Symbol	Semantic	Numeric	Name
#		#	Hash mark or number symbol
%		%:	Percent sign
×	×	×	Multiplication sign
÷	÷	÷	Division sign
+	+	+	Plus sign
–	−	-	Hyphen/minus sign
±	±	±	Plus/minus sign
≡	≡	≡	Equivalent to symbol
≈	≈	≈	Approximately equal to symbol
≠	≠	≠	Not equal to sign
<	<	<	Less than (angle bracket) symbol
>	>	>	Greater than (angle bracket) symbol
≤	≤	≤	Less than or equal to symbol
≥	≥	≥	Greater than or equal to symbol
∴	∴	∴	Therefore
¬	¬	¬	Logical Not symbol
…	&helip;	…	Ellipsis (horizontal)
µ	µ	μ	Micro symbol
π	π	π	Pi symbol
Ω	Ω	Ω	Omega symbol
ϑ	&theta-sym;	ϑ	Theta symbol
°	°	°	Degree symbol
∏	∏	∏:	Product sign
∑	∑	∑:	Summation sign
∞	∞	∞:	Infinity sign
¼	¼	¼	Fraction 1/4
½	½	½	Fraction 1/2
¾	¾	¾	Fraction 3/4
^{1}	¹	¹	Superscript 1
^{2}	²	²	Superscript 2
^{3}	³	³	Superscript 3
º	º	º	Masculine ordinal number
ª	ª	ª	Feminine ordinal number

5. Currency

Symbol	Semantic	Numeric	Name
¢	¢	¢	Cent sign
£	£	£	British Pound sign
€	€	€	Euro sign
¥	¥	¥	Yen sign
¤	¤	¤	General currency sign

6.Language Symbols
Letters with *Accent Grave*

Symbol	Semantic	Numeric	Name
`	`	`	Grave accent
À	À	À	Capital A, accent grave
à	à	à	Lowercase a, accent grave
È	È	È	Capital E, accent grave
è	è	è	Lowercase e, accent grave
Ì	Ì	Ì	Capital I, accent grave
ì	ì	ì	Lowercase i, accent grave
Ò	Ò	Ò	Capital O, accent grave
ò	ò	ò	Lowercase o, accent grave
Ù	Ù	Ù	Capital U, accent grave
ù	ù	ù	Lowercase u, accent grave

Letters with *Accent Acute*

Symbol	Semantic	Numeric	Name
´	´	´	Acute
Á	Á	Á	Capital A, accent acute
á	á	á	Lowercase a, accent acute
É	É	É	Capital E, accent acute
é	é	é	Lowercase e, accent acute
Í	Í	Í	Capital I, accent acute
í	í	í	Lowercase i, accent acute
Ó	Ó	Ó	Capital O, accent acute
ó	ó	ó	Lowercase o, accent acute
Ú	Ú	Ú	Capital U, accent acute
ú	ú	ú	Lowercase u, accent acute
Ý	Ý	Ý	Capital Y, accent acute
ý	ý	ý	Lowercase y, accent acute

Letters with *Accent Tilde*

Symbol	Semantic	Numeric	Name
~		~	Tilde
Ã	Ã	Ã	Capital A, accent tilde
ã	ã	ã	Lowercase a, accent tilde
Ñ	Ñ	Ñ	Capital N, accent tilde
ñ	ñ	ñ	Lowercase n, accent tilde
Õ	Õ	Õ	Capital O, accent tilde
õ	õ	õ	Lowercase o, accent tilde

Letters with *Accent Circumflex*

Symbol	Semantic	Numeric	Name
Â	Â	Â	Capital A, accent circumflex
â	â	â	Lowercase a, accent circumflex
Ê	Ê	Ê	Capital E, accent circumflex
ê	ê	ê	Lowercase e, accent circumflex
Î	Î	Î	Capital I, accent circumflex
î	î	î	Lowercase i, accent circumflex
Ô	Ô	Ô	Capital O, accent circumflex
ô	ô	ô	Lowercase o, accent circumflex
Û	Û	Û	Capital U, accent circumflex
û	û	û	Lowercase u, accent circumflex

Letters with *Accent Umlaut*

Symbol	Semantic	Numeric	Name
¨	¨	¨	Umlaut
Ä	Ä	Ä	Capital A, accent umlaut
ä	ä	ä	Lowercase a, accent umlaut
Ë	Ë	Ë ;	Capital E, accent umlaut
ë	ë	ë	Lowercase e, accent umlaut
Ï	Ï	Ï	Capital I, accent umlaut
ï	ï	ï	Lowercase i, accent umlaut
Ö	Ö	Ö	Capital O, accent umlaut
ö	ö	ö	Lowercase o, accent umlaut
Ü	Ü	Ü	Capital U, accent umlaut
ü	ü	ü	Lowercase u, accent umlaut
Ÿ	Ÿ	Ÿ	Capital Y, accent umlaut
ÿ	ÿ	ÿ	Lowercase y, accent umlaut

Letters with Other Language Symbols

Ç	Ç	Ç	French C cedille
ç	ç	ç	French C cedilla
Æ	Æ	Æ	A-E ligature
æ	æ	æ	A-E ligature
Œ	Œ	Œ	O-E ligature
œ	œ	œ	O-E ligature
ß	ß	ß	German Sharp/Double S
Ø	Ø	Ø	Nordic O slash
ø	ø	ø	Nordic O slash
Å	Å	Å	Nordic A ring, Angstrom sign
å	å	å	Nordic A ring, Angstrom sign
Þ	Þ	Þ	Old English Thorn
þ	þ	þ	Old English Thorn
Ð	Ð	Ð	Old English Eth
ð	ð	ð	Old English Eth
Š	Š	Š	Czech S hachek (S Caron)
š	š	š	Czech S hachek (S Caron)
Ž	Ž	Ž	Czech S hachek (Z Caron)
ž	ž	ž	Czech S hachek (Z Caron)

Appendix C

Cascading Style Sheets: CSS Properties and Syntax

Cascading Style Sheets: CSS Properties and Syntax

Hidden "inside" all HTML browsers are the rules that specify how each element will be presented. Using style sheet *selectors* and their *declarations* one can alter the rule defaults that are included in the browser's DTD (document type declaration).

An HTML page's style rules can be changed in several ways. Located within the **head** element can be link(s) to external style sheet files using the **link** element and/or specific internal or imbedded stylization using the **style** element. Within the **body,** specific portions of the content can be additionally stylized, or have their current style overridden using inline style *attributes* in a specific element's opening tag.

Cascading style sheets (CSS) provide a robust set of tools that are used to add formatting to your content with control at the pixel level! Full information is available on the World Wide Web Consortium website at: **www.w3.org/Style/CSS.**

CSS enables increased typographic and page layout control and easier customization at the web, page, and character levels while separating the HTML content from its CSS presentation in a web document.

These style rules are intended to change the default styles of the browser. This method permits standardizing the style of a web page at the site (external), page (internal/embedded), or instant (inline) of invoking an HTML element. These layers create a cascading effect which is why the technique is dubbed Cascading style sheets or CSS. The hierarchy of the style changes is:

Browser defaults (DTD)
User "Content" Changes to *their* Browser (e.g., default language, font, color palettes)
<link> Linkages to external style sheets
@import "at-rule" links in the **style** container to "imported" external style sheets
<style> Embedded or Internal Style Sheets within the **head** of the document
<element style=" ... " > Inline style changes within the opening tag of an **element**

CSS informs the browser that the contents in an HTML element must be changed from the default. Thus, if all forms of CSS styling are used, one could have the initial default overridden at the website level, then that new default overridden at the individual document or web page level and finally, as needed within that document, for one or more of the instances of that particular HTML element:

Inline style changes: **<element style=" ... " >** ends with the **element** closing
Embedded or Internal Style: **<style>**
Imported external style sheets **@import**
External Style: File links **<link>**
User "Content" Changes to *their* Browser (e.g., default language, font, color palettes)
Browser defaults (DTD)

The effect of using CSS is to have several layers of potential style changes from the HTML browser's built-in default values stacked one on top of the other with the rule change closest to the actual content being marked up being the style used. All of these optional style sheets override the current default. Once invoked, they can NOT be removed. Inline changes are the only ones that, when the element closes, are removed and whatever is left on the stack will be the new default.

Comments in Style Sheets

To avoid confusion with the HTML comment technique, whenever we want to provide design notes or comments inside of a CSS file or in the internal CSS area at the **head** of a document, we use the following set of opening and closing tags:

/* . . . */

At-Rules ("@rule") in Style Sheets

In addition to providing link elements that can access style sheet files, the **@import** rule accesses an external CSS file from within the **style** container in the **head** of an HTML document.

CSS Syntax

The CSS style syntax begins with a "selector" whose property and value pairs create a rules "declaration" that will change the defaults of the HTML element/selectors they define. Semicolons are used to separate each property—value pair rule declaration, with the semicolon on the last property—value pair optional:

selector {property:value; property:value;}

Selectors can be elements, classes, and ids used to create limitations on what elements are included or excluded from the change in stylization.

The result of changing a particular element at the web or page level includes all of a document's elements, elements inside of specific parent elements (e.g., elements that are within the paragraph container). Selectors can be created to define the special

style attribute values of **class** and **id** and there are also several special predefined pseudo-selectors. Selectors fall into two types: **fully defined selectors** and **generic** selectors.

Fully Defined Selectors

Fully defined selectors use a specific HMTL element you wish to stylize. For example, the style on a page for all the **h1** content using a CSS rule with multiple style rules looks like:

h1 {color:red; font-size:12px;}

It will change the style rule for all **h1** elements to a default text style of 12 pixels in red. Since browsers ignore line spacing, this multiple style rule can also be seen in either an external or imbedded sheet as:

h1
{color:red; font-size:12px;}

or can have each style rule exist as a separate line of style:

h1
{
color:red;
font-size:12px;
}

or even as separate rules:

h1 { color:red; }
h1 { font-size:12px; }

It may be that your style requires several elements to have the same style, for example, all odd-numbered headings to be colored "red." That can be accomplished separating the element names by commas:

h1, h3, h5 {color:red;}

If the bold element is to be styled green, but *only* when used inside of a list item, the CSS syntax for that fully defined selector would be:

li b {color:green;}

which will render only the list item bolded content green with all other bolded content in the document displayed in the current default color (typically black for the DTD default).

Generic Selectors

Specifying the specific element that will be stylized is useful, but occasionally we might want to create a general style that could be used in several elements, but only at the content level rather than the page level. Generic selectors create either a **class** or

id "code" that is not tied to a specific HMTL element. For example defining a **class** of sematic styles "red" would look like:

red {color:red;}

Then, to use the "red" style for a particular element's content, we would include a **class** attribute in the opening tag of that element:

<element class="red"> content </element>

The same technique applies for **id**s.

Inline style statements use **style** as an attribute in an element's opening tag. Using the **element** element as an example, the coding would look like:

<element style="property:value; property:value;"> content to be styled **</element>**

Unlike external and internal style sheeting, inline stylization is only effective as long as the container styled is still open. Once closed, the element style reverts back to the previous defaults. In addition, opening up the same element without using the style attribute does not normally result in a change in style.

This appendix is subdivided into three parts; Part 1 is a chart, **CSS Selectors and At-Rules,** the user may find helpful in deciding which selectors to use and how to use them, Part 2, **CSS Properties,** illustrates the property-value pairs that can be used to create style sheet rules, and Part 3, **CSS Units,** is a chart helpful in deciding which units to use and how to use them when creating the value for a property-value pair.

As always, feel free to improve your knowledge of CSS by reviewing the wealth of materials available on the World Wide Web Consortium's pages at: **www.w3.org** in general, and the CSS pages beginning with the page at

www.w3.org /TR/tr-technology-stds#tr_CSS.

Appendix C: CSS Selectors and At-Rules

a. Selection of CSS Selectors

Selector Name	Syntax [e = elementname]	Description
Universal	*	Matches ALL element types
Type	**e**	Matches every instance of the **element (e)**
Descendant	**e1 e2**	Matches **element2** when inside **element1**
Child	**e1 > e2**	Matches **element2** when inside **element1**
Adjacent Sibling	**e1 + e2**	Matches **element2** only when after **element1**
Attribute Selector	**e [att]**	Matches when element uses att
Class	**.classname**	Defines a new **class** for attribute **classname**
	<e class="classname"> content </e>	The **classname** style is "called" for in the opening tag of the element "e"
ID Selector	**#value**	Defines an ID named **value** for element style
	<e id="value"> content </e>	The id **value** style is "called" for in the opening tag of the element "**e**" (*note "value" not used*)
Pseudo-Class First-Child	**e1 > e2:first-child**	Defines a new style for the first **element2** "child" of the element **element1**
	e1:first-child e2	Defines a new style for the first element2 for any element element1
Pseudo-Class Anchor Link	**a:link**	Defines a style for anchor links not visited
	a:visited	Defines a style for anchor links visited
Pseudo-Class Dynamic	**a:hover**	Defines a style when mouse over an area
	a:active	Defines a style between mouse press & release
Pseudo-Elements: First-Line	**e:first-line**	Defines a new style for the first line of **e**
First-Letter	**e:first-letter**	Defines a new style for the first letter of **e** (use for dropped caps)

See also: http://www.w3schools.com/cssref/css_selectors.asp

b.CSS At-Rules (@rules)

Function	Syntax	Description
Import Rule	**@import "style.css" ;**	Imports a local external CSS style sheet
	@import URL ("style.css");	Imports an external CSS style sheet with in the URL
Character Set	**@charset "ISO-8859-1"**	Identifies character set to use
Page Rule	**@page**	Defines paged media
Target Media	**@media type**	Specifies media type for style rules where **type** is: **all**, **print**, **screen**, **projection**, etc.

Appendix C: CSS Property-Value Pairs

c. CSS Properties

Type	Property	Values
TEXT PROPERTIES	**color**	[color] I inherit
	letter-spacing	left I right I center I justify
	text-align	normal I length I inherit
	text-decoration	none I underline I overline I line-through I blink I inherit
	text-indent	length I [percentage] I inherit
	text-shadow	none I [color] I length I inherit
	text-transform	capitalize I uppercase I lowercase I none I inherit
	vertical-align	baseline I sub I super I top I text-top I middle I bottom I text-bottom I [percentage] I length I inherit
	word-spacing	normal I length I [percentage] I inherit
FONT PROPERTIES	**font-family**	[font name] I [generic name] I inherit
	font-size	xx-small I x-small I small I medium I large I x-large I xx-large I [length] I [percentage] I larger I smaller I [relative measurement] I inherit
	font-size-adjust	[number] I none I inherit
	font-stretch	ultra-condensed I extra-condensed I condensed I semi-condensed I normal I expanded I extra-expanded I ultra-expanded I inherit
	font-style	normal I italic I oblique I inherit
	font-variant	normal I small caps I inherit
	font-weight	normal I bold I lighter I bolder I 100 I 200 I 300 I 400 I 500 I 600 I 700 I 800 I 900 I inherit
	line-height	normal I [number] I [length] I [percentage] I inherit
BACKGROUND PROPERTIES	**background-color**	transparent I [color value] I inherit
	background-image	none I [url] I inherit
	background-repeat	repeat I repeat-x I repeat-y I norepeat I inherit
	background-attachment	scroll I fixed I inherit
	background-position	[percentage] I [length] I top I center I bottom I left I center I right I inherit
DISPLAY PROPERTIES	**display**	block I inline I list-item I run-in I compact I marker I table I inline-table I table-row-group I table-header group I table-footer group I table-row I table-column group I table-column I table-cell I table-caption I none I inherit

(Continued)

Type	Property	Values
List Styles	**list-style-image**	url I none I inherit
	list-style-position	inside I outside I inherit
	list-style-type	disc I circle I square I decimal I lower-roman I upper-roman I lower-alpha I upper-alpha I none I inherit
	white-space	normal I pre I nowrap I inherit
BOX PROPERTIES	**clear**	none I left I right I both I inherit
	float	left I right I none I inherit
	height **width**	[length] I [percentage] I auto I inherit
Borders	**border-bottom-width**	[length] I thin I medium I thick I inherit Same for: **border-left-width; border-right-width; border-top-width**
	border-color	[color value] I [color name] I transparent I inherit
	border-style	none I hidden I dotted I dashed I solid I double I groove I ridge I inset I outset I inherit
	border-width	[length] I thin I medium I thick I inherit
Margins	**margin-[top**	[length] I [percentage] I auto I inherit Same for: **margin-right; margin-bottom; margin-left**
Padding	**padding-top**	[length] I [percentage] I inherit Same for: **padding-right; padding-bottom; padding-left**
SHORTHAND PROPERTIES	**background**	[background-color I background-image I background-repeat I background-attachment I background-position] I inherit
	border	[border-width] I [border-style] I color I inherit
	border-top	[border-width] I [border-style] I color I inherit Same for: **right, bottom, left**
	font	[font-weight] I [font-style] I [font-variant] I [font-size] I [line-height] I [font-family] I caption I icon I menu I message-box I small caption I status-bar I inherit
	margin	margin-width I inherit (*)
	padding	padding-width I inherit (*)
	(*)NOTES	If single value: apply to all sides Two values: apply to top, bottom Three: 1=top, 2=right/left, 3=bottom Four: Apply to top, right, bottom, left

Appendix C: CSS Units

d. Font Size values

Property/Value Type	Value Abbreviation	Value Description
font-size	**font-size:12px**	Property:value pair example
Length Values	**Px**	Pixels (1 pixel = 0.75 points)
	Pt	Points (1 point = 1/72 of an inch)
	Pc	Picas (1 pica = 12 points)
	em	Roughly width of a capital letter "M"
	en	Roughly width of a lowercase letter "n"
	ex	Roughly height of a lowercase letter "x"
	cm	Centimeters
	in	Inches (1 inch = 2.54 centimeters)
	mm	Millimeters
Percentage	**n%**	Font size relative to previous default
Relative Sizes	**larger**	Increases one font size relative to default
	smaller	Decreases one font size relative to default
Absolute Size Values	**xx-small**	Font Size "7"—unreliable, avoid using
	x-small	Font Size "6"—unreliable, avoid using
	small	Font Size "5"—unreliable, avoid using
	medium	Font Size "4"—unreliable, avoid using
	large	Font Size "3"—unreliable, avoid using
	x-large	Font Size "2"—unreliable, avoid using
	xx-large	Font Size "1"—unreliable, avoid using

Index

Absolute file addressing, 24–25, 80–82, 81 (fig.), 87, 89, 162, 164, 194, 213, 222, 229, 232
Accessibility of web pages to disabled patrons Section 508 requirements, 168, 170
Address for files: absolute addresses (*see* Absolute file addressing); relative addresses (*see* Relative file addressing)
Adobe Acrobat, 34
Adobe Photoshop, 75, 83, 107, 163, 245
Adobe Reader, 34
Align attribute, 60, 62–64, 85–86, 96, 128–29, 132, 134, 144, 154, 155, 166; in span tag, 62 (fig.)
Alignment of images and text, 64, 64 (fig.), 131, 166
Alt attribute, 15, 26, 35, 81–82, 89, 163; adding information with, 82 (fig.); insertion of, 28 (fig.)
Ampersand, 70, 151, 226
Angle brackets, 23, 39, 54
Animation Factory, 36, 77, 92
Area attribute, 162
Attributes, 9, 21–22, 25, 31, 39–42, 44, 46, 50, 51–53, 55, 59–64, 67, 69–70, 73, 80, 82–86, 89, 95–101, 105–6, 109, 115, 117–19, 124, 127–28, 132–33, 142, 144–46, 162, 164, 166–68, 174–75, 177, 182, 185, 191–93, 195–97, 210–12, 215, 221, 224–27, 232, 236; align, 60, 62–64, 62 (fig.), 85–86, 96, 128–29, 132, 134, 144, 154, 155, 166; alt, 15, 26, 28 (fig.), 35, 81–82, 82 (fig.), 89, 163; area, 162; border, 15, 16, 40, 84, 89, 96–97, 106, 108–9, 113, 128, 132, 135, 138, 142, 166; float, 95, 111–13, 137; height, 82–83, 86, 89, 96, 109, 112, 137, 147, 162, 166–67, 178, 184, 210, 266; http-equiv attributes, 7, 48–50; http-equiv = "refresh", 50; image maps, 159, 161–62, 164; inline style, 31, 95–98, 110, 115, 118, 124–25, 128, 160, 182, 209; language, 26, 42, 44, 51, 195–96, 206, 213, 230; name, 25, 48–49, 87, 88 (fig.), 90, 145, 162–63, 196, 225, 226; noshade, 63, 96; size, 46, 60, 63, 68–69, 130; source, 80; style, 95–98, 109, 115, 118–19, 121, 124, 142, 148, 160, 182; text direction, 42, 44, 52; width, 15, 63–64, 82–83, 93, 130

Background for page: images, 36, 56, 58, 91–92, 97, 110; solid, 55–56, 57 (fig.), 72, 103, 107–8, 173, 176 (fig.); tiled graphic, 58 (fig.)
Base element, 45
Blank space character, 70, 129, 225
Blind patrons Lynx browser, usefulness of, 26
Block formatting element, 60, 64, 66
Block quotations, 65; indented paragraphs, view of, 65, 65 (fig.); single line quotation, view of, 65 (fig.)
Body of document, 41–42, 54–56; color, 56, 57 (fig.)
Body tag, 8–9
Bold element. *See* Strong element
Bold tag. *See* Strong element
Border attribute, 15, 16, 40, 84, 89, 96, 128
Borders, 16, 91, 96, 108–9, 184; horizontal rules used with, 96; image border stylization, 16, 97, 108–9, 111 (fig.); table with border (basic), addition of, 19 (fig.), 128, 135, 138; text border stylization, 110, 110 (fig.), 111 (fig.)
Boxes: borders (CSS), 184; boxes (CSS), 184; CSS box margin shorthand, 184; definitions, 185 (fig.); for text, 110, 147, 186
Breaks. *See* Line breaks
Broken links, 82. *See also* Hyperlinking
Browser, 1, 2, 6–14, 25–31; opening new window, 88–89; nested font changes, 71 (fig.); view of box definitions, 185 (fig.); view of collapsed tree structure, 215 (fig.); view of comment delimiters, 55 (fig.); view of CONTENTdm Administration Pages, 250 (fig.), 251 (fig.),

250 (fig.); view of HTML file, 11 (fig.); view of inline font color, 70 (fig.); view of inline font face, 69 (fig.); view of inline font size, 68 (fig.); view of pre tag, 64 (fig.); view of semantic recipe elements, 203 (fig.); view showing Page Title, 45 (fig.); view of web page, 10 (fig.); view of XML recipe file, 201 (fig.); view of XML tree structure, 214 (fig.); word processor compared, 9, 65, 127
Browsers: Chrome, 2, 26, 39, 82; Firefox, 2, 20, 26, 37, 39, 82, 88, 95, 97–98, 125, 152, 153 (fig.), 179, 234–35, 235 (fig.); Internet Explorer, 2, 26, 37, 39, 82, 98, 125, 127, 152, 177, 184, 230; Lynx (non-GUI), 26, 27, 28 (fig.), 82; Safari, 2, 26
Browser types: graphical user interface (GUI), 25, 26, 27; non-GUI, 27. *See also* Browsers
Buttons on forms, 143, 145, 145 (fig.), 148 (fig.)
Buzz words, 265
Bytes (file sizes), 4, 84, 109

Cable modems, 4
Cached pages: instruction to browser to ignore saved pages, 49
Calendars: cascading style sheet (CSS) one-month table template, 141 (fig.); cascading style sheet (CSS) one-week table template, 140 (fig.); cascading style sheet (CSS) seven-day event table, 140 (fig.); form calendar, annual version, 156 (fig.); form calendar, quarterly version, 155 (fig.); forms graphics, use of, 154–55; one-day event calendar, 135, 138 (fig.); one-month table template, 141 (fig.); one-week activity calendar, 139 (fig.); one-week calendar table, 140 (fig.); one-week table template, 133 (fig.); seven-day event table, 133 (fig.); simple monthly calendar, 134 (fig.); tables, use of, 130–41; weekly planner, 139 (fig.)
Caps: dropped caps, 111–12
Captions: table captions, 128, 129, 131
Cascading style sheet (CSS) techniques, 96–115, 171–88; addition to single web page, 98; application to home page, 104; background images, 107–8; border around image, 108–9; buttons in forms, 145, 145 (fig.); changes, 175–76, 176 (fig.), 182; classes, use of, 125; cookbook, CSS-Structured XML, 198; creating HTML element styles in, 209; dropped caps, 111–12, 112 (fig.); embedded style sheet, 178, 181; external CSS techniques, 96, 103–4, 106 (fig.), 175, 176 (fig.), 212, 214; external style sheet, use of, 104, 106 (fig.), 107; floating images, 112, 113 (fig.); h1 style definitions, making change in, 99, 100 (fig.), 101–2, 137, 173, 209; image borders, 108–9, 111 (fig.); in-file embedded style definitions, 178, 181; inline style attributes, 95–98, 110, 118 , 182; internal CSS techniques, 211 (fig.); internal style sheet, use of, 98, 181–83, 211, 211 (fig.); linking to, 179–80, 193; links, defining, 174–75; margins, 106–7, 184–86, 185 (fig.); multiple style sheets, 175 (fig.); one-month table template, 141 (fig.); one-week table template, 140 (fig.); paragraph, 97, 106–7, 108 (fig.); pseudo-classes, 111, 172; resources, 113; rules, 172, 173 (fig.); sample home page incorporating styles, 106 (fig.); seven-day event table, 133 (fig.); softened logo for watermarking, 108 (fig.); specifications, 172; style declarations, 31, 67, 209, 211 (fig.), 212; sub-attributes of style attributes, 95, 97; table creation, 127–41; table effects, 127; table with seven columns, 133 (fig.); templates from online resource, 104; textarea box forms, 147, 147 (fig.); text boxes, 110; watermarking, 109 (fig.), 110
C/C++ programming language, 149
CDATA, 44, 216, 217, 218, 226
Center tag, 13, 14, 63; centering text, 63; web page view, 17 (fig.); WordPad view, 16 (fig.)
CGI. *See* CGI Scripts
CGI Scripts, 157; client-side mapping software, 154, 161; form applications, 144
Character data (CDATA). *See* CDATA
Character formatting, 61, 63–64, 66
Checking for browser type: IE Conditional Comments, 184
Children content specifications. *See* Content specifications
Chrome browser, 2, 26, 39, 82. *See also* Browsers
Classes: definition, 101; fully defined element class method, 101, 102 (fig.); generic class method, 101–2, 102 (fig.); stylizing, 102; use of, 101–2
ClickArt® graphics tool, 35
Client-side processing of forms, 104, 154, 161–62
Clip art collections, 37, 91, 76 (fig.); fee-based, 75, 77, 79, 92; format tricks, 72 (fig.); free, 36, 37; logo creation, 77 (fig.), 78 (fig.); public domain, 75; royalty-free, 36, 37; spicing up web page, 80; subscriptions, 36, 77; URLs, 76 (fig.), 91–92

CMS. *See* Content management systems
Closing tag, 8, 39; contents of, 8; defined, 8
Color: background, 55; body, 47, 55, 56; color chart, use of, 47; combinations of, 56; common color values, 46; default color, 56, 59, 100, 147, 176; for font face, 46, 69, 70 (fig.), 98, 100, 106; how best to colorize web page, 47; for hyperlinks, 59 (fig.); table borders, 127–28; textarea box form, addition to, 147, 147 (fig.); text hyperlinks, 166
Color chooser, 47
ComicCMS, 259. *See also* Content management systems
Comments: browser view, 55 (fig.); delimiter sets, 54–55; use of, 45, 53–54, 54 (fig.)
Common Gateway Interface (CGI) program, 144, 149–50
Compression algorithms, 79; graphics compression, 79; image compression, 79; lossless image compression, 79; lossy image compression, 79; LZW (Lempel, Ziv, and Welch) lossless compression algorithm, 79
Computer code fragments element, 67
Conditional comments, IE, 184 (fig.)
Connection to Internet, 4, 28, 80. *See also* Modem
Content management systems (CMS), 241–60; basic process, 245, 246 (fig.); content, what is, 245; databases, 243 (fig.), 244 (fig.); DreamHost CMS Server, 252, 253 (fig.); other DreamHost CMS options, 258; web design methodology, 247; WordPress, in Dreamhost, 252
Content of web page: metadata, description with, 48–50
Content specifications: ALL and EMPTY, 216; children and mixed specifications, 216; element rules, 216, 217 (fig.)
Content specification occurrence rules, 216, 217 (fig.)
CONTENTdm, 247–52; how it works, 248, 252 (fig.); collections tab administration interface, browser, 251 (fig.); CONTENTdm Content Management System, 249; items tab administration interface, browser, 253 (fig.); project client interface, 248 (fig.); server tab administration interface, browser, 250 (fig.). *See also* Content management systems
Copyright infringement, graphics, 75–76
Copyright symbol, 70
Databases: MySQL, relational databases, 243–46, 243 (fig.), 244 (fig.), 256, 261, 269; SQL, structured query language databases, 242, 245
DC. *See* Dublin Core
DCMES. *See* Dublin Core Metadata Element Set
DCMI. *See* Dublin Core Metadata Initiative
Default fonts, 46, 60, 69. *See also* Font element
Definition lists, 117, 121–23; event template, 123 (fig.); with hyperlinks to full event descriptions, 122 (fig.); images in, 123; indented portion, 121; monthly activities, list of, 122 (fig.); non-indented portion, 121; program page template, 122 (fig.); unordered list embedded in, 123 (fig.)
Dial-up modems, 4
Digital subscriber line (DSL) connections, 4
Directions page, 136 (fig.), 137 (fig.); map image, 136 (fig.)
Directories. *See* Folders (directories)
Disabilities, people with accessibility of web pages, Section 508 requirements, 168; sight-impaired patrons, usefulness of Lynxbrowser for, 26
Document type definitions (DTDs), 23, 31–32, 42, 171, 189, 197, 215, 219–23, 228–30, 236; default DTD table, 174 (fig.); inline style commands to modify rule (*see* Attributes); modification of rule set, 31; style sheet techniques to modify rules (*see* Cascading style sheet [CSS] techniques)
Dreamhost, 252: CMS setup, 253 (fig.). *See also* Content management systems
Drop-down lists, 143, 146, 146 (fig.)
Dropped caps, 111–13; ways to define and use dropped caps, 112 (fig.)
Drupal, 258. *See also* Content management systems
DSL. *See* Digital subscriber line (DSL) connections
DTDs. *See* Document type definitions (DTDs)
Dublin Core (DC), 44–49; description of web page, 44; ISO15836 Standard, Dublin Core metadata elements, 48; XML tree diagrams, 203–4
Dublin Core Metadata Element Set (DCMES), 190, 196, 205, 206, 207 (fig.), 223, 223 (fig.), 230, 232
Dublin Core Metadata Initiative (DCMI) Specification, 223–24
Dublin Core specification. *See* Dublin Core Metadata Element Set (DCMES)

EAD. *See* Encoded Archival Description XML vocabulary
Element occurrence rules. *See* Content specifications
Elements, 7–9; base, 45; body, 41–42, 54–56, 59, 62, 86, 107, 175, 190, 209; block formatting, 60, 64, 66, 210; block quotations, 117–18, 121; bold face, 13, 16 (fig.), 17 (fig.), 62; center, 13, 16 (fig.), 17 (fig.), 59; character formatting, 66; classes, use of, 101–103, 107, 138, 183; default fonts, 46; div, 61–62, 216; empty, 23, 44, 191; font, 46, 67–70, 67 (fig.), 68 (fig.) 69 (fig.), 70 (fig.), 71 (fig.), 78 (fig.), 79, 96–106, 160; form element, 144–45, 151, 152 (fig.); head, 41, 44, 190; heading, 60, 60 (fig.), 62, 68, 79, 101, 128, 131–32, 173; horizontal rules, 16, 40, 62–63, 63 (fig.), 96–97, 96 (fig.), 160; hyperlink anchor, 60; image, 17–19 (fig.), 27, 28 (fig.), 40, 80–86, 82 (fig.), 83 (fig.), 84 (fig.), 109, 110 (fig.), 111 (fig.), 112, 113 (fig.), 120, 121, 123–24, 124 (fig.), 136, 225; image map, 161–66, 162 (fig.), 164 (fig.); inline style attributes, addition of, 95–96, 97–99, 99 (fig.), 110, 125, 160, 182, 207, 208 (fig.); input element, 145, 145 (fig.), 147, 149 (fig.), 151; italics, 66, 67 (fig.), 72 (fig.), 173; line breaks, 40, 60–62, 64; linking to other documents, 44, 50, 103–4, 174–84; lower case, use of, 9, 39, 41; metadata, 41, 47–49, 48 (fig.), 55, 242–43, 248–50 (*see* Dublin Core); occurrence rules (*see* Content specifications); paragraph, 11–14, 14 (fig.), 15 (fig.), 60 (fig.), 61–67; preformat, 11, 14 (fig.), 15 (fig.), 55, 61, 63–64; quotations, block, 117–18, 121; "root," 8, 41, 42, 44, 50, 190, 193–97, 199, 203, 204, 220, 221–22, 233; select element, 146; span, 61–62, 62 (fig.), 102–3, 111; strong, 13–14, 60, 66, 66 (fig.), 100, 173; style, 44, 86, 98, 103, 124, 177, 179, 181–82, 212; table, 15–16, 19 (fig.), 21 (fig.), 40, 120, 127–41, 156, 157 (fig.), 184; textarea element, 144, 147, 148 (fig.); text style, 60, 67, 90, 106; title, 8, 9, 11 (fig.), 44–45, 45 (fig.), 48, 54–55, 104, 179, 190; underline, 13, 66, 235
E-mail address, addition to web page, 34, 49, 90, 152 (fig.); automatic e-mail to webmaster, 90, 152
E-mail programs: receiving program, through Netscape, 152–53; sending program, through Outlook Express, 153 (fig.)
Empty tag, 23, 40, 54, 61–62, 89
Encoded Archival Description XML vocabulary (EAD), 194
Entity characters, 71, 71 (fig.), 215; DTD parameter syntax in XML, 228; entity, parameter syntax (XML), 228; entity declarations (XML), 227; entity references (XML), 226; external file syntax (XML), 228
Expiration date for page: setting date, 49
Explorer (Windows). *See* Windows Explorer
Explorer Browser (Windows). *See* Internet Explorer Browser
Extensible Hyper Text Markup Language. *See* XHTML
Extensible Markup Language. *See* XML
External CSS style: processing, 212; XML-like documents, 212

File location: absolute addressing, 24–25, 80–82, 81 (fig.), 87, 89, 162, 164, 194, 213, 222, 229, 232; file-naming conventions, 24; long file names, 24; relative addressing, 25, 40, 80–81, 81 (fig.), 87, 194; 8.3 filename specification, 24
File sizes (bytes), 4, 80, 84
Firefox browser, 2, 26, 82, 88, 95, 98, 179; alt attribute, 82; border stylization, 97; forms and results submitted using e-mail, 152, 153 (fig.); horizontal rules, 97; list style, 125; namespace syntax, 234, 235 (fig.); Outlook Express e-mail generated by form in Firefox, 153 (fig.); style definitions and, 97, 98; style sheet selection using link, 179, 181 (fig.). *See also* Browsers
Float attribute, 112–13, 113 (fig.)
Floating images: example of how images float around text, 113 (fig.)
Folders (directories): structure, 2–3, 2 (fig.), 3 (fig.), 14, 24, 29–30, 30 (fig.), 80–81; subfolders, creation of, 2 (fig.); website with common subfolders, 3 (fig.)
Font element, 46, 67–70, 67 (fig.), 68 (fig.), 69 (fig.), 70 (fig.), 71 (fig.), 78 (fig.), 79, 96–106, 160; color, 69–70, 70 (fig.), 96, 98, 100, 166; color change, browser view, 70 (fig.); default fonts, 46, 60, 69, 132; font face, 69 (fig.); multiple attributes in, 70–71; nesting of, 70–71; nested font changes, browser view, 71 (fig.); size changes, browser view of, 68 (fig.)
Font face, 46, 64, 68–69; default fonts, 46, 60, 69, 132; examples, 69; inline changes on browser, 69 (fig.); types of, 69
Font style, types of, 68–69
Font tag. *See* Font element

Font typefaces, 66–67; changing from default or base font, 66–69, 69 (fig.); monotype text display, 67 (fig.)
Form element, 144–45, 151, 152 (fig.). *See also* Forms
Formatting: character formatting, 66–67; enhancements to web page, 72 (fig.), 77 (fig.); format tricks, 71
Forms, 143–58; action buttons, 147–48; buttons, addition to form, 149 (fig.); buttons, stylization of, 145 (fig.); calendar, annual version (portrait print out), 156 (fig.); calendar, graphics in, 154–56; calendar, quarterly version, 155 (fig.); CGI form applications, 149; check box button, 145 (fig.); client-side processing, 154; creation of, 144–48; drop-down form for hotel reservations, 146 (fig.); drop-down lists, addition of, 146, 146 (fig.); e-mail-creating form responses, 151–53; e-mail form elements, 152 (fig.); e-mail response generators, 149–50; e-mail techniques for forms processing, 151–53; form elements and their attributes, 144; graphics in calendar pages, 154–56; hosted CGI form applications, 149; hosting services, 149–50; input element, 145; JavaScript URL selection form, 155 (fig.); online surveys, 151; preselectable responses, forms with, 146, 146 (fig.); puzzle, addition of, 156, 157 (fig.); radio button, 145 (fig.); select element, 146; server-side processing, 149–53; stylization of buttons, 145 (fig.); surveys, 151; text button, 145 (fig.); textarea element, 147; URL, selection of, 155 (fig.)
Fortran programming language, 149
Freshness date: setting date, 49
Fully defined element class method, 101; class definitions, 102 (fig.)

Generic class method: class definitions, 102 (fig.)
GetSimple, 259. *See also* Content management systems
Gif. *See* Graphics Interchange File (gif file)
Glossary listing, 121. *See also* Definition lists
Google, 75, 159. *See also* Search engines
Government websites: Section 508 accessibility requirements, 168
Graphical user interface (GUI) browser, 25, 26, 27
Graphics, 35–36: compression of, 79; copyright and, 75; enlargement of, 82–84; file types, 79; how to place graphic on web page, 17 (fig.); linking to web pages, 89; permission to use graphics, 75; shrinking of, 82–84; table elements, use of, to place graphic, 19 (fig.); webpage with, 17 (fig.). *See also* Images; Photographs
Graphics Interchange File (gif file), 79
Graphics tools: Adobe Photoshop, 75; ClickArt, 35; clipart (*see* Clip art collections); iStockphoto, 36; Paint, 75; Paint Shop Pro, 75; PowerPoint, 32, 77; Print Shop, 35; PrintMaster, 35
GUI browser. *See* Graphical user interface (GUI) browser

Head section of document: base URL, 45; cached (saved) pages, instruction to ignore, 49; color values, 46–47; fonts, default, 46; freshness date, setting of, 49; head element, 44; header information, 44, 47–48; ISBN, addition of, 50; latest files, request for, 49; links to other documents, 50; makeup of, 41; metadata, 47–48; redirecting patrons to new site, 49; search engine, instruction not to index page, 49; title element, 44–45
Headings, 60–61; changing style definitions, 98; defaults, change in, 98 (fig.); elements of, 60–61; examples, 60 (fig.); table headings, 131–33; height attribute, 82–84; high-speed connection, 28; home page file, 30, 30 (fig.); getting page on line, 5; information to include, 3–4; hypothetical library home page, contents of, 28–32; top links for libraries, 32–34
Home page, 3, 4, 32, 33, 33 (fig.), 45, 104, 105 (fig.), 123, 159, 161, 161 (fig.), 163, 165, 166, 249
Horizontal rules, 62–63; attributes, 62–63; border attributes, use with, 96–97; examples of horizontal rules, 63 (fig.); inline style examples, 96 (fig.)
Hovering, 86, 105–6
HTML, 1, 5, 235: anchor element, 86; attributes, 39, 40, 41; background, 55; base URL, 45; basic markup elements, 6–18; block formatting, 60; block-level element types, 173; body of document, 41, 54–60; browser view of newsletter HTML file, 10 (fig.); centering text, 63; character formatting, 66–71; color, 46, 54–60; default fonts, 46; default styles, 174; document requirements, 191 (fig.); document structure, 41; document type definitions, 28 doctypes, 171; doctype

declaration, 194 (fig.); elements, 39–41; empty tag set, 23, 40, 44, 54, 61–62, 89, 191; entities, 71, 215; file-naming conventions, 20–21; file structure, 9 (fig.), 41, 43 (fig.); fonts, 46, 67–70; font typefaces, 66–68, 69 (fig.); freshness date, 49; header information, 44; heading, 44; head section, 41, 44; horizontal rules, 62–63; hyperlinking, 87; inline-level element types, 173; instruction to search engine not to index page, 49; ISBN, addition of, 50; line breaks, 61; link, 50; lists, 117–24; markup, basic elements, 8–18; metadata, 47–48; no caching, 49; page structure, 8–11, 9 (fig.), 43 (fig.); paragraphs, making text into, 61; preformatting, 64–65; quoted text as block, 65–66; redirecting patrons, 50; root element, 41; sections of document, 41; skeleton of page, WordPad view, 9 (fig.); special characters, 70; standard element tag set, 23; standards, 31; structure of document, 41, 43 (fig.); structure of page, 43 (fig.); style sheet (CSS) techniques; style sheets, 95–96 (*see also* Cascading style sheet [CSS] techniques); tables, 127–34; tags, 7–8, 39–40, 43 (fig.); text file change to HTML file, 4; title element, 44–45; type faces, changing, 67, 68, 69 (fig.); word processing, simulating, 86
HTML DTD link standard, 33
HTML elements, 2, 6, 7, 18, 23, 31, 33, 39–41, 53, 65, 95–96, 117, 136, 171, 174, 201–203, 210–212, 229
HTML tag. *See* HTML elements
http. *See* Hypertext transfer protocol (http)
http-equiv attributes, 7, 48–50
http-equiv = "refresh" attribute, 50
Hypergraphic links, 25, 84, 87–90, 106, 159, 261
Hypergraphics, 106, 159
Hyperlink anchor, 60
Hyperlinking, 47; broken links, 82; colors, customized, 59 (fig.); colors, default, 59 (fig.); e-mail address, addition to web page, 89; external, 86; global, 86; of graphics, to web pages, 87
Hypertext links, 75, 87, 88 (fig.), 89, 104–6, 123, 129, 159–61, 247
Hyper Text Markup Language. *See* HTML
Hypertext navigation bar, 160–61, 160 (fig.), 161 (fig.), 162 (fig.); internal, 86; linking graphics to web pages, 87; local, 86; mailto: hyperlink, use of, 90, 91 (fig.); navigation bar, 160 (fig.), 161 (fig.), 162 (fig.); other documents, linking to, 50; relative links within web page, 90; stylized navigation bar, 161 (fig.); top links for library home page, 32–35
Hypertext transfer protocol (http), 29
Hypertext transfer protocol reference link, 86

ID selectors, 183–84, 183 (fig.), 188. *See also* Selectors
Image element, 80–85, 109; addition of tag, 18 (fig.); relative and absolute addressing in, 81 (fig.); web page view, 18 (fig.)
Image maps, 161–65; area attributes, 162–65; attributes, 162–65; common navigation bar, 162 (fig.); correlation between hyperlinks and files, 163 (fig.); defined, 161; elements, 162–65; files and hyperlinks, correlation between, 163 (fig.); hyperlinks and real file names (border at "0"), home page with, 166 (fig.); image map navigation, home page with, 165 (fig.); navigation bar image, 162 (fig.), 164 (fig.); navigation tools, home page with, 159–60; restyled hyperlinks for "finished" look (underlining removed), home page with, 167 (fig.)
Image tag. *See* Image element
Images, 29, 31, 35–36, 75: adding img tag, 18 (fig.); adjusting height to fit space, 83 (fig.); alignment with text, 85–86, 85 (fig.); automatic border around image, 85; background images, 107–8, 108 (fig.), 109 (fig.); borders, 108–9; borders, styling of, 111 (fig.); box around image, 84, 84 (fig.); compression of, 79; copyright infringement, 35–36, 75–76; copyright symbol, 70; in definition lists, 121, 123; enlargement of, 82–84; fancy borders, 110 (fig.); floating images, 95, 112, 113 (fig.); flowing text around image, 86 (fig.); height, 79–81, 83 (fig.); horizontal space between images, addition of, 84 (fig.); how to place image on web page, 18 (fig.); linking to, 87–90; Lynx view, 27, 27 (fig.); missing images, 81–82; multiplying images, 82; shrinking of, 82–83; sizing, 82–83; stylization of, 106; web page with graphics, 18 (fig.); white space around images, 85; width, 82–83. *See also* Graphics; Photographs
Indentation, 107
Indented paragraphs. *See* Block quotations
Index page. *See* Home page
Inline style attributes, 31, 95–98, 96 (fig.), 99 (fig.), 100 (fig.), 110, 118, 125, 128, 160,

182, 207–9, 208 (fig.): use of, to modify DTD rules, 31. *See also* Attributes
Input element, 145, 145 (fig.), 147, 149 (fig.), 151
Interaction with patrons. *See* Forms
International Standard Book Number (ISBN): addition of, 50; identifying ISBN for document, 50, 195
International Standards Organization (ISO): ISO639 Standard, HTML native language, 42; ISO8859 Standard, Latin-1 character set, 192; ISO15836 Standard, Dublin Core, 48; ISO18004 Standard, QR Codes, 263; ISO19136 Standard, Geography Markup Language, 238
Internet connection. *See* Connection to Internet
Internet Explorer Browser, 2, 26, 37, 39, 82, 98, 125, 127, 152, 177, 184, 230; border stylization, 109–10; folder structure, 2–3, 2 (fig.), 3 (fig.), 14, 24, 29–30, 30 (fig.), 80–81; forms and results submitted using e-mail, 152; horizontal rules, 96; image maps, 164; list style, 125; style definitions, 98; table effects, 128, 129
Internet service provider (ISP), 2, 4, 28, 143
Internet Software Consortium, 27
Interoperability, 39, 196
ISBN. *See* International Standard Book Number
ISO. *See* International Standards Organization
ISP. *See* Internet service provider
iStockphoto, 36, 79
Italics tag, 66–67, 67 (fig.), 90, 120, 173, 210

JavaScript, 31, 44, 154, 177, 235, 242; scripting language, 154, 159, 266; URL selection form, 155 (fig.)
Joint Photographic Editors Group (jpg or jpeg file extension), 79, 84
Joomla, 258. *See also* Content management systems
JPEG. *See* Joint Photographic Editors Group
JPG. *See* Joint Photographic Editors Group

Keyboard element, 67

Language attribute, 42: ISO639 Standard native language default, 42
Latest files, request for, 49
Line breaks, 61
Linking. *See* Hyperlinking
List: basic lists, 117–18; definition list, 117, 121–23; directory list style, 118 (fig.); drop-down lists, addition to forms, 143, 146, 146 (fig.); external style sheet properties, 124; glossary listing, 121; graphical list items, 120; hypergraphic list quiz, 121 (fig.); hypertext, 123; image list item styles, use of, 124, 124 (fig.); internal style sheet properties, 124; link element, 174–75; long lists, 118, 119; menu list style, 118 (fig.); nesting lists, 119–21, 119 (fig.), 120 (fig.); ordered list, 118, 119, 119 (fig.), 120 (fig.); outlines, 117–19; short lists, 117; stylization of, 120, 124 (*see also* Cascading style sheet [CSS] techniques); unordered list, 117–18, 118 (fig.), 120 (fig.)
Lossless image compression, 79
Lossy image compression, 79
Lower case, use in element type, 9, 39, 41
Lynx browser, 26, 27, 82: image, Lynx view of, 28 (fig.); newsletter, Lynx view of, 27 (fig.); nongraphic web page output seen by, 27 (fig.); sight-impaired patrons, usefulness for, 26, 27 (fig.). *See also* Browsers
LZW (Lempel, Ziv, and Welch) lossless compression algorithm, 79

MapEdit, 161
Mapping software, 161
Maps. *See* Directions page; Image maps
Margins, styling of, 85, 96, 98, 106–7, 110, 137, 168, 184–86
Markup language interpreters, browsers as, 31
Markup tags, 29, 40
Marquees, 159, 166–68; styling of, 166–68; three-line scrolling display, 168 (fig.)
Media (CSS): alternate style sheets, 180 (fig.); attributes, 176–77; media blocks, 179, 180 (fig.)
MediaWiki, 259. *See also* Content management systems
Metadata, 41, 47–49, 48 (fig.), 55, 190, 196, 205, 206, 207 (fig.), 223 (fig.), 242, 243, 248–50, 252; describing page with, 47–48
Missing images, 81
Mixed content specifications. *See* Content specifications
Mobile applications, 263
Modem: cable modem, 4; connection to Internet, 28; dial-up modem, 4
Moodle, 260. *See also* Content management systems
Monotype text display, 67, 67 (fig.)
Mouseover, 105, 106
MySQL (My Structured Query Language), 245, 254, 258, 266

Name attribute, 88 (fig.), 90
Namespaces, 205, 232; namespaces for science and math, 237
Navigation techniques, 159; hyperlinks and real file names, border at "0", 166 (fig.); hypertext navigation bar, 160 (fig.), 161 (fig.), 162 (fig.); image map navigation, 173–79, 165 (fig.); logo and hypertext navigation bar, 162 (fig.); navigation tools on home page, 165–68; restyled hyperlinks for "finished" look, underlining removed, 167 (fig.)
Nesting, 36; of font tags, 8, 12, 41 (fig.), 70–71, 127, 202 (fig.); improper nesting, 40, 41 (fig.); of list elements, 119–21, 119 (fig.), 120 (fig.), 124; nested font changes on browser, 67, 71 (fig.); proper nesting, 8, 12, 41; of table elements, 128; well-formedness, 202 (fig.)
Netscape Navigator; browser, 26; e-mail receiving program, 152
Network card: Internet connection, 28
Newsletter designs: browser view of HTML file, 10 (fig.); floating images for, 95, 112, 113 (fig.); HTML file, browser view of, 11 (fig.); Word document file, 5 (fig.); WordPad view of newsletter, 10 (fig.)
Noshade attribute, 63, 96
Notepad, 88, 103

Occurrence rules. *See* Content specification occurrence rules
Offline use of web page, 29
Omeka, 258–59. *See also* Content management systems
Online public access catalog (OPAC), 3, 143
OPAC. *See* Online public access catalog (OPAC)
Opening tag, 8, 23, 25, 39–40, 42, 46, 56, 61, 63, 87, 90, 97–99, 102, 107, 112, 119, 128, 136, 174, 181–84, 201, 208, 225; contents of, 8; defined, 8
Operating systems: Linux, 1–2, 26; Mac, 1, 2, 161, 261. *See also* MacOS or Macintosh; Macintosh, 26, 161. *See also* Mac or MacOS; MacOS, 161. *See also* Mac or Macintosh; Windows, 2, 7, 26, 30 (fig.), 161, 248, 248 (fig.), 265
Ordered lists, 118–19; nesting lists, 120 (fig.); types of, 119 (fig.). *See also* Lists
Outlook Express e-mail program: e-mail generated by form in Firefox browser, 153 (fig.); e-mail sending program, 152; forms and results submitted using e-mail, 152, 152 (fig.)
Overlapping tags, 40, 191, 221, 243

Paint, 75, 79, 163, 235
Paint Shop Pro, 75, 83, 107, 163
Paragraph element, 11–13; addition of, 14 (fig.); effect of, 15 (fig.)
Paragraphs, 53, 60–61, 97, 98, 111–12, 173, 209; defining classes, 108 (fig.); indentation, 65, 107; margin, 106–7; styling of, 106–8, 112; use of, 60 (fig.)
Parsed Character Data. *See* PCDATA
PCDATA, 44, 217, 218, 219, 221–22
PDAs, 31, 177
Periodical table, table techniques in, 134, 135 (fig.), 136
Perl programming language, 149, 150
Permission to use graphics, 29, 75, 88, 134
Photographs. *See also* Graphics; Images; digital photographs, 75, 110, 110 (fig.); stock photographs, 36, 79–80; stylizing photos, 109; template for stylizing photo, 110 (fig.)
PHP (PHP: Hypertext Preprocessor), 266
Plain-text browser, 27. *See also* Lynx browser
PNG. *See* Portable Network Graphics
Pop-up windows, 26, 77, 266
Portable Digital Assistants. *See* PDAs
Portable Network Graphics (png file), 31, 79–80, 162, 245
PowerPoint, as graphics tool, 36, 79–80
Pre element. *See* Preformat element or preformat tag
Preformat element, 11–12, 29, 55, 61, 63–65, 64 (fig.), 215. *See also* Preformat tag; Web page view, 13 (fig.); WordPad view, 12 (fig.)
Preformat tag, 11–12, 64–65; browser view of, 64 (fig.)
PrintMaster, 35
Print Shop, as graphics tool, 35
Programming languages: Perl, 149, 150; C/C++, 149; Fortran, 149; JavaScript, 31, 44, 154, 177, 235, 242
Programs (software): Adobe Acrobat, 34; Adobe Photoshop, 75, 83, 107, 163, 245; Adobe Print Shop, 35; Adobe Reader, 34; Common Gateway Interface (CGI) software program, 144; MapEdit, 161; Notepad, 88, 103; Paint, 75, 79, 163, 235; Paint Shop Pro, 75, 83, 107, 163; Word, 2, 4–5, 5 (fig.), 7, 24, 34, 49, 245
Program types: art, 75; e-mail, 151, 152; graphics, 35, 36, 245; mapping, 161; "paint," 75, 79, 163,

235; word processing, 2, 4, 5 (fig.), 7, 24, 34, 86, 127, 245, 260
Protocol interpreters, browsers as, 24, 29, 31
Puzzles: forms element, creation with, 156, 157 (fig.)

QR code, 263–64, 264 (fig.), 265 (fig.)
Quotations. *See* Block quotations

Redirecting patrons to new site, 50
Refresh techniques, 49–50, 151
Registered trademark symbol, 70, 71 (fig.)
Rehabilitation Act of 1973: accessibility of web pages, 168; disabilities, patrons with, 168; Section 508 accessibility requirements, 168
Relative file addressing, 24, 25, 40, 80–81, 81 (fig.), 87, 89–90, 162, 164, 194, 213, 222, 229, 232
"Root" element, 8, 41, 42, 44, 50, 190, 193–97, 199, 203, 204, 220, 221–22, 233

Safari browser, 2, 26. *See also* Browsers
Saving web page from Internet, 28–29
Scrolling text or characters, 166–67; infinite scrolling, 167. *See also* Marquees
Search engines, 44, 48–49; categorizing and finding content, 159; getting web pages noticed, 159; instruction not to index page, 49
Section 508 accessibility requirements, 168
Select element, 146
Selectors, 101, 172–73, 178; ID selectors, 183–84, 183 (fig.), 188; XML selectors, 233
Server-side processing of forms, 149–53
Shareware program, 161
Sight-impaired patrons: Lynx browser, usefulness of, 25
Size attribute, 46, 56, 60, 63, 67–71, 68 (fig.)
Social media, 260–61, 261 (fig.). *See also* "Web 2.0"
Software programs. *See* Programs (software)
Source attribute, 80, 196, 206, 223, 225
Span element, 61–63, 62 (fig.), 102–3, 111–12, 173, 182; align attribute in span tag, 62 (fig.); div element compared, 62 (fig.)
Spanning: advanced table technique, 133
Special characters, 71
Specification occurrence rules. *See* Content specification occurrence rules
SQL, 242, 245
Stock photographs, 36, 79
Strong element, 13, 14, 60, 66, 100, 173; how characters are displayed, 13, 66 (fig.), 175
Strong tag. *See* Strong element
Structured Query Language, 254. *See also* SQL
Style element. *See* Cascading style sheet (CSS) techniques
Style sheets: alternate style sheets, 181 (fig.); external CSS, 175; internal CSS, 182; inline styling, 181–82; XML style sheets, 193
SuDoku puzzle: input buttons and color, use of, 156, 157 (fig.); large table, 156, 157 (fig.)
Surveys: creation of, 146, 151; large surveys, 151; online creation tool, 151; online surveys, 151; short surveys, 151; types of, 151

Table element, 15–16, 19 (fig.), 40, 86, 120, 127–28, 131, 132, 135–38, 140
Tables: advanced table techniques, use of, 135 (fig.); with border attribute, 15–16, 19 (fig.), 40, 128; with border attribute at "0", 16, 20 (fig.), 106, 137 (fig.); with borders in color, 129–30, 130 (fig.); building a table, 127–36; calendar design, 130–40, 133 (fig.), 134 (fig.), 138 (fig.), 140 (fig.), 141 (fig.), 144, 154–56, 155 (fig.), 156 (fig.); calendar for one-day event, 141, 138 (fig.); captions, 128, 129–32; cascading style sheets, use to create tables, 127–41; color borders, 129–30, 130 (fig.); column attributes, 133; column spanning for odd and even column rows, 134 (fig.); directions page, 136 (fig.), 137 (fig.); directions page, basic, 136 (fig.); directions page, border removed, 137 (fig.); element equivalents for style sheet table, 136–37, 139 (fig.); four-cell table, 131 (fig.); headings, 129–32; hyperlinks, 135; map image, 137 (fig.); multiple-row, double-column calendar, 137, 138 (fig.); one-cell tables, 129 (fig.); one-row, seven-cell table, 132 (fig.); one-week activity calendar, 133 (fig.); one-week calendar table, 133 (fig.); one-week table tem plate, 140 (fig.); row attributes, 134–36; seven-column table using CSS, 140 (fig.); simple monthly calendar, 134 (fig.); single-color table border, 130 (fig.); spanning rows and columns, 133–36; style sheet table based on W3 example, 139 (fig.); style sheet table element equivalents, 127–41; stylization of, 127–31; titles, 132–33; two-cell table, 131 (fig.); weekly planner, 139 (fig.); width attribute, 130, 138
Table tag. *See* Table element

Tags: closing, 7, 8, 12, 13, 39–41, 87, 103, 132, 171–72, 218; empty, 23, 40, 44, 89, 191, 218; html, 8, 29, 32, 39–40, 54 makeup of, 8, 39; markup, 40; nesting, 40, 41 (fig.); opening, 78, 12–13, 39–40, 87, 103, 107, 128, 132, 171–72, 218; overlapping, 39; tags inside other tags, 39–40, 41 (fig.). *See also* Elements
TEI. *See* Text Encoding Initiative XML vocabulary
Teletype element, 67
Textareaelement, 144, 147, 147 (fig.); box form, addition of color, 147; color addition to box, 147; stylization of, 147
Text border, styling of, 111 (fig.)
Text boxes, styling of, 110–11
Text direction attribute, 42
Text Encoding Initiative XML vocabulary (TEI), 194
Text file: direct view of, 6 (fig.); using Wordpad to change HTML file, 5
Text style, 60, 67, 90, 106, 131
Title element, 7–8, 44, 203, 207, 211, 231; attributes in the link tag, 179; browser view, 45 (fig.)
Title of document, 44; browser's title window, view in, 45 (fig.)
Title tag. *See* Title element
Trademark: registered trademark symbol, 70
Transitions, addition to pages, 50, 156, 266
Tree displays, XML: Browser XML tree displays, 214, 203 (fig.), 204 (fig.), 215 (fig.)
Typefaces: bold, 66, 71, 132; changing fonts, 66; italics, 66–67, 71, 90, 120, 173

Underline element, 13, 16 (fig.); web page view, 17 (fig.); WordPad view, 16 (fig.)
Underline tag. *See* Underline element
Uniform Resource Identifier (URI), 205, 232
Uniform Resource Locator (URL), 24–25, 44–45, 49–50, 80–82, 162, 164–65, 190, 194, 205, 229, 237, 245, 246, 263–65; absolute URL, 24–25; base URL, 44–45; case sensitivity, 25; full URL, 24–25, 80–82. *See also* Absolute file addressing; Relative file addressing
Unordered lists, 117; definition list, embedded in, 123 (fig.); nesting lists, 119 (fig.), 120 (fig.); types of, 118, 118 (fig.)
URI. *See* Uniform Resource Identifier (URI)
URL. *See* Uniform Resource Locator (URL)
URL selection form, 155 (fig.)
Usability, web page, 262

Vocabularies (XML): EAD (*see* Encoded Archival Description XML Vocabulary); library-oriented vocabularies, 194; namespaces for science and math, 237; TEI (*see* Text Encoding Initiative XML vocabulary)

Watermarking: softened logo for, 108 (fig.); style sheet watermarking, 109 (fig.)
"Web 2.0," 260, 260 (fig.)
Web browser. *See* Browser
Web page, generally with all content, 21 (fig.); content of, 47–48; creation of, generally, 11–18; expiration date, setting of, 49; freshness date, 49; with graphics, 18 (fig.); long page, navigating through, 90; metadata, description with, 47–48; navigation (*see* Navigation techniques); offline use of, 28; recreation of, for offline use, 28; saving page from Internet, 28; transitions, 50, 156, 266; up-to-date information, importance of, 49
Web site: creation of, 3–4; design of, 29–31; file sizes (bytes), 4–5; opening page, 29; shell directory setup, 2–3
Width attribute, 15, 63–64, 82–83, 93, 130
Windows Explorer: suggested folder structure, 29, 30 (fig.)
Word, 4, 24, 34
Word document saved as web page, 5 (fig.)
WordPad, 2, 5, 9, basic skeleton of HTML page, WordPad view, 9 (fig.); table with border, addition of, 19 (fig.); use of, to change text file into HTML file, 5 (fig.)
Wordpress, 241, 252, 254–60, 255 (fig.), 256 (fig.), 257 (fig.), 258 (fig.); planning your WordPress theme, 256–57; quick setup, 255 (fig.); themes, 258 (fig.); "Twenty-Ten" Template, 257 (fig.); website differences, 256 (fig.); widgets, 257 (fig.); WordPress, what is it, 254; WordPress.com or WordPress.org?, 254–56. *See also* Content management systems
Word processing program, 2, 5, 9, 24, 34, 86; browser compared, 10–11
Word-to-web method of getting page on line, 4–5
World Wide Web Consortium (W3C), 31–32, 104
W3C. *See* World Wide Web Consortium (W3C)
WYSIWYG (what-you-see-is-what-you-get), 4, 25, 245

XHTML, 1, 6, 7, 23, 31–32, 41, 95, 189–90, 194, 232; cascading style sheet (CSS) upward compatibility with, 95; empty tags and, 40; unordered lists and, 117; upward compatibility with, 9, 23, 31–32, 40, 41, 63, 95, 146

XML: ALL and EMPTY content specifications (*see* Content specifications); applications, 190; element attributes, 224; attribute declaration syntax, 225; attribute, Required, Fixed, and Implied defaults, 225; attribute, String, Enumerated, and Tokenized types, 226; attributes, class, 182 (fig.), 183 (fig.); basic web document requirements, 190; body, 197; browser tree displays, 215; character and entity references, 226–27; comments in, 193; declarations, 227; doctype declaration, 194 (fig.); doctypes, 193; document, 191; document construction, 199; document tree, 203; document, using CSS, 206; documents, creating without DTDs, 198; documents, creating an XML-like, 201; DTD stack, 183 (fig.) (*see also* XML DTDs); element declarations, 216; encoding, 192; entity, external file syntax, 229; entity, parameter syntax, 228; entity declarations, 227; entity references, 226, 227 (fig.); epilog, 197; examples (*see* XML examples); extensions, which to use .htm or .xml?, 214; file extensions, which to use .htm or .xml?, 214; ID selectors, 183 (fig.); library-oriented vocabularies, 194; prolog, 191; style sheets, 193, 211 (fig.), 213 (fig.); unicode transformation format, 192; vocabularies, 190; what is, 189; XML-like (*see* XML-like presentations)

XML DTDs, 193; cookbook, 218; cookbook, internal DTD, 229; document type definition vocabularies, creating, 215; documents, creating without DTDs, 198; Dublin Core DTD, 207 (fig.), 223, 223 (fig.), 224 (fig.); external DTDs, 222; internal DTD Subsets, 197; internal XML DTD, 219–20, 222 (fig.); internal XML DTD, creating an , 219–20; multiple DTDs, 230; unordered list, 220–21

XML Examples: books, 204 (fig.); cookbook, DTD element set, 199 (fig.), 200 (fig.), 201 (fig.), 205 (fig.), 208 (fig.), 209 (fig.), 218, 220 (fig.), 229 (fig.), 230 (fig.), 231 (fig.); Dublin Core DTD, 207 (fig.), 223, 223 (fig.), 224 (fig.); play, 206 (fig.); recipe, 201 (fig.), 202 (fig.), 203 (fig.), 205 (fig.), 209 (fig.); records, 206 (fig.); unordered list, 220–21

XML-like presentations, 206; documents, creating without DTDs, 198; documents, creating XML-like, 201; documents, external CSS style processing in, 212; documents, using CSS, 206

Yahoo, 75. *See also* Search engines

About the Author

CHARLES P. RUBENSTEIN, PhD, is professor of engineering and information science in the Graduate School of Information and Library Science and the Department of Mathematics and Sciences of the School of Liberal Arts and Sciences at Pratt Institute in New York City. He has also been a visiting professor of engineering at the Farmingdale State College (SUNY). His published works include Library Unlimited's *Crash Course in Web Design for Libraries* (the first edition of this text).

He has an earned doctorate in bioengineering (NYU-Polytechnic University) and a master's in library and information science (Pratt Institute). He is a life senior member of the Institute of Electrical and Electronics Engineering—IEEE—and was elected as an IEEE director (2010–2011) and an honorary member of the Board of the IEEE Technology Management Council (2007). He currently serves on the IEEE Publications Services and Products Board and chairs the IEEE-USA Conferences Committee. He is a Fellow, Chartered Engineer and International Professional Registration Advisor (FIET, CEng and IPRA) of the Institution of Engineering and Technology (IET) in the UK.

Dr. Rubenstein is an internationally known distinguished lecturer in web design, leadership skills, Android App Design and wireless technologies, as well as a organizer and established technical conference leader. He has received many honors for his IEEE professional society volunteer efforts, notably the IEEE Robert S. Walleigh Distinguished Professionalism Award, an IEEE-USA Citation of Honor, an IEEE Centennial Outstanding Young Engineer Award, an IEEE Third Millennium Medal, and an IEEE Regional Activities Board Innovation Award. He is a member of the Eta Kappa Nu and Tau Beta Pi engineering honor societies.